THE COMPLETE ROMAN LEGIONS

NIGEL POLLARD AND JOANNE BERRY

THE COMPLETE ROMAN LEGIONS

with 212 illustrations, 204 in colour

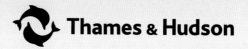

Thames & Hudson

To Maria and Livia Pollard

Half-title page Roman helmet of 'Imperial-Italic G' type, found near Hebron in the Palestinian West Bank. 2nd century AD, perhaps from the Second Jewish Revolt of AD 132–35.

Title pages Relief fragment from a column pedestal (*left*), from the headquarters of the legionary fortress at Moguntiacum (Mainz), showing two legionaries with helmet and shield. One carries a *pilum* and the other is stabbing with a sword (*gladius*). Detail (*right*) of the funerary monument of Titus Calidius Severus, centurion of *XV Apollinaris*, showing helmet with centurion's transverse crest, greaves and a mail or scale armour cuirass; mid-1st century AD; from vicinity of the legionary fortress at Carnuntum (Vienna, Kunsthistorisches Museum).

Right Bronze statuette of a legionary wearing *lorica segmentata* armour and a crested helmet (probably 2nd century AD. British Museum).

First published in the United Kingdom in 2012 by Thames & Hudson Ltd, 181A High Holborn, London WC1V 7QX

First paperback edition 2015

British Library Cataloguing-in-Publication Data
A catalogue record for this book is available from the British Library

ISBN 978-0-500-29183-2

Printed and bound in China by Toppan Leefung Printing Ltd

CONTENTS

The Legions of Rome

Describing the Roman imperial army in the reign of the second emperor, Tiberius, in AD 23, the Roman historian Tacitus lists the twenty-five legions that made up the core of the army, with the provinces of the empire in which they were deployed. He also states that there were allied naval units and units of supporting ('auxiliary') cavalry and infantry 'not much inferior to them in strength'. It is clear that the legions constituted only about half the military strength of the Roman empire.

However, Tacitus devotes most attention to the legions, describing their deployment province by province, while he glosses over the other elements of the armed forces in a couple of sentences. And it is precisely the legions of the Roman army that come to our minds when we think about Roman military strength. In many modern languages and cultures, the word 'legion' has become synonymous with Roman military power, and more generally with 'elite military unit' (the French Foreign Legion, for example) or simply 'military power'. It has even taken on a meaning beyond the purely military sense, namely to denote a multitude or mass, an image of overwhelming strength.

So why, when we think of the Roman armed forces, do we think of the legions rather than the 'other half'? For Tacitus, the legions were paramount because they were the high-status units of the army. They were composed of Roman citizens, with full Roman legal and political rights, and, in Tacitus' day, they still represented the Roman people under arms. Auxiliary troops, by contrast, were recruited largely from allies and subjects, men of inferior status who aspired to Roman citizenship after a lifetime in the army. Equally important is the fact that in AD 14 the legions already had a history of over three centuries of success. They had formed the heart of an army that had propelled Rome from obscurity – a modest central Italian city-state – to domination of the Mediterranean basin and beyond. They had beaten Hannibal, the Macedonians, the Gauls and many others.

They had suffered defeats too, but one Roman characteristic was an ability to endure losses and reconstitute fighting strength, so the legions lived on. They lived on, and fought, well beyond the age of Augustus. Legions were still important fighting units in the 5th century AD, when the western empire was in military and political decline. And they survived even longer in the armies of Rome's eastern successor state, the Byzantine

Opposite Detail from the Ludovisi Sarcophagus, showing a Roman officer and Germanic captive, mid-3rd century AD. Rome, Palazzo Altemps.

empire. A Byzantine historian writing in the early 7th century AD describes a soldier belonging to a unit known (in Greek) as the *Kouartoparthoi* (*Quartoparthoi*), clearly the descendant of *legio IV* (*Quarta*) *Parthica*, the Fourth Legion *Parthica*, based in the same region two centuries earlier. Thus, the Roman legions existed as elite military units for an unprecedented thousand years or so.

This book is a history of the Roman legions, from their origins by the 4th century BC, to Late Antiquity. Part I examines the origins of the legion, and its character and exploits through the expansion of the Roman empire in the Republican period, to *c.* 31 BC. However, these legions were ad hoc units within a citizen army, raised on a temporary basis for particular campaigns, and had no lasting identities that we can describe over a period of centuries. Legions as units with stable, long-term histories emerged from the armies of Julius Caesar in Gaul in the mid-1st century BC and of Octavian and Mark Antony in the civil wars of the 40s and 30s BC. These legions' identities became more

Relief sculpture depicting members of the Roman army (including an officer in muscled cuirass). Perhaps late 1st–2nd century AD. Rome, Capitoline Museum.

View of the Roman Forum, with the triumphal arch of Septimius Severus (right) and the Temple of Saturn (left). The route for processions celebrating Roman triumphs ran along the Sacred Way under the arch, turning left alongside the Temple of Saturn, and then climbed the Capitoline Hill to finish at the Temple of Jupiter.

permanent and distinct with the creation of a professional standing army by Rome's first emperor, Augustus (formerly Octavian), as part of the imperial system of government that replaced the Republic.

Part II of this book is made up of 'biographies' of 45 legions that we can identify by name and number or by number alone, and follow through three centuries of their history in the early and middle imperial period ('the Principate'). Many continued to exist into Late Antiquity, alongside numerous newly created legions.

The fragmented and often under-documented nature of the late antique legions makes it difficult to sustain a 'biographical' approach, so Part III takes a broader perspective on the units termed 'legions' in later centuries of Rome's history.

Note to the reader

Standard Roman numerals are used for the numbers of individual legions, though to reflect the evidence from inscriptions, IIII may be used in place of IV. Sources for the ancient works referred to in the text as well as a glossary of terms may be found at the back of the book.

ATLANTIC OCEAN
BRITANNIA
GERMANIA
Colonia Claudia Ara Agrippinensis
LOWER GERMANY
BELGICA
LUGDUNENSIS
Rhine
Danube
Carnuntum
RAETIA
NORICUM
UPPER GERMANY
AQUITANIA
Lugdunum (Lyon)
ALPES POENINAE
ALPES COTTIAE
ALPES MARITIMAE
PANNONIA
Sirmium
DALMATIA
NARBONENSIS
Bononia (Bologna)
Massilia (Marseilles)
Salonae
LUSITANIA
TARRACONENSIS
Tarraco
ITALIA
CORSICA
Roma
Neapolis (Naples)
Pompeii
BALEARES
SARDINIA
Corduba
BAETICA
Carthago Nova
Carthage
SICILY
Syracuse
MAURETANIA TINGITANA
MAURETANIA CAESARIENSIS
NUMIDIA
AFRICA PROCONSULARIS
AFRICA PROCONSULARIS (TRIPOLITANIA)
Italy
Roman acquisitions to 201 BC
Roman acquisitions to 100 BC
Roman acquisitions to 44 BC
Roman acquisitions to AD 14
Roman acquisitions to AD 96
Roman acquisitions to AD 106
Roman acquisitions to AD 200
Boundary of the Roman empire
Provincial boundary
Provincial capital
0 100 200 300 400 km
0 100 200 300 miles

General map of the Roman empire showing its expansion between 201 BC and AD 200.

PART I

The Legions in the Republican Period

The Roman Legions from Romulus to Marius

Previous pages Detail from the eastern relief of the Mausoleum of the Julii at Glanum (St Rémy de Provence, c. 30–20 BC), probably commemorating the military achievements of Gaius Julius in the army of Julius Caesar or Augustus, in the guise of a mythological scene.

'Legion' comes from a Latin verb meaning 'choose' or 'select', which suggests that the army was originally drawn selectively from particular groups in Roman society, defined by age, wealth and social and political status. Ancient authors looking back at the earliest origins of Rome, when history and myth are largely indistinguishable, thought legions existed from the very beginning of its history. Plutarch (*Romulus* 13.1), writing in the late 1st–early 2nd centuries AD, claimed that Rome's founder, Romulus, divided up men who could bear arms into 'legions' of 3,000 infantry and 300 cavalry, explaining the term as denoting that the men were 'selected' for their warlike characters. This account may well be anachronistic. Later writers such as Livy and Dionysius of Halicarnassus, describing the earliest Roman armies of the 6th–5th centuries BC, suggest they were based, in part at least, on the contemporary Greek hoplite phalanx.

Polybius and the 'Manipular' Legion

The earliest contemporary description of a Roman legion was written by the Greek writer Polybius in *c.* 150–120 BC. He describes a military organization that is distinctively Roman, and specifically refers to it as a 'legion'. It consisted of 4,200 infantry (5,000 in times of emergency), subdivided into units of 120 or 60 men called maniples ('handfuls'), and so modern scholars often refer to it as the 'manipular' legion, to distinguish it from later legions organized in larger subunits called cohorts.

This 'manipular' legion emphasized the role of small, flexible subunits of heavy infantry and the swordsmanship of individual soldiers, in contrast to the massed phalanx formation and tactics employed by Greek and Macedonian armies. It perhaps emerged as a distinctively Roman formation in the 4th century BC (as Livy suggests), due to problems the Romans encountered fighting against enemies who fought in looser formations than the phalanx and in rougher terrain, to which the phalanx was unsuited. These included Gauls, who sacked Rome in 390 BC, and upland central Italian peoples like the Samnites, against whom the Romans fought a sequence of difficult wars in 343–290 BC. As Rome defeated external enemies and its power grew, so did the size of its army. Livy tells us that the Romans fielded two legions from 362 BC, and four from 311 BC. By the time Polybius was writing, their numbers had expanded considerably more.

The manipular legion formed the core of the Roman Republican armies that defeated Hannibal in the second Punic war (218–202 BC) and conquered Greece and the kingdoms that Alexander the Great's successors had established in the eastern Mediterranean. The Roman army of this period was a citizen army, with soldiers called up for specific campaigns rather than serving as a long-term career. However, lengthy wars fought in defence of Italy and then to expand Roman control throughout the Mediterranean meant that even notionally part-time military service was a significant commitment. Polybius records that men were obliged to serve a total of 10 to 20 years throughout their lifetime. The individual legions lacked long-term identities, and existed only as long as they were needed for a particular campaign.

Under normal conditions, not all Roman citizens served in the legions, only those wealthy enough to provide their own weapons and equipment. Poorer individuals served as oarsmen in the fleet. In emergencies, however, as after the disastrous defeat by Hannibal at Cannae in 216 BC, even these less wealthy citizens might be conscripted into the army.

Organization of the Manipular Legions

Polybius (6.22–23; 25) describes how the legion in this period was divided into four types of infantry. There were three different groups of heavy infantry: 1,200 *hastati* ('spearmen'), 1,200 *principes* ('leading men') and 600 *triarii* ('third-

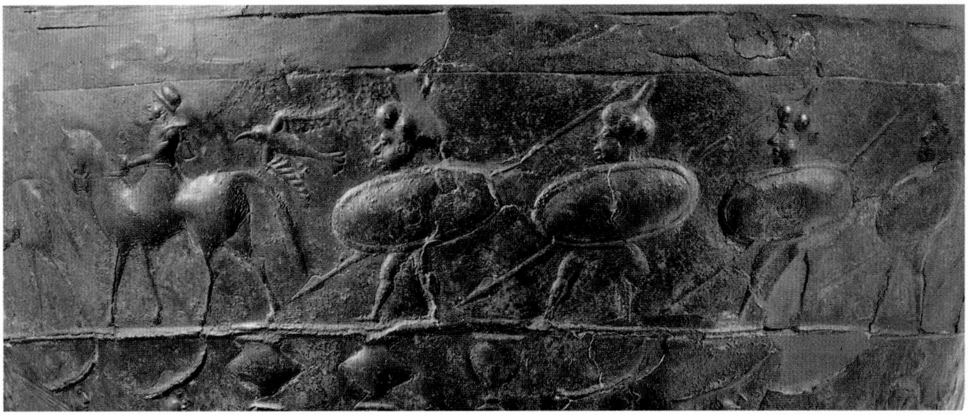

Detail from the Certosa Situla, a bronze vessel depicting cavalry and variously equipped groups of infantry. This may be evidence for an early (6th–5th centuries BC) Italian preference for heterogeneous army organization, foreshadowing the Roman manipular legion. Bologna, Museo Civico.

line men'). They were equipped in broadly similar fashion, with bronze helmets and greaves and either a simple square bronze chest-guard, or more elaborate body armour such as a mail tunic, according to each individual's wealth and ability to provide his own protection.

Legionaries carried a distinctively Roman shield, a long (4 Roman feet, *c.* 1.17 m) oval type called a *scutum*, of laminated wood and canvas with an iron rim and boss. As an offensive weapon, they employed a short-bladed 'Spanish' sword optimized for stabbing. *Hastati* and *principes* also carried a pair of *pila* (singular *pilum*), heavy (thus armour-piercing) throwing spears with a long iron head set in a wooden shaft. *Pila* were thrown at short range before the legionaries engaged their enemies at close quarters with the sword. This combination of offensive weapons characterized Roman legionaries for almost half a millennium to come, as similar equipment continued to be used throughout the Principate. *Triarii* were equipped like the other heavy infantry except that they used a thrusting spear instead of *pila*. The fourth group of infantry was composed of 1,200 *velites*, skirmishers integral to the legion. Polybius describes them as drawn from the youngest recruits, equipped with a 3-Roman-feet-diameter (88 cm) round shield, sword and light javelins, sometimes with a wolf skin worn for identification over a plain helmet.

Each legion also had an attachment of 300 Roman cavalry. While these were drawn from the wealthiest members of society, and formed a social elite, cavalry was never a particular strength of Roman armies. Polybius states that, before his day, they had been lightly armoured and poorly equipped, whereas now they were armed and equipped according to contemporary Macedonian practice, with a Greek-style lance and shield.

The *hastati* and *principes* were divided into ten maniples of 120 men, the *triarii* into ten of 60 men. The *velites* were also organized into ten subunits, and assigned to the heavy infantry. The command structure of the legion emphasized maturity and experience: each was headed by six officers called tribunes, who had to have completed a minimum of five or ten years' military service before appointment. The officers who commanded the maniples, two for each, were the centurions, elected by the soldiers themselves. Polybius notes of these men:

> They want their centurions not to be men who are audacious and reckless, but individuals who are natural leaders, steady in spirit, with the power to endure. They don't want men who will rush forward and provoke combat before the main battle lines meet, but ones who will hold their position when their comrades are getting the worst of the battle and hard-pressed, and even die at their posts.
>
> Polybius, *The Histories* 6.24.8–9

This emphasis on tenacity rather than élan characterized Roman armies throughout much of their history, and their ability to endure and keep on fighting, on a strategic as well as tactical level, was a key factor in their ultimate defeat of Hannibal in the second Punic war. Polybius also records the ferocious discipline of the legions,

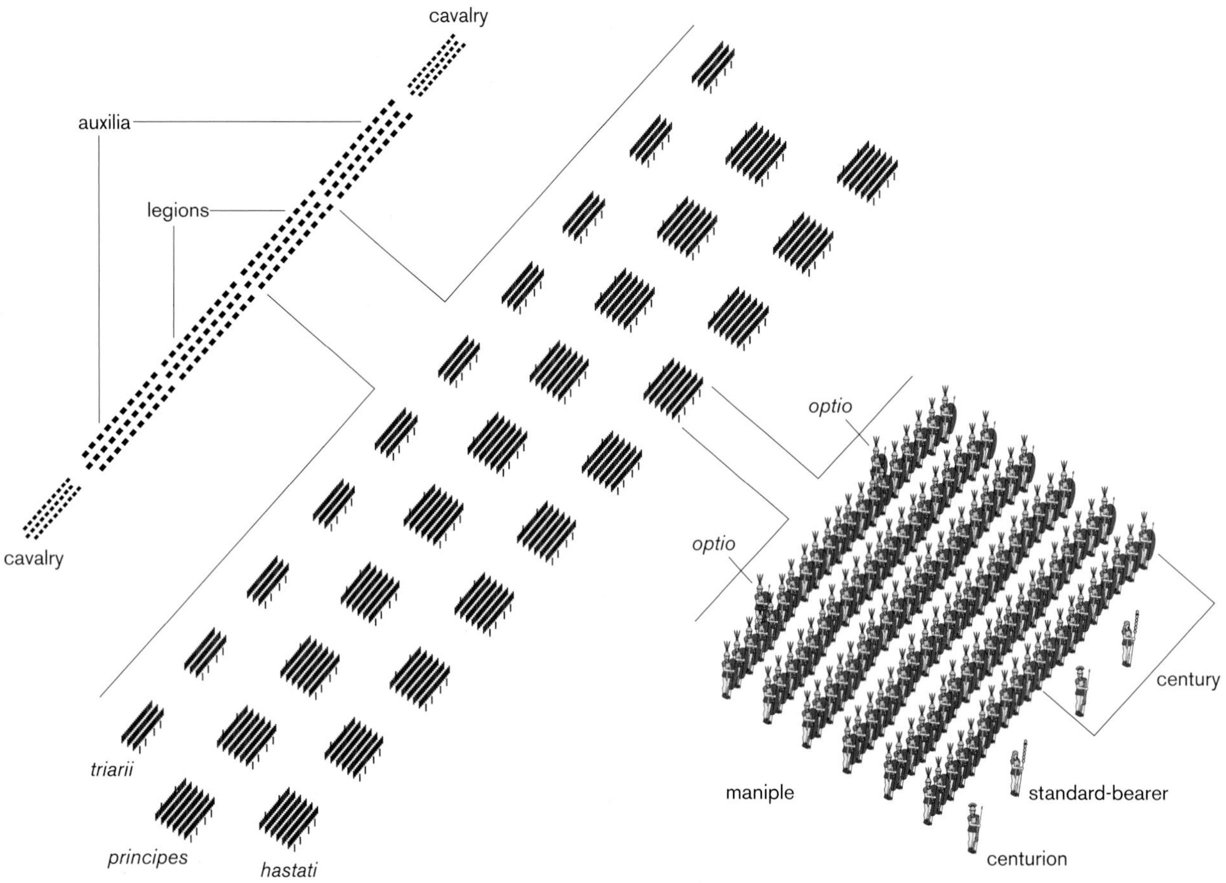

Deployment of manipular legion: a full Roman army, with the legions at the centre, the *auxilia* on each flank and the cavalry beyond them. The close-up of a legion shows three ranks of ten maniples. A maniple of *hastati* or *principes* consisted of two centuries of 60 men, with the centurion and standard-bearer standing in front of their respective centuries and the *optio* behind the century.

describing how men were beaten to death by their comrades for lapses on guard duty and entire units subjected to 'decimation', execution of every tenth man, for breaking in battle. The importance of centurions in providing an experienced cadre within each legion is another recurrent theme in the army of the later Republic and Principate.

Polybius' account also emphasizes that the legions did not fight alone. As the Romans expanded their political control of Italy, they compelled allies and subjects to provide military contingents to fight alongside them. Polybius (6.26.7) records that allies provided the army with infantry equal in number to the Romans', and about three times as much cavalry. The greater number of allied cavalry reflects the fact that Rome was traditionally weak in cavalry, while some allies and subjects (notably the Campanians of south-central Italy) inhabited plains more suited to raising and maintaining horses. Rome's use of 'auxiliary' or supporting troops is a consistent theme throughout her history. While all legions formed the high-status core of Roman armies, they invariably fought alongside lower-status and often more lightly equipped infantry, and cavalry, provided by allies and subjects.

The Manipular Legion in Battle

Contemporary accounts of ancient battles are rarely clear or detailed. Ancient writers (except, perhaps, Julius Caesar) gloss over technicalities, either because they assumed their audiences were familiar with them, or because technical detail did not go well with the grand rhetorical tone adopted by Roman historians. We have to piece together how the manipular legion functioned in battle from scattered evidence and a lot of guesswork.

It is clear that the *hastati*, *principes* and *triarii* normally fought in three separate lines in that order, each of ten maniples, with gaps between them. The maniples of *hastati* formed the first line and the *triarii* (as their name suggests) the third. Within each maniple, individual soldiers typically formed up in three or four ranks, for combat at least. Roman writers describe the maniples within the legion as forming a *quincunx*, or chessboard pattern. The great strength of the manipular legion was its flexibility (see pages 18–19): units from the second and third lines could support or relieve troops in the first line, or deploy onto their flanks to outflank an enemy as at Zama (202 BC) and Cynoscephalae (197 BC). Again, the practical details of how all this was done are not entirely clear. It seems unlikely that gaps within the maniples were retained when the first line came into contact with the enemy, or individual maniples would find themselves outflanked. Presumably there was a standard manoeuvre that a maniple used to increase frontage before coming into contact with the enemy, but no details of this survive. Nor are the mechanics clear of how a fresh line of troops might relieve a line already engaged. To have sufficient room to use their *pila* and swords effectively, individual Roman legionaries fought in relatively loose order compared with soldiers in a Macedonian phalanx, a point specifically made by Polybius.

What happened when two formations of legionaries (or other soldiers of the ancient world) engaged in hand-to-hand combat is a problem widely discussed by modern scholars, since ancient writers do not provide details. Some modern historians characterize ancient (particularly Greek) hand-to-hand combat as a large-scale shoving match by two close-packed bodies of men. This does not go well with the idea that Roman legionaries fought in fairly loose order and required space to use their swords effectively. Another possibility is that hand-to-hand combat was essentially a series of extended duels between the men in each front rank. This

Legion Against Phalanx: Romans Encounter the Macedonian Military

The other major military system in the 3rd–2nd-centuries BC Mediterranean, besides those of Rome and Carthage, was that of the successors to Philip II of Macedon and Alexander the Great. They developed an army emphasizing cooperation between heavy cavalry and heavy and lighter infantry. The cavalry, typically 'Companions' of the king, provided a striking force that attacked a weak point in the enemy line. Meanwhile the heavy infantry, whose function was to fix the enemy battle line, formed a phalanx armed with the sarissa, a pike some 6 m (*c.* 18 ft) long, wielded in both hands. Later commanders typically had access to fewer cavalry and emphasized the role of the phalanx in battle. They also made use of elephants, first encountered by Alexander in India. These could be effective in intimidating and disordering enemy forces, but often panicked causing casualties and disruption among their own side.

Polybius (18.29–30) compared the relative effectiveness of legion and phalanx in the context of the battle of Cynoscephalae in 197 BC. He noted that a Macedonian phalanx required half the frontage of a Roman legion, and that the sarissas of the succeeding four ranks protruded in front of the first, so each Roman soldier effectively had to fight against ten pikemen. This made the phalanx virtually unbeatable in frontal combat.

On the other hand, the looser and more flexible Roman maniples had an advantage in uneven terrain, where the phalanx could become disordered and the Roman legionaries could attack into gaps between the Macedonian troops. The length of the sarissa made it difficult for a frontally engaged phalanx to meet a threat from flank or rear, so the Romans could draw reserves from the second and third lines of the legion formation to move against the vulnerable enemy flanks.

Detail of a plate from Capena, Italy, 3rd century BC. Elephants were difficult opponents, but defeated by the Romans, e.g. at Zama in 202 BC, where Scipio deployed velites *between the legionary maniples to harass Carthaginian elephants and channel them between the subunits of heavy infantry. Rome, Villa Giulia Museum.*

The Rise of the Manipular Legions: From Defeat to Victory

These battles show how Roman commanders learned to exploit the flexibility of the manipular army and the weaknesses of their enemies.

Asculum (Italy), 279 BC: King Pyrrhus of Epirus narrowly defeated a Roman army that struggled to stand up to his elephants and the frontal attack of his phalanx.

Cannae (Italy), 216 BC: An outnumbered Carthaginian army under Hannibal won a decisive victory over the Romans whose unusually dense formation led to heavy casualties when their infantry was lured forward into a trap and encircled.

Ilipa (Spain), 206 BC: Publius Cornelius Scipio exploited the discipline and flexibility of the maniples to undertake a complex redeployment in the course of the battle against the Carthaginians, moving his best troops to the flanks of his infantry line to attack and defeat his enemy's weaker troops.

Zama (Tunisia), 202 BC: Scipio won the decisive victory of the second Punic war (and won the title *Africanus*) by using a novel manipular formation and *velites* to defeat Hannibal's opening elephant charge. He harnessed the flexibility of the maniples to support his own first line of infantry and outflank the enemy.

A gold stater coin depicting T. Quinctius Flamininus, the victor of the battle of Cynoscephalae against Philip V of Macedon in 197 BC, perhaps minted to commemorate that battle. He is named on the reverse side.

Cynoscephalae (Greece), 197 BC: T. Quinctius Flamininus defeated Philip V of Macedon by manoeuvring maniples to attack the enemy phalanx in the rear.

Magnesia (Lydia, Turkey), 190 BC: The Romans defeated the Seleucid king Antiochus III when his phalanx was disordered by his own elephants, and the more flexible Roman maniples struck into gaps in its formation.

Pydna (Greece), 168 BC: Aemilius Paullus defeated a Macedonian army under King Perseus when the phalanx was disordered on rough ground and the maniples exploited gaps in its formation.

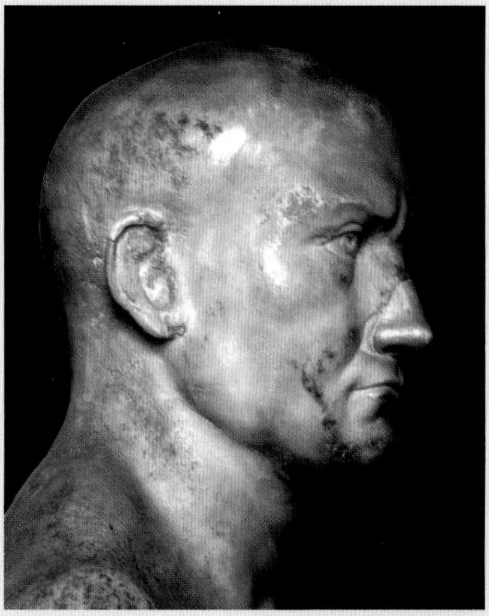

Below *Bust identified as that of Scipio Africanus, victor of the battle of Zama. Rome, Capitoline Museum.*

Left *A portrait bust identified as King Pyrrhus of Epirus (in northwest Greece), from the Villa of the Papyri in Herculaneum. Naples, Museo Archeologico Nazionale.*

corresponds more closely with what we know about legionary formations and Roman infantry training, although ancient writers imply that some battles involving Roman armies lasted for many hours before one side broke, a long time for soldiers to sustain brutal close-quarter fighting, if continuous.

The military historian Philip Sabin suggested that units involved in such long battles were not in continuous combat. If, after an initial charge, neither unit broke on first contact they may have fought until the strain forced one or both sides to break off temporarily. Then, after a period of recovery, they may have resumed fighting, only to break off again when once more exhausted or over-stressed. This cycle repeated itself until one side broke decisively. The possibility that hand-to-hand combat involved periods in which both sides stood off at a short distance from one another, interspersed with bouts of actual fighting, makes it easier to understand how fresh troops from the second and third lines of a manipular legion could relieve the first.

Normally the *velites* fought as skirmishers in front of the heavy infantry, using their javelins to disorder the enemy before they engaged the main Roman battle line and preventing enemy skirmishers from doing the same in turn.

In his account of the legions' organization, Polybius (6.24.6) mentions that each maniple had two standard-bearers and hence, presumably, two standards. We know nothing about their form in this period, although they may have been similar to the familiar 'pole with discs and crescents' used by legionary subunits in the later Republican period, or *vexilla*, with a flag hanging from a crossbar on a pole. However, the Roman encyclopaedist the Elder Pliny (*Natural History* 10.16), looking back from the 1st century AD to the early legions, implies that each had five animal standards. These depicted an eagle (described by Pliny as the 'first' of the standards), wolf, minotaur, horse and wild boar, and Pliny states that each was carried before a different subdivision (*ordo*) of the legion. These must have been different from the standards of each maniple, and, if the animal standards existed in Polybius' day, perhaps each belonged to a major division of the manipular legion (the *hastati*, *principes*, *triarii* and perhaps the *velites* and legionary cavalry) and/or the legion as a whole.

Besides the organization of the legion, Polybius records the engineering skills of the Roman army and the effort put into constructing marching camps when in enemy territory. An emphasis on engineering and construction remained characteristic of Roman armies through the subsequent imperial period.

Bronze statuette depicting a standard-bearer with eagle standard, from the Roman town of Alba Fucens (Abruzzo, Italy). Perhaps 1st century BC.

The 'Marian' Reforms of the Legions

The 2nd century BC was a period of imperial expansion, with legions defeating Macedonian and Seleucid armies in the East and pacifying and expanding former Carthaginian territories in North Africa, Spain and southern Gaul. Some legionaries may have become de facto professional soldiers as they served in one campaign after another. By the early decades of the 1st century BC, while the Roman legions remained units of about 5,000 infantry recruited from Roman citizens, they had undergone a number of changes in their organization, equipment and recruitment. These included an emphasis on the eagle as the primary symbol of the legion, a shift from the maniple as the basic subunit of the legion to the cohort of about 500 men, and homogenization of the troop types and equipment within the legion. Troops were recruited from a broader economic range of Romans as well as, eventually, from all over Italy.

Traditionally the great Republican general Gaius Marius (156–86 BC) has been seen as the driving force behind many of these innovations. Born in Arpinum, south of Rome, Marius was a political outsider (a 'new man') who exploited military success as a general to gain political power with popular support. He may have been a military reformer, but it is likely that some changes took

Denarius coin of the moneyer Lucius Sentius, minted in 101 BC, the year of Marius' victory over the German Cimbri (at Vercellae, northwest Italy) and his triumph over them and the Teutones, whom he defeated at Aquae Sextiae (Aix-en-Provence) in 102 BC. Marius made his name by victories over the Numidian king Jugurtha (107–6 BC).

place gradually over previous decades, and were assigned to Marius as a suitably renowned figurehead.

One important symbolic reform assigned to Marius (by Pliny the Elder) was the establishment of the eagle as the principal standard of each legion. As already noted, Pliny records that before Marius' second consulship in 104 BC the eagle standard had been one of five used by each legion, and Marius eliminated the other four. However, Pliny records that 'a few years before' it had become usual for the other four standards to be left in the camp while the eagle alone was carried into battle, so even this may have been the culmination of a process that began before Marius rather than a sudden innovation.

The Homogenization of the Legions

One important change by the first decades of the 1st century BC was the homogenization of legions into units composed of heavy infantry, without the differentiation of equipment and troop types seen in the manipular legion. While the

distinction between *hastati*, *principes* and *triarii* was preserved in centurions' titles, by Marius' day it ceased to have any significance in how legionaries were equipped and fought. The *triarii* disappeared as a distinctively equipped group by the early 1st century BC, when they used the *pilum*, like other legionaries, instead of the thrusting spear that had characterized their weaponry in Polybius' day. Likewise, *velites* disappeared as a distinctive light-infantry element. They are last mentioned in Sallust's account of the war against Jugurtha (*Jugurthine War* 46.7), shortly before Marius assumed full command. Henceforth Roman legions were composed entirely of heavy infantry.

A tendency towards homogenization of weapons and equipment had been encouraged already by the popular tribune Gaius Gracchus' law of 123 BC, granting state provision of soldiers' equipment (Plutarch, *C. Gracchus* 5.1). The equipment of the 1st-century BC legionary was similar to that of the earlier *hastati* and *principes*. The main offensive weapons remained the *pilum* and the short sword. Legionaries of this period continued to use the elongated oval *scutum* shield. The famous relief sculpture sacrifice scene from the so-called Altar of Domitius Ahenobarbus (below) provides an early depiction of such a shield, with its prominent reinforcing rib and boss. It also shows legionaries wearing tunics made of mail, a type of armour that the Roman writer Varro suggests was adopted from the Gauls, and helmets of the 'Montefortino' type (named after a site where examples were found).

The Roman cavalry assigned to each legion had also disappeared by the later 2nd century BC and the last reference to Italian allied cavalry is at about the same time as the last mention of *velites*.

This relief from the 'Altar of Domitius Ahenobarbus' (Rome, late 2nd/early 1st century BC) provides rare contemporary visual evidence for Republican legionaries, depicting *lorica hamata* mail armour, Montefortino helmets, the *gladius* sword carried on the right-hand side, and details of the *scutum* shield's exterior and its interior hand grip. Louvre, Paris.

The functions of light infantry and cavalry, once performed by specialists within the legions, were taken on by units of auxiliary troops outside the legionary structure, provided by non-Italian allies, subject peoples and mercenaries. Accounts of wars through the 1st century BC contain contingents already familiar from the Punic wars and Hellenistic armies of the past, including slingers from the Balearic Islands, archers from Crete and cavalry from Numidia and Gaul.

The Cohort

The maniples of 120 or 60 men that formed the primary tactical subunits of the manipular legion were subsequently replaced by larger subunits called cohorts. In the imperial period, these cohorts each had a nominal strength of 480 men,

Examples of 'Montefortino' helmets have been found on archaeological sites in Italy and Spain. They are characterized by a hemispherical bowl beaten from bronze, with a short neck guard, a knob (depicted on the Domitius Ahenobarbus relief as the base for a crest) and separate cheek pieces.

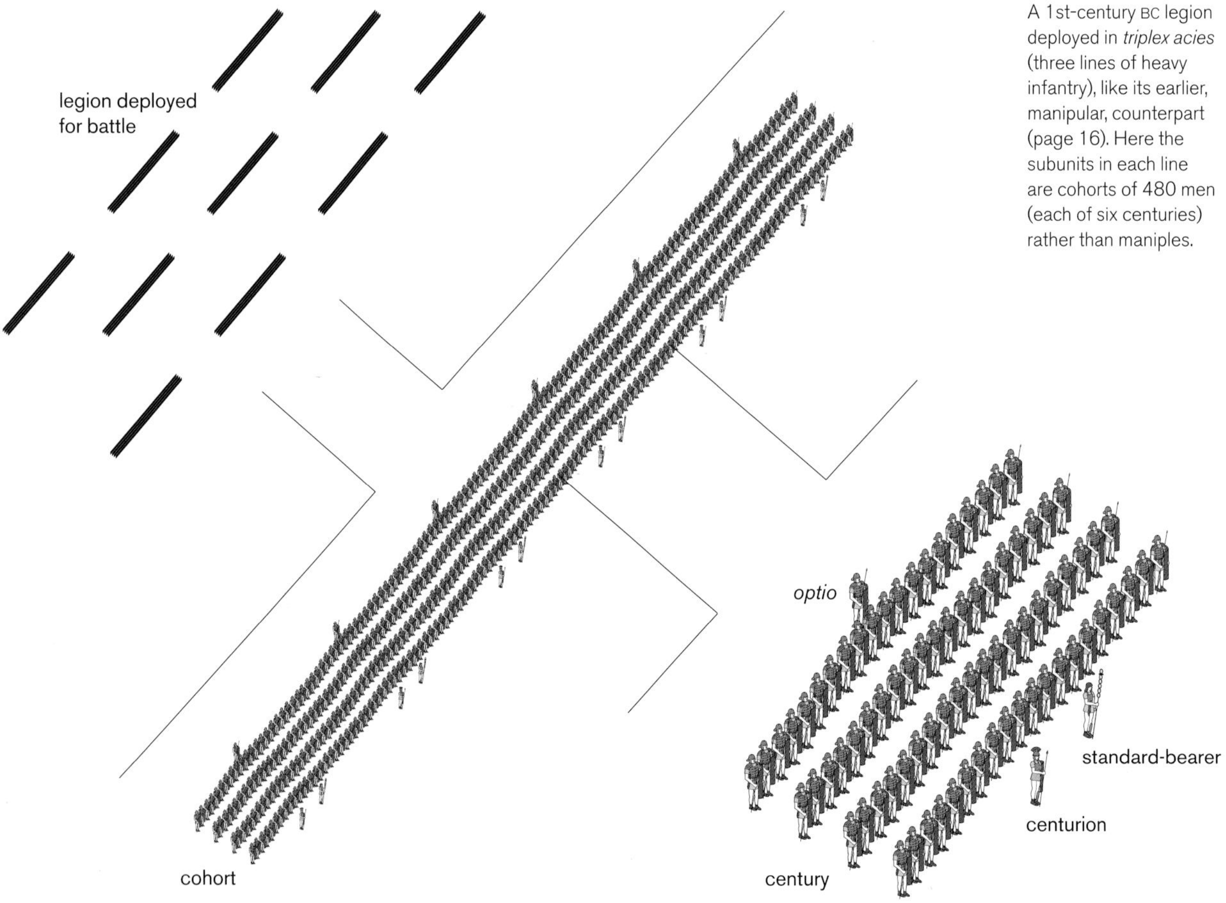

A 1st-century BC legion deployed in *triplex acies* (three lines of heavy infantry), like its earlier, manipular, counterpart (page 16). Here the subunits in each line are cohorts of 480 men (each of six centuries) rather than maniples.

This silver *denarius* coin was issued by Italian rebels against Rome during the Social war ('War of the Allies') of 91–88 BC. The obverse shows a female head, labelled *Italia*, as a personification of Italy. The reverse depicts men swearing an oath by holding out their swords towards a kneeling figure holding a pig.

divided into six centuries of 80, and this is likely to have been true of late Republican cohorts too. There were ten cohorts in each legion, so a full-strength late Republican legion had 5,000 or so men, all equipped as heavy infantry. We do not know exactly when the cohort became the principal subdivision of the legion, except that it was normal by the time of Caesar's Gallic wars. From this time onwards the maniples only appeared in the titles of the centurions within each legion.

Probably we should not think of a sudden switch to the cohort system coordinated by a single innovator like Marius. The two formations may have coexisted for some time, until the cohort became standard. Why this change took place is another important but difficult question. Some scholars argue that the change was a tactical one, and that the larger cohort was easier to control and more resilient against large formations of irregular enemy troops, such as Marius' opponents, the Cimbri and Teutones. Others suggest that the change related to imperial expansion and that cohorts were more versatile than maniples, more suited to detached service when legions were subdivided to conquer and pacify large territories.

Recruitment of the Legions

The later 2nd and early 1st centuries BC saw diversification in the range of men recruited into the legions, including the more regular use of poorer Roman citizens and also Italians who had previously served in allied contingents. As we have seen, service in the Republican army was a privilege and duty for Roman citizens with sufficient wealth to equip themselves for battle.

However, when Marius was elected consul for 107 BC promising a successful end to the war against the Numidian king Jugurtha, he recruited volunteers from the poorest members of society, the landless *proletarii*, rather than men who fulfilled the formal property qualification. The writer Sallust (*Jugurthine War* 86.3), presents this as a turning point in Roman politics and professionalization of the army, since, he claims, the poor were encouraged to volunteer by the prospect of booty from successful warfare and were malleable in the hands of politically ambitious commanders like Marius, because they had no economic stake in the state and would do anything for pay.

Marius' act has been viewed as a crucial one in the unravelling of the Republican political system as a succession of 1st-century BC commanders like Marius, Sulla, Pompey and Julius Caesar exploited the personal loyalty of their troops to achieve extra-constitutional power by threat or actual use of force. However, one can view Marius' actions not as revolutionary, but as a logical continuation of what had occurred previously.

The property qualification for legionary service had gradually been reduced over the previous century and in emergencies (as after Cannae in 216 BC) even the poorest citizens were recruited. Furthermore, there is no evidence that Marius' recruitment of the *proletarii* was intended to be a permanent reform and legions down to Augustus' reign probably included a mixture of volunteers (including *proletarii*, some of whom were effectively professional soldiers) and traditional propertied conscripts. In this, as in other aspects of Marius' military career, his action was less of a radical change than is sometimes presented.

The other change in legionary recruitment at this time resulted from the so-called Social war of 91–88 BC. This was a revolt by some of Rome's Italian allies, support for which was undercut by the Romans granting citizenship to those who remained loyal or laid down their arms. This swept away the political and judicial distinctions between Romans and most Italian adult males. Since citizenship was the main prerequisite for legionary service, Italians now joined the legions rather than providing separate allied contingents. As we have seen, the auxiliary troops, light infantry and cavalry that supported the legions then came from foreign allies and subjects.

Caesar's Legions, 58–44 BC

The campaigns of Julius Caesar provide an important background to the imperial legions, not because he was a great military innovator, but because many legions that served with him in Gaul (58–51 BC) and his subsequent civil war against Pompey the Great had a long-term existence that lasted into the imperial period.

Caesar in Gaul

In the Republican period, men who had served their year in Rome as consul or praetor typically left Italy for a period to govern part of the empire or even conquer new territories. They bore the titles *proconsul* ('with powers equivalent to a consul's') or *propraetor*. Following his consulship in 59 BC, Caesar was appointed to a proconsulship that allowed him to focus his activities on Transalpine Gaul, the area north of the Alps, mostly within the borders of modern France. At this time, the Romans only controlled Cisalpine Gaul (south of the Alps – modern northern Italy) and a narrow coastal strip linking Italy to Spain through the south of France (Provincia, 'the Province', hence modern Provence). Beyond lay Gallia Comata, 'hairy Gaul', with tribal peoples and proto-states subject to little or no Roman control. East of them (with the Rhine as a nominal boundary) was Germany, with peoples that were, for the most part, culturally distinct from the Gauls, and, to the northwest, Britain, with strong cultural and even political ties to Gaul.

Caesar started out with four legions under his command, numbered *VII*, *VIII*, *IX* and *X*. Their initial deployment was defensive, in northeastern Italy, but Caesar's military activities from 58 to 50 BC were conducted north of the Alps.

As his campaigns in Gaul developed, Caesar raised new legions and added them to the existing four. Most of his new legionaries were Roman citizens recruited in Cisalpine Gaul (northern Italy) and 'the Province' in the winter, after the campaigning season was over. The new legions raised continued the existing number sequence of *VII–X*, peaking at 12 legions in 52–50 BC.

58 BC: *XI*, *XII* added
57 BC: *XIII*, *XIV* added
54–53 BC (winter): *XIV* destroyed (later reconstituted)
53 BC: *XV* added and an additional legion borrowed from Pompey
By 52 BC: *V* and *VI* added
50 BC: former Pompeian legion returned to Pompey for Parthian war (never undertaken), along with Caesar's own *XV*

Statue of Julius Caesar. Rome, Capitoline Museum.

Major Events during Julius Caesar's Campaigns in Gaul

58 BC
- Campaign against the Helvetii; Roman victory near Bibracte (Mont Beuvray).
- Campaign against Ariovistus and the Suebi.

57 BC
- Campaign against the Belgae; Caesar's army narrowly escapes defeat when ambushed by the Belgic Nervii at the river Sambre.

56 BC
- Caesar's command extended for a further five years (to 50 BC) by agreement with Pompey and Crassus.
- Campaigns on the west coast of Gaul, against the Veneti and others.

55 BC
- Campaigns in northeast Gaul and against the Germans, both west and east of the Rhine.
- (Autumn) First expedition to Britain; withdrawal to Gaul.

54 BC
- (July) Second expedition to Britain.

53 BC
- (Winter 54–53 BC) Legion *XIV* attacked and destroyed in its camp by the Eburones in the Meuse Valley; another legion under Quintus Cicero (the brother of the politician and orator) survives a similar attack by the Nervii and is relieved by Caesar.
- Second crossing of the Rhine.

52 BC
- Defeat of the Bituriges' Revolt in central Gaul.
- Outbreak of Vercingetorix's Revolt.
- Battle at Gergovia.
- Siege of Alesia.

Caesar's account of his war in Gaul emphasizes the importance of his legions. He describes campaigns and battles in terms of their movements and actions, barely mentioning his auxiliaries (Numidians, Cretan archers, Balearic slingers (*Gallic War* 2.7) and Gallic and German cavalry). Sometimes the legions were concentrated into a single force for a campaign or battle. When Caesar fought the Helvetii near Bibracte (Mont Beuvray) in 58 BC, he drew up his four veteran legions (*VII–X*), their cohorts deployed in three lines, on the middle slopes of a hill, with the recently recruited legions *XI* and *XII* in reserve with the auxiliaries on the summit of the hill. In the following year, the army was gathered to campaign against the Belgic Nervii and, when it was attacked near the river Sambre (*Gallic War* 2.19), it included all eight of the legions (*VII–XIV*) recruited up to that time, along with auxiliaries.

However, Caesar also divided the army as necessary. He took only two (*VII* and *X*) of his eight legions to Britain in 56 BC, leaving the rest to garrison Gaul (*Gallic War* 4.22), and in the following year he took five legions on his second British expedition (*Gallic War* 5.8), leaving Labienus, his legate (a subordinate, with delegated powers; Caesar had ten in 56 BC), with three legions to guard his rear in Gaul. At other times the army could be dispersed, with legates sent to campaign or pacify a region with a force of anything from one to three legions.

Typically the onset of winter and the end of the campaigning season led Caesar to disperse his legions to winter quarters in Gallic *oppidum* settlements spread throughout Gaul, so they could live on the relatively meagre supplies available in any particular area. However, this dispersal of legions in barely pacified territory made the legions vulnerable to surprise attack. At the end of 54 BC, the recently raised *XIV*, commanded by the legates Q. Titurius Sabinus and L. Aurunculeius Cotta, wintered in the Eburones' territory in the Meuse Valley. Their camp was attacked and, when they tried to break out, they were ambushed. Cut off, the Romans tried to surrender to Ambiorix, the enemy commander, who killed Sabinus and launched a general attack on the Romans. Cotta was also killed, as was *XIV*'s eagle-bearer, who managed to throw the eagle back into the camp before he perished. Some men escaped back to the camp, but committed suicide. Only a few escaped (*Gallic War* 5.37).

In contrast, when the Nervii attempted to repeat the success of the Ambrones, against the winter quarters of *XI* commanded by Quintus

Cicero, they met with fierce resistance, until the camp was relieved by Caesar. Caesar recounts (*Gallic War* 5.44) how two senior centurions, Lucius Varenus and Titus Pullio, competed to outdo one another in bravery, leaving the safety of the camp to take on the enemy. Eventually, having killed numerous enemies though vastly outnumbered, the two men helped one another retreat into the camp, to the cheers of their watching comrades.

Two Brothers in Caesar's Legions

'Gaius Canuleius, son of Quintus, an *evocatus* (reservist) of Legion *VII*, decorated with necklaces, armbands, discs and a crown, died at the age of 35. Quintus Canuleius, son of Quintus, of Legion *VII*, was killed in Gaul aged 18. Their father set up this monument to the two brothers.' (*ILS* 2225)

Quintus, probably the elder brother, was killed serving in Gaul. Gaius fought in Gaul and was recalled as a veteran by Octavian to fight in the civil war before retiring to Capua (in Italy, where this inscription was found) where he died.

Caesar's Legions in Civil War

Civil war broke out on 10 January 49 BC, when Caesar led *XIII* from his province of Cisalpine Gaul across the river Rubicon into Italy, claiming the need to vindicate his name and position against Pompey and enemies in the Senate. The speed of his advance, even with such a small force, disconcerted Pompey, who quickly abandoned Rome, then fled Italy entirely, to Greece.

This gave Caesar full access to the legionary recruitment grounds of Italy, and so began the large-scale mobilization that typified the period to 30 BC. Caesar already had legions numbered *V* to *XV*. As consul in 48 BC, he added *I–IV* and equally quickly extended the (probably continuous) sequence beyond *XXX*. Caesar left Italy in summer 49 BC for Spain, where he employed legions from his Gallic army as well as newly raised forces to defeat Pompey's allies, then returned, and crossed the Adriatic to confront Pompey. After a clash at Dyrrhacium (Durrës, Albania) where a cohort of the Sixth Legion distinguished itself (see page 151), the decisive battle was fought at Pharsalus (in Thessaly, Greece).

Caesar's Tenth Legion

The Tenth Legion, already in Cisalpine Gaul when Caesar took up his provincial command, became an elite unit in his army – the legion on which Caesar could always depend.

As early as 58 BC, when elements of the army expressed doubts about following Caesar to fight Ariovistus' Suebi, Caesar proclaimed (*Gallic War* 1.40–41) that he would fight without them, taking just the Tenth Legion as his 'praetorian cohort'. Repaying the compliment, the Tenth expressed their enthusiasm for battle and the other legions fell back in line. A praetorian cohort was the unit of picked legionaries that acted as a Republican general's bodyguard, later evolving into the permanent Praetorian Guard of Roman emperors.

When Caesar and Ariovistus met to negotiate, they agreed to bring just a cavalry bodyguard. Caesar, distrusting his own Gallic cavalry, mounted some men of the Tenth to accompany him instead, joking (*Gallic War* 1.43) that first he had made them praetorians, now he was making them 'knights'. Like the English 'knights', the Latin *equites* meant 'cavalry' but also implied social status, as the *equites* were among Rome's richest citizens. Subsequently the legion was sometimes called *X Equestris* ('Mounted' or 'Knights').

The Tenth Legion was also important in preventing a Roman defeat at the hands of the Nervii at the Sambre (57 BC), when a Gallic surprise attack forced both leader and army to scramble into action at short notice. Caesar's own account (*Gallic War* 2.21, 23) describes how he fired up the Tenth by reminding them of their past achievements: the Tenth was one of two legions that Caesar had taken with him to Britain late in 55 BC. Famously, when the Roman troops hesitated to disembark from their ships on the British coast, the eagle-bearer encouraged them by leaping ashore himself with their standard, challenging his comrades not to abandon it to the enemy (*Gallic War* 4.25).

Caesar's former legate Labienus fought for Pompey and the senatorial forces in the subsequent civil war. His encounter with a man of the Tenth during the Thapsus campaign is related in *The African War* 16 (written perhaps by Aulus Hirtius, another of Caesar's legates). Caesar's army largely consisted of raw recruits, stiffened with men of veteran legions including the Tenth. Labienus is said to have hailed some of Caesar's men as novices, but a veteran identified himself proudly as a man of the Tenth, at the same time hurling a *pilum* at Labienus, whose horse it killed.

Caesar's Tenth Legion was the forerunner of the imperial legion *X Gemina*.

The small river Rubicon was important as the boundary between Caesar's province of Gaul and Roman Italy. By crossing it with *legio XIII* in January 49 BC, Caesar exceeded his authority and precipitated civil war.

PHARSALUS (central Greece, August 48 BC)
Caesar (*Civil War* 3.89) records the number of men (22,000) and of cohorts (80) in his army. This means that units were significantly under-strength, with an average of 275 men per cohort, or 2,750 men per legion. He only specifically lists three legions: the Tenth, and the Ninth, which was so under-strength that it was combined with the Eighth for the battle. Undoubtedly other Caesarian legions participated, however.

Pompey's army comprised 110 cohorts (equivalent to 11 legions), giving a total of 45,000 men plus 2,000 *beneficiarii* (recalled veterans). Among the legions were the First and Fifteenth (by this time renumbered the Third) that Caesar had given up for the Parthian war in 50 BC.

Caesar deployed in the usual three lines, but with a fourth, reserve, line of one cohort per legion to counter outflanking by Pompey's superior cavalry. Pompey's legions met Caesar's infantry at the halt, in a deep formation, while his cavalry drove off Caesar's. However, Caesar's fourth line defeated the enemy cavalry and flanked Pompey's legionaries, winning a decisive victory for Caesar.

Pompey lost 15,000 dead in contrast with Caesar's 200 (according to Caesar). Some 24,000 Pompeian troops surrendered and were incorporated into Caesar's army as four new legions, numbered up to *XXXVII*.

Gnaeus Pompeius Magnus, Pompey the Great, depicted in this portrait, was quickly and decisively defeated by Julius Caesar in the civil war of 49–48 BC. However, he had proved himself an effective general in previous decades, and had conquered substantial territories in the eastern Mediterranean for the Roman empire.

Veterans of Legion *XIV* in Africa

Reinforcements including the veteran legions *XIII* and *XIV* were sent to Africa to join Caesar before the battle of Thapsus. *The African War* (44–46) describes how men of *XIV* were captured by Scipio's army when their ship was blown off-course. Scipio offered to spare them if they changed sides. A veteran centurion of *XIV* refused and offered to take on a whole cohort of Scipio's men with just ten of his comrades. Scipio had him killed on the spot and the other veterans taken outside the camp, tortured and executed. Some recent recruits to the legion did defect to the enemy, however.

ALEXANDRIA (Egypt, winter 48–47 BC)
Pompey fled to Alexandria, but was assassinated on the orders of advisors to the teenage king, Ptolemy Philopator. Caesar pursued with two very under-strength legions, including *VI*. Siding with the king's sister Cleopatra, he was besieged by hostile citizens and Ptolemy's army of 20,000. He was relieved by *XXXVII* (ex-Pompeian troops) and then others, sent by sea and by land from Asia (*Alexandrian War* 9). The Romans won, despite losing 400 legionary dead in one episode of fighting alone (*Alexandrian War* 21).

Ptolemy allegedly drowned while crossing the Nile in flight, Caesar departed for Syria (with the Sixth Legion) leaving Cleopatra as ruler of Egypt.

ZELA (Pontus, north Anatolia, August 47 BC)
Caesar went on to Pontus and defeated its king Pharnaces, using his own legions *VI* and *XXXVI* (ex-Pompeians sent to garrison Asia) and a local 'imitation legion' of King Deiotarus, perhaps the predecessor of the imperial legion *XXII Deiotariana* (see page 123). This was the occasion on which Caesar famously said 'I came, I saw, I conquered'.

THAPSUS (Tunisia, April 46 BC)
After a brief return to Rome, during which he suppressed a mutiny of discontented veterans (including the Tenth Legion), addressing them as *Quirites* ('Citizens', a term normally applied to civilians – Suetonius, *Caesar* 70), Caesar made a risky winter landing in Africa with six legions (including the recently recruited *XXV*, *XXVI*, *XXVIII* and *XXIX*) to take on Pompeian supporters commanded by Pompey's father-in-law, Q. Metellus Scipio. The army was later reinforced and the decisive battle was fought at Thapsus, in which *II*, *V*, *VIII*, *IX* and *X* played important roles (*African War* 81). Scipio's army employed elephants in the battle and *The African War* (84) recounts an anecdote in which a legionary of *V Alaudae* continued to strike at an elephant that had picked him up in its trunk, until it dropped him and ran off. *V Alaudae* used an elephant emblem in the imperial period to commemorate this and other feats at Thapsus.

MUNDA (Spain, March 45 BC)
After Caesar's victory in Africa, his army fought the decisive final battle of the civil war at Munda (Spain) in March 45 BC, where Pompey's forces had rallied under his sons Gnaeus and Sextus, and Caesar's former legate Labienus. Caesar's victorious army included *V Alaudae* again, as well as men of the Tenth Legion who had already been discharged to establish colonies in Gaul. Labienus was killed in battle.

After Munda, Caesar returned to Rome, where he continued to exercise the supreme political power he had wielded since Pompey's departure from the city in 49 BC. Demobilization of veterans was intensified, but for many of them retirement was short-lived, as Caesar's assassination by senatorial opponents on 15 March 44 BC brought about another phase of civil war.

V Alaudae was unusual because of its distinctly Gallic character, including its cognomen *Alaudae*, 'The Larks', probably reflecting a Celtic practice of wearing feathers or bird crests on the helmet. It was recruited in Transalpine Gaul, but subsequently passed into Mark Antony's army, as shown by this *denarius* of Antony's legionary series (*c*. 33–31 BC), with the legion's eagle flanked by other standards and *LEG V*.

Imperial Legions with Likely Caesarian Origins

From the Gallic war period, 58–50 BC:

V Alaudae	*IX Hispana (?)*	*XII Fulminata*
VI Ferrata	*X Gemina*	*XIII Gemina (?)*
VII Claudia	*XI Claudia (?)*	*XIV Gemina (?)*
VIII Augusta		

From the civil war period, 49–44 BC:

I Germania (?) *III Gallica*

The Legions of the Triumviral Period, 44–31 BC

Julius Caesar's assassination began another phase of civil war lasting until Octavian (later the first emperor, Augustus) achieved supreme power after the battle of Actium in 31 BC. This is known as the triumviral period, after the 43 BC political alliance of three men, or 'triumvirate': Caesar's lieutenant Mark Antony, Caesar's great-nephew and heir Octavian, and Caesar's patrician supporter Marcus Aemilius Lepidus. These joined forces in order to eliminate Caesar's assassins, and the subsequent unravelling of the triumvirate led to a final confrontation between Octavian and Antony in 31 BC. Many of Caesar's legions were re-established, since the triumvirs drew on the support of his veterans to raise armies quickly, and many more new legions were created too, so the majority of the imperial legions traced their origins to this period.

Huge numbers of men served in the war and Augustus himself (*Res Gestae* 3.3) claimed that half a million men, the equivalent of 100 legions, had taken the soldier's oath to him. Inevitably some of these legions were disbanded during or at the end of the civil war. Others survived and formed the basis of the imperial standing army created by Augustus after 31 BC, so when we write the 'biographies' of the imperial legions (in Part II), we see that many of them started as legions commanded by Caesar or those recruited for the civil war that followed his death.

Bust identified as Mark Antony (Kingston Lacy, Dorset). Antony had shown his ability as a commander under Caesar in Gaul, was Caesar's political agent in Rome in the lead-up to civil war, and his second-in-command when he was dictator. He stood to inherit Caesar's political and military support, but was unexpectedly challenged by the young Octavian, Caesar's personal heir.

The War of Mutina and the Philippi Campaign, 43–42 BC

After Caesar's assassination, Mark Antony was faced with a hostile Senate and competition from Octavian, Caesar's 19-year-old great nephew and personal heir who had returned from studying in Greece not only to claim his family inheritance, but also to present himself as Caesar's political heir. Both Antony and Octavian drew on Caesar's past supporters and Octavian quickly raised an army from Caesar's veterans of *VII* (which would become the imperial *VII Claudia*) and *VIII* (imperial *VIII Augusta*), who had retired and settled in Campania, along with *IIII* (imperial *IIII Macedonica*) and *Martia* that had been on their way to join Antony. Initially Octavian allied himself with the Senate and linked up with the armies of the consuls Hirtius and Pansa who were seeking to relieve Mutina (Modena in northern Italy), where Decimus Brutus (one of Caesar's assassins) was under siege by Antony. The two armies fought two separate battles near the besieged city. An officer in the consuls' army wrote to Cicero, recounting the final stages of the first battle (at Forum Gallorum, 15 April 43 BC) as Antony's legions *II* and *XXXV* fought successfully against the *Martia* legion and Octavian's praetorian cohort (personal guard), only to come up against the veterans of *VII* and *VIII*:

Octavian's guard cohort was deployed on the Aemilian Way itself and the battle there was long. The left wing was our weaker one, with two cohorts of the legion *Martia* and the guard cohort. These began to retreat because they were out-flanked by Antony's cavalry.... When all our ranks had withdrawn, I retreated to our camp, the last to do so. Antony acted as if he had won the battle and thought he could take our camp too. But he failed and suffered a number of casualties. When Hirtius heard what was going on, he brought 20 veteran cohorts and attacked Antony as he was withdrawing to his own camp, and killed or routed all his men, in the same place as the earlier clash. Antony, along with his cavalry, retreated to his camp at Mutina at about 10pm....Thus Antony lost the majority of his veteran troops, but at the cost to us of casualties among the guard cohorts and the legion *Martia.* Two of Antony's eagles and 60 other standards were captured. The battle went well.

Cicero, *Letters to his Friends* 10.30

Major Events of the Triumviral Period

43 BC
- Conflict between Mark Antony and senatorial forces commanded by Octavian, and the consuls Hirtius and Pansa killed at the battle of Mutina (Modena, Italy).
- Establishment of the triumvirate between Antony, Octavian and Lepidus.

42 BC
- Octavian and Antony defeat Caesar's assassins Brutus and Cassius at the battle of Philippi (Greece).

41 BC
- Mark Antony in the East; Octavian resettles veterans in Italy.
- Conflict between Octavian and Mark Antony's brother (Lucius) and wife (Fulvia); siege of Perusia (Perugia, Italy; the 'Perusine war') ending in Octavian's victory.

40 BC
- War with Parthia (to 34 BC).

38–36 BC
- Octavian's war against Pompey the Great's son Sextus Pompey, centred on Sicily, won by Octavian in 36 BC.

31 BC
- Octavian defeats Antony (and Cleopatra) at the naval battle of Actium and begins the establishment of a new imperial political system.

Pansa was killed in this first battle, followed by his colleague Hirtius in the second, a few days later. While Antony lost both battles, he and Octavian were strengthened politically, and came together (with Lepidus) in a triumvirate, later in 43 BC. After purging their enemies, they crossed over to Greece with 22 legions, most of which derived to some extent from Caesar's former legions.

Caesar's assassins Brutus and Cassius gathered an army from the eastern part of the empire, but they were engaged by Octavian and Antony at Philippi, in eastern Macedonia, and defeated in two engagements in October 42 BC.

From the Perusine War to Actium, 41–31 BC

After Philippi, Antony stayed in the eastern empire, where he and his lieutenants fought against the Parthian empire. The first campaign (40–39 BC) was one of defence and counter-attack in Anatolia and Syria, as the Romans sought to ward off the forces of the Parthian king Pacorus and his Roman ally Q. Labienus (the son of Caesar's legate). In 36 BC, Antony invaded the Parthian empire. His army included two future imperial legions, *III Gallica* and *VI Ferrata* (see pages 133ff and 151ff), and it is likely that there were others. Antony advanced deep into the Persian heartland, but was forced to undertake a disastrous retreat in which his forces suffered heavy casualties.

In 41 BC Octavian returned to Italy with part of his army and also veterans of the Philippi campaign whom he was charged with settling in rural areas of Italy, including colonies in Campania (such as Benevento and Capua) and northern Italy (including Rimini and Bologna).

The confiscation of land that ensued caused unrest in Italy, and Antony's brother, the consul Lucius Antonius, and Antony's wife Fulvia advertised themselves as the champions of the dispossessed and of discontented veterans, and raised an army against Octavian. This was trapped and besieged by Octavian in Perusia (modern Perugia, see box opposite). Sling bullets from the site marked with legionary numbers provide evidence for the composition of the armies, including on Octavian's side *IIII* (later *Macedonica*), *VI* (*Victrix*), *VIII* (*Augusta*), *XI* (*Claudia*) and *XII* (possibly the later *XII Fulminata*).

After Lucius Antonius' defeat, Octavian and Antony were reconciled temporarily, and Octavian undertook a naval and land war against Sextus Pompey, the son of Pompey the Great, who had established a base on Sicily (see page 146). Both Octavian and Antony built up their armies, incorporating Caesar's legions and those raised by others (such as their colleague Lepidus and the consuls of 43 BC) as well as newly raised units. These sometimes duplicated numbers, leading to the complexities of the imperial army, when the triumviral numbers were preserved, giving rise to multiple legions with the same number.

Antony's legions before Actium are conveniently summarized by an issue of silver coins (probably to pay his forces), depicting a ship's prow (on the reverse) and eagle standards along with the numbers, and sometimes titles, of his legions (on the obverse). His army at Actium consisted of some 23 legions and may have included the forerunners of such imperial legions as *III Gallica*, *III Cyrenaica*, *V Alaudae*, *VI Ferrata*, *X Gemina* (Caesar's *X Equestris*) and perhaps *IIII Scythica* and *XII Fulminata*.

We lack such a convenient source for Octavian's legions, but they may have included the imperial legions *I* (*Germanica*), *II Augusta*, *III Augusta*, *IIII Macedonica*, *IIII Scythica* (?), *V Macedonica*, *VI Victrix*, *VII Claudia*, *VIII Augusta*, *IX Hispana*, *X Fretensis*, *XI Claudia*, *XII Fulminata*, *XIII Gemina*, *XIV Gemina*, *XV Apollinaris* and perhaps the rest of the sequence from *XVI* (originally *Gallica*, re-formed as *Flavia Firma*) to *XXI* (*Rapax*).

The final clash between Octavian and Antony took place at Actium, off the west coast of Greece, in September 31 BC. The decisive action was a naval battle, although their respective armies also took part in the campaign. Octavian won and took control of both forces. Some legions were disbanded and many soldiers retired, but many remained in service in the imperial army that took shape in the first decades of the reign of Octavian (or Augustus, as he subsequently became known). During this time, Augustus gradually developed a new political system focused on himself as emperor. And just as he instituted political, administrative, social and moral reform, so too he reformed the army, creating a professional standing force in which legions took on long-term identities and created individual histories.

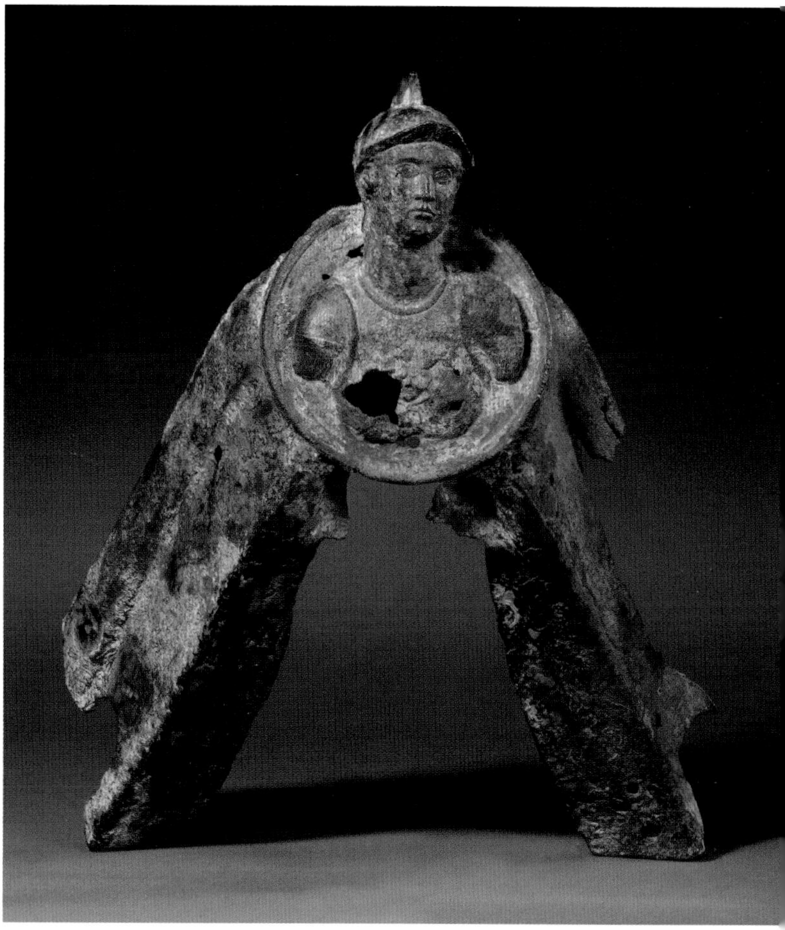

Bronze prow of a boat or small ship, found at Actium, perhaps from the battle of 31 BC. The helmeted female figure probably represents the goddess Athena / Minerva. (1st century BC? London, British Museum.) While Actium was primarily a naval battle, legions of both sides were deployed on land nearby, and some (such as *X Fretensis*) may have fought as marines.

PART II

The Legions in the Imperial Age

The Legions from the Time of Augustus

After the defeat of Mark Antony at Actium and his subsequent suicide in 30 BC, Octavian was left in sole control of the Roman empire. As the first Roman emperor, he created a new system of government, taking the name Augustus ('Revered One'). To ensure that he could not be overthrown in another round of civil war, he established himself as commander-in-chief of the army, with *imperium* (the power to raise and command armies) greater than that of the senators who typically governed the provinces and commanded armies in the field. These senators were mostly imperial appointees (legates) rather than the independent proconsuls and propraetors of the Republican period. Many emperors did not command armies in the field themselves, but almost invariably they took credit for their generals' victories and celebrated triumphs for campaigns undertaken in their name.

Augustus also demobilized the large armies of the triumviral period, reducing the number of legions to 28. There were never more than 33 legions in existence at any one time until the later 3rd century AD, with a total of about 150,000 legionaries and a similar number of supporting auxiliary troops. Some legions were disbanded or destroyed and some new ones raised in this time, but most took on a long-term and stable identity that enables us to recount in some detail their histories over almost three centuries, from the triumviral period to *c.* AD 250.

Augustus' main military reforms had the effect of turning the army into a standing force of long-service professionals, instead of the part-time citizen force of the Republic. This was intended to focus the loyalty of the troops on the state and the emperor as head of state, and reduce the potential for disloyalty among legions who might be tempted to throw in their lot with rebellious commanders, as they had in the civil wars of the 1st century BC. Augustus' professionalization of the army entailed creating regular, empire-wide terms of service. In theory, at least, soldiers signed up for a fixed length of service, received regular pay at standard rates set by the state and retired with a bonus provided by the state.

Previous pages
The spiral reliefs of Trajan's Column in Rome commemorate his victories in Dacia in AD 101–2 and 105–6, and provide important evidence for the equipment and activities of the Roman legions.

The emperor Augustus had a poor reputation as a battlefield commander, but his reorganization of the Roman army established it as a long-service professional standing force, with regular terms of service.

The Imperial Legions: Terms of Service

Length of Service

The normal length of service for legionary soldiers throughout the imperial period was 25 years. Augustus had experimented with shorter periods, starting with 16 years (from 13 BC, according to Cassius Dio 54.25) and then 20 years (AD 5, Dio 55.23), but he or one of his immediate successors settled on 25 years, probably to put off for as long as possible the payment of retirement bonuses.

Pay

The annual salary of 225 *denarii* a year for an ordinary legionary attested at the end of Augustus' reign (Tacitus, *Annals* 1.17) may have been established by Julius Caesar. Domitian (probably

AD 83–84) increased this to 300 *denarii*, and there were subsequent increases, under Septimius Severus and Caracalla (late 2nd–early 3rd centuries AD), probably to 450 and then to 675 *denarii*. However, the army took substantial deductions from pay for items such as clothing.

Legionaries also received sporadic but substantial additional income from imperial cash distributions when emperors came to power and at other important times. For example, Augustus left legionaries 75 *denarii* each in his will (Suetonius, *Augustus* 101.2), while Septimius Severus allegedly gave 2,500 *denarii* each to the legionaries who brought him to power (*SHA Severus* 7.6). Soldiers could also enrich themselves from looting and extortion.

Retirement

Augustus introduced a regular retirement bonus for soldiers. This was a response to the unrest caused by confiscations of land in Italy for the resettlement of veterans, a typical late Republican practice that he had undertaken himself after the Philippi campaign (42 BC). After Actium, he used his own tremendous wealth either to give veterans a cash bonus, or to buy land for them. In AD 6, he established a regular state-operated military treasury funded by auction and inheritance taxes to provide cash bonuses for veterans.

Other veterans were settled in *coloniae* (colonies), urban communities of veterans founded outside Italy. This continued through the 1st and early 2nd centuries AD, but largely died out after Hadrian's reign. Other Roman cities acquired the title *colonia* in later decades, purely as a mark of honour, although sometimes these were communities with a close association with the army. One such example is Eboracum (York, in Britain), where the city had developed alongside the legionary fortress.

The Roman theatre at Augusta Emerita (Mérida) in Spain, a *colonia* of discharged veterans founded by Augustus. The theatre was initially built by Marcus Agrippa in 16–15 BC and reflects the cultural impact of the settlement. Other imperial veteran colonies include Berytus (Beirut, Lebanon), Glevum (Gloucester, England) and Aelia Capitolina (Jerusalem), established by Augustus, Nerva and Hadrian respectively.

Theory and Reality of Military Service

Despite all this, there is evidence that the system did not always function as advertised. In particular, the state had a vested interest in delaying payment of soldiers' salaries and retirement bonuses for as long as reasonably possible. However, delays might lead to discontent, mutiny or even revolt. The historian Tacitus sets out a range of soldiers' complaints in his account of a mutiny of the Pannonian legions in AD 14 (*Annals* 1.17) – probably exaggerated for rhetorical effect, but presumably at least plausible to his listeners and readers. The main complaints besides the general harshness of military life, are that soldiers were kept on beyond their retirement age; that veterans were given land in undesirable frontier regions; and that pay was insufficient, with deductions taken for clothing and equipment. In addition, as we have seen, general pay rises were very infrequent.

Nevertheless, it is clear that service in the legions was an attractive option for many. Soldiers were fed at least reasonably well and regularly, in contrast to many of their peasant contemporaries, the social group from which most soldiers were drawn. And, despite complaints about pay and retirement, a veteran's bonus and savings that accumulated over 25 years of service, together with the prestige and status of military service, meant that an ex-soldier was a comparatively wealthy and important man in civilian society.

There is some evidence of conscription in the imperial period (notably, but not exclusively, for the emergencies of the Pannonian Revolt of AD 6 and after the defeat of Varus' army in the Teutoburg Forest in AD 9), but this is probably more relevant to the auxiliary forces than to the legions. For the most part, service in the legions was a desirable enough occupation that they could be kept up to strength with volunteers, and conscription was unnecessary.

In theory, recruits were all Roman citizens – in contrast with the auxiliary forces, initially composed of free non-citizens of the empire. This was largely true in practice, although in the eastern empire, where there were few Roman citizens early on, non-citizens seem to have been recruited, becoming citizens on enrolment (see page 124). Legionaries who served in the East tended to be recruited in other eastern provinces and spoke Greek in private. Legionaries serving in the West tended to be recruited in western provinces and spoke Latin. Latin was the official language of the army (in official inscriptions, documents and orders) throughout the empire.

Scholars such as Giovanni Forni and J. C. Mann have shown that that most legionaries across the empire were of Italian origin until the reign of Claudius (AD 41–54). Through the reigns of Claudius and Nero, about half were Italian and half of provincial origin. By Trajan's reign (AD 98–117), legionaries from the provinces outnumbered Italians by four or five to one, although these provincial recruits often came from culturally Roman regions and communities such as *coloniae*. In the later 2nd and 3rd centuries, recruitment became more localized, and many legionaries were recruited *castris*, 'from the camp', typically sons of soldiers.

The Organization and Command Structure of the Imperial Legion

Evidence for the structure of the imperial legion is wide-ranging, including inscriptions, papyrus documents, and archaeological evidence of legionary camps and fortresses, along with literary texts, notably *Concerning the Fortification of a Camp* by Hyginus (or 'Pseudo-Hyginus') whose date is uncertain. Broadly speaking, paper organization of imperial legions was very similar to that of the late Republican period and remained so until the 3rd century AD. A legion was still organized in ten cohorts, each typically made up of six centuries of 80 men each. The centuries were subdivided into *contubernia* (singular, *contubernium*) of eight men. This much is relatively clear, and implies a legion of 4,800 at full strength.

The legion also had a detachment of 120 horsemen (*equites legionis*), typically employed as messengers and similar roles, rather than as cavalry in combat. It is unclear whether they were included in the legion's notional strength of 4,800, or supernumerary.

In some periods the first cohort of some (or all) legions was double strength. This is stated by both 'Pseudo-Hyginus' and Vegetius (writing in Late

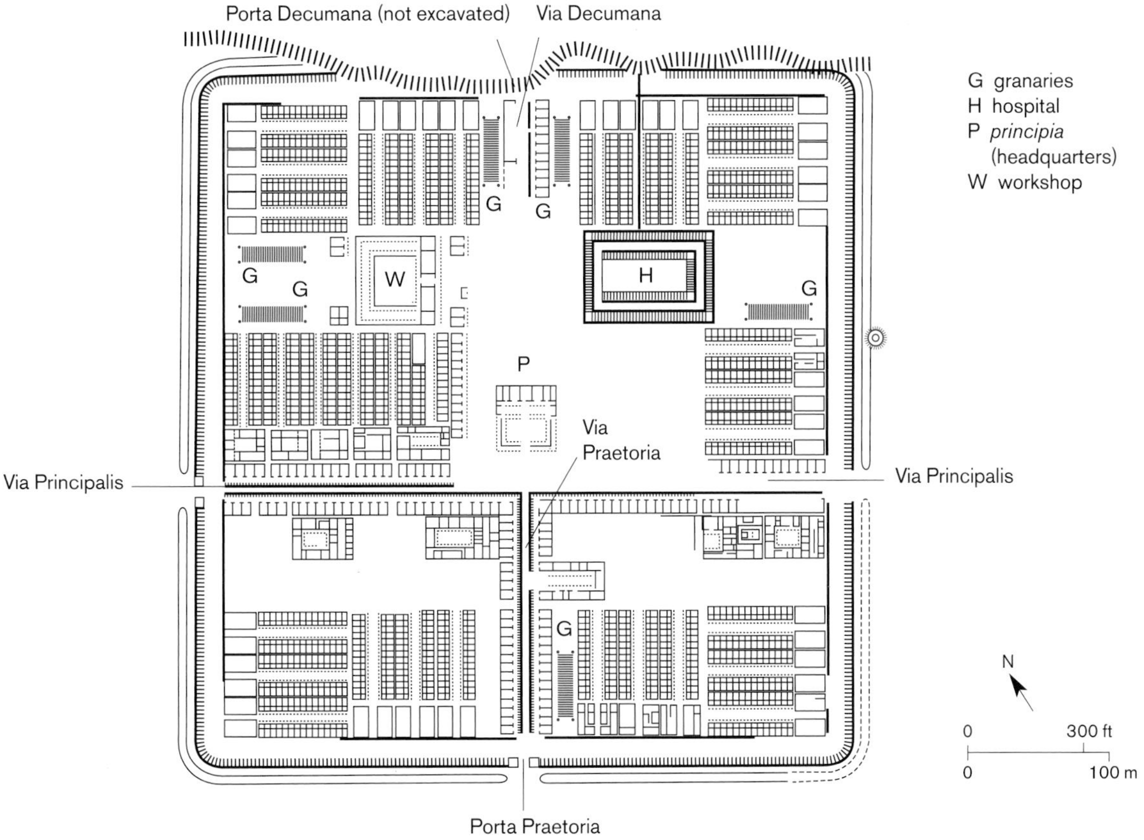

Aerial photography (see pages 46–47) and excavation of the fortress of Inchtuthil in Scotland have provided our clearest evidence for the layout of an imperial legionary base. The elongated rectangular barrack blocks are mostly in groups reflecting the six centuries of a standard cohort. The larger group of barracks for the first cohort is to the left of the *principia* (headquarters).

Antiquity, but reflecting past as well as contemporary practice). This is confirmed by one of the best-preserved and excavated legionary fortresses, at Inchtuthil in Scotland, datable to *c.* AD 84–86 (see above and image on page 47). Its plan shows normal barracks for nine cohorts and a larger group west of the central headquarters building, with barracks for five (rather than six) double-sized centuries. This suggests a first cohort of 800 (rather than 480) men and a nominal legion strength of 5,120. This may not have been true for all legions in all periods. Other excavated fortresses lack special arrangements for the first cohort and scholars have argued that the larger first cohort was a creation of the Flavian period, or a feature of early imperial legions abandoned after the Flavian period.

Cohorts, centuries and *contubernia* were the regular subunits of the legion, but it could also be broken down into vexillations, temporary (in theory, at least) detachments named after the *vexillum* (flag) standard they carried in place of the legion's eagle. Using vexillations, typically 1,000 or 2,000 men drawn from a particular legion, was common practice to avoid moving the whole legion far from its post when troops were needed to deal with a crisis or mount a campaign in another province. This was particularly common from the 2nd century AD, when legions tended to settle into long-term locations and permanent fortresses, but we find evidence of their vexillations across the empire, for example in the Jewish Revolt of AD 66–70.

Large legionary vexillations, with attached auxiliaries, were typically commanded by senatorial commanders with titles such as *dux*, *praepositus* or legate, or sometimes by very senior centurions. Smaller detachments for policing or construction duties might be commanded by centurions.

Emperors, Army Commanders and Legionary Commanders

At the top of the hierarchy was the emperor himself, commander-in-chief of the Roman army by virtue of his possession of *imperium maius*, a

power to raise and command armies that outranked that of anyone else. Some emperors commanded armies in the field themselves, others did not, but emperors of both categories adopted the trappings of military command in the form of the title imperator ('victorious general') and victory titles such as *Germanicus, Dacicus, Parthicus* ('Conqueror of Germany, of Dacia, of Parthia' – in this case the titles in AD 117 of Trajan, a particularly active conqueror).

The imperial system of provincial government ensured that provinces with a legionary garrison were governed by a *legatus Augusti pro praetore*, or 'imperial legate with praetor's powers'. He was drawn from the Senate as a personal appointee of the emperor, governing and commanding in the name of the emperor. If there was just one legion in a province, the imperial legate also commanded that legion and was typically of *praetorian* status (he had been praetor in Rome). If there were multiple legions in a province, they were commanded by men with powers delegated to them by the provincial governor, and each legionary commander was known as a *legatus legionis* ('legionary legate'). In a multi-legion province, the governor (imperial legate) typically was of *consular* status (i.e. had been consul at Rome). All served at the will of the emperor and undertook military activity under his auspices – any successes they won were in his name.

Typically the men who commanded armies and legions were senators. There were no military specialists in Roman government and no imperial high command. All senators alternated brief periods of military command with administrative posts, participation in domestic politics and careers as legal advocates. As military commanders they were, to a great extent, amateurs, even though most did a brief spell as a junior officer (tribune) in a legion. They would have depended on the professional junior officers (tribunes and centurions) as well as the training and discipline of the legionaries themselves to win battles.

The governors of a few provinces (notably Egypt, but also Mesopotamia) were *equites* ('knights'), members of the next wealthiest group in Roman society after the senators, the equestrian order. Not only were the governors of these provinces *equites* (such as the prefect of Egypt, who doubled as Egypt's principal military commander), but also the commanders of

This detail from Trajan's Column shows a *testudo* of legionaries (see page 46) assaulting a Dacian fortification. Trajan commanded his army in person – he is depicted at the extreme right of the image. In the imperial period, only the emperor as commander-in-chief (or, sometimes, members of his family) could celebrate a full triumph even if a subordinate actually commanded in the field.

individual legions within those provinces. Equestrian officers were often more experienced than senators, having served as commanders of auxiliary infantry and cavalry units and as junior legionary officers before achieving higher command.

Officers within the Legion: Tribunes and Centurions

Officers within each legion can be divided into two groups. Tribunes, like the legionary legate (commander), were drawn from Rome's social and political elite, the senatorial and equestrian orders, and were not professional soldiers. They alternated military service with political, judicial and administrative duties. Others, principally centurions, were career soldiers.

Tribunes

One tribune per legion came from the senatorial order and was known as *laticlavus*, 'broad striper', from the striped toga distinguishing members of that order. Typically he was a young man (in his twenties), and only served for a year in a particular legion to give him a brief exposure to military life. Before he became emperor, the young Hadrian served as tribune in three different legions (*II Adiutrix*, *V Macedonica* and *XXII Primigenia*), but such military experience was exceptional, and most young aristocrats would have served as tribune once or twice only, with little further military service before (perhaps) commanding a complete legion later in life.

Five tribunes were drawn from the equestrian order, and were known as *angusticlavi*, 'narrow stripers' from the distinctive togas worn by *equites*. Typically they had more military experience than their senatorial counterparts, as equestrian military officers commanded a cohort of auxiliary infantry and (sometimes) an auxiliary cavalry unit before becoming tribune in a legion. A few might even be former centurions promoted to the equestrian order and serving in command positions. These five equestrian tribunes may have been assigned to command two cohorts each in battle, since Josephus (*Jewish War* 6.131) mentions 1,000 men assigned to each tribune during combat in Jerusalem in AD 70. Josephus also discusses (*Jewish War* 3.87) their role as intermediaries between centurions and the legionary legate, implying that each tribune had regular responsibility for a particular part of the legion, in battle and in camp.

The *praefectus castrorum* ('prefect of the camp') was effectively third-in-command of the legion (after the senatorial legate and senatorial tribune) and had special responsibility for fortifications, sieges and artillery. He was also a member of the equestrian order, and might be a former *primus pilus* (senior centurion).

Career Officers: The Centurions

Each of the ten cohorts in a legion, except for the first, had six centurions with titles in part derived from the organization of the old manipular army described by Polybius.

Cohorts II–X

pilus prior	*princeps prior*	*hastatus prior*
pilus posterior	*princeps posterior*	*hastatus posterior*

In this terminology, *pilus* derives from a word for a spear (like *pilum*), *prior* means 'former' and *posterior* 'latter', deriving from the order in which centurions were chosen in the old manipular army. *Princeps* and *hastatus* derive from the *principes* and *hastati* of the old manipular army. Most scholars believe that the titles of centurions in the second to tenth cohorts did not denote any particular rank or seniority. However, the five centurions of the first cohort, the *primi ordines* ('men of the first rank') were of higher rank than any other centurion and there was progression within that cohort.

Cohort I

primus pilus	*princeps prior*	*hastatus prior*
	princeps posterior	*hastatus posterior*

The *primus pilus* was the highest-ranking centurion in the legion, followed by the *princeps prior*, *hastatus prior*, *princeps posterior* and finally *hastatus posterior*. The term *primipilaris* (plural *primipilares*) was applied collectively to men who had held the rank of *primus pilus*.

Some centurions were promoted from the ranks, while others entered the army as centurions. Studies of *III Augusta* in Africa and *VII Gemina* in Spain suggest that many were recruited directly from the municipal landowning class and a few from the equestrian order in Rome. Centurions normally spent about three years in a particular legion, then moved on to another. Their careers could take them to several different provinces. Most did not achieve the rank of *primus pilus*, but those who did might move up into the equestrian career structure, serving as auxiliary commanders, tribunes in legions or the garrison of Rome (praetorians, urban cohorts or *vigiles* – nightwatchmen) and even as civilian financial officials (procurators) within the imperial administration.

Immunes and *Principales*

The ordinary soldiers of the legions were known as *milites* ('soldiers', singular *miles*), but among the rankers there were men with titles denoting special responsibilities and technical specializations. Over the 2nd century AD their statuses were formalized. There was a basic distinction between *immunes*, men who received no additional pay but were excused heavy labour, and *principales*, who received additional pay.

Principales typically received pay-and-a-half (sometimes double pay) and included men with

Centurion's Careers

Latin inscription *CIL* 3, 14387, from Heliopolis (Baalbek)

'To [Lucius] Antonius Naso, son of Marcus, of the tribe Fabia, [centurion] of *Legion III Cyrenaica*, [centurion] of Legion *XIII Gemina*, honoured by the emperor in the White Parade [?], of the community of the Colaphiani, *primus pilus* of Legion *XIII Gemina*, tribune of the Legion *I Italica*, tribune of the Fourth Cohort of Nightwatchmen, tribune of the Fifteenth Urban Cohort, tribune of the Eleventh Urban Cohort, tribune of the Ninth Praetorian cohort, decorated by the emperor [Nero?] with a mural crown, a gold crown, two flags, two untipped spears, [*primus pilus* for a second time] in Legion *XIV Gemina* [tribune] of the First Praetorian Cohort, in charge of the veteran soldiers of numerous armies staying in Rome, procurator of the emperor in Bithynia and Pontus.'

Antonius Naso had an exceptional career as centurion, and beyond. He went from Egypt to Pannonia, where he served as centurion, then *primus pilus*. He then became a tribune of *I Italica* (probably when it was raised in Italy) and held a number of tribunates in Rome. He was dismissed as tribune of the Ninth Praetorian Cohort (Tacitus, *Histories* 1.20) by Galba in AD 69, but returned to the army to do a second stint as *primus pilus*, in *XIV Gemina*, once more served as a tribune in the Praetorian Guard, and eventually became a procurator (financial official) in modern Turkey. The 'White Parade' is not attested elsewhere and its significance is unknown.

Latin inscription *CIL* 8, 2877 from Lambaesis, Numidia (Africa)

'To the spirits of the departed. Titus Flavius Virilis, centurion of Legion *II Augusta*, centurion of Legion *XX Valeria Victrix*, centurion of Legion *III Augusta*, centurion of Legion *III Parthica Severiana* as *hastatus posterior* of the ninth cohort. He lived for 70 years and served for 45 years. Lollia Bodicca, his wife, and Victor and Victorinus his sons and heirs had this made at a cost of 1200 sesterces.'

This is a more ordinary, but lengthy, career. The length of his service suggests he was a legionary before achieving promotion. His first two appointments were in legions in Britain, then he moved to Africa and finally Mesopotamia. The title of *III Parthica* dates this inscription to the 3rd century AD. Presumably on retirement he returned to his previous station at Lambaesis in Africa, where he died. His wife's name, Bodicca (like Boudica) suggests she was British.

Far left Tombstone of Cn. Petronius Asellio (*CIL* 13, 6816, Moguntiacum), an officer from the equestrian order who served as legionary tribune, cavalry officer and *praefectus fabrum* (chief of engineers) for Tiberius.

Left Relief fragment from the fortress of Moguntiacum (Mainz), depicting legionary and *signifer* on the march. (Late 1st century AD, Mainz, Landesmuseum.)

the title *optio* ('orderly', typically assisting a centurion), *tesserarius* (bearer of the password), standard-bearers (*aquilifer, signifer, imaginifer*) and senior clerical officials. An impression of the range of activities undertaken by *immunes* is provided by a 2nd-century AD legal scholar, preserved in the Roman legal compilation *The Digest* (50.6.7). It includes medical orderlies, surveyors, metalworkers, clerks, musicians and others. Some of these titles (and more besides) are also attested in inscriptions and papyrus documents.

The Equipment of the Imperial Legions

Legions of the imperial period were predominantly composed of heavy infantry and formed the core of Roman armies. Lighter infantry, specialists such as archers, and cavalry were provided by (infantry) cohorts and (cavalry) *alae* of auxiliary troops. These were lower-status units recruited, initially at least, from peregrines, free non-citizen individuals within the Roman empire.

Offensive Weapons

The offensive weapons used by legionaries of the first two centuries AD were very similar to those used in Marius' time and show strong continuities from as far back as the Punic wars and Polybius' 2nd-century BC account of legionary equipment. Imperial legionaries were primarily swordsmen who employed a heavy throwing spear (*pilum*) to disrupt their enemy before engaging in hand-to-hand combat. Imperial battle accounts tend to be rather vague and general, but the *pilum*-and-sword combination is described vividly in Caesar's account of the battle of Bibracte in 58 BC, one equally applicable to the imperial period:

> Caesar's soldiers threw their *pila* from higher ground and easily broke up the enemy's phalanx. When this was disrupted, they charged with swords drawn. The Gauls were greatly disadvantaged in combat, as many of their shields were pierced or pinned together by a single *pilum* cast. The iron heads had bent over, so the Gauls could not pull them out or fight effectively with their left arms weighed down. Many Gauls, having tried for a while to shake off the *pila*, preferred to throw away their shields and fight unprotected. Eventually, worn out by their wounds, they began to retreat and withdrew to a hilltop about a mile away.
>
> Caesar, *Gallic War* 1.25

This modern re-enactor is dressed as a centurion, with his characteristic transverse helmet crest and vine staff. He also wears military decorations: *phalerae* (discs on his chest), torques (on his shoulders) and *armillae* (wristbands).

The importance of the sword is seen in Polybius' account of the legionaries' *gladius hispaniensis* (Spanish sword), and early imperial swords of the Mainz type (so-called because examples were found in the Rhine at Mainz, in Germany) are quite similar to Republican examples. The Mainz-type sword was a short sword, primarily (but not exclusively) for stabbing rather than cutting. From the AD 60s or so, the Mainz type was increasingly replaced by the Pompeii type, so-called because examples were found at Pompeii (and Herculaneum), buried by the eruption of Vesuvius in AD 79. It has a shorter point than the Mainz type and, while it too was primarily a stabbing weapon, it was perhaps more versatile as a cutting weapon than the Mainz type.

By the later 2nd or early 3rd century AD, the short stabbing sword was largely replaced by the longer *spatha*, a cutting weapon previously used by Roman cavalry (who required longer swords to cut down their opponents) and probably adopted from Rome's Celtic enemies. Legionaries carried the *spatha* on the left side (so it could be drawn across the body) rather than the right, where they had carried the shorter sword for a straight draw from its scabbard.

The importance of swordsmanship for imperial legionaries is emphasized by written evidence and artistic depictions such as a relief from Mainz that shows a legionary employing a characteristic underarm thrust with a short stabbing sword. Vegetius' late antique military manual describes (1.1) how Roman recruits were trained to fence against a post, using a double-weight wooden sword to develop skills and stamina. Legionaries carried a dagger as a secondary weapon.

The brutality and physical and psychological stress of hand-to-hand sword combat between two Roman armies is vividly described by the writer Appian:

> The two sides fell on one another, inspired both by anger and by their passion for honour, treating the battle as a personal issue rather than one between their generals. Both sides were experienced and neither raised a battle-cry, knowing it wouldn't inspire fear in their enemy. Nor did they utter a sound in the battle itself, regardless of whether they were winning or losing. There was no room for outflanking or

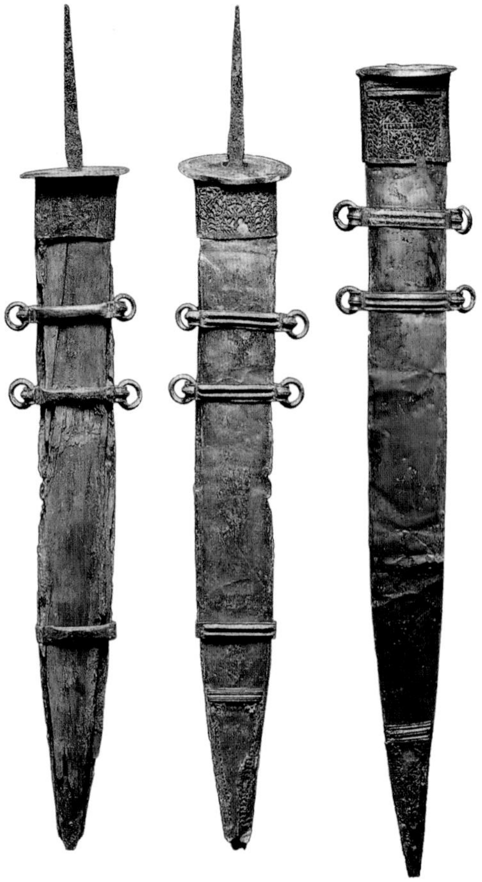

Examples of scabbards for Mainz-type swords that were typified by their tapering blade (sometimes with a 'waisted' profile), contrasting with the 'Pompeii' type with its parallel-edged blade. The hand guard, grip and pommel were riveted on to the tang of the sword.

This legionary wears *manicae*, arm protection against the sickle-like *falx* of his Dacian opponent. Relief from the AD 108 *Tropaeum Traiani* at Adamklissi (Romania), commemorating Trajan's conquest of Dacia.

charging among the marshes and ditches, so the armies met in close order. Neither side could dislodge the other, as they engaged at close-quarters with the sword, as if in a wrestling bout. No blow was unaimed and men were wounded and slaughtered, uttering groans rather than shouting out. When a man fell he was carried off at once and another took his place. These veterans did not need instructions or encouragement – each man was, in effect, his own general. When they got tired, the two sides drew a short distance apart from one another, as if drawing breath in a gymnastic competition, then resumed the close-quarter battle again. The new recruits who had come up were awe-struck to see such deeds done with such discipline, and in silence.

Appian, *Civil War* 3.68

The account by Caesar of the battle of Bibracte (see page 41) shows that the sword was used to close with the enemy after throwing *pila*, heavy javelins designed for short-range fighting, with a maximum range probably of about 30 m (*c.* 100 ft), and effective armour-piercing range probably rather less, to penetrate armour and disorder and encumber the enemy. While Polybius states that legionaries in his time carried two *pila* of different weights, Josephus (*Jewish War* 3.95), writing in the later 1st century AD, says they carried one, and depictions of legionaries typically show one.

Examples surviving from the Augustan legionary fortresses on the Rhine show that imperial *pila* typically had an iron pyramidal head (for penetrating armour) and shank riveted into a wooden shaft. Depictions and surviving examples often show a pyramidal extension of the shaft where it attached to the shank, and sometimes weights, to increase penetration. The weight of the wooden shaft and the thin iron shank meant the latter often bent on use, making it impossible for an enemy to throw it back, and (as Caesar describes) encumbering their shields. The *pilum* had been used in the Punic wars and eastern wars of expansion, was a primary weapon of legionaries in the late republic and early empire, and remained in use into the 3rd century AD. However, by then it was no longer the only type of spear used by legionaries, since the *pilum* had been supplemented by the *lancea* (a lighter javelin) and other shafted weapons.

These legionaries depicted on the *Tropaeum Traiani* at Adamklissi are marching bare-headed and apparently unarmoured, perhaps wearing *subarmales*, padded garments normally worn under armour, made of felt or similar materials.

Shields and Armour

The large *scutum* shield had been characteristic of Roman legionaries since before Polybius' day. Republican shields were of elongated oval form, some 3 by 4 Roman feet (*c.* 88 by 117 cm), designed to cover a soldier's left side. The characteristic imperial legionary *scutum*, rectangular in frontal view, is familiar to us from Trajan's Column and modern Roman army re-enactment groups. Such shields existed by Augustus' time, perhaps initially alongside curved oval versions like Republican examples. They were made largely of perishable materials that have not survived well in Europe, but the written evidence of Polybius, and a Republican example found in Egypt, suggest they were made of plywood laminated with leather and canvas, bound together at the edges with iron or bronze. The shield also had a central boss made of iron or copper alloy. Artistic depictions (such as the sculpted reliefs on Trajan's Column) suggest shields were generally decorated with thunderbolt, wing, star and crescent motifs, probably painted on the canvas facing.

Later Republican legionaries typically wore iron mail (*lorica hamata*) tunics, a technique adopted from the Gauls before Polybius' day. This continued to be used in the imperial period and is depicted on legionary tombstones and on the Trajanic victory monument at Adamklissi (Dacia, in modern Romania). It is also found on numerous military sites. Scale armour is also depicted in the Adamklissi reliefs. This consisted of small metal scales wired together and sewn onto a fabric backing. Of course, the type of armour typically associated with imperial legionaries, thanks to Trajan's Column and re-enactment societies, is the so-called *lorica segmentata*. This was made up of strips of iron held together and articulated with leather straps and copper alloy fittings. This provided particularly good protection for the shoulders,

and could be extended with *manicae* ('sleeves') protecting the arms. These are depicted on the Adamklissi monument and on the tombstone of Sextus Valerius Severus of *XXII Primigenia* at Mainz.

Helmets were another important element of legionaries' protective equipment. While the Republican 'Coolus' and 'Montefortino' types continued into the early imperial period, the main features of the so-called 'Imperial-Gallic' and 'Imperial-Italic' types were a bowl with broad-ribbed neck-guard beaten from a single piece of iron. It had a pronounced brow ridge to protect the forehead and large hinged cheek guards.

Roman soldiers, including legionaries, wore other distinctive pieces of equipment. Greaves are typically associated with centurions, but some legionary rankers are depicted wearing them as lower-leg protection too. Legionaries also wore a distinctive heavy belt, the *balteus*, with a metal belt-plate, and, for the earlier part of the imperial period at least, hobnailed open leather boots called *caligae*.

Artillery

Besides the individual weapons discussed above, Roman imperial legions also employed artillery, mostly descendants of torsion catapults that first came into widespread use in the Hellenistic period (4th–1st centuries BC). Looking back to the imperial legion, Vegetius (2.25) reports that each had 55 *carroballistae* (small bolt-shooters) and ten *onagers* (stone-throwers). Their use in open battle and in siege warfare is described by ancient writers. In his account of the siege of Jerusalem, Josephus (*Jewish War* 5.269–70) singles out artillery of *X Fretensis*, both bolt-shooters and stone-throwers, as particularly powerful, noting its use to repel sorties and clear the defenders from the walls rather than attack the walls themselves. Tacitus (*Histories* 3.23) describes the Vitellian artillery at the second battle of Bedriacum (Cremona, in northern Italy) in AD 69, including a particularly large stone-thrower belonging to *XV Primigenia*.

There is a good deal of archaeological evidence for such machines, although its interpretation is often difficult. Mostly it consists of metal washers and square-section bolt heads, but sometimes it is more substantial. Of particular interest, in the light of Tacitus' account, are finds from near Cremona of elements of a bolt-shooter and a stone-thrower, the former including an inscribed metal shield of the Vitellian *IIII Macedonica* with a date (presumably of its construction) of AD 45 (see page 62). Such machines were wooden-framed as well as shielded (like the familiar design

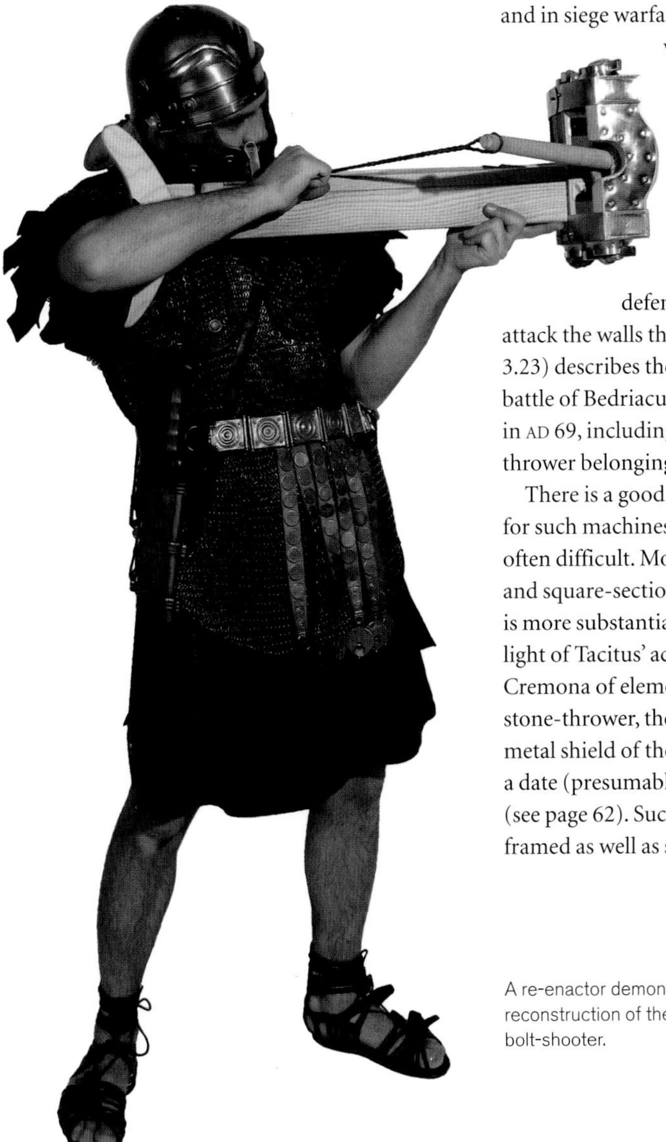

A re-enactor demonstrating a reconstruction of the Xanten bolt-shooter.

Opposite, above Lorica segmentata armour from the fort at Coria (Corbridge, just south of Hadrian's Wall). This is the most famous example of such armour, and dates to the 2nd century AD. However, finds from German sites show *lorica segmentata* was already in use in the reign of Augustus.

Opposite, below left A legionary on the *Tropaeum Traiani* at Adamklissi wearing *lorica squamata* (scale armour), correcting the impression given by Trajan's Column that all legionaries in the Dacian wars wore *lorica segmentata*.

Opposite, below right This image of modern legionary re-enactors provides a good view of the broad neck guards typical of imperial helmets, as well as the substantial shoulder protection of the *lorica segmentata*.

on the funerary monument of Vedennius Moderatus in Rome), but examples of a new design with an iron frame and open aperture are depicted on Trajan's Column mounted on carts (probably the *carroballista* mentioned by Vegetius and others) and may have been a Flavian innovation. The torsion frame of a small bolt-shooter found recently near the legionary fortress of Xanten in Germany may have belonged to a hand-held weapon, a type perhaps more common than previously suspected.

The Legions in Action

Tactics

We don't have much detailed information about the Roman imperial army in battle. Historians such as Tacitus provide some information, but tend to omit technical details as inimical to their high-flown, literary style. Caesar's *Commentaries* on the Gallic and civil wars were a different kind of literature and do include more useful technical detail, which can be extrapolated to later centuries. Military manuals and other technical treatises, like the works of Vegetius, Arrian and others, are not as useful as one might hope, as they are often theoretical and sometimes anachronistic. However, one can make some general observations about the tactics employed by Roman legions in battle.

For the most part, Roman armies formed up with the infantry – particularly the heaviest infantry, the legionaries – in the centre of their battle-line, flanked by lighter auxiliary infantry with cavalry on the extreme flanks. We see this in Tacitus' description (*Annals* 14.34) of a battle between the Roman army and Boudica's British rebels in AD 60–61. Tacitus' description (*Agricola* 35) of the battle of Mons Graupius in Scotland (AD 84) also places the legionary troops in the centre, but in a second, reserve, line, behind the auxiliary infantry. Tacitus claims this was to avoid the spilling of Roman blood, but it may have been to provide a reserve line against the possibility of outflanking.

Like manipular legions, imperial legions typically deployed in multiple lines, with cohorts in three (or sometimes two) lines, known as a *triplex acies* ('triple battle-line') or *duplex acies* ('double battle-line') respectively. As in the manipular legion, subunits from the second and third lines could relieve engaged troops, protect against outflanking by the enemy, or, conversely, deploy to outflank that enemy. Individual cohorts were typically deployed in three or four ranks of legionaries that might occasionally be doubled to defend against cavalry or for shock effect.

The *triplex acies* is mentioned regularly in Caesar's accounts of his battles in Gaul and the subsequent civil war. At Bibracte in 58 BC (*Gallic War* 1.24), he deployed his four veteran legions in a *triplex acies* on a hillslope. In the subsequent battle against Ariovistus (*Gallic War* 1.51–53) the army was again deployed in a *triplex acies*, and when the Roman right flank was pressured by the Germans, Publius Crassus deployed the third line to support them, showing the flexibility of the Roman formation. At Pharsalus in 48 BC, against Pompey, Caesar deployed his army in three lines (*Civil War* 3.89), and the impetus of the third line, brought up when the rest of the army was engaged, was decisive in the main infantry battle (3.94). Caesar had also detached cohorts from the third line to form a fourth, that played a crucial role in defeating Pompey's superior cavalry.

It is very likely that the *triplex acies* continued to be used through the imperial period, but battle descriptions of that period are so vague and lacking in detail that it is not surprising that it isn't specified. The *duplex acies* is not mentioned very much in accounts of imperial battles for the same reason. However, Vegetius (2.6), writing in Late Antiquity, presents the *duplex acies* as the normal battle-order of what he describes as the 'ancient legion', with the First Cohort, the strongest, on the right flank of the first line.

Specialized formations for subunits of the legion are mentioned on occasion. The famous *testudo* ('tortoise') formation, in which legionaries interlocked their shields for mutual protection from missiles fired or dropped from above, as well as from the front and flanks, was clearly best suited to siege or assault situations. A *cuneus* ('wedge') formation, presumably deep, with a narrow frontage, is also mentioned occasionally, such as in the battle against Boudica's British rebels mentioned above (Tacitus, *Annals* 14.37).

There are suggestions that 2nd–3rd-century legionary infantry sometimes employed a pike-

armed phalanx formation, like that of Macedonian infantry five centuries earlier (see pages 168 and 206). However, there is no reason to believe this became the norm, if it was ever used in battle at all.

Many legionary fortresses attracted civilian settlements that became modern cities (for example, Bonn, Budapest, York) that in turn obscure the remains of the Roman fortress. To see the layout of a complete legionary fortress we must turn to a more remote site, pictured here: Inchtuthil in Scotland, occupied briefly in the AD 80s and excavated in the 1950s and 1960s. See also diagram on page 37.

Construction, Engineering and Siege Warfare

Another aspect of continuity between the Republican and imperial legions was their expertise in, and emphasis on, construction and engineering skills. Just as Polybius, writing in the 2nd century BC, presented Roman camp construction as a characteristic feature of the legions of his day, so too did Josephus, writing over two centuries later. Legionary bases (known by modern scholars as fortresses, to distinguish them from the smaller bases – forts – typically constructed and used by auxiliary units) initially started as temporary structures for defence on campaign, but, particularly through the 2nd century AD, tended to become more permanent structures. This increasing permanence, often

Detail from Trajan's Column, showing legionaries building a fort. The two standing figures in the foreground with oval shields are auxiliary troops, apparently guarding the soldiers engaged in construction.

characterized by a transition from turf and timber to stone construction, can be seen in the development of Rhine legionary fortresses such as Xanten (Roman Vetera, Germany), Haltern (Germany) and Nijmegen (Noviomagnus, Netherlands). The earliest phases at Haltern and Nijmegen were large enough to accommodate two or more legions together, and Tacitus' accounts of campaigns in Germany in the reign of Tiberius make it clear that such brigading of legions on campaign was normal. Later fortresses were intended to house individual legions, for military and political reasons.

Legionaries' engineering and construction skills were put to use for obviously military purposes (fortifications), but also sometimes for improving infrastructure by building canals or bridges, or in mining and quarrying. Inscriptions and Roman literature (such as Pliny the Younger's letters when governor of Bithynia-Pontus) show that military specialists, such as surveyors, also participated in these activities.

The Roman army excelled at siege warfare, on account of its soldiers' construction and engineering skills, as well as its effective use of artillery. The sieges of Jerusalem and Masada in Judaea provide particularly vivid examples of this (see *X Fretensis*).

The Legions in the Roman Empire

There are three accounts of the deployment of the legions across the Roman empire:

(1) Tacitus (late 1st–early 2nd century AD, looking back to AD 23) records the total number of legions, rather than listing their individual identities and gives only general locations.

(2) Cassius Dio (late 2nd–early 3rd century AD, reflecting the situation in his own day) provides a

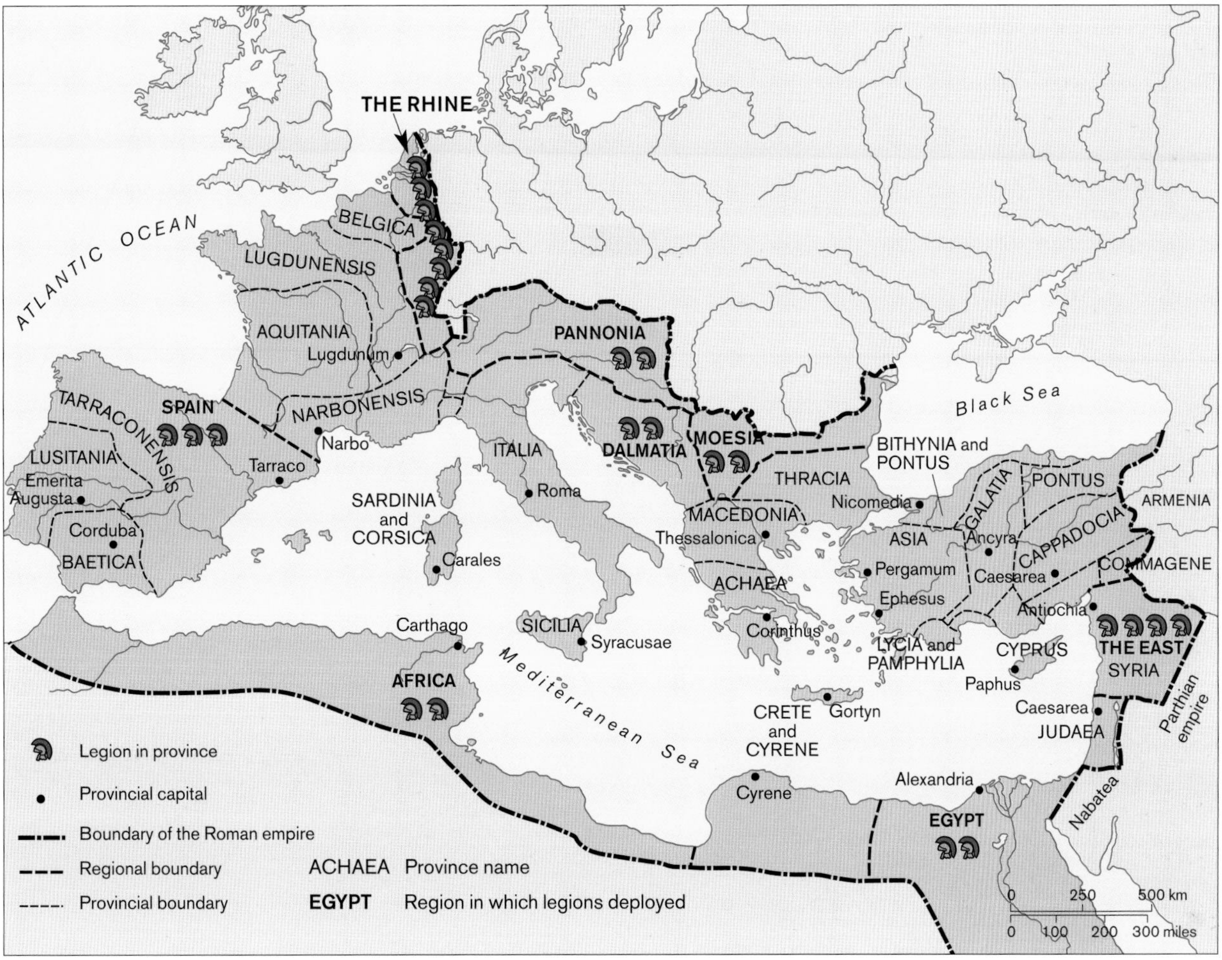

Map showing the dispositions of the legions in AD 23, as described by Tacitus (*Annals* 4.5).

list naming individual legions and provinces, specifying whether they were Augustan or later creations.

(3) An inscription from the Roman forum (*ILS* 2288), names the legions individually, in a logical order by location. This inscription was probably originally compiled early in the reign of Marcus Aurelius (AD 160s) as *II* and *III Italica*, and the Severan (late-2nd-century AD) legions *I–III Parthica* were added out of sequence at the bottom of the list, presumably at a later date.

These are empire-wide 'snapshots' of legionary deployment at particular times. The detailed picture is much more complicated, with legions moving around, being destroyed or disbanded, and new legions being created. We can fill in some detail by using individual references in Roman literature, inscriptions and archaeological evidence, much of it set out in the 'biographies' of individual legions in this book. In other cases, we lack information to be sure of a particular legion's location or movements at a given time.

These 'snapshots' provide us with interesting information. We get an approximate idea of the size of the legionary core of the army in the 1st to 2nd centuries AD, some 25 to 33 legions (125,000 to 165,000 men), and find that they were spread throughout the frontier provinces (or close to them), rather than at the centre of the empire. There are also striking differences between AD 23 (Tacitus) and the early-3rd-century AD picture (Cassius Dio). Provinces recently conquered or pacified, or subject to recent unrest in AD 23, such as Spain, Africa and Egypt, all had garrisons reduced to a single legion by Dio's time. The Rhine frontier was heavily garrisoned in AD 23, but that garrison was reduced by half. However, the garrisons of the Danubian and Balkan

The Disposition of the Legions, 1st Century to Early 3rd Century AD

Region	Tacitus, *Annals* 4.5	*ILS* 2288 (inscription)	Province	Cassius Dio 55.23
Rhine	8 legions	*VIII Augusta* *XXII Primigenia*	**Upper Germany**	*VIII Augusta* [*XXII Primigenia*]
		I Minervia *XXX Ulpia*	**Lower Germany**	(*I Minervia*) [*XXX Ulpia*]
Spain	3 legions	*VII Gemina*		(*VII Gemina*)
Africa	2 legions	*III Augusta*	**Numidia**	*III Augusta*
Egypt	2 legions	*II Traiana*		(*II Traiana*)
The East	4 legions	*XII Fulminata* *XV Apollinaris*	**Cappadocia**	*XII Fulminata* *XV Apollinaris*
		III Gallica *IIII Scythica* *XVI Flavia*	**Syria**	*III Gallica* *IIII Scythica* (*XVI Flavia*)
	(not annexed)	*III Cyrenaica*	**Arabia**	*III Cyrenaica*
		VI Ferrata *X Fretensis*	**Judaea**	*VI Ferrata* *X Fretensis*
	(not conquered)	*I Parthica* *III Parthica*	**Mesopotamia**	(*I Parthica*) (*III Parthica*)
Pannonia	2 legions	*I Adiutrix* *X Gemina* *XIV Gemina*	**Upper Pannonia**	*X Gemina* *XIV Gemina*
		II Adiutrix	**Lower Pannonia**	(*I Adiutrix*) (*II Adiutrix*)
Moesia	2 legions	*IIII Flavia* *VII Claudia*	**Upper Moesia**	*VII Claudia* (*IIII Flavia*)
		I Italica *V Macedonica* *XI Claudia*	**Lower Moesia**	*XI Claudia* (*I Italica*)
		II Italica	**Noricum**	(*II Italica*)
		III Italica	**Raetia**	(*III Italica*)
	2 legions		**Dalmatia**	
	(not conquered)	*XIII Gemina*	**Dacia**	*V Macedonica* *XIII Gemina*
	(no legions)	*II Parthica*	**Italy**	(*II Parthica*)
Britain	(not conquered)	*II Augusta* *VI Victrix* *XX Victrix*	**Upper Britain**	*II Augusta* *XX Valeria Victrix*
			Lower Britain	*VI Victrix*

Notes:
Tacitus sets out the disposition of the legions in broad geographical terms ('regions', in the first column), while the inscription and Cassius Dio assign them to specific provinces (in the fourth column).

Dio suggests that legion *XXII* in Upper Germany existed under Augustus, but he confuses the Augustan *XXII Deiotariana* (that spent all of its existence in Egypt, and disappeared in the first half of the 2nd century AD) with *XXII Primigenia*, raised after Augustus' death for service in the West. He also omits the location of the Trajanic *XXX Ulpia*, located in Lower Germany by other sources.

Square brackets denote errors or omissions that can be corrected/supplied from other sources.

Curved brackets in the Cassius Dio column denote legions that Dio says were formed after the reign of Augustus.

provinces had been doubled in size from 6 to 12 legions, reflecting Trajan's conquest of Dacia (in AD 106) and (from the AD 160s) for conflict during the reign of Marcus Aurelius. The eastern frontier legions increased with the garrisoning of Judaea/Syria Palaestina and annexation and garrisoning of new provinces like Cappadocia, Arabia and Mesopotamia. Britain, too, was invaded in AD 43, after the AD 23 date of this list, and garrisoned with three legions.

The Functions of the Imperial Legions

The deployment of imperial legions in frontier provinces shows they were used in part to defend the empire against hostile peoples on its frontiers, particularly Germanic peoples on the Rhine and Danube frontiers, and the Persian empire in the East. They also undertook offensive wars to expand the empire, such as Trajan's invasions of Dacia (modern Romania) in AD 101–2 and 105–6. The army, including the legions, also played an

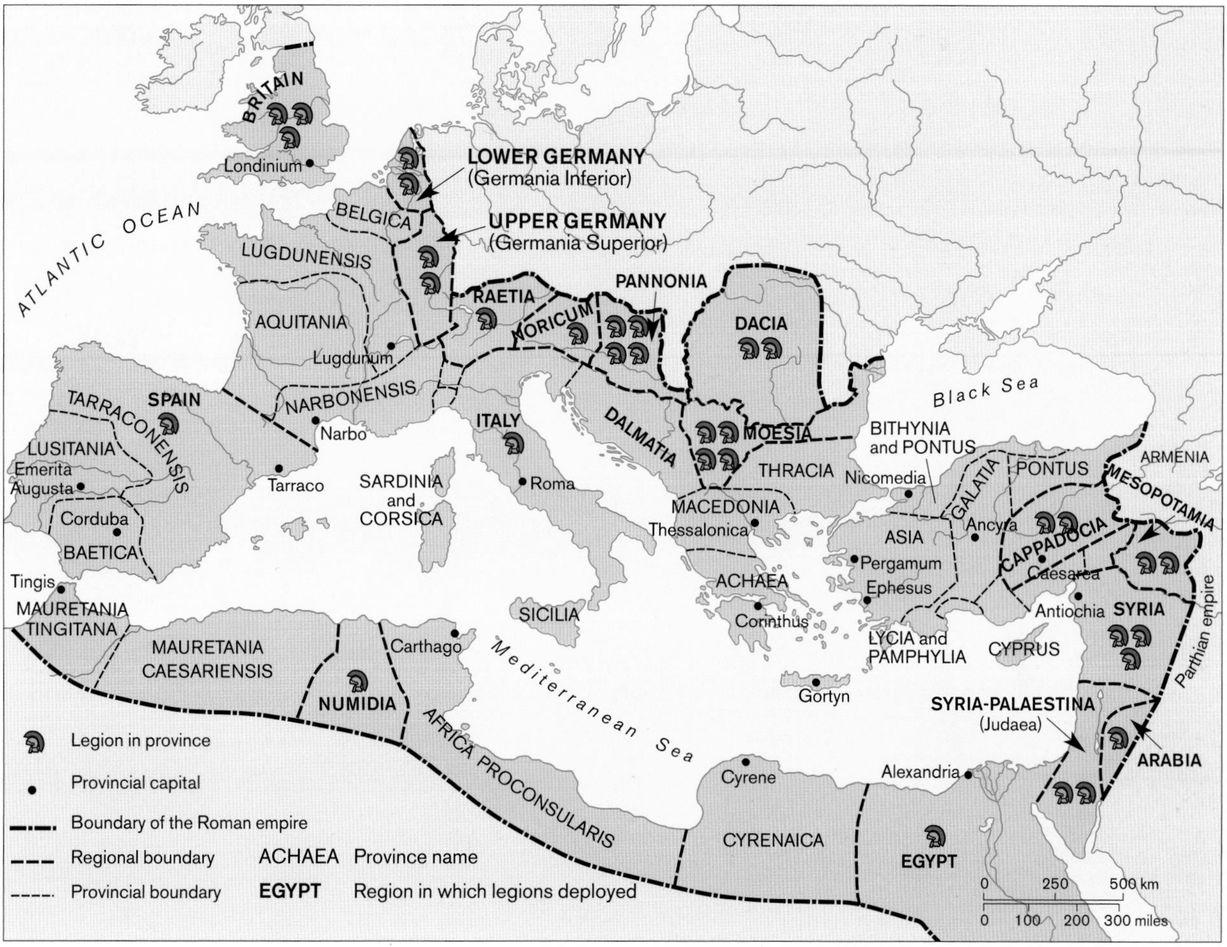

important role in maintaining the internal security of the empire. This involved suppression of large-scale revolts (like those in Judaea in AD 66–70 and AD 132–35), low-level conflict against nomads (in Africa, for example) and even policing duties in large cities and rural areas. These last activities are particularly well-attested in Egypt and other eastern provinces.

Legions sometimes played an important role in imperial politics too. In the early decades, the Praetorian Guard (in Rome and thus close to the emperor) was the most important military force in bringing emperors to the throne, maintaining them and overthrowing them. However, the civil war of AD 68–69 (the so-called 'Year of the Four Emperors', see page 59) saw legionary forces of three frontier regions (the Rhine, the Danube and the East) proclaiming emperors and fighting to put their candidates on the throne. Vespasian, proclaimed by the eastern legions and supported by the Balkan legions, was ultimately successful, and Tacitus (*Histories* 1.4) wrote that a secret of empire had been revealed – an emperor could be made outside Rome. While the Praetorian Guard remained important, it was a privileged rather than necessarily a battle-hardened body and incapable of resisting numerically greater and more experienced legionary forces. This was demonstrated in the civil war of AD 193–97, when Septimius Severus and the Balkan legions suppressed first the Praetorians in Rome, then the eastern legions, most of which supported Pescennius Niger, the governor of Syria, and finally defeated the legions from Britain brought across to Gaul by Clodius Albinus. Such civil wars became more frequent in the 3rd century AD, contributing to a sense of political and military crisis in the empire.

Map showing the dispositions of the legions in the early 3rd century AD, as described by Cassius Dio (55.23).

The Legions of the Rhine Frontier and Gaul

Augustus' Lost Legions: *XVII, XVIII, XIX*

Legions in the Batavian Revolt, AD 69–70: *I Germanica, IIII Macedonica, XV Primigenia, XVI Gallica*

The *Exercitus Germaniae Inferioris*: *I Minervia, XXX Ulpia Victrix*

Other Legions on the Rhine Frontier: *VIII Augusta, XXII Primigenia, V Alaudae, XXI Rapax*

Gaul (modern France, Belgium and parts of Germany) was conquered by the legions of Julius Caesar from 58 BC and quickly assimilated into the Roman empire (see Part I). Between 58 and 51 BC, the legions pushed the frontier of the empire to the banks of the Rhine. This new frontier remained unstable.

In Augustus' reign Gaul was divided into three provinces, Gallia Aquitania (southwest France), Gallia Lugdunensis (the rest of modern France) and Gallia Belgica (the Rhine frontier and its hinterland – the modern southern Netherlands, Belgium, Luxembourg, northeast France and western Germany). Augustus' stepson Drusus divided the Rhine corridor into two military zones: Germania Inferior (Lower Germany) and Germania Superior (Upper Germany). The entire Rhine frontier was the scene of conflict for centuries to come. It was the jumping-off point for campaigns against Germanic tribes, a major focus of frontier conflicts, and the scene of rebellions and mutinies by Roman soldiers and Rome's German allies. The concentration of legions on the Rhine meant they were an important force in the civil wars of AD 69, and even as the the focus of legionary deployments gradually shifted from the Rhine to the Danube, the Rhine legions remained crucial in the civil conflicts from the late 2nd century onwards.

Reconstruction of the Roman fort of Saalburg in Germany, as it would have looked under the Romans in the 1st century AD. The fort could accommodate a cohort and probably fell under the command of the legionary fortress at Moguntiacum (Mainz).

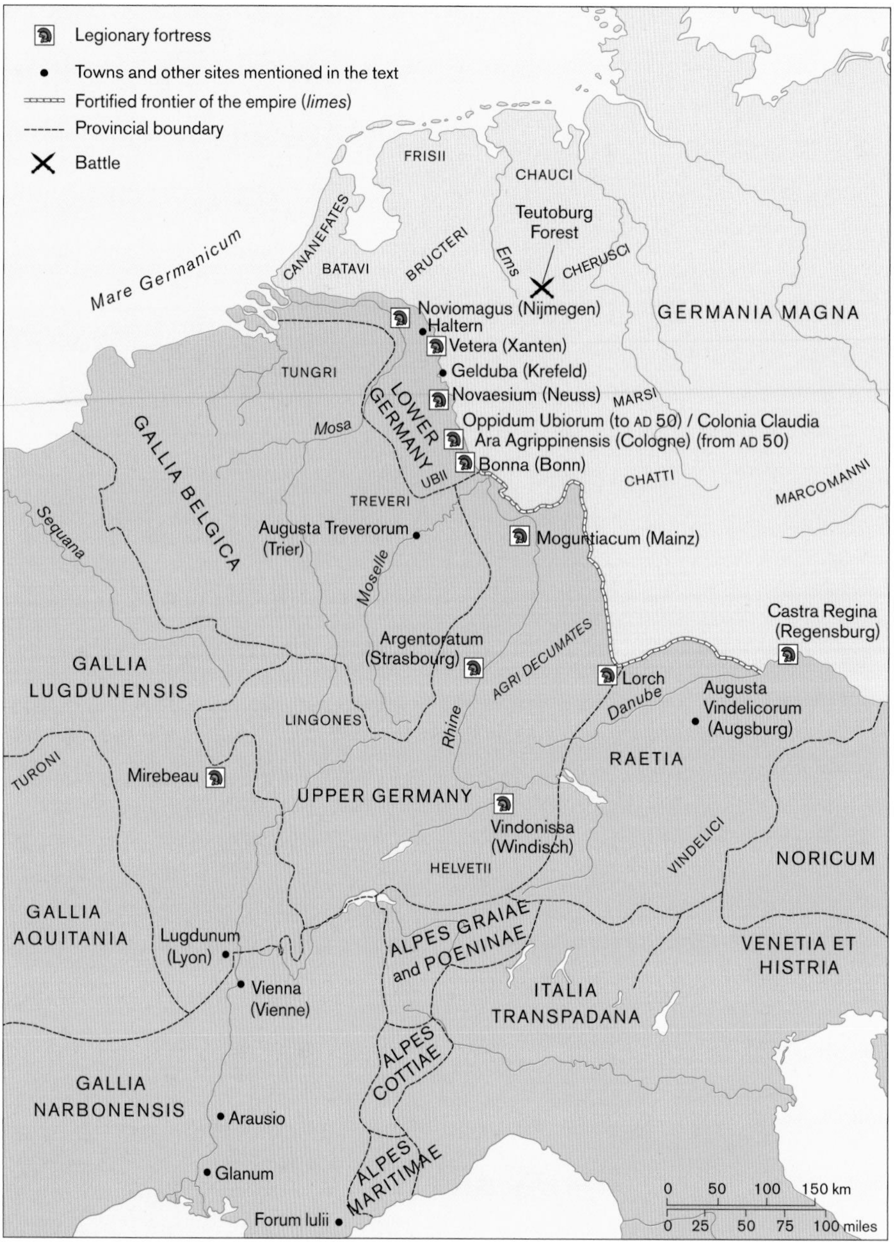

Map showing the Rhine Frontier and Gaul during the Principate. Lower Germany (Germania Inferior) covered the west bank of the Rhine in the area of modern Luxembourg, the southern Netherlands, parts of Belgium and North Rhine-Westphalia. Upper Germany (Germania Superior) spanned western Switzerland, the French Jura and Alsace, and southwest Germany.

Augustus' Lost Legions

In AD 9 three legions, the Seventeenth, Eighteenth and Nineteenth, were massacred in the Teutoburg Forest by the Cheruscі tribe.

> It was the bravest army of all, the very best corps of Roman soldiers in discipline, skill and experience in battle. But because of the indolence of its commander, the treachery of its enemy and the perfidy of fate, it was trapped.... It was hemmed in by forests, swamps and ambushes, and was slaughtered in a massacre by an enemy that in the past it had itself slaughtered like cattle, that had depended for life or death on the fury or the pity of the Romans.
>
> Velleius Paterculus, *Roman History* 2.119.2

The early history of all three legions is unclear. Julius Caesar raised legions with these numbers in 49–48 BC, during his civil war against Pompey. However, both Octavian and Antony also had legions with these numbers. Since all we know of the imperial legions *XVII* to *XIX* comes from the West, it is most likely they were raised by Octavian (Antony was based in the East), perhaps with cadres of Caesar's veterans.

Legio XVII (*Gallica* or *Germanica*?)

There is no firm evidence for the existence for *XVII*, but as Augustus' legions were numbered I to XXII, there must have been a Seventeenth Legion. It was probably raised by Octavian and, eventually, transferred to the Lower Rhine. Perhaps it took part in the campaigns of Drusus (13–9 BC) and Tiberius (8 BC and AD 4–5). Since we know three legions were destroyed in the Teutoburg Forest – *XVIII*, *XIX*, and another, and no other legion disappears from the historical record at this time, it is likely that the third was *XVII*.

Legio XVIII (*Gallica* or *Germanica*?)

Inscriptions document that veterans of this legion settled in the Veneto in either 30 or 14 BC. At some point the legion was sent to the Rhine, where it must have taken part in Drusus' and Tiberius' campaigns, and in AD 6 formed part of Tiberius' army for his planned assault on the Marcomanni. The legion was probably based at Vetera (Xanten), where the tombstone of Marcus Caelius (see box overleaf) was found.

Legio XIX (*Gallica* or *Germanica*?)

Veterans of the Nineteenth settled in the vicinity of Pisa after Actium. An inscription (*AE* 1994, 1323) on an iron catapult bolt found at Döttenbichl may be evidence that the legion was part of the army that conquered Raetia from 15 BC. Finds including a small bronze plaque that names the legion were found at Dangstetten, a fortress on the Upper Rhine, north of modern Basel, and suggest that the legion was based here

Legio XVII

Cognomen	*Gallica* or *Germanica*(?)
Emblem	Unknown
Main base	Unknown
Major campaigns	Rhine, 13–9 BC(?), 8 BC(?) and AD 4–5 (?)

Legio XVIII

Cognomen	*Gallica* or *Germanica*(?)
Emblem	Unknown
Main base	Vetera (Xanten)
Major campaigns	Rhine, 13–9 BC, 8 BC and AD 4–5

Legio XIX

Cognomen	*Gallica* or *Germanica*(?)
Emblem	Unknown
Main base	Unknown
Major campaigns	Raetia, 15 BC; Rhine, 8 BC and AD 4–5

Publius Quinctilius Varus

In AD 6, Publius Quinctilius Varus, a friend of Augustus and important senator, was sent to Germany as imperial legate. Velleius Paterculus (*Roman History* 2.117.2, writing in AD 29) describes him as a 'man of gentle character and quiet habits, rather inert in both mind and body, more familiar with a leisurely life in the camp than with service on campaign'.

This description may have been distorted by Velleius' knowledge of subsequent events, since Varus was an experienced administrator and commander and (as governor of Syria) had used his army quite effectively to deal with unrest in Judaea in 4 BC (see page 134).

Germany was recently pacified, but not reconciled to Roman domination. Varus' job was to turn the region into a peaceful province, introducing Roman administration and taxes. The Germans were infuriated by the new taxes and responded by exploiting the new laws Varus had imposed. They made up fictitious lawsuits or provoked disputes, and then thanked Varus when he settled their quarrels. Varus was lulled into a false sense of security, perhaps seeing himself as governor of a peaceful province rather than a general in hostile territory.

The Germans saw their opportunity, and a plot to crush the Romans was hatched by Arminius, son of Sigimer, a German prince of the Cherusci. Arminius had fought with the Romans and been awarded equestrian rank. News of his plans quickly spread through the German ranks, reaching Varus himself – who refused to believe that one of his allies would turn against him. Thus the plot succeeded.

Marcus Caelius

In 1638 the sculpted funerary relief of Marcus Caelius, a centurion of the Eighteenth (written as XIIX), killed in the Teutoburg Forest, was discovered at Vetera, a Roman legionary fortress near Xanten. Caelius and his legion were perhaps stationed there before the disaster.

A native of Bologna, Marcus Caelius was 53½ at the time of the disaster and had campaigned throughout the empire. He is depicted with all his military awards, wearing an oak wreath, two gold torques, and *phalerae* (gold discs) displayed on his cuirass. Flanking him are the portrait busts of his freedmen, Privatus and Thiaminus, and the three are framed by a decorated temple pediment and columns.

The inscription reads: 'To Marcus Caelius, son of Titus, of the Lemonia voting tribe, [born in] Bologna, centurion of the Eighteenth Legion, who lived 53½ years. He died in the Varian War. The bones of his freedmen may be buried [here]. His brother, Publius Caelius, son of Titus, of the Lemonia tribe, set this up.' (*CIL* 13, 8648)

The relief of Marcus Caelius was commissioned and paid for by his brother, Publius. It measures 1.37 m (4 ft 6 in.) in height and 1.08 m (3 ft 6½ in.) wide, and is made of limestone from Lorraine.

Aureus coin, depicting crossed oblong shields, was struck by the emperor Claudius to commemorate his father Drusus' victories on the Rhine during the reign of Augustus.

before 9 BC. Inscriptions relating to the legion also have been found at Cologne and Haltern. Thus the legion must have participated in the German campaigns of Drusus and Tiberius.

Massacre in the Teutoburg Forest

From various written accounts – most, apparently, based on the recollections of survivors of the massacre – it is possible to reconstruct a broad outline of the events of September AD 9. Varus and three legions – *XVIII*, *XIX*, and probably *XVII* – were in Cheruscan territory, about to return to their winter quarters on the Rhine. The other legions in Germany – *I Germanica* and *V Alaudae*

– were in the south with Varus' nephew, Lucius Asprenas. Hearing about a minor rebellion, Varus gathered his forces and headed for the trouble-spot.

This rebellion had been engineered by Arminius so that Varus and his army would have to march north through the Teutoburg Forest, instead of following the military road back to the Rhine. Arminius and his fellow conspirators began the march with Varus, but then left the main army to collect their forces. Varus believed that they would return to help him suppress the rebellion. Instead Arminius and his father Sigimer raced ahead to ambush the Romans in the *saltus Teutoburgiensis* (Teutoburg Forest), an area of marshy narrows bounded on one side by a hill and on the other by broad wetlands. With them were several renegade Germanic tribes (notably the Cherusci, Bructeri and Marsi).

The Romans were marching in scattered groups, with wagons and pack animals, as well as women, children and servants. Bad weather spread them out even more and the ground became treacherous. Thus, when they were suddenly surrounded by the Germans, they were unable to group together to resist the attack. Outnumbered, they suffered huge losses over the next three days.

The German forces swelled as new tribesmen joined the fight, hoping for plunder, and the fourth day brought even more troubles to the surviving Romans as a violent rainstorm made it difficult for them to keep their footing and use their weapons effectively.

At this point, the Roman officers realized their situation was hopeless. Varus and many of his officers committed suicide and resistance ceased. Some Romans killed themselves, others allowed their comrades to kill them. A few officers deserted their men in their attempt to flee. Others attempted to negotiate surrender, but were sacrificed to German deities or simply butchered.

> They put out the eyes of some men and cut off the hands of others. They cut off the tongue of one man and sewed up his mouth, and one of the barbarians, holding the tongue in his hand, exclaimed 'That stopped your hissing, you viper.'
>
> Florus, *Epitome* 2.30.37

Ordinary Roman soldiers who were captured were either killed or enslaved. Some would eventually be ransomed or rescued.

The entire Roman force of 12,000 to 15,000 legionaries was destroyed, along with six cohorts of auxiliary infantry and three *alae* of cavalry. The Germans captured the Roman standards, including the three eagles. The Germans dug up Varus' body (buried by his loyal soldiers), cut off his head and sent it to Maroboduus, king of the Marcomanni, hoping to persuade him to join the insurrection. Maroboduus instead sent it to Augustus, who had it buried in his own family mausoleum.

The Aftermath

News of the Teutoburg disaster spread quickly south. Varus' nephew Asprenas immediately sent *V Alaudae* and *I Germanica* north, and Tiberius marched *XX Valeria Victrix* and *XXI Rapax* from the Danube to the Rhine.

The biographer Suetonius famously described Augustus' reaction to the news:

> He was so upset that for months afterwards he let his beard and hair grow, and sometimes hit his head against the door, shouting: 'Quintilius Varus, give me back my legions!' He also marked the anniversary of the disaster as a day of grief and mourning.
>
> Suetonius, *Augustus* 23

Fearing riots in Rome and rebellion elsewhere in the empire, Augustus ordered a watch to be kept throughout the city by night, took measures to appease the gods and prolonged the terms of governors so that experienced men remained in control of Rome's provinces. Tiberius campaigned in Germania for the next three years, celebrating a triumph in AD 12. Eight legions (*I Germanica, II Augusta, V Alaudae, XIII Gemina, XIV Gemina, XVI Gallica, XX Valeria Victrix* and *XXI Rapax*) were left to guard the German frontier under the command of Tiberius' nephew Germanicus, but no further efforts were made to conquer the areas east of the Rhine during Augustus' reign.

Augustus died in AD 14, and Germanicus invaded 'free' Germany, winning a series of battles against the German tribes and capturing many who had taken part in the ambush in the

Kalkriese: The Site of the Battle

For almost two millennia, the location of the battle of the Teutoburg Forest remained hidden. In the 17th century, Roman coins were accumulated by farmers in the Barenau estates of Kalkriese in Lower Saxony. Speculation grew over the next 250 years that the coins – all Augustan in date, and newly minted – related to the disaster: none dated to after AD 9, the year of the massacre. Further finds led to systematic excavations. In 1990, the remains of a rampart were excavated and more coins and fragments of military equipment dating to the Augustan period were also found.

Then, in 1994, five pits were excavated, containing the disarticulated remains of humans and animals. To date, eight pits have been uncovered. These were probably the mass graves dug by Germanicus' soldiers in AD 16 for the remains of the massacred soldiers, which had been left exposed on the surface until then. The human bones show deep cuts.

The Germans undoubtedly looted the bodies of the fallen Roman soldiers, stripping them of weapons, armour and other valuables. However, some military equipment was excavated at the site.

Excavations have been taking place at Kalkriese (below) since 1987, and finds have been made both in the open field and in the forest that surrounds it. This silver-plated mask from a cavalry helmet (left) is one of the more famous discoveries.

Some finds were spectacular, including the silver-plated mask of a cavalry helmet. A silver beaker and silver spoon were also found, along with more mundane objects, such as keys, razors, rings, surgical instruments, a stylus, cooking pots, buckets and even jewelry and hairpins – evidence perhaps of the women, children and servants who were following the army back to its winter bases.

Teutoburg Forest. He then marched to the site of the massacre, wishing to honour the fallen soldiers. Tacitus describes the scene that met him:

> In the centre of the field were whitening bones, lying where men had fled or stood and fought back. Some were scattered around, others lay in heaps. Nearby lay broken weapons and horses' limbs, as well as soldiers' heads nailed to trees in full view. In the woods nearby were the barbarous altars, where the Germans had slaughtered the tribunes and leading centurions. The survivors of the disaster, who had escaped from the battle itself or from subsequent captivity, showed where the legates had fallen, where the eagles had been captured, where Varus had suffered his first wound and where he had met his death with his own ill-omened hand. They showed the mound from which Arminius had addressed his men, the gibbets and the pits for the prisoners and where, in his arrogance, he had insulted the standards and the eagles.
>
> Tacitus, *Annals* 1.61.2–4

Germanicus' men buried the bones of their comrades. The three lost legions were never reconstituted. The eagle of *XIX* was recovered from the Bructeri in AD 15 (Tacitus, *Annals* 1.61). The following year the Marsi revealed the location of a second eagle (*Annals* 2.25). The third was recovered in the reign of Claudius during action against the Chauci (Cassius Dio 60.8).

Legions in the Batavian Revolt, AD 69–70

The Batavian Revolt is described in detail in Tacitus' *Histories*. The Batavians were pro-Roman members of the Chatti tribe, renowned for their warlike character and settled by the Romans in the Rhine delta, which became known as the 'island of the Batavians'. Skilled horsemen, they supplied the Roman army with large numbers of auxiliary troops in return for exemption from taxes. In addition to their fame as the best of auxiliary troops, Batavians formed the Roman emperor's personal bodyguard.

The revolt of AD 69–70 was led by Julius Civilis, a Roman auxiliary officer of 25 years' service and a hereditary prince among his people. In AD 66 Civilis and his brother were arrested by the governor of Lower Germany on suspicion of treason. The charges were false, but Civilis' brother was executed. Civilis himself was sent to Rome to be tried. He remained there until AD 68, when Nero committed suicide, starting the 'Year of the Four Emperors' (AD 68–69; see box).

Below left Items from the Kalkriese hoard. It included Roman swords, spears, sling bullets, arrowheads, fragments of plate armour, chain mail, hobnails and military belt buckles.

The Year of the Four Emperors

Between Nero's suicide in June AD 68 and Vespasian's accession in December AD 69, the Roman empire endured another civil war. Emperor followed emperor in swift succession.

In AD 67–68, Gaius Julius Vindex, governor of Gallia Lugdunensis, rebelled against Nero, supporting the claim to the throne of Servius Sulpicius Galba, governor of Spain. This rebellion was crushed by the German legions, but the Senate declared Galba emperor, driving Nero to suicide. Galba accused the German legions of attempting to block his accession. On 1 January AD 69 they refused to swear loyalty to him, acclaiming instead their own commander, Aulus Vitellius.

In Rome, Marcus Salvius Otho took advantage of the tense situation to bribe the Praetorian Guard. They killed Galba, and Otho became emperor in his place. But the German legions were already marching on Rome, and defeated Otho's army at the first battle of Bedriacum near Cremona (April AD 69). Vitellius was now proclaimed emperor by the Senate.

Meanwhile, the legions of Egypt and the East had acclaimed Titus Flavius Vespasianus emperor. While Vespasian remained in the East, part of his army set out for Italy, commanded by the governor of Syria, Mucianus. The Balkan legions also declared for Vespasian and marched on Rome, defeating Vitellius at the second battle of Bedriacum (October AD 69). Vitellius was killed and Vespasian proclaimed emperor.

Galba acquitted Civilis and sent him home. However, when he reached Germany he was arrested again, this time by the new governor, Vitellius, and the local legions demanded his execution. At about the same time, Galba disbanded the emperor's Batavian bodyguard – a grave insult to the Batavians. The situation grew so tense that on two occasions the Batavian cohorts and soldiers of *XIV Gemina* (who had fought side by side for 25 years) fought one another openly.

Civilis was eventually released by Vitellius early in AD 69 because Vitellius needed Batavian support for his challenge against Otho. The Batavians fought for Vitellius at the first battle of Bedriacum, and were then ordered to return home. At this point Vespasian entered the fray. Vitellius badly needed more troops to hold off his rival, and ordered the general of Lower Germany to conscript more Batavians. The number required was greater than the maximum stipulated in their treaty with Rome, and this provoked the Batavians to revolt.

Left Bust of Aulus Vitellius, briefly emperor in AD 69. Vitellius was governor of Lower Germany and his claim to the throne was supported by most of the legions stationed in Germany: *I Germanica*, *IIII Macedonica*, *V Alaudae*, *XVI Gallica*, *XX Primigenia*, *XXI Rapax* and *XXII Primigenia*.

I Germanica

Cognomina *Augusta*; *Germanica*
Emblem Unknown
Main base Bonna (Bonn)
Main campaigns Octavian's campaign against Sextus Pompey (36 BC), Cantabrian wars (27–19 BC); Vindex' Revolt (AD 67); civil war (AD 69); Batavian Revolt (AD 69–70)

I Germanica

The first legion (later *Germanica*) was either raised by Julius Caesar as consul in 48 BC, or by Pansa in 43 BC for the campaign fought by the Senate and Octavian against Antony. It may have been with Octavian at the battles of Mutina (43 BC) and Philippi (42 BC), but we lack clear evidence. However, Appian (*Civil Wars* 5.112) mentions the legion in Octavian's campaign against Sextus Pompey in Sicily in 36 BC.

Coins minted in Spanish colonies suggest that a 'First' legion took part in Augustus' Cantabrian Wars, and it may have earned the cognomen *Augusta* at that time. This legion then disappears from the sources and it has been argued that it was disbanded. Cassius Dio (54.11.5) describes the disciplinary problems encountered by Augustus' general Agrippa, and mentions that he 'ordered that the entire Augustan legion, as it was called, should no longer carry that name'. The historian Ronald Syme argued that it was the First Legion that was deprived of its cognomen for mutinous behaviour, but that it continued in existence or was re-formed by Tiberius as governor of Gaul in 19–18 BC.

By AD 6, the First was stationed on the Rhine frontier, as part of the army under the command of Sentius Saturninus for Tiberius' aborted campaign against the Marcomanni. In AD 9 it was with Lucius Asprenas when the Varian disaster took place. Asprenas used the legion (and *V Alaudae*) to garrison the fortresses of Lower Germany.

The first clear evidence for the activities of the First Legion comes in the context of the Rhine mutinies on the death of Augustus (and accession of Tiberius) in AD 14. Tacitus (*Annals* 1.42.6) reports how Germanicus remonstrated with

Right Copper *as* coin of the *colonia* of Acci (modern Guadix, Spain) that depicts the standards of *I Germanica* and *II Augusta* either side of two legionary eagles. Together these legions seem to have been involved in the construction of Acci during the early Augustan period.

the rebellious First and Twentieth Legions as 'the men who took their standards from Tiberius'. This supports the idea that the legion was re-established by Tiberius, but ultimately the date of any such re-formation is uncertain, and it may have happened much later than 19–18 BC.

Move to Germania

From AD 6, and possibly earlier, *I Germanica* was stationed on the Rhine frontier, remaining there until AD 69, and thus acquiring the cognomen *Germanica*. This title is first attested in two inscriptions, one (*AE* 1976, 169) perhaps of Augustan date (suggesting it was awarded the cognomen for its actions after the Varian disaster), the other Claudian (*ILS* 2342). After the Varian disaster, the legion was stationed at Oppidum Ubiorum (Cologne), the capital of Lower Germany, before being transferred to Bonna (Bonn).

In AD 21 there was a rebellion of the Treveri and Turoni in Gaul against Roman taxation, led by Julius Florus and Julius Sacrovir. The German legions were sent to suppress the revolt. An inscription (*CIL* 14, 3602) reveals that the Roman forces included a mixed vexillation of *I Germanica*, *V Alaudae*, *XX Valeria Victrix* and *XXI Rapax* under the command of an officer of *I Germanica*.

The legion is next heard of in AD 67 when, with the other legions of Lower Germany, it marched south to suppress the governor of Gaul, Gaius Julius Vindex, who had revolted against Nero and was supporting the claim to the throne of Galba, the governor of Spain. The legions defeated Vindex, but in AD 68 Galba became emperor anyway, with the help of the newly raised Seventh Legion from Spain. The legions of Lower Germany would not support Galba and were persuaded by the commander of *I Germanica*, Fabius Valens, to declare for Vitellius, the governor of Lower Germany. Valens then led the First Legion to Italy, where it helped to defeat Otho at the first battle of Bedriacum. They were later defeated by Vespasian's army at the second battle of Bedriacum (see pages 134–35) and eventually disbanded after the Batavian Revolt.

Tombstone of Publius Clodius of *I Germanica*, found at Bonn. Originally from Alba Helvia (Viviers, Provence) in Gallia Narbonensis, he served 25 years, and died at the age of 48 (*ILS* 2245).

IIII Macedonica

The Fourth Legion's emblem was the bull, which implies that it was raised by Julius Caesar, probably as consul in 48 BC. It was stationed in Macedonia at the time of Caesar's assassination in 44 BC and must have gained its title there, although the use of its cognomen in inscriptions was mostly later, when the legion was based in Germany. In the summer of 44 BC, the legion was shipped back to Brundisium in Italy, along with three other legions, as Antony planned to send them north to Cisalpine Gaul, where he had been appointed governor. But during the march north, *IIII Macedonica* and the legion *Martia* declared for Octavian and moved to Alba Fucens, 100 km (*c.* 62 miles) east of Rome (Cicero, *Philippics* 3.6–7). Octavian had been at Apollonia in Macedonia in 45–44 BC, and so perhaps had been able to sow the seeds of defection among the legions there.

IIII Macedonica was in the army that defeated its former commander, Antony, at Mutina, and later fought at Philippi against Brutus and Cassius. After Philippi, Octavian returned to Italy with three legions, including the Fourth. Legends on sling bullets show the legion at the siege of Perusia (Perugia) in 41 BC. It probably also took part in the final defeat of Antony at Actium (31 BC).

IIII Macedonica must have been one of eight legions that participated in Augustus' Cantabrian wars (27–19 BC), although the first inscription naming it there dates to 9–8 BC. Boundary markers recording the *prata legionis*, the legion's pasture land, have been found at Aguilar de Campóo on the Pisuerga river (Aguilar derives from the Latin *aquila*, 'eagle'). The legion itself was stationed at nearby Herrera de Pisuerga, where tile stamps name the legion, with the legion's presence there dated archaeologically from 15 BC to the mid-1st century AD. Thus *IIII Macedonica* was stationed in the region for a long time and its soldiers saw service all over Spain.

IIII Macedonica

Cognomen	*Macedonica*
Emblem	Bull
Main base	Moguntiacum (Mainz)
Main campaigns	Mutina (43 BC); Philippi (42 BC); Perusia (41 BC); Cantabrian wars (27–19 BC); Rhine frontier (AD 43–69); civil war (AD 69)

The Rhine Frontier

IIII Macedonica remained in Spain until at least AD 43, when the legions were reorganized in preparation for the invasion of Britain. It moved to Moguntiacum (Mainz) in Upper Germany, replacing *XIV Gemina*, and shared the fortress with the newly founded *XXII Primigenia*. This remained its base until AD 70. Numerous tile stamps and stamped ceramics from Moguntiacum testify to the legion's presence there. The presence of its soldiers elsewhere in Germany is revealed by several other inscriptions, including a tombstone in Bingium (Bingen) near Moguntiacum (*CIL* 13, 7506), and an altar in Marienhausen near Bonn (*CIL* 13, 7610).

The Fourth and Twenty-Second were the first legions to side with Vitellius, and a large mixed vexillation of the two marched to Italy with him and fought at the first battle of Bedriacum. The legions continued to Rome, where some of their soldiers were rewarded with transfer to the Praetorian Guard. After its involvement in the Batavian Revolt, *IIII Macedonica* was disbanded by Vespasian (see page 66).

An embossed catapult shield found at Bedriacum, now in the Museo Civico di Cremona. The inscription reads: 'Belonging to *IIII Macedonica* (built) in the year when Marcus Vinicius, for the second time, and Taurus Statilius Corvinus were consuls (AD 45), Gaius Vibius Rufinus was legate, and Gaius Horatius was centurion in charge of headquarters' (*ILS* 2283).

XV Primigenia

The Fifteenth was a short-lived legion and there is little evidence for its activities. It was probably formed along with *XXII Primigenia* in AD 39 by Caligula (or perhaps by Claudius in AD 42) in preparation for the invasion of Britain. Four inscriptions (*AE* 1911, 234; *CIL* 13, 11853, 11855, 11856) from Moguntiacum (Mainz) of soldiers who died in their first year of service suggest that the legion was first based there, in Upper Germany. It may then have been transferred to Bonna (Bonn) in Lower Germany, as a stamp bearing the legion's numeral was found there, and then to Vetera (Xanten) where numerous brick stamps relating to the legion have been found.

Brick stamps also suggest that a detachment was sent to Toul in Belgium. A monument in Colonia Claudia Ara Agrippinensis (modern Cologne) dedicated to Nero in AD 66 by the legionary legate Publius Sulpicius Scribonius Rufus implies that men from the legion were stationed there, but does not prove that the entire legion was present (*CIL* 13, 11806). The Fifteenth was destroyed in the Batavian Revolt and never re-formed (see page 66).

XV Primigenia

Cognomen	*Primigenia*
Emblem	Unknown
Main base	Vetera I (Xanten)
Main campaigns	Batavian Revolt (AD 69–70)

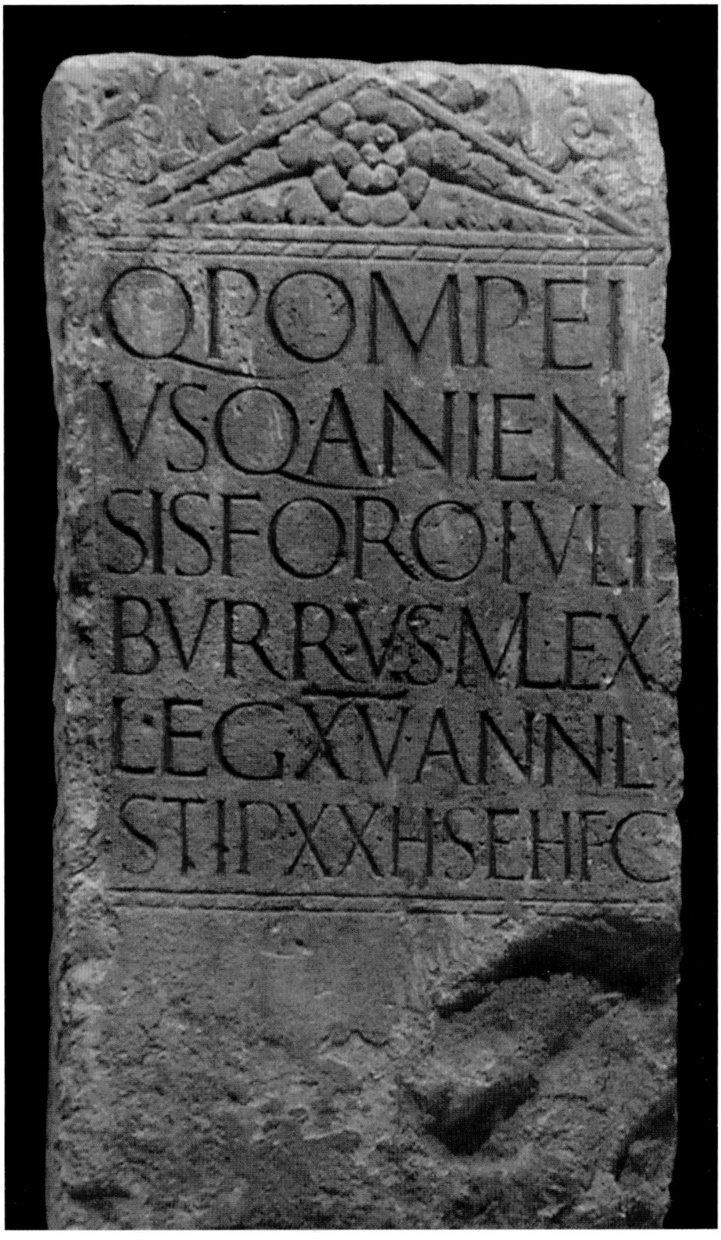

This tombstone found at Cologne commemorates Quintus Pompeius of *XV Primigenia* who died at the age of 50. He came from Forum Iulii (Fréjus) and served in the Roman army for 20 years (*CIL* 13, 8284).

XVI Gallica

A small silver coin found in Roman Africa, bearing the head of a young Octavian on the obverse and a leaping lion with the legend *LEG XVI* on the reverse, is usually taken as evidence that *XVI Gallica* was raised by Octavian in the years before the battle of Actium in 31 BC, and that its emblem was the lion (the zodiac sign related to Jupiter). The provenance of the coin also suggests that the legion spent some time in Africa, but there is no other evidence for this.

The legion's title *Gallica* implies that the legion was stationed in Gaul, possibly during Drusus' campaigns (13–9 BC). It has been suggested that the legion was then deployed on the Danube. If so, then along with *XXI* it formed the initial garrison of Raetia (the new province on the Upper Danube created by Tiberius in 16–14 BC), and was only later transferred to the Rhine where it was probably stationed at Moguntiacum (Mainz) in Upper Germany. Many inscriptions referring to the Sixteenth Legion have been found there, none more than a few years earlier than the Varian disaster in AD 9.

On the Rhine

In AD 6, *XVI Gallica* was one of the legions assembled by Tiberius for a campaign against King Maroboduus of the Marcomanni, but the operation was abandoned at the outbreak of the Pannonian Revolt. In the aftermath of the Varian disaster of AD 9, *XVI* may have garrisoned Oppidum Ubiorum (Cologne) but by AD 14 it was definitely at Moguntiacum (Mainz) in Upper Germany, where Tacitus relates that it swore loyalty to the new emperor Tiberius 'without demur' (unlike many of the other legions).

Before the death of Claudius in AD 54, *XVI Gallica* moved from Moguntiacum to Novaesium (Neuss) in Lower Germany. This move may have been connected with the war against the Chauci and Frisii in AD 47, or to the redistribution of legions at the time of the invasion of Britain in AD 43. *XVI Gallica* thus took the place of *XX Valeria Victrix* which was included in the force that moved from Novaesium to take part in the invasion. Most of the evidence for the legion's presence at Novaesium consists of brick stamps, some of which depict the legion's lion emblem.

XVI Gallica

Cognomen	*Gallica*
Emblem	Lion
Main base	Novaesium (Neuss)
Main campaigns	Drusus' German campaigns? (13–9 BC); civil war (vexillation, AD 69)

The legion is next mentioned in literary sources during the civil war of AD 68–69: Tacitus (*Histories* 1.55) records its reluctance (with the other German legions) to swear an oath of allegiance to Galba. Detachments of the legion later fought in Italy for Vitellius and entered Rome with him, where (an inscription shows) some of the soldiers became members of the Praetorian cohorts.

Tacitus describes the low morale of the troops as they were despatched from Rome back to Cremona to prepare to fight Vespasian's army in October AD 69:

Bust of Vespasian (Capitoline Museum, Rome). Tacitus (*Histories* 4.13) claims he initially encouraged the Batavian Revolt to prevent the German legions helping his rival Vitellius, but the Batavian leader Civilis only pretended to support him.

> The soldiers had no energy or enthusiasm. They marched in a column that was sluggish and strung-out, their weapons carried carelessly, their horses worn out. They could not endure the sun, the dust or the storms. The less ready the soldiers were to face exertion, the more ready they were to quarrel.
>
> Tacitus, *Histories* 2.99

Unsurprisingly, Vitellius' army was defeated (see pages 134–35) and the vexillation of *XVI Gallica* was probably destroyed. The remaining soldiers of the legion were still at Novaesium and were soon embroiled in the Batavian Revolt.

The Batavian Revolt: The Role of *I Germanica*, *IIII Macedonica*, *XV Primigenia* and *XVI Gallica*

In summer AD 69, Julius Civilis was in command of Batavian auxiliary troops attached to the Rhine legions. Encouraged by Vespasian, who wanted to prevent the German legions from joining Vitellius' forces, he persuaded the Cananefates tribe (that lived between Batavia and the North Sea) to attack Roman forts in their territory. As Civilis had hoped, the commander of the Rhine legions, Marcus Hordeonius Flaccus, sent auxiliary troops to deal with this revolt – troops that were commanded by Civilis himself. Civilis took command of the rebellion, more auxiliary troops deserted to his side and he defeated Roman forces near modern Arnhem in the Netherlands.

Flaccus then ordered *V Alaudae* and *XV Primigenia* to deal with the situation. The legions were accompanied by Ubian and Treveran auxiliaries, and by a Batavian cavalry unit whose commander was thought to be hostile to Civilis. Instead the Batavians defected to their fellow countrymen. The other German auxiliaries deserted, and the legions withdrew to the fortress at Vetera (Xanten) (Tacitus, *Histories* 4.18).

More Batavian auxiliary troops now deserted to the rebels, and began the march north to join Civilis, passing the legions stationed at Moguntiacum (Mainz) and Bonna (Bonn). Uncertain what to do next, Civilis had his forces swear allegiance to Vespasian, and sent a delegation to Vetera to persuade the legions there to follow suit. They refused, re-stating their loyalty to Vitellius, and Civilis decided to blockade the fortress (Tacitus, *Histories* 4.21).

Flaccus ordered *IIII Macedonica* to hold Moguntiacum, and sent for reinforcements from Gaul, Spain and Britain. He then sent Gaius Dillius Vocula, commander of *XXII Primigenia*, to Novaesium with his legion and elements of *IIII Macedonica*. There they linked up with Flaccus, *I Germanica* (based at Bonna) and *XVI Gallica* (based at Novaesium) and began the march to Vetera to rescue the beleaguered legions there. However, the army halted at Gelduba (modern Krefeld), where they received news that Vespasian's legions had reached Italy. They remained there, ostensibly engaging in training exercises, waiting to find out who would win the civil war in Italy.

Vespasian defeated Vitellius. Civilis now took the initiative, deciding to lead his rebel forces in an attack on the Roman legions at Gelduba to prevent them reaching Vetera. The attack failed, but Roman losses were heavy, confirmed by the discovery of a mass grave of men and horses at modern Krefeld. The Romans under Flaccus marched on to Vetera and lifted the siege.

Almost immediately came news of a threat to Moguntiacum; the Romans headed there, leaving Vetera seriously undermanned. En route they reached Novaesium and Flaccus decided to celebrate Vespasian's accession by distributing money to the legionaries. The soldiers had been loyal to Vitellius, however, and, taking offence, murdered Flaccus.

Repenting of his men's act, Vocula took the legionaries of the First, Fourth and Twenty-Second to Moguntiacum, broke the siege there and, leaving *IIII Macedonica* and *XXII Primigenia* behind, set off for Vetera, where Civilis had renewed the siege. However, when Vocula heard of a new uprising (the Treveri and Lingones had revolted against Rome) he withdrew to Novaesium. Encouraged by rebel envoys, Vocula's legions defected and murdered their commander. The leader of the Treveran cavalry, Julius Classicus, entered the Roman fortress dressed as a Roman general and administered an oath of loyalty to a new Gallic empire to the legionaries.

Now with no hope of relief, the besieged legions at Vetera yielded. Marching out under terms of surrender, they were ambushed and massacred by the rebel leader Civilis (Tacitus, *Histories* 4.60). Coins have been found commemorating the destruction of *V Alaudae* and *XV Primigenia*. Even though they had sworn allegiance to the Gallic empire, Civilis sent the First and Sixteenth from Novaesium to the colony of the Treveri (modern Trier), a dismissal that caused them great shame (Tacitus, *Histories* 4.62).

However, the Romans were now in a position to muster an army large enough to suppress the revolt and sent troops under the command of Petillius Cerialis. The Treveri were quickly defeated, and Trier captured. Here Cerialis found the First and Sixteenth Legions, shamed by their defection (Tacitus, *Histories* 4.72). They were given amnesty and joined with Cerialis to fight the rebels, but they performed badly. Tacitus describes how, despite being hard-pressed, Cerialis managed to recover the bridge over the Moselle.

> Returning to the camp soon afterwards, he saw the companies of the legions captured at Novaesium and Bonna hanging around, with hardly any of the men fallen in with their standards .... He was furious and said 'There's no treachery here ... nor can I be held at fault except for my foolish belief that you had forgotten your agreement with the Gauls and remembered your oath to Rome.'
>
> Tacitus, *Histories* 4.77

Civilis with his rebels retreated to Vetera and Cerialis brought against him a huge army consisting of *XXI Rapax*, *II Adiutrix*, *VI Victrix* and *XIV Gemina*. Civilis fled to the island of the Batavians and was eventually forced to negotiate a peace with the Romans. His fate is unknown.

Vespasian dealt next with the dishonoured Rhine legions. He disbanded *IIII Macedonica* and *XVI Gallica*, but reconstituted them as *IIII Flavia Felix* and *XVI Flavia Firma*. They were sent to Dalmatia and Syria respectively. Vespasian also disbanded *I Germanica*: its remaining soldiers may have joined the Seventh Legion, henceforth known as *VII Gemina* ('Twin'). *XV Primigenia*, destroyed at Vetera, was never reconstituted. The fate of *V Alaudae* remains uncertain.

The *Exercitus Germaniae Inferioris*

I Minervia and *XXX Ulpia Victrix* are referred to in inscriptions as *exercitus Germaniae Inferioris* (abbreviated as EXGERINF), 'The Army of Lower Germany'.

EXGERINF tile stamp from Vetera (Xanten). Examples have been found throughout Lower Germany, including Cologne, Laurum (Woerden), Novaesium (Neuss) and Traiectum (Utrecht).

I Minervia

Cognomina	*Flavia*; *Minervia*; *Pia Fidelis Domitiana*
Emblems	Minerva; boar
Main base	Bonna (Bonn)
Main campaigns	Domitian's war against the Chatti (AD 83); Saturninus' Revolt (AD 89); Trajan's Dacian wars (101–6); Lucius Verus' Parthian war (161–66); Marcus Aurelius' Marcomannic wars (166–80); Severus' second Parthian war (197); Severus Alexander's German wars (235); against the Franks (256–58)

I Minervia

We know from the historian Cassius Dio (55.24.3) that the emperor Domitian raised a new legion during his reign. The exact date is uncertain, but it is likely that the legion was formed for Domitian's campaigns against the Chatti in AD 83. The legion's full name at this time was probably *I Flavia Minervia*, advertising Domitian's family name, Flavia, and his protecting deity, Minerva.

In AD 89 *I Minervia* was one of the legions of Lower Germany (along with *VI Victrix*, *X Gemina* and *XXII Primigenia*) sent to Moguntiacum (Mainz) to defeat Lucius Antonius Saturninus, the rebellious governor of Upper Germany (see page 80). As a reward all four legions received the title *Pia Fidelis Domitiana* ('Dutiful and Loyal, of Domitian'). After Domitian's assassination in AD 96 the legion's name changed to *I Minervia Pia Fidelis*, eliminating the reference to this unpopular emperor.

The Legion at Bonna

I Minervia's main base was the fortress at Bonna (Bonn). This fortress was constructed after the Varian disaster in AD 9, near the site of a previous auxiliary fort built by Drusus between 16–13 BC. Initially the fortress was garrisoned by *I Germanica*. After the Batavian Revolt (AD 69–70) it was rebuilt in stone and became the base of *XXI Rapax*. A few years later, after AD 83, *XXI Rapax* was transferred to Upper Germany and *I Minervia* was sent to Bonna. It remained there until the 4th century AD. The fortress now lies beneath the modern city of Bonn, but excavations have revealed the *principia* (administrative

Tombstone of Gaius Julius Maternus, a veteran of *I Minervia*, and his wife Maria Marcellina (*CIL* 13, 8267a), found at Colonia Claudia Ara Agrippinensium (Cologne) and now in the Römisch-Germanisches Museum, Köln. The relief depicts Maternus and Maria at a banquet. Slaves stand to either side.

building), *valetudinarium* (hospital), *horrea* (warehouses) and barracks. Many inscriptions relating to *I Minervia* have been found here.

Other inscriptions have been found at nearby Colonia Claudia Ara Agrippinensium (Cologne) in Lower Germany, the provincial capital, and soldiers from Bonna probably served there on the governor's staff. Inscriptions also show that soldiers from the legion were sent all over Lower Germany, including Iversheim (*CIL* 13, 7943), Mannaricium (Maurik; *AE* 1975, 639d), Lottum (*AE* 1987, 778) and Rigomagus (Remagen; *CIL* 13, 7795).

Campaigns in Germania and Beyond

The legion saw action with Trajan against the Dacians (101–6) and towards the end of these wars it was commanded by the emperor Hadrian. Its boar emblem can be seen on standards carried by standard-bearers on Trajan's Column, the monument erected in Rome to commemorate Trajan's great victory over Dacia. After the Dacian wars, the legion returned to Bonna. From this time it regularly operated with Trajan's new legion, *XXX Ulpia Victrix*, which was based at Vetera (Xanten).

For the most part, *I Minervia* remained in Bonn until the 3rd century AD, but soldiers did occasionally see service in other parts of the empire. Tombstones (*CIL* 8, 9654 and 9662) of two soldiers from the legion have been found at Cartenna (Tenes, Algeria), suggesting that a vexillation was sent to Mauretania. Another inscription (*CIL* 6, 41142) found in Trajan's Forum in Rome suggests that the entire legion, under M. Claudius Fronto, fought in Lucius Verus' Parthian campaigns (162–66). The legion, or part of it, probably also took part in Marcus Aurelius' war against the Marcomanni in 166–80.

The 3rd Century

When civil war broke out in 193, *I Minervia* supported Septimius Severus, and later fought with him against Clodius Albinus. Inscriptions reveal that during Severus' reign (198–211), subunits of the army of Lower Germany and the two legions from Upper Germany (*VIII Augusta* and *XXII Primigenia*) garrisoned Lyon, the capital of the Gallic provinces. An inscription (*AE* 1957, 123) records that Claudius Gallus commanded a vexillation of four German legions in Septimius Severus' second Parthian war (197).

In the first half of the 3rd century, the legion's titles changed several times, reflecting service under various emperors. Between 211 and 222 the legion received the name *Antoniniana*, from the family name of Caracalla (211–17) or Elagabalus (218–22). The name was probably acquired during the reign of Elagabalus, since it was dropped after his assassination. The legion seems to have fought under the emperor Severus Alexander (222–35), because an altar found at Bonn, dedicated in 231, refers to it as *I Minervia Pia Fidelis Severiana Alexandriana* (*CIL* 13, 8017). After Severus Alexander was killed in 235, *I Minervia* became *I Minervia Maximiniana Pia Fidelis Antoniniana* (*AE* 1939, 11, also found at Bonn), reflecting its service against the Alamanni for the next emperor, Maximinus Thrax (235–38).

When Maximinus was murdered, *Maximiniana* was dropped, and the legion acquired the title *Gordiana*, after the next emperor, Gordian III (*CIL* 13, 6763). Coins minted by Gallienus (253–68) reveal that he awarded the legion the cognomen *VI Pia VI Fidelis* ('Six times Dutiful and Loyal'), and the legion must have fought for him during the Frankish invasions of Lower Germany in 256–58. Nevertheless, the legion supported the breakaway Gallic empire, formed by Postumus, the governor of Lower Germany, from 260 to 274.

Bonna was destroyed in 353 by another Frankish invasion, but the fate of the legion is unclear. It is not known if the legion returned to Bonna when the town was recaptured by the emperor Julian a few years later.

Originally this inscription (*AE* 1931, 11) found in Bonn read '*Legio I Minervia Maximiniana Pia Fidelis Antoninana*', but the name '*Maximiniana*' was erased after the emperor Maximinius was overthrown in 238.

XXX Ulpia Victrix

According to Cassius Dio (55.24.3), *XXX Germanica* was formed by the emperor Trajan with the cognomen *Ulpia*, from Trajan's family name. The legion was probably raised in anticipation of his Dacian wars (AD 101–6) and its third cognomen *Victrix* will have been a reward for acts of bravery during those wars. Based on the evidence of coins from the reigns of Gallienus (253–68) and Carausius (286–93), the legion's emblems may have been Neptune and Capricorn.

Pannonia and Lower Germany

The Thirtieth's role in the Dacian wars is unknown, but when they ended the legion was apparently sent to Upper Pannonia, to replace *XI Claudia*. Brick stamps of the Thirtieth have been found at *XI Claudia*'s vacated base at Brigetio (Szöny) and also at Carnuntum (Petronell-Carnuntum) and Vindobona (Vienna). Together these suggest that the legion was involved in rebuilding legionary forts in Pannonia in the wars' aftermath. At the end of Trajan's Parthian war in 118 the Thirtieth and the other legions of Pannonia and Dacia were commanded by Quintus Marcius Turbo, close friend of the future emperor Hadrian who was charged with reorganizing the northern provinces. Shortly afterwards it was sent to Lower Germany.

Once in Lower Germany, the legion took over the legionary fortress at Vetera (Xanten), formerly the winter base of *VI Victrix*. It remained there for the next 200 years.

Evidence of the activities of members of the Thirtieth Legion has also been found in other parts of the province. From a dedication he made to Jupiter Optimus Maximus at Colonia Ara Agrippinensis (Cologne) (*CIL* 13, 8197), and a later inscription from Rome (*CIL* 6, 1333), we know that Lucius Aemilius Karus commanded the legion before AD 142. From other inscriptions, we know the names of centurions who served on the staff of the provincial governor (based at Colonia Ara Agrippinensis), such as Priscus, who restored a sanctuary to Jupiter Dolichenus on behalf of the governor in 211 (*CIL* 13, 8201). Other members of the legion served elsewhere in Lower Germany, for example, in Rigomagus (Remagen) (*AE* 1995, 1110 and *CIL* 13, 7789), Erkelenz (*CIL* 13, 7896),

XXX Ulpia Victrix

Cognomina	*Germanica; Ulpia; Victrix*
Emblems	Neptune; Capricorn
Main base	Vetera (Xanten)
Main campaigns	Trajan's Dacian wars (AD 101–6); Antoninus Pius' war against the Moors (*c.* 150); Lucius Verus' Persian war (162–66); Severus' Caledonian campaign (208); Severus Alexander's Persian war (235); against the Franks (240 onwards)

Dedication to the god Silvanus by Cessorinus Ammausius, a bear-handler or bear-keeper of *XXX Ulpia Victrix*, from Xanten (*CIL* 13, 8639. 3rd century AD; Römer Museum, Xanten).

The Fortresses at Vetera

There were two legionary fortresses at Vetera (Xanten), known to us as Vetera I and Vetera II. Vetera I was constructed on the west side of the river Lippe before 12 BC; it was rebuilt in stone as a two-legion fortress during the reign of Nero and became the base of *V Alaudae* and *XV Primigenia*. This fortress was destroyed during the Batavian Revolt of AD 69–70 (see pages 65–66). After this, Vetera II was constructed at a nearby site, closer to the Rhine, and was the base of *XXX Ulpia Victrix* from *c.* AD 120. A town grew up around the fortress, eventually becoming a *colonia* during the reign of Trajan.

Only parts of Vetera I have been excavated, including the *via principalis*, which ran between the two sections of the double fortress, and buildings such as the two *principia* (headquarters) and some peristyle houses. Vetera II was destroyed in the early Middle Ages when a branch of the Rhine flooded and changed course, submerging the remains of the fortress and town.

Reconstructed section of the city walls in Xanten (Archaeological Park). Excavations have shown that the original wall was built in AD 105/6 and enclosed the entire city that developed around the legionary base.

Merten (*CIL* 13, 8156) and Noviomagus (Nijmegen; e.g. *CIL* 13, 8719), and at sites in Upper Germany, such as Moguntiacum (Mainz) (e.g. *CIL* 13, 6763), Kruft (e.g. *AE* 1926, 21) and Vinxtbach (*CIL* 13, 7732). A handful of inscriptions name *XXX Ulpia Victrix* alongside its sister-legion, *I Minervia*, and reveal that they worked together on construction projects at Bonna (*I Minervia*'s fortress), and in different parts of the Netherlands.

Evidence of the Legion outside Germany

It is not until the reign of Antoninus Pius (138–61) that there is evidence for members of the Thirtieth Legion operating outside Germany. A tombstone of a legionary was found in Caesarea (Cherchell in Algeria) (*CIL* 8, 21053) and probably relates to a campaign against the Moors in Antoninus' reign. Another vexillation may have joined *I Minervia* when it took part in Lucius Verus' Parthian war in 162 and, like its sister-legion, it must have sent vexillations to fight for Marcus Aurelius against the Marcomanni (166–80).

During the civil war that eventually brought Septimius Severus to sole power, the Thirtieth supported Severus and fought with him against Clodius Albinus in AD 196–97. With *I Minervia* it garrisoned Lugdunum (Lyon) in this period. As a reward, it was given the cognomen *Pia Fidelis* ('Dutiful and Loyal'), which can be seen on coins minted during Severus' reign and occasionally on later monuments.

The 3rd Century AD and Beyond

Between *c.* 206 and 208 a vexillation of the legion formed part of the army commanded by Julius Castinus that subdued troublemakers in Gaul and Hispania (*CIL* 3, 10471–73). The tombstone of a legionary found in Ancyra supports the suggestion that the legion took part in Severus Alexander's Persian war of 235 (*CIL* 3, 6764).

Just a few years later, in 240, the Rhine frontier was overrun by the Franks, although eventually they were pushed back. Sixteen years later the Franks again invaded Gaul, and were repelled by the emperor Gallienus, presumably with the help of the 'Army of Lower Germany' since coins minted by Gallienus give both legions the cognomina *VI Pia Fidelis* and *VII Pia Fidelis*.

In 260 the Franks invaded again and this time it was the turn of the governor of Lower Germany, Postumus, to drive them back. *XXX Ulpia Victrix* and *I Minervia* supported Postumus when he was proclaimed emperor of the breakaway Gallic empire immediately after his success. The Gallic empire remained separate from the Roman empire until 274 when Aurelian reconquered Gaul. However, this led to another Frankish invasion of the Rhine region. It was not until *c.* 300 that the emperor Constantius Chlorus was able to restore peace to the region.

Little more is known of the legion. It is last attested on coins minted by Carausius in the late 3rd century AD. The legion probably remained in its fortress at Vetera until the collapse of the Rhine frontier in 407. A legion XXX shows up in the East in the mid-4th century, in Ammianus Marcellinus' account of the siege of Amida in Mesopotamia. Probably this refers to a vexillation that had been detached from the main body of the legion to become part of the mobile field army (*comitatus*) before the loss of Lower Germany.

Members of the re-enactment group '*XXX Ulpia Victrix*' at their summer camp in Tillsonberg, southern Ontario.

Other Legions on the Rhine Frontier

VIII Augusta

Cognomina	*Gallica*; *Mutinensis*; *Augusta*; *bis Augusta*; *Pia Fidelis Constans Commoda*
Emblem	Bull
Main base	Argentoratum (Strasbourg)
Main campaigns	Caesar's Gallic and civil wars (58–46 BC); Mutina (43 BC); Philippi (42 BC); Perusia (41 BC); Actium? (31 BC); Pannonian Revolt (AD 6–9), Britain? (AD 43); against Vindex' Revolt (AD 68); civil war (AD 69); Marcus Aurelius' Marcomannic wars (166–80); Severus' civil war against Clodius Albinus (196–97); Caracalla's war against the Alamanni (213); Severus Alexander's Persian war (vexillation?, 233); Severus Alexander's German war (235); late-3rd- and 4th-century campaigns against the Alamanni and other Germanic peoples

VIII Augusta was descended from Julius' Caesar's legion of that number. The legion used a bull as its emblem, the zodiac sign associated with Venus, the legendary founder of the Julian family. In return for its service during the civil wars of 58–46 BC, veterans of the legion are thought to have been given land at Casilinum in Campania in southern Italy (Appian *Civil Wars* 3.40; Cicero *Philippics* 2.102).

In 44 BC, these veterans were recalled by Octavian seeking to bolster his position against Mark Antony after Caesar's assassination. In 43 BC the Eighth fought against Mark Antony at Mutina (Modena in Italy). An inscription from Teano (southern Italy) gives the legion the cognomen *Mutinensis* ('of Mutina', *CIL* 10, 4786). Veterans may have been given land there after Philippi in 42 BC, a battle in which the legion certainly took part. The legion probably also participated in Octavian's siege of Perugia in 41 BC, since some of the sling bullets found here bear the numeral VIII.

The Augustan Period

There is no specific evidence that the legion was at the battle of Actium in 31 BC, but it is likely. Coins with the legion's numeral and inscriptions of its veterans show that *VIII Augusta* took part in the settlement of the *colonia* at Berytus (Beirut) by Agrippa, probably in 15–14 BC. One inscription from the site (*CIL* 3, 14165) refers to the legion by its old cognomen *Gallica*.

The date of the legion's transfer to Illyricum is uncertain, but it must have been sent to Pannonia or Noricum by AD 6. Its cognomen *Augusta* is first attested in Noricum at Virunum (near Magdalensberg, Austria) on the funerary monument of a veteran (*ILS* 2466).

Probably *VIII Augusta* was in the army mustered by Tiberius at Carnuntum in AD 6 to campaign against King Maroboduus of the Marcomanni. However, this expedition was abandoned on the outbreak of the Pannonian Revolt and *VIII Augusta* would have been engaged in combating the rebellious Pannonian tribes for the next three years. It was one of the legions stationed in Pannonia at the end of the revolt, at Poetovio (Ptuj), which it shared with *XV Apollinaris* and *IX Hispana*. Tacitus (*Annals* 1.23) describes how the Eighth was one of the legions involved in the mutinies that followed the death of Augustus in AD 14 (see page 78).

Moesia and Beyond

VIII Augusta's history in the next few decades is uncertain. Aulus Plautius, who led the invasion of Britain in AD 43, was governor of Pannonia and so may have taken a vexillation of the legion with him. But the evidence is not conclusive. At about the same time, Claudius sent the legion to Moesia. Inscriptions of the mid-1st century AD from Novae (Svištov, Bulgaria) naming soldiers of *VIII Augusta* suggest that it established a legionary fortress there. While in Moesia, the Eighth may have been sent to take part in the Crimean campaigns of Plautius Silvanus, perhaps being awarded the cognomen *bis Augusta* ('twice Augustan') at this time. This is found on a single inscription in Italy (*CIL* 11, 3004), and presumably was dropped after Nero's death.

During the Year of the Four Emperors (AD 69; see page 59), *VIII Augusta* initially sided with Otho, and set off for Italy with the other legions of Moesia. They were too late for the first battle of Bedriacum and, after Otho's defeat, joined the Pannonian legions in support of Vespasian against Vitellius. Commanded by Marcus Antonius Primus of the Seventh Legion (see pages 109 and

Opposite The tombstone of Gaius Valerius Crispus, a soldier of *VIII Augusta*. The inscription, which was found at Wiesbaden, reveals that he came from Macedonia, served 21 years and died at the age of 40 (*CIL* 13, 7574).

133–34), they defeated Vitellius in the second battle of Bedriacum and later entered Rome.

Tacitus (*Histories* 4.68) tells us that during the Batavian Revolt of AD 69–70 *VIII Augusta* was sent from Rome to Gaul to deal with unrest, but there is also archaeological evidence for the legion's presence at Burnum in Dalmatia at this time.

VIII Augusta in Upper Germany

The aftermath of the Batavian Revolt saw Vespasian reorganize the deployment of Rome's legions. *VIII Augusta* was sent to Upper Germany along with *I Adiutrix*, *XI Claudia* and *XIV Gemina*. It was once thought that the Eighth was based at Argentoratum (Strasbourg) from the start of its service in Upper Germany. However, a fortress has since been found at Mirebeau-sur-Bèze in Burgundy, constructed at the start of the AD 70s, with stamped bricks of *VIII Augusta*. It seems likely that the legion was based initially at Mirebeau, to watch over the Lingones, who had played an important part in the Batavian Revolt. The evidence suggests a long stay at Mirebeau, until the start of the war with the Chatti (AD 83) or, possibly, the revolt of, Saturninus, governor of Upper Germany, in AD 89. Afterwards the legion was based at Argentoratum (Strasbourg), where it remained until the 5th century AD.

There is scattered evidence through the late 1st century AD for the presence of soldiers of *VIII Augusta* throughout Germany, engaged in a range of construction projects. For example, a milestone (*CIL* 13, 9082) found in the Kinzig river near Offenburg reveals that legionaries under Cornelius Clemens built a road through the Black Forest from Augusta Vindelicorum (Augsburg) in Raetia, to Moguntiacum (Mainz) in Upper Germany. Some soldiers were sent to military outposts along the Rhine. *Beneficiarii* on detached duties dedicated altars that have been found in Osterburken (*AE* 1985, 686, 690, 692, 695) and and Obernburg (*AE* 1957, 48), as well as a column and altar to Jupiter at Heidelberg (*CIL* 13, 6397). A legionary's shield-boss was also found at Vindonissa.

Little is known of the legion's activities during the 2nd century. The emperor Hadrian sent a vexillation to Britain, which was based on Hadrian's Wall. The legion must also have been involved in the Marcomannic wars of Marcus Aurelius. In the 180s it was given the cognomen *Pia Fidelis Constans Commoda*. This new title perhaps relates to its suppression of a band of deserters, led by Maternus, which terrorized the region in *c.* 186 (Herodian 1.10). After Commodus' death in 192, *Commoda* was dropped.

We have more evidence for the legion in the 3rd century AD. Caracalla used it against the Alamanni in 213, and 20 years later a vexillation went east with Severus Alexander to fight against the Sasanians. While it was away from the Rhine frontier, the Alamanni attacked Roman territory, drawing Severus Alexander back from the East. *VIII Augusta* undoubtedly was part of the emperor's army that crossed the Rhine to combat the invaders, and subsequently defected to Maximinus (in 235; Herodian 6.7–9). Conflict with the Alamanni recurred throughout the 3rd and 4th centuries, and after the abandonment of the Agri Decumates (the territory between the Rhine and Danube) in 260, *VIII Augusta* remained at Argentoratum to guard the Rhine frontier. Its role in the struggle between the emperor Gallienus and the pretender Postumus (based in Gaul) is unclear. The legion was honoured by Gallienus with the title *V Pia V Fidelis* ('Five times Dutiful and Loyal'; this cognomen also appears with *VI* and *VII* and is found on coins), yet Postumus controlled Upper Germany.

The legion was still garrisoned at Strasbourg (Argentoratum) in the 4th century, with a

Above Model of *VIII Augusta*'s legionary fortress in the Archaeological Museum of Strasbourg.

Below An inscription (*left*) recording building work by the Eighth Legion at Zugmantel (to the north of Wiesbaden) and a tile (*right*) stamped with 'Leg VIII', both now at the Saalburg Museum.

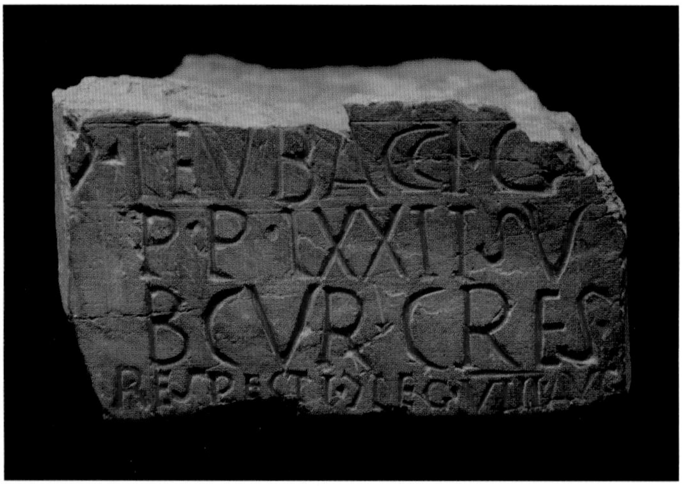

vexillation at Divitia (modern Deutz) in Lower Germany with soldiers of *II Italica*. An inscription (*AE* 2002, 1051) from Etzgen (Switzerland) dating to 371 proves that the legion was still in Upper Germany, and *VIII Augusta* may well have fought against the Alamannic invasion that culminated in the emperor Julian's victory at Strasbourg in 357. However, it does not appear in any identifiable form in the *Notitia Dignitatum*, a late antique document that lists the legions throughout the empire (see Part III) suggesting it was swept away in events of the late 4th–early 5th centuries AD.

Denarius coin minted during the reign of Septimius Severus, depicting an eagle between two standards with the legend *LEG VIII AUG*. The legion was quick to support Severus in his civil war with Clodius Albinus (196–97), and part of it was sent to Lyon, the principal city of Gaul, when that city's urban cohort sided with Albinus.

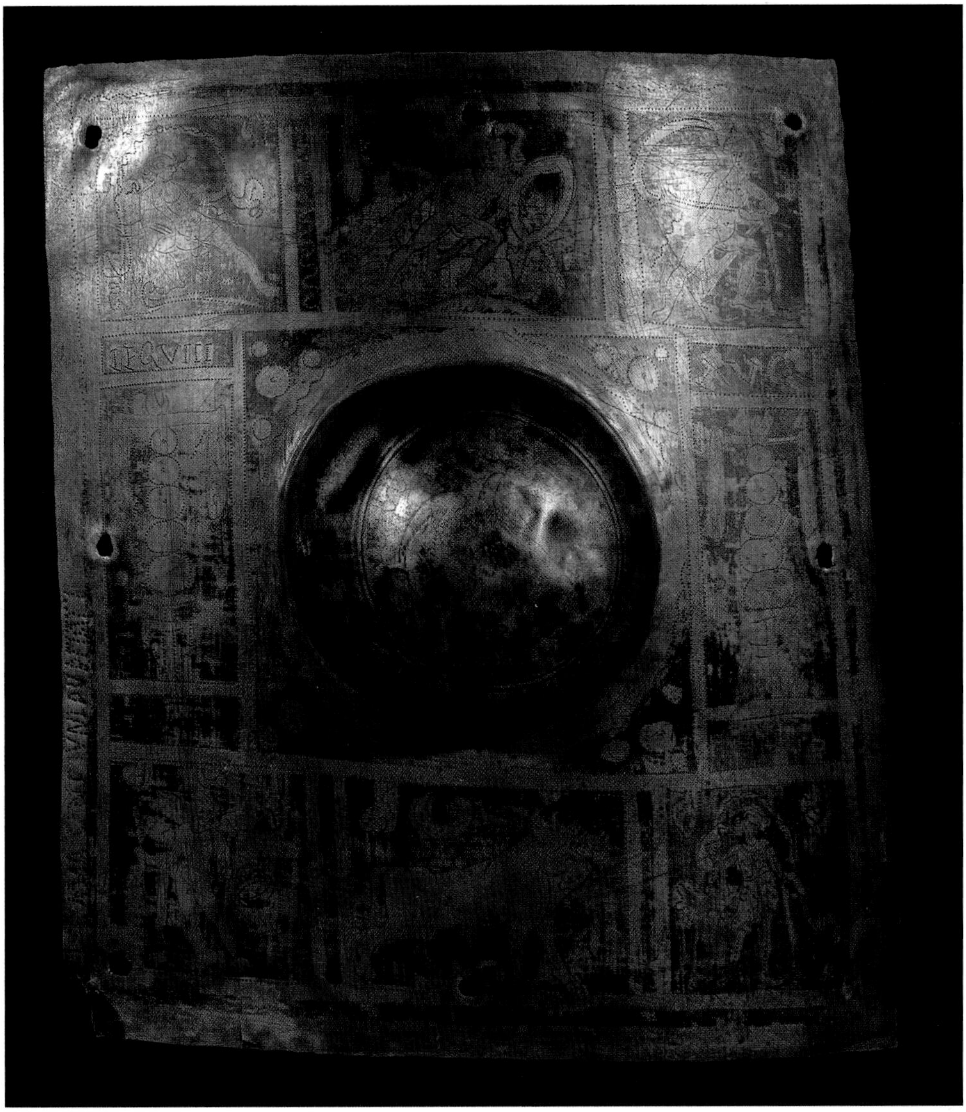

Shield boss of Junius Dubitatus, a soldier of *VIII Augusta* on Hadrian's Wall (early 2nd century AD), found in the river Tyne in 1867 (British Museum). It depicts the four seasons, military standards, the god Mars and a bull (the legion's emblem). It is inscribed *Iul Magni Iuni Dubitati* (recording its owner and his membership of Julius Magnus' century) and *Leg VIII Aug*.

XXII Primigenia

XXII Primigenia existed by AD 43, when inscriptions place it at Moguntiacum (Mainz) with *IIII Macedonica*. It may have been one of two legions (the other was *XV Primigenia*) raised either in AD 39 by Caligula in anticipation of an invasion of Britain, or (less likely) in AD 42 by Claudius, to replace legions earmarked for his invasion army. Little is known of its activities before AD 69, the Year of the Four Emperors.

XXII Primigenia

Cognomina	*Primigenia*; *Pia Fidelis Domitiana*; *Antoniana*; *Alexandriana*; *Pia VI Fidelis VI*
Emblems	Capricorn, Hercules
Main base	Moguntiacum (Mainz)
Main campaigns	Civil war (AD 69); Batavian Revolt (AD 69–70); Saturninus' Revolt (AD 89); Trajan's Parthian war (vexillation, 115–17); Lucius Verus' Parthian war (vexillation?, 161–66); Marcus Aurelius' Marcomannic wars (vexillation?, 166–80); Septimius Severus' civil wars against Clodius Albinus (196); Septimius Severus' second Parthian war (vexillation, 197); Caracalla's war against the Alamanni (213); Severus Alexander's Persian and German wars (vexillation, 233; 235); Philip the Arab's Dacian war (246); Gallienus' Gothic war? (vexillation, 267–69)

Troublesome Years on the Rhine

One of the contenders for the throne in AD 69 was Vitellius, commander of the armies of Lower Germany. The legions there naturally supported his claims and Tacitus (*Histories* 2.100) records that a vexillation of *XXII Primigenia* fought at the second battle of Bedriacum (October 69). The legions of the Rhine were defeated by Vespasian's army at that battle.

While the civil war was going on, the Batavian Revolt had broken out (see pages 65–66) and *V Alaudae* and *XV Primigenia* were besieged at Vetera (Xanten). *XXII Primigenia*, commanded by Gaius Dillius Vocula, was sent with *IIII Macedonica* to relieve them, though ultimately it was left to guard Moguntiacum and did not engage the rebels. In autumn AD 70, Petillius Cerialis reached Moguntiacum with a huge army, and went on to crush the Batavians and their allies.

Within a year, the Twenty-Second Legion had moved to a new base at Vetera (Vetera II – the old fortress was destroyed in the revolt). From there, in AD 89, the legion rushed south with the rest of the army of Lower Germany (*I Minervia*, *VI Victrix*, *X Gemina*) to defeat Lucius Antonius

Remains of the aqueduct at Moguntiacum. The fortress there was first established during the reign of Augustus at the confluence of the Main and the Rhine. It was occupied by a succession of legions before becoming the permanent base of *XXII Primigenia*.

Saturninus, the rebellious governor of Upper Germany. In recognition of their swift action, all four legions were awarded the cognomina *Pia Fidelis Domitiana* ('Dutiful and Loyal, of Domitian'). *Domitiana* was dropped after the emperor's assassination in AD 96.

At Moguntiacum and Bonna

By AD 97 *XXII Primigenia* had returned to its old base at Moguntiacum (Mainz), where it remained for the next two centuries. But vexillations served frequently elsewhere. Inscriptions reveal that one unit garrisoned Bonna in Lower Germany, when *I Minervia*, its usual garrison, was sent to the Lower Danube to take part in Trajan's Dacian wars (101–6). At Bonna an architect specialist of the legion built an altar to the deities Nemesis and Diana (*AE* 1960, 160). A vexillation apparently took part in Trajan's Parthian war, since its *primus pilus* Marcus Iulius Maximus, was awarded *dona militaria* for service in Armenia and Parthia (*AE* 1962, 311).

Service Elsewhere in the Empire

Further inscriptions reveal that legionaries of *XXII Primigenia* were involved in the construction of Hadrian's Wall in Britain (in 119, under the command of Titus Pontius Sabinus) and the Antonine Wall (139–42), and there is evidence that the legion was involved in building new forts on the east bank of the Rhine.

Vexillations also served elsewhere, apparently fighting against the Parthians during the reign of Lucius Verus (161–66) and the Marcomanni in the reign of Marcus Aurelius (166–80). At this time (170–71), the future emperor Didius Julianus commanded the legion (*SHA Didius Julianus* 1.6).

XXII Primigenia defended Trier when it was attacked by Septimius Severus' rival Clodius Albinus in 196. There it was commanded by Claudius Gallus, who also commanded a mixed vexillation of the four Rhine legions later, in Septimius Severus' second Parthian war.

The legion probably saw action during Caracalla's German campaign of 213. It was certainly involved in the preparations made for this campaign, helping to rebuild the bridge across the Rhine at Mainz, and it was probably during this campaign that it earned the cognomen *Antoniniana*. Fragmentary inscriptions from Piercebridge suggest that soldiers of the legion also served in Britain during Caracalla's reign.

A vexillation fought with Severus Alexander against the Sasanians in 233, when the legion gained the title *Alexandriana*, after the emperor. While the emperor was engaged with the Persians, the Alamanni attacked, and Alexander returned to the West and crossed the Rhine to campaign against them until his army defected to Maximinus. *XXII Primigenia* must have been one of the legions involved in these events. An inscription found in Romula (Resca, Romania, *AE* 1945, 77) gives the titles *XXII Primigenia Pia Fidelis Philippiana*, showing the legion took part in Philip the Arab's Dacian war (in 246).

During more German invasions in 260, Postumus, governor of Germany, was acclaimed emperor by his troops and declared an independent Gallic empire. The Twenty-Second supported the emperor Gallienus against Postumus. A vexillation may have served in Gallienus' campaign against the Goths, since an inscription (*CIL* 3, 14207) relating to it was found at Perinthus on the northern shores of the Sea of Marmara. Like other legions loyal to Gallienus, *XXII Primigenia* was awarded titles like *Pia VI Fidelis VI* ('Six times Dutiful and Loyal') and *Pia VII Fidelis VII* ('Seven times Dutiful and Loyal').

After Gallienus died, Moguntiacum briefly became an independent city-state under the leadership of Laelianus, thought to be *XXII Primigenia*'s commander (*SHA The Thirty Pretenders* 5). This lasted for two months before being conquered by Postumus and incorporated into his Gallic empire, which was in turn crushed by the emperor Aurelian in 274, but the legion survived. It was still in existence at the beginning of the 4th century AD, but disappears from our sources after the reign of Constantine (306–37).

1st-century AD dagger (*pugio*) found in the Rhine near Mainz. Its sheath has silver, brass and enamel inlay decoration. Mainz, Landesmuseum.

Brick stamped *LEG XXII PR* (Saalburg Museum). The fort was manned by an auxiliary cohort, but probably lay under the command of the fortress of *XXII Primigenia* at Moguntiacum.

V Alaudae

V Alaudae was raised by Julius Caesar in *c.* 52 BC (see page 24) from Gallic recruits, and its cognomen 'the larks' may reflect distinctive helmet crests worn by its members. After the Gallic war, it fought right through the civil war to the battle of Munda (45 BC), and gained its emblem of an elephant from fighting enemy elephants at Thapsus (46 BC). It served under Mark Antony until its incorporation into the imperial army after Actium.

The Augustan Period

Coins naming the legion show that *V Alaudae* was used by Augustus in his Cantabrian campaigns of 27–19 BC (see pages 107–8), and its veterans received land at Colonia Augusta Emerita (Merida) in 25 BC. There is also evidence of veterans at Hispalis and Corduba. The legion itself was stationed with *X Gemina* in Hispania Ulterior.

In 17 BC *V Alaudae* was sent to Gaul, where it met with humiliating defeat. Cassius Dio (54.20)

V Alaudae

Cognomina	*Alaudae*; *Gallica*
Emblem	Elephant
Main base	Vetera (Xanten)
Main campaigns	Caesar's Gallic and civil wars (52–45 BC); Mutina (43 BC); Philippi (42 BC); Actium? (31 BC); Spain (from 30 BC); Gaul (17 BC); Rhine frontier (AD 9); Frisian Revolt (AD 28); civil war (AD 69); Domitian's Dacian and/or Sarmatian wars? (AD 85–86; 92); Trajan's Dacian wars? (101–6)

Denarius of Julius Caesar after the victory at Thapsus. It depicts symbols of Caesar's status as *pontifex maximus*, and an elephant trampling a snake. The elephant became *V Alaudae*'s emblem.

The Mutinies of AD 14

In AD 14 the legions of Pannonia and Lower Germany mutinied, triggered by the death of Augustus and spurred on by poor conditions of service (Tacitus, *Annals* 1.31–49). The mutiny in Germany began with the Fifth and Twenty-First legions, and soon swept up the First and Twentieth, who were camped together. Tacitus describes the mutiny as disciplined white hot anger – there was no chaos or disorder. The men whipped their centurions and threw them over the fortress walls or into the Rhine.

The commander of the German legions was Germanicus, nephew of the new emperor Tiberius. He rushed back from Gaul to deal with the mutinous legions. He found them waiting for him outside their fortress, heads hung in shame. But the mutiny was not over and the men voiced their grievances loudly. Germanicus discharged all men who had served over 20 years, but withheld the pay owed to the soldiers until they had dispersed to their winter fortresses. The First and Twentieth legions were led away; the Fifth and Twenty-First refused to move until they had been paid.

After several setbacks, all the mutinous legions had been satisfied except the Fifth and Twenty-First. Germanicus collected an army to move against them; on hearing of this, loyal men of these legions cut down the leaders of the mutiny. Tacitus describes how mess-mates fought one another with no restraint by their officers. Eventually the mutiny was suppressed and Germanicus entered the fortress. Subsequently he gave the mutinous legions an opportunity to regain their honour by campaigning against German tribes who had been hoping to exploit the legionary unrest.

The so-called 'Sword of Tiberius', found at Mainz, dates to c. AD 15 and depicts Tiberius presenting a statuette of Victory to the emperor Augustus, who is flanked by Victory and Mars Ultor.

and Velleius Paterculus (*Roman History* 2.97) describe how the Romans were defeated by the Sugambri and other German raiders, and *V Alaudae* lost its eagle. Augustus himself travelled to Gaul to deal with the crisis, and the Germans withdrew and agreed terms.

In AD 6 *V Alaudae* was in the army assembled by Tiberius to campaign against the Marcomanni, but this was forestalled by the Pannonian Revolt. In AD 9, at the time of the Varian disaster, the legion was commanded by Varus' nephew, Lucius Asprenas. He marched north to rescue the garrison that Varus had left at Aliso, and took up positions on the Rhine to defend the river crossings and check any potential unrest in Gaul.

The 1st Century AD

In AD 14 *V Alaudae* was at Vetera in Lower Germany, with *XXI Rapax*, and was one of the legions that mutinied at the news of the death of Augustus (see box opposite).

In AD 28 the Frisians rebelled against Rome. In one battle of the ensuing campaign the auxiliary troops of the Roman army got into difficulties, and had to be relieved at a crucial moment by the main body of legionary troops, *V Alaudae* attacking with particular ardour. Tacitus (*Annals* 4.73), records the important role played in the battle by the Fifth's legate, Cethegus Labeo.

Under Claudius the legion was still based in Lower Germany. It may have sent a vexillation to Britain in AD 43: an unnamed tribune of the Fifth received decorations from Claudius, but it is not clear if this was for service in Britain or Germany (*ILS* 974). There are other glimpses of the activities of members of the legion in the mid-1st century AD. For example, an inscription from Tarraco in Spain records a military tribune, Aemilius Fraternus taking a census there in the reign of Nero (*CIL* 2, 4188).

When Galba became emperor in AD 68, the Fifth and its fellow legions in Germany were reluctant to swear allegiance, and even stoned the new emperor's images (Tacitus, *Histories* 1.55).

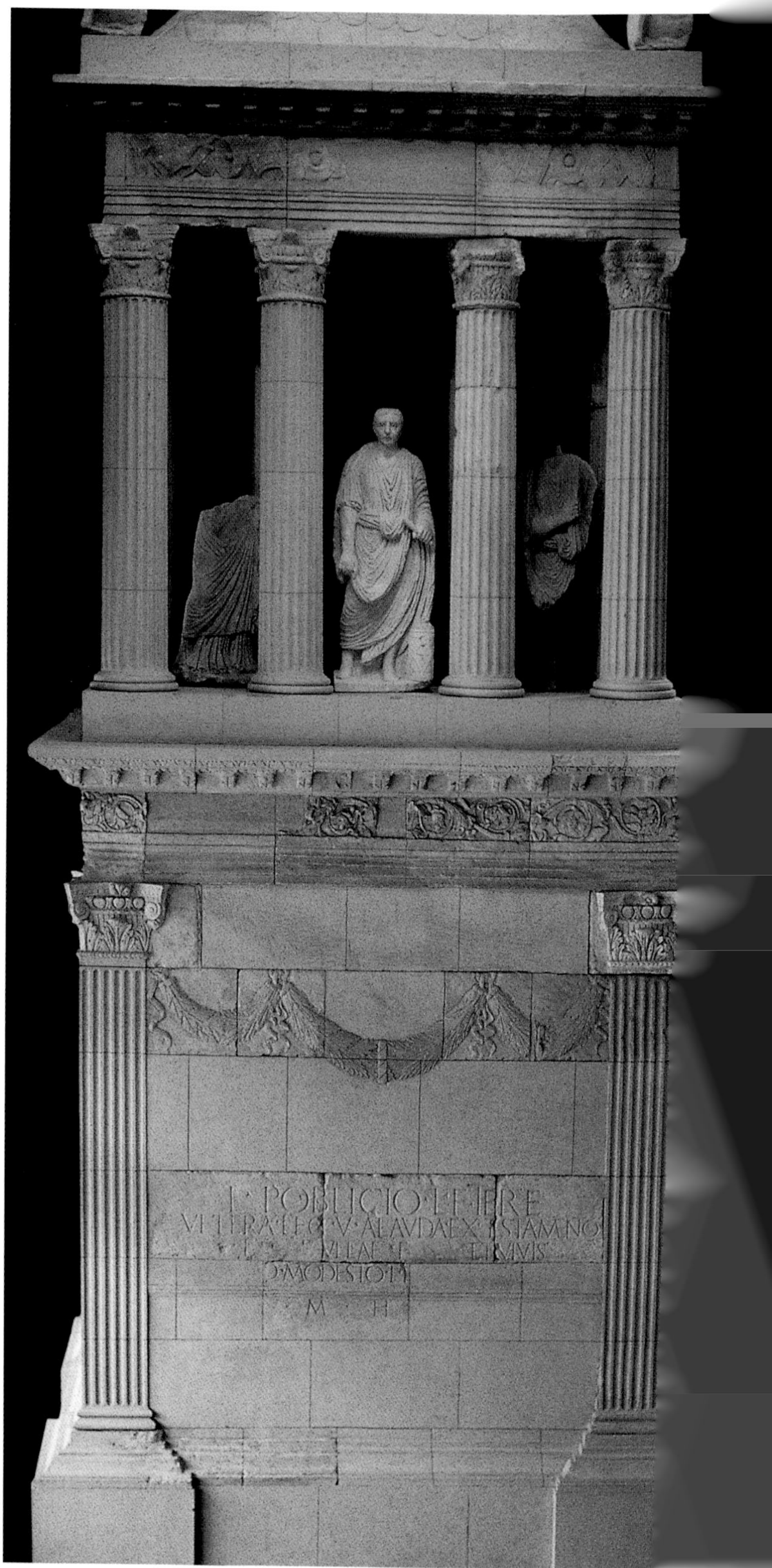

Tomb of Lucius Poblicius, a veteran of *V Alaudae*, reconstructed in the Römisch-Germaniches Museum, Cologne (*AE* 1979, 412).

They were quick to transfer their loyalty to Vitellius. Along with the other legions of Germany, part of the Fifth fought for Vitellius against Otho's forces at the first battle of Bedriacum and, according to Tacitus, routed the Thirteenth Legion. But even after victory soldiers of the Fifth were involved in trouble: Tacitus (*Histories* 2.68) records how a drunken wrestling match between a legionary and a Gallic auxiliary provoked a full-scale battle in which two cohorts were destroyed.

Later in the same year, *V Alaudae* was in the army sent back to Cremona by Vitellius to prevent the advance of Marcus Primus' Flavian (pro-Vespasian) force on Rome. On hearing that the fleet based at Ravenna had defected to Vespasian, the army commander, Aulus Caecina Alienus, decided to change sides. However, the soldiers of the Fifth remained loyal to Vitellius, and threw Caecina in chains, replacing him with their own legate, Fabius Fabullus (Tacitus, *Histories* 3.14). When subsequently the Vitellian force was defeated, *V Alaudae* was sent to Illyricum, along with the other defeated legions, to keep them out of further action until the civil war was over.

Part of *V Alaudae* had remained on the Rhine and was swept up in the events of the Batavian Revolt in AD 69–70, eventually being massacred by the rebel leader Julius Civilis (see page 66). The fate of the remaining soldiers of *V Alaudae* after AD 70 is unknown. The legion was once thought to have been disbanded in AD 70, along with *I Germanica* and *XV Primigenia*, in the aftermath of the Batavian Revolt. However, there are suggestions that the legion was transferred to the Balkans after AD 70. An altar found at Adamklissi in Dacia bears the names of 3,800 legionaries, and it has been suggested that these were all soldiers of *V Alaudae*, who died fighting during Trajan's Dacian wars. More recently, an inscription commemorating Gaius Julius Velox, a veteran of the legion of 35 years' service, has been found at Scupi (modern Skopje) and seems to date to the reign of Domitian (*IMS* 6, 41). Thus the legion may have met its end on the Danube *c.* AD 85–86 at the hands of the Dacians (during Domitian's Dacian campaign), or in AD 92 during the war against the Sarmatians, in which an unknown legion and its general were massacred.

XXI Rapax

Cognomen	*Rapax*
Emblem	Capricorn
Main base	Moguntiacum (Mainz)
Main campaigns	Pannonian Revolt (AD 6–9); Germanicus' war against the Chatti (AD 9–14); against the Turoni (AD 21); civil war (AD 69); Batavian Revolt (AD 69–70); Domitian's war against the Chatti (AD 83); Domitian's Sarmatian war (AD 92)

XXI Rapax

The early history of *XXI Rapax* ('Rapacious') is obscure. Emil Ritterling believed it was formed by Augustus for the conquest of the Alps, but it might have been formed in the triumviral period. Augustus may have used the legion in his Cantabrian campaigns in Hispania, but there is no firm evidence. After 15 BC it was based in the newly annexed Raetia, possibly at Castra Regina (Regensburg), and in AD 6 it prepared to take part in Tiberius' abandoned invasion of Bohemia to crush Maroboduus' Marcomanni. Instead it must have been involved in the suppression of the Pannonian Revolt of AD 6–9.

Move to Germania

After the Varian disaster of AD 9, the legion was sent to Lower Germany, where it shared the fortress at Vetera with *V Alaudae* and took part

The Revolt of Saturninus, 1st January AD 89

The details of this revolt are sparse, but involved the two legions stationed at Moguntiacum (Mainz), *XIV Gemina* and *XXI Rapax*. Suetonius (*Domitian* 6.2) reports that 'a civil war provoked by Lucius Antonius, governor of Upper Germany, was brought to an end in the emperor's absence by miraculous good fortune. For at the very hour of the battle, the Rhine suddenly thawed and prevented a barbarian force from crossing to join Antonius.'

The reason for Lucius Antonius Saturninus' revolt at his Moguntiacum base is unknown, and there is no other evidence for support by barbarian allies. It was swiftly put down by the legions of Lower Germany, led by their governor Lappius Maximus, and Domitian used the uprising as an excuse to execute many of his enemies.

in Germanicus' German campaigns against the Chatti until AD 14. On the death of Augustus in AD 14 it was one of the legions that mutinied over poor conditions and terms of service, and was slow to surrender to Germanicus (see page 78).

The legion remained at Vetera until *c.* AD 43, but a mixed vexillation of *XXI Rapax, I Germanica,* and *XX Valeria Victrix* was sent to put down a rebellion by the Turoni in Gaul in AD 21, commanded by an officer of *I Germanica* (*CIL* 14, 3602). The legion also seems to have taken part in Caligula's German war.

In the reorganization of the German legions that took place in preparation for Claudius' invasion of Britain in AD 43, *XXI Rapax* was transferred to Upper Germany, where it perhaps stayed briefly at Strasbourg (Argentoratum, where it is named in tile stamps) before garrisoning Vindonissa (Windisch), vacated by *XIII Gemina.* Alternatively a vexillation may have been stationed at Strasbourg while the main body was at Vindonissa. The legion was certainly at Vindonissa by AD 47 and was responsible for rebuilding the wooden fortress in stone and brick. A few inscriptions have been found attesting to its building activities, at Vindonissa and the surrounding region.

In the Year of the Four Emperors, *XXI Rapax* sided with Vitellius, the governor of Lower Germany. With him and other legions of the province, it marched on Italy and defeated Otho at the first battle of Bedriacum before moving on Rome. Before the end of the year, however, the army had been defeated at the second battle of Bedriacum by the Danubian legions supporting Vespasian (see pages 134–35). After this defeat all the vanquished legions that had supported Vitellius were sent to Illyricum, but quickly returned to Germany to help suppress the Batavian Revolt (AD 69–70). The Twenty-First played a decisive role in defeating the rebels at Augusta Treverorum (Trier) and was part of the victorious army at Vetera.

XXI Rapax was then sent to Bonna (Bonn) in Lower Germany, where it took the place of *I Germanica.* The fortress was rebuilt in stone in this period. In AD 83 the legion was sent back to Upper Germany once more to take part in Domitian's war against the Chatti. Its permanent base was probably Moguntiacum (Mainz), but brick stamps naming the legion have been found in smaller forts along the frontier. By AD 88, *XXI Rapax* was certainly based at Moguntiacum, where – along with *XIV Gemina* – it supported the rebellion by the provincial governor, Lucius Antonius Saturninus.

It has been argued that, after the Revolt of Saturninus, *XXI Rapax* was sent to Pannonia. Here, according to Suetonius (*Domitian* 6), a legion – often identified as the Twenty-First – was destroyed by the Sarmatians in AD 92. More recently it has been suggested that the legion was disbanded after the revolt of Saturninus.

The tombstone of Quintus Marcius Balbus and his son, Celer, legionaries of *XXI Rapax* (*CIL* 13, 6951a). They both died while the legion was based at Moguntiacum, and the tombstone can be seen in the Landesmuseum, Mainz.

The Legions of Roman Britain

II Augusta, VI Victrix, IX Hispana and XX Valeria Victrix

At the beginning of the imperial period, Britain lay beyond the frontiers of the Roman empire – but after its conquest in AD 43, it became a major focus of legionary activity. Widespread archaeological and epigraphic evidence reflects the impact of the legions in this province, where they both actively campaigned to expand Roman territory and policed the border against hostile northern tribes.

Little is known of the composition of Claudius' invasion force in AD 43, but by AD 60 there were four legions in Britain: *II Augusta, IX Hispana, XIV Gemina* and *XX Valeria*

Victrix. During the AD 60s, *II Adiutrix* replaced *XIV Gemina.* Twenty years later *II Adiutrix* was removed, reducing the garrison to three legions. By the end of the Roman occupation of Britain, there was only one legion in the province: *VI Victrix.*

The presence of four legions reflects the unsettled situation in Britain during the 1st century AD. The invasion established a permanent Roman military presence, but much of Britain refused to accept Roman rule. Roman treatment of their subjects exacerbated the problems and culminated in the Boudican Revolt of AD 60, in which the Ninth Legion was routed and *XIV Gemina* rushed to save the day.

The legions continued their conquests in Wales and the north of Britain, advancing into Scotland and establishing garrisons in the Highlands in an attempt to consolidate their hold on the north. Ultimately this failed and the legions pulled back to Hadrian's Wall which became the frontier for the rest of the Roman period.

Hadrian's Wall was constructed along the Tyne-Solway line in the AD 120s. The northern border remained a trouble-spot for the rest of the 2nd century and was policed by detachments of three legions.

Map of Britain showing the legionary fortresses and other places mentioned in the text.

Each legion eventually settled into a permanent base, but individual legionaries moved around, serving on the staff of the provincial governor in London, undertaking duties on Hadrian's Wall, or fighting in Septimius Severus' Scottish campaign. Into the 4th century AD the British legions remained a strong military force and were called upon by usurpers such as Clodius Albinus, Carausius and Allectus, who sought to wrest control of the empire or establish their own breakaway empires.

II Augusta

II Augusta perhaps owes its origins to Caesar's Second Legion, raised in 48 BC and employed by Mark Antony at Mutina in 43 BC, or a Second Legion recruited by the consuls Hirtius and Pansa for the same campaign. Otherwise it may have been formed or re-formed later by Octavian (Augustus). The Capricorn (Augustus' conception sign) supports this idea, as does the cognomen *Augusta*. Alternatively *Augusta* may refer to a victory in his reign. It is first attested in an inscription from Spain, before AD 9 (*ILS* 6948).

Octavian settled veterans at Arausio (Orange) in France, and an inscription there mentions a *II Gallica* ('of Gaul'), presumably stationed in the province before 30 BC. Colonists of a *II Sabina* are known from Venafrum (Venafro, Italy). Both may be the same legion as *II Augusta*.

II Augusta

Cognomen	*Augusta*
Emblems	Capricorn; Pegasus
Main base	Isca Silurum (Caerleon, Wales)
Major campaigns	Cantabrian wars (26–19 BC); Germanicus' German campaigns (AD 9); invasion and pacification of Britain (AD 43 onwards); Scottish campaigns of Septimius Severus (208–11)

Early History in Roman Spain

Our earliest secure knowledge of the legion comes after 26 BC, as part of an army of at least seven legions led by Augustus against the Cantabrians of northwest Spain, perhaps resulting in its title 'Augustan'. It remained in Spain after the war, but its subsequent movements are unclear. A gravestone found in Barcino (Barcelona), which

The Conquest of Britain

Julius Caesar's invasion of Britain was an embarrassing near-disaster, but hailed as a great triumph in Rome. In summer 55 BC he sailed to Britain with two legions. After hard fighting, Caesar agreed terms with the British tribes and withdrew. The following year Caesar took five legions to Britain in a face-saving campaign. This time he marched inland to the Thames, but in the face of strong resistance withdrew once more. Another invasion of Britain was planned by Augustus and Caligula, but finally undertaken by Claudius.

In late summer AD 43 the Romans invaded Britain again, under the command of Aulus Plautius. We lack precise information about the size and composition of his army, although by AD 60 four legions are attested in Britain. Tacitus and Suetonius record that *II Augusta*, led by the future emperor Vespasian, was part of the invasion force. Inscriptions suggest that the Ninth and Twentieth Legions were involved and it is likely that *XIV Gemina* was also part of the invading army, resulting in a force of four legions or more, at full strength or as vexillations.

Ancient writers record that the troops were reluctant to cross the Channel – for Britain was at the edge of the empire, beyond the limits of the civilized world. Only when Claudius sent his freedman Narcissus to harangue the troops were they shamed into embarking. After a rough crossing, the Romans landed with no initial resistance. The legions then advanced into Catuvellaunian territory, crossing the river Thames. Claudius received the formal surrender of tribal leaders and entered Camulodunum (Colchester), establishing a military base there. Aulus Plautius became the first governor of Britain. In the following years, the Romans expanded their control to the north, west and southwest, their movements traceable from the forts and fortresses they built.

Plaque recording building by II Augusta *at Condercum (Benwall), with its Capricorn and Pegasus emblems (RIB 1, 1341).*

became a *colonia* under Augustus, suggests that veterans of the legion may have settled there. Others must have settled at Cartenna in Mauretania (Tenes, Algeria; then part of Roman Spain), since according to Pliny the Elder (*Natural History* 5.20), this was a 'colony founded under Augustus by the Second Legion'.

Transfer to Upper Germany

The disastrous defeat of Varus in Germany in AD 9 (see pages 54–59) had wide ramifications. Spain's garrison was reduced to three legions and *II Augusta* moved to Upper Germany. Initially it was based near Moguntiacum (Mainz), as attested by the tombstone of Gaius Iulius, set up by his comrades in the Second Legion (*CIL* 13, 7234).

Tacitus says that the legion was involved in the mutiny of the Rhine legions after Augustus' death in AD 14. In the following year it was part of the army that Germanicus led deep into Germany against the Chatti and Cherusci. However, *II Augusta* (with *XIV Gemina*) suffered severely from storms and flooding as it returned to Roman territory along the North Sea coast (Tacitus, *Annals* 1.70). Germanicus' German campaigns ended in AD 16. The Second Legion moved from Moguntiacum to Argentoratum (Strasbourg), where tombstones of some of its soldiers, of Italian origins, have been found: Babuleius Garrulus from Mediolanum (Milan) died aged 45, after 22 years' service (*CIL* 13, 5976); Titus Iulius from Alba died aged 35, after serving 16 years (*CIL* 13, 5977); and Gaius Largennius from Luca died aged 37, having served 18 years (*CIL* 13, 5978).

In AD 21 the German legions under the governor of Upper Germany, Gaius Silius, crushed a rebellion in Gaul led by Julius Sacrovir and Julius Florus. The Second Legion must have been part of this Roman force and the triumphal arch at Orange – decorated with the Capricorn emblem – was perhaps set up to commemorate its role in the victory.

Invasion of Britain

From literary evidence we know that the future emperor Vespasian commanded *II Augusta* from AD 42, and thus he was with the legion when it invaded Britain in AD 43. An honorific inscription from Antioch in Pisidia sheds some light on *II Augusta*'s role in the invasion of Britain:

> To Publius Anicius Maximus, son of Publius, of the voting tribe Sergia, prefect of Gnaeus Domitius Ahenobarbus, *primus pilus* of Legion *XII Fulminata*, camp prefect of Legion *II Augusta* in Britannia, prefect of the army which is in Egypt, granted military decorations by the emperor because of the campaign, honoured with a mural crown and an untipped spear because of of the British war. His home city is Alexandria in Egypt. (This was set up) to honour him.
>
> *CIL* 3, 6809

Originally these decorations were for storming a stronghold and saving a citizen's life respectively, but by this time they were awarded for more general acts of bravery.

After a number of tribes capitulated to Claudius, Vespasian led his legion westward along the south coast of England to suppress further resistance. Between AD 43 and 47, at least 30 battles were fought against British tribes, and more than 20 native towns, along with the Isle of Wight, were captured. Vespasian and *II Augusta* almost certainly participated in fighting at Maiden Castle and Hod Hill in Dorset, Ham Hill in Somerset and Hembury in Devon. By AD 47, much of southern Britain was subdued, and Vespasian left *II Augusta*. The legion remained in Britain, at first probably at Isca Dumnoniorum (Exeter), then at Glevum (Gloucester), although there is little specific evidence from either site that can be related directly to the legion.

The legion played no part in suppressing Boudica's revolt of AD 60–61 (see page 97) despite being summoned by the governor, Suetonius Paulinus. Its camp prefect Poenius Postumus later committed suicide because 'he had cheated his own legion of its share of the glory and had failed to obey his commander's orders, contrary to military tradition' (Tacitus, *Annals* 14.37).

Civil War

In AD 69, the Year of the Four Emperors, a vexillation of *II Augusta* fought first for Otho and then for Vitellius against Vespasian at Bedriacum, near Cremona in northern Italy (see page 59). Tacitus states that the British vexillations were drawn up in the centre of the battleline, but poor leadership led to their defeat (*Histories* 3.22). Most of the British garrison remained in Britain and when it became apparent that Vitellius' cause was doomed, *II Augusta* declared for their former commander Vespasian. Tacitus claims that the legion was crucial in persuading the other British legions to do the same (*Histories* 3.44).

One senatorial officer of *II Augusta* known from this period is Lucius Antistius Rusticus, then a military tribune (*AE*, 1925, 126 = 1926, 78). Later he received decorations normally reserved for legionary legates, implying that he commanded the legion in the absence of its regular legate. It is likely that Rusticus was rewarded for his part in securing the allegiance of the British legions to Vespasian. That would explain his distinguished subsequent career, as consul and governor of Cappadocia in AD 90.

The Fortress at Isca Silurum

The pacification of Wales was now a priority and Julius Frontinus, governor of Britain in AD 74–78, launched a series of campaigns against the Silures. A new fortress was established for *II Augusta* at Isca Silurum (Caerleon), at the mouth of the river

Later literary sources, like Ptolemy's *Geography* (2nd century AD), suggest that *II Augusta* was stationed in the lands of the Dumnonii. Excavations at Isca Dumnoniorum (Exeter) have indeed revealed the remains of a fortress (*above*), though perhaps too small (*c.* 15 ha) for an entire legion. Excavated structures include the Neronian *principia* (headquarters) and a bath-house (*left*). A stamped roof tile, also dating to the Neronian period, identifies the Second Legion. The fortress was abandoned, probably in the late AD 60s. The tribal capital of the Dumnonii grew up in its place.

Excavations at Caerleon

Formal excavation at Caerleon began in 1908, on land, originally intended for houses, that the National Museum of Wales had succeeded in buying up. In 1926 excavations began in the amphitheatre and subsequently a row of barracks was uncovered in a neighbouring field. Both can still be visited today, along with the western defences and the fortress baths. In recent years geophysical surveys have produced an almost complete outline of the stone fortress, while the original timber structure is buried deeply beneath it.

Many finds were made during the excavations, including military equipment, pottery, glass, coins and jewelry. Numerous inscriptions, inscribed building stones and stamped tiles link *II Augusta* to Isca Silurum and the surrounding area over the centuries. The earliest, a marble slab, dates to AD 99/100:

> To Imperator Caesar Nerva Trajan Augustus, son of the deified Nerva, Victor over the Germans, High Priest, holding tribunician power, Father of his Country, Consul for the third time, (dedicated) by Legion *II Augusta*. (*RIB* 1, 330)

There is also evidence of veterans settling near the fortress. A tombstone (probably 2nd- or 3rd-century) was found at Great Bulmore, a few miles from Isca Silurum. It records that Julius Valens, a veteran, lived to the age of 100. However, Roman funerary inscriptions often exaggerated or rounded up ages.

Aerial view of the remains of the barracks at Isca Silurum (Caerleon). The whole base encompassed some 20.5 ha (50.5 acres) and was initially built from turf, clay and timber, with a ditch and walled rampart. By AD 100, the original construction was replaced with stone.

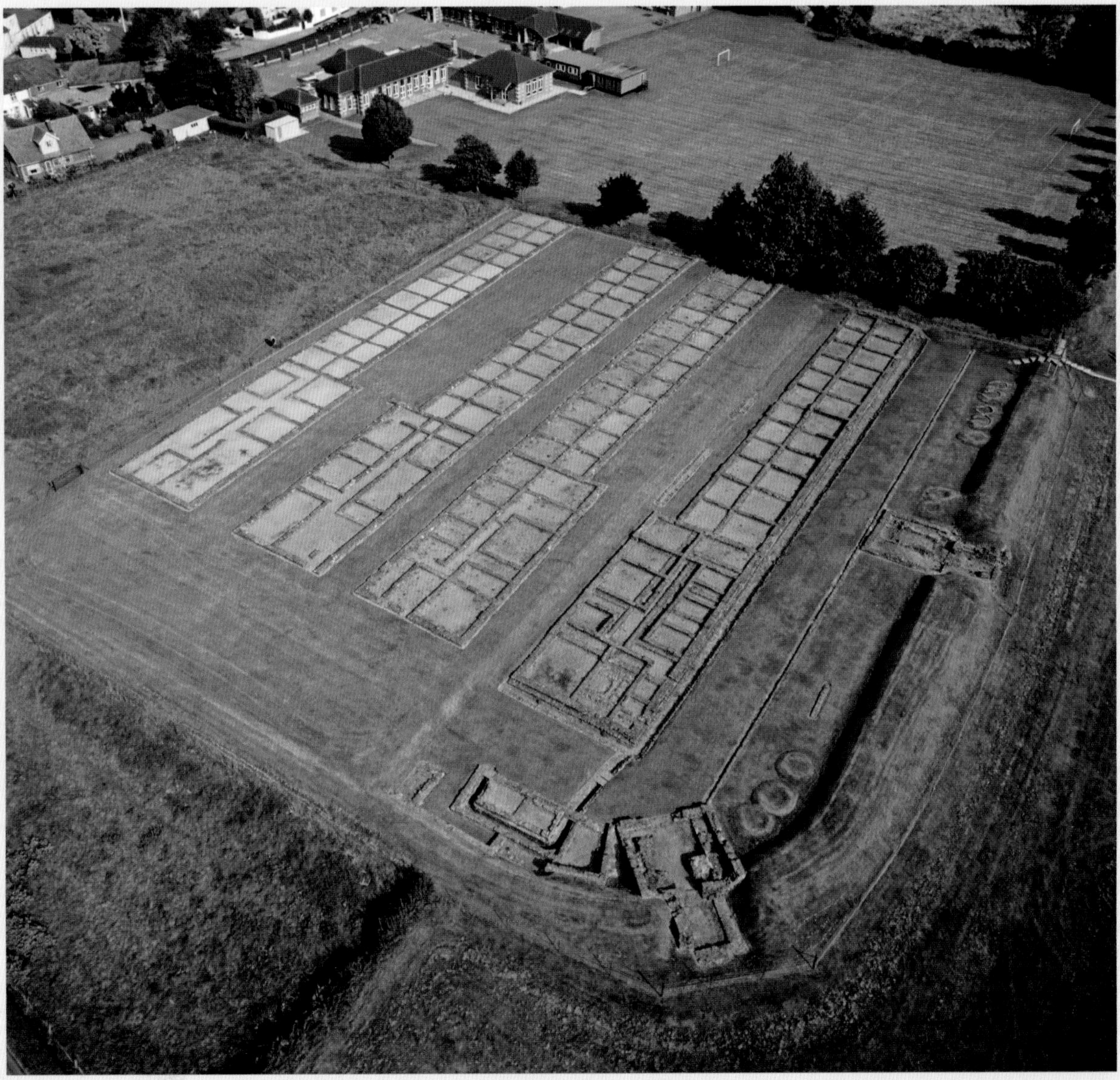

Usk, where it could easily be supplied by sea. This fortress was occupied by *II Augusta* for over 200 years.

II Augusta in Northern Britain

While *II Augusta* settled down in its long-term fortress at Isca Silurum, elements of the legion were detached to other locations, assuming various roles within the province. In AD 77–84 at least part of *II Augusta* moved north under the new governor Gnaeus Julius Agricola. It was present at his final victory at Mons Graupius, but did not engage the enemy. The battle was won by the efforts of auxiliary troops, and the Romans set about establishing garrisons in the Scottish Highlands to consolidate their hold on the north. Archaeological remains of some of the forts can be seen at places like Cardean, Stracathro, Fendoch, Strageath, Dalginross and Bochastle.

The 2nd Century

Archaeological evidence from the 2nd century AD suggests considerable movement of troops within Britain, as well as deployment of vexillations abroad. While the three British legions had permanent fortresses at Isca Silurum, Eboracum (York) and Deva (Chester), many soldiers were on more-or-less permanent detachment near Hadrian's Wall (at Corbridge and Carlisle, for example). Others served in London on the governor's staff. Detachments of non-British legions were sent to reinforce British garrisons in times of crisis or active campaigning. Vexillations of the Twenty-Second and Eighth Legions came from Upper Germany and were responsible for construction at Birrens fort in southwest Scotland during Antoninus Pius' reign. Meanwhile, vexillations of the British legions may have served temporarily in Germany.

In the 160s (during the reign of Marcus Aurelius), news reached Rome of an imminent war in Britain. A new governor, Sextus Calpurnius Agricola, was sent to deal with the situation (*SHA Marcus Aurelius* 8.6–7), but there is no specific archaeological evidence for this conflict. Later in his reign, Marcus Aurelius sent 5,500 cavalry to Britain (Cassius Dio 72.16), but it is not until the governorship of Ulpius Marcellus (*c.* 177) that we have an explicit account of troubles in Britain:

> But the most difficult of his wars was the one in Britain. For when the barbarians in that island had crossed the wall that separated them from the Roman encampments and had done a great deal of harm, slaughtering a general with his troops, Commodus was fearful, and sent Ulpius Marcellus against them.
>
> Cassius Dio 73.8

Ulpius Marcellus defeated the tribes and engaged in punitive action, but no details are known.

Septimius Severus

In 192 the emperor Commodus was assassinated and civil war began again. One of the contenders for the throne was Clodius Albinus, the governor of Britain. He took some British legions to the continent, but was defeated by Septimius Severus near Lyon. After defeating Albinus, Severus divided Britain in two: Superior (Upper, to the south) and Inferior (Lower, to the north), splitting the legionary command. In 208 Severus himself (with his wife and sons) arrived in Britain to reinvade Scotland with additional troops from Europe.

Isca Silurum remained the Second's main base throughout the Severan period and there is evidence of rebuilding within the fortress at this time. However, much of the legion moved to Scotland to take part in Severus' campaigns and the garrison remaining at Isca Silurum was greatly reduced in numbers. *II Augusta*'s soldiers who went north helped to construct the Carpow fortress, on the south bank of the river Tay.

When Severus died at Eboracum (York) in 211, his sons Caracalla and Geta abandoned his British conquests. Subsequently, the frontier remained at Hadrian's Wall, although outpost forts retained contact with lowland Scotland. The northern frontier was relatively peaceful through the 3rd century AD.

The 3rd and 4th Centuries

Cassius Dio states that *II Augusta*'s winter quarters were in Upper Britain (i.e. Isca Silurum), but inscriptions suggest it also spent time at Carlisle (Luguvalium), in the north. Individual soldiers and vexillations of different legions frequently moved around and served together. This probably explains the joint dedication to *Concordia* of

Hadrian's Wall and the Antonine Wall

After Agricola's governorship we lack major historical sources for Britain and have to piece together its story from fragmented and diverse evidence. With the Romans engaged in Parthia and Dacia, there was no attempt to hold on to Agricola's remote conquests. The Roman army pulled back to the Tyne–Solway line, a process that culminated in the construction of Hadrian's Wall. The Wall was probably begun in AD 122, when Hadrian visited Britain. It was not an impenetrable frontier but designed to control movement, creating secure crossing points where traffic could be searched and taxed. To support this frontier there were forts in northern England. Legions remained at Isca Silurum, Eboracum (York) and Deva (Chester), and some troops were stationed in London with the governor.

It is unclear why a second wall was built. It may have been connected with trouble in Britain at the time of Antoninus Pius' accession. In or around AD 139 the governor, Quintus Lollius Urbicus, had to repel barbarians and build another wall of stone and turf, the Antonine Wall, which became the northern frontier of Roman Britain. Lollius Urbicus is named on two inscriptions found at Balmuildy (*RIB* 1, 2191 and 2192). The wall's construction was

Above *Distance slab on the Antonine Wall: 'The Second Augustan Legion built 4140 feet' (RIB 1, 2203). Hunterian Museum, Glasgow.*

Below *For around 20 years in the mid-2nd century AD, the Antonine Wall was the northern frontier of Britain.*

Opposite above *A milecastle on Hadrian's Wall. There were 80 of them over the 74 miles (119 km) of the wall.*

accompanied by a reoccupation of lowland Scotland and the building of numerous forts and small forts, particularly along main roads to the north, attested by inscriptions and archaeological remains. In 161, however, the Romans were forced to abandon the Antonine Wall, and Hadrian's Wall became the definitive frontier.

Milecastle inscriptions show cohorts of *II Augusta* (along with *VI Victrix* and *XX Valeria Victrix*) participating in the construction of Hadrian's Wall in the 120s and 130s. *II Augusta* also helped to build the Antonine Wall in *c.* 139. Beautifully carved distance slabs record the legions involved in the wall's construction. These were apparently set up in pairs, marking each end of a section built by a legion. *II Augusta* also rebuilt forts in this area, including Corbridge.

Right *Inscriptions from Hadrian's Wall. LEG(io) II AUG(usta) can be read clearly on the largest.*

statues of two legionaries by *II Augusta* and *XX Valeria Victrix*. The remains were discovered in the foundations of Carlisle cathedral in 1988 (*RIB* 3, 3459). This suggests elements of both legions were stationed at Carlisle and hints at tension between them – *Concordia* ('Harmony') was typically invoked because of conflict. Other evidence also shows soldiers of different legions serving together. At Piercebridge in Durham, a dedication reveals Marcus Lollius Ventor, centurion of *II Augusta*, in command of vexillations of *VI Victrix* and 'the armies of both the Germanies' (*RIB* 3, 3253), while the 3rd-century funerary inscription of Gabinius Felix, a soldier of *II Augusta*, was found at Deva (Chester), fortress of *XX Valeria Victrix* (*RIB* 1, 488).

By the mid 3rd century, the whole legion was back in Isca Silurum. In 244 its *primus pilus* set up an inscription celebrating Augustus' birthday and in 255 its legate Titus Flavius Postumius Varus restored a temple to the goddess Diana. Rebuilding within the Isca Silurum fortress also took place. Subsequently much less is known of the legion's movements and activities. The early-5th-century *Notitia Dignitatum* records *II Augusta* at Richborough (southeast England), under the command of the Count of the Saxon Shore. By this time, Isca Silurum had been abandoned.

Officers of *II Augusta* in the 2nd Century AD

Vittius Adiutor, an eagle-bearer of *II Augusta*, is named on a writing-tablet from Vindolanda (Tablet 214), c. AD 92–97.

Aulus Claudius Charax from Pergamon (Turkey), a scholar and historian, commanded the legion at the time of the construction of the Antonine Wall. His career is recorded on an inscription from his home town (*AE* 1961, 320).

Marcus Cocceius Firmus was a centurion of *II Augusta* in the 2nd century AD. He dedicated five altars to 11 different deities. He may be the same man mentioned in an intriguing text by the legal scholar Pomponius, where one of Cocceius' slave women, serving a term of hard labour in salt works, was seized by bandits from 'across the border'. The bandits sold her back to Cocceius, who promptly claimed the purchase price back from the treasury, presumably on the grounds that it failed to protect his property while she served her sentence. The border involved may have been the northern British frontier, as salt-works existed on the coast of Fife (*RIB* 1, 2174–7).

Marcus Iulius Quadratus was also a centurion in the 2nd century AD. He died in combat in Britain aged 38, and was commemorated in his hometown, Castellum Arsacalitanum (Mechtet 'Ain Hallouf) in Numidia (modern Algeria):

> To the Spirits of the Departed. Marcus Julius Quadratus, son of Gaius, of the voting tribe Quirina lies here. He was granted a horse at public expense and was selected for the Board of Five Judges. He was centurion of the legion *XIII Gemina* in Dacia, centurion of the legion *III Augusta* in Africa and centurion of the legion *II Augusta* in Britain. He died in Britain, on active service. He lived 38 years. (*AE* 1957, 249)

Publius Septimius Geta, brother of the future emperor Septimius Severus, was tribune in *II Augusta* in the AD 170s.

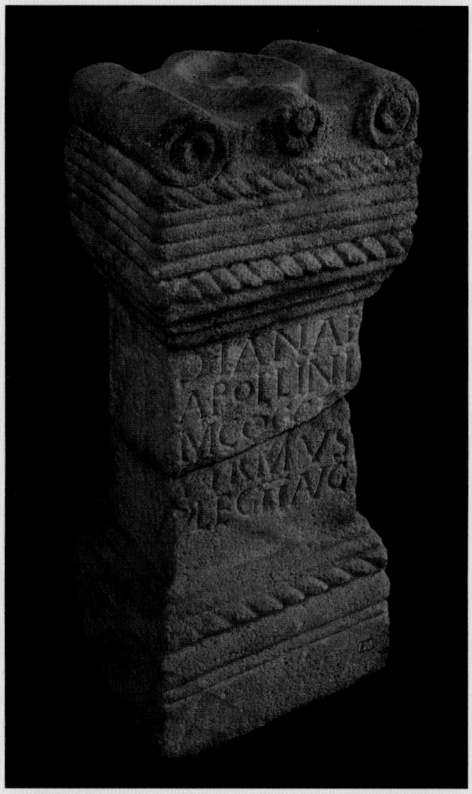

One of five altars set up by Marcus Cocceius Firmus, a centurion of the Second Legion. The altars are dedicated to Jupiter, Diana, Apollo, Mars, Minerva, the Campestres, Hercules, Epona, Victory, Silvanus and the Genius (divine spirit) of Britain. They were discovered in 1771 by workmen digging the Forth and Clyde Canal, just south of the fort at Auchendavy on the Antonine Wall.

VI Victrix

This legion was probably founded by Octavian during the civil war. Sling bullets with its number from Perusia (Perugia, Italy) suggest it took part in Octavian's siege of that city in 41 BC and no doubt it was present at Actium in 31 BC.

Activities in Spain

The legion moved to Hispania Tarraconensis (northeastern Spain) after 30 BC. Its main base may have been Legio (León). It participated in Augustus' campaigns against the Cantabrians (27–19 BC), along with *I Germanica*, *II Augusta*, *IIII Macedonica*, *V Alaudae*, *IX Hispana*, *X Gemina* and *XX Valeria Victrix*. *VI Victrix* remained in Spain until AD 70. Inscriptions reveal that soldiers of *VI Victrix* and *X Gemina* were among the first settlers at Colonia Patricia (Cordoba), Emerita Augusta (Mérida) and Caesaraugusta (Saragossa). The legion was given the name *Hispaniensis* ('Stationed in Spain'). The name *Victrix* ('Victorious') is first attested in the Neronian period, but may relate to earlier successes under Augustus.

In AD 68 *VI Victrix* was the only legion in Hispania Tarraconensis, under the command of its governor, Servius Sulpicius Galba. When news arrived of Vindex's rebellion in Gaul against Nero, Galba had the legion proclaim him 'legate of the Senate and the Roman people'. He then raised another legion, numbered *VII*. After Nero's suicide, Galba went to Rome as emperor with his newly raised Seventh Legion, leaving *VI Victrix* in Spain.

The Move North

After Vespasian's victory and accession in AD 69, he sent a large force commanded by Quintus Petillius Cerialis, including *VI Victrix*, to suppress the Batavian Revolt. The rebels were defeated at Vetera (Xanten) in AD 70, and in AD 73 *VI Victrix* set up a monument, possibly on the site of the victory, dedicating it to the new emperor, and his son Titus:

> [To Vespasian and] to Titus, son of Imperator Vespasian Augustus, holder of tribunician power, acclaimed Imperator for the fourth time, Consul twice and appointed as Consul for a third time, appointed as Censor. *Legio VI Victrix* dedicated this, when Aulus Marius Celsus was pro-praetorian legate of the emperor and Sextus Caelius Tuscus was legate of the emperor.
>
> *AE* 1979, 413

VI Victrix

Cognomina	*Hispaniensis*; *Victrix*; *Pia Fidelis*; *Fidelis Constans*; *Britannica*
Emblem	Probably a bull
Main base	Eboracum, York
Major campaigns	Perusia (41 BC); Actium (31 BC); Cantabrian wars (27–19 BC); Batavian Revolt (AD 69–70); against Saturninus' Revolt (AD 89); Dacian wars? (101–6); British Revolt (155–58); against Septimius Severus (191); Severus' Scottish campaigns (209)

VI Victrix subsequently remained in Lower Germany, occupying the former base of *XVI Gallica* at Novaesium (Neuss). This fortress was destroyed by the Batavians, and rebuilt. Brick stamps confirm that *VI Victrix* undertook the reconstruction. In AD 89, the governor of Upper Germany rebelled against the emperor Domitian. Four legions (*I Minerva*, *VI Victrix*, *X Gemina* and *XXII Primigenia*) were sent to defeat him, each subsequently awarded the title *Pia Fidelis Domitiana* ('Dutiful and Loyal, of Domitian'). *Domitiana* was dropped after Domitian's assassination and *damnatio memoriae* in AD 96.

At the end of the 1st century or very beginning of the 2nd century, Novaesium was abandoned and *VI Victrix* transferred to the rebuilt fortress at Xanten, known as Vetera II, replacing *XXII Primigenia*. Part of the legion may have been sent to the Danube during Trajan's Dacian wars (101–6).

Portrait bust of the emperor Galba, now in the Antikensammlung im Königlichen Palast, Stockholm. Galba was governor of Spain in AD 68 and was declared emperor by the Sixth Legion (Cassius Dio 63.23).

Distance slab of the Sixth Legion found at Braidfield Farm near Duntocher Fort in Scotland in 1812. The inscription reads: 'For the Emperor Caesar Titus Aelius Hadrianus Antoninus Augustus Pius, Father of his Country, a detachment of the Sixth Victorious, Loyal and Faithful Legion built the wall for a distance of 3240 feet' (*RIB* 1, 2200).

Transfer to Britain

In AD 122, Hadrian went to Britain taking with him the governor of Lower Germany, Aulus Platorius Nepos (who now became governor of Britain) and the Sixth Legion. A military tribune of the legion at this time was Marcus Pontius Laelianus, whose career is recorded in a funerary inscription found in Rome (*CIL* 6, 41146). In Britain the legion set about building the stretch of Hadrian's Wall from Newcastle to Carlisle, including a bridge across the river Tyne near Newcastle. The legion is first attested in Britain on a building stone from Haltonchesters that names the legion and Platorius Nepos and thus dates to between 122 and *c.* 126 (*RIB* 1, 1427).

Building inscriptions show that vexillations of *VI Victrix* participated in the construction of the Antonine Wall from 139. An inscription of 158 records that the Sixth Legion engaged in repairs on Hadrian's Wall near Heddon, perhaps resulting from a revolt in Britain at that time. A few years later, in 161, the Romans were forced to abandon the Antonine Wall and return to Hadrian's Wall. Part of the legion can now be placed at Corbridge on the basis of an inscription (*RIB* 1, 1137) recording that during the governorship of Sextus Calpurnius Agricola (162–68) an altar was set up to Sol Invictus ('the Unconquered Sun') by a vexillation. Tombstones and dedications suggest that the fortress at Eboracum (York) – originally built by *IX Hispana* – had become the legion's main base by this period.

The Severan Period

In 191 Clodius Albinus became governor of Britain. With the onset of civil war in 193, he took *VI Victrix* from Britain to join the fight against Septimius Severus. Clodius Albinus proclaimed himself emperor in winter 195/96 and established his base at Lugdunum (Lyon). The two armies fought a decisive battle here a year later. It was evenly matched and Clodius Albinus' infantry came close to victory. Cassius Dio (76.6–7) describes how they lured Severus' men into hidden pits and trenches in front of their lines, inflicting heavy casualties. Severus' army was on the verge of flight when his cavalry attacked Albinus' flank, winning the battle and the war.

Severus returned *VI Victrix* to Britain, as the only legion in the newly created province of Britannia Inferior (Lower Britain). During their absence, Scottish tribes had overrun Hadrian's

Wall. Troubles with northern tribes continued and in AD 208 Septimius Severus himself came to Britain with the aim of conquering Scotland. The Sixth moved north and shared a new legionary fortress with *II Augusta* at Carpow on the river Tay. More than 200 stamped roof tiles found here reveal that the legion's full cognomen was now *Victrix Britannica Pia Fidelis*, but the reason for and date of these new titles are unknown.

The legion remained at Eboracum after Severus' Scottish conquests were abandoned. Information about it now becomes scarcer, though it may have sent vexillations to the Rhine and Danube to serve with Gallienus against the Germans (253–68). An inscription reveals that a detachment of the legion served at Piercebridge near Hadrian's Wall along with men from both Upper and Lower Germany. They were commanded by a centurion of *II Augusta* (*AE* 1967, 259). In 286 Carausius declared himself emperor of a breakaway empire based in Britain. The Sixth Legion appears to have remained at Eboracum and it is not known if it supported the usurper (the legion is not found on the coins minted by Carausius).

Britain rejoined the Roman empire in 297. When Constantius I Chlorus (305–6) died at Eboracum in 306, the soldiers of *VI Victrix* proclaimed Constantine emperor.

Little is known of *VI Victrix* subsequently, although in the *Notitia Dignitatum* it is listed as part of the army of the *Dux Britanniarum* early in the 5th century AD.

IX Hispana

Cognomina	*Triumph(alis?); Macedonica; Hispana*
Emblem	Bull?
Main base	Eboracum (York)
Major campaigns	Philippi? (42 BC); Cantabrian wars (27–19 BC); Numidian campaigns (AD 20); invasion of Britain (AD 43); Boudican Revolt (AD 60–61); first battle of Bedriacum (AD 69); against the Brigantes (AD 71); against Scottish tribes (AD 83)

IX Hispana

The origins of *IX Hispana* are unclear. Julius Caesar had a Ninth Legion in Gaul by 58 BC, which was disbanded in 46–45 BC. A later legion may have been raised by Octavian from Caesarian veterans settled in Italy. The titles *Triumph(alis?)* and *Macedonica* are found on early inscriptions naming the Ninth, probably relating to activities in the civil wars. *Macedonica* suggests service in Macedonia, probably at Philippi (42 BC).

The legion served under Augustus in Spain during the Cantabrian war (27–19 BC) and must have stayed there for a long time because *Macedonica* was substituted with *Hispaniensis* ('Stationed in Spain'); this was later modified to *Hispana* ('Spanish'), as seen in an inscription from Aquileia in northern Italy (*CIL* 5, 911). The tombstones of other soldiers of the legion were found in Aquileia, the base for operations in Illyricum (the modern Balkans). It seems that, after its service in Spain, *IX Hispana* was posted to the Balkans and Aquileia served as its base.

The legion was definitely in Pannonia in AD 14, when Augustus died. Tacitus (*Annals* 1.16–30) says that all three Pannonian legions, including the Ninth, were together in a single fortress when they mutinied over poor conditions. Tiberius' son Drusus executed the ringleaders, and the three legions departed to separate winter camps (see page 166).

In AD 20 *IX Hispana* was sent to Africa to reinforce *III Augusta* in its campaigns against native Numidian rebels led by Tacfarinas (Tacitus, *Annals* 3.8.1 and 4.23.2; see pages 115–16). After a major Roman victory in AD 22, *III Augusta* was left to deal with Tacfarinas and *IX Hispana* returned to Pannonia, probably settling at Siscia (Sisak, Croatia).

The Legionary Fortress at Eboracum

The legionary fortress at Eboracum (York) must have been established by Petillius Cerialis as a base for operations against the Brigantes, although only a handful of inscriptions connect it to *IX Hispana*. The base was located in the Vale of York, at the confluence of the Fosse and Ouse rivers, a strategically important position that could be supplied from the North Sea.

Its original defences consisted of a single ditch and rampart, surmounted by a timber palisade, enclosing *c.* 20 hectares (50 acres). Inscriptions reveal that these defences were replaced in stone in the early 2nd century AD, providing the last evidence of the Ninth's presence in Britain. By the AD 120s *VI Victrix* had replaced the legion at Eboracum, though no building inscriptions of this legion have been found there and *IX Hispana* was probably responsible for all the major construction at the base.

Above *Inscription from a gate of the Roman fortress at Eboracum, recording its construction* c. *107 by* VIIII *(i.e.* IX*)* Hispana *(*RIB *1, 665).*

Below *The fortress now mostly lies under the modern city of York, but the Multangular Tower (here) at its west corner is still visible, along with part of the basilica and legionary baths.*

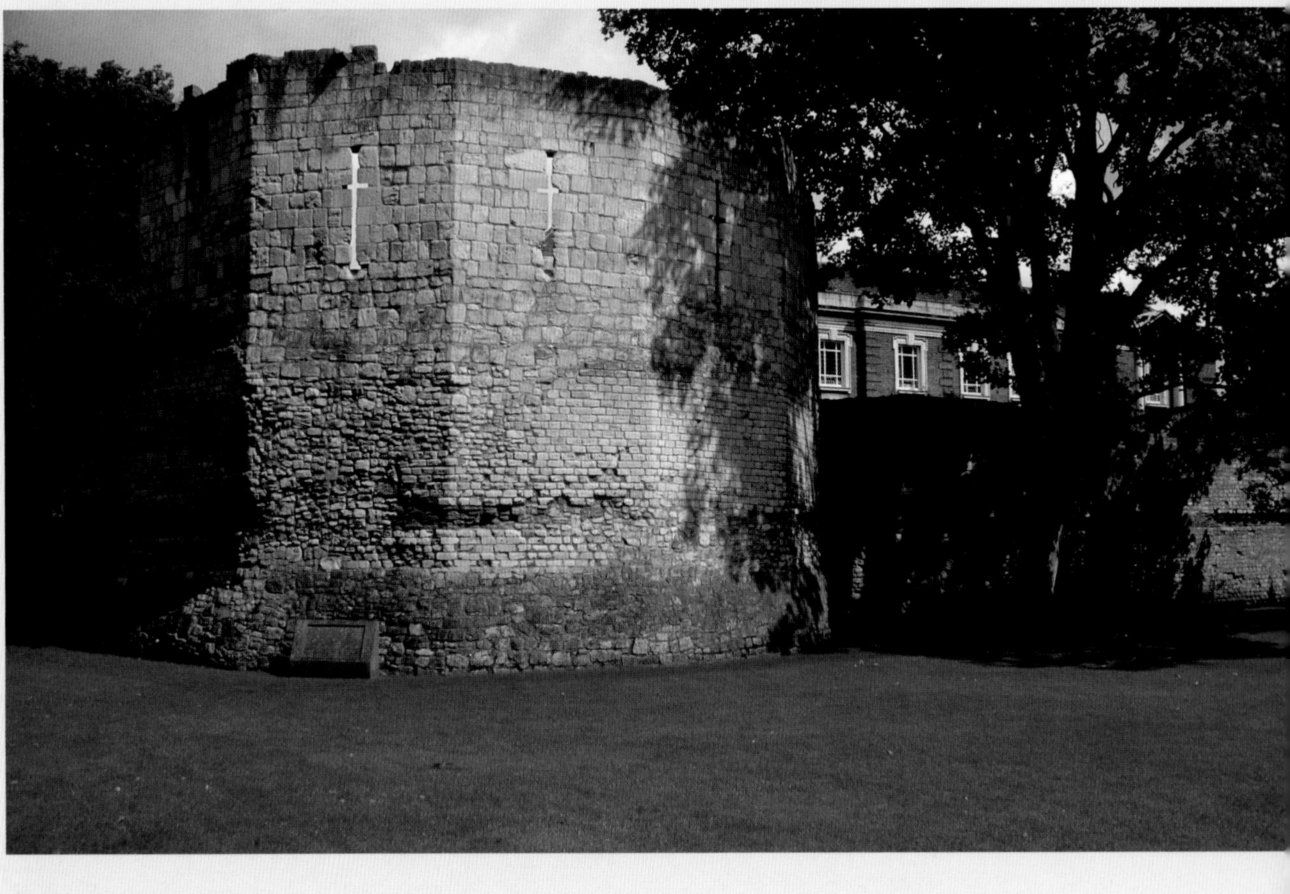

Move to Britain

In AD 42 Aulus Plautius was governor of Pannonia, and *IX Hispana* apparently accompanied him when he left to command the invasion of Britain. Vexillations from the other Pannonian legions may have joined the invasion force, which crossed the Channel in AD 43. Inscriptions suggest that *IX Hispana* was present in Britain from the start, initially at Londinium (London). It then advanced north into the territory of the Brigantes. It has been suggested that the legion now established a base at Lindum (Lincoln), but the funerary inscriptions that form the basis of this suggestion are of uncertain date (*CIL* 7, 183, 188, 196).

IX Hispana is not mentioned in Britain by literary sources until AD 61, during the Boudican Revolt. The legion, commanded by Petillius Cerialis, attempted to relieve the colony of Camulodunum (Colchester), but was routed by the Britons. The Roman infantry was destroyed, but Cerialis escaped. The Fourteenth and Twentieth were left to deal with Boudica's forces.

During the Year of the Four Emperors (see page 59), a vexillation of *IX Hispana* supported Vitellius in his march on Rome in AD 69 and was with him at his defeat at Bedriacum. By the end of the year Vespasian was emperor. Funerary inscriptions found at Rieti, Vespasian's birthplace, suggest that some men of the Ninth were later settled there.

In AD 71 Vespasian sent Petillius Cerialis back to Britain as its governor, where he campaigned against the Brigantes. Inscriptions show that *IX Hispana* established a new base at Eboracum (York). The legion's commander in the latter half of Vespasian's reign was Gaius Caristanius Fronto, whose career is recorded in an honorific inscription found in Pisidian Antioch (Turkey). He was still in command when Agricola became governor of Britain.

The Boudican Revolt, AD 60–61

The Boudican Revolt occurred after the death of King Prasutagus of the Iceni. Roman soldiers took the opportunity to plunder the kingdom, enslave his subjects and rape his daughters. The historian Cassius Dio (62.2) also claims that the Romans had forced loans onto the Britons and now called them in. Thus the Boudican Revolt can be explained largely as caused by Roman mismanagement of Britain. Many Britons had supported Rome in AD 43, but were alienated by the Romans. The role of Prasutagus' wife, Boudica, in this famous revolt is unknown, since our only accounts are by Roman writers, but at the very least she seems to have inspired it.

The governor of Britain at the time of the revolt, Suetonius Paulinus, was fighting against the Druids in Wales. He had left the province in the hands of Decianus Catus (who fled to Gaul once the uprising began). Camulodunum (Colchester) was destroyed by the British rebels; they then sacked Londinium (London) and Verulamium (St Albans) and defeated *IX Hispana*. Eventually they were overcome by the Fourteenth and a vexillation of the Twentieth. Forts were built throughout the region. No tribe of southern, central or eastern Britain ever revolted again.

This famous statue by the Victorian sculptor Thomas Thornycroft depicts Boudica with her daughters in her war chariot. It can be seen by Westminster Bridge near the Houses of Parliament in London.

To Gaius Caristanius Fronto, son of Gaius, of the voting tribe Sergia, military tribune, commander of the *Ala Bosporana* of cavalry, co-opted into the Senate among the men of tribunician status and promoted among those of praetorian rank. Imperial legate with praetor's powers in Pontus and Bithynia, legate of the legion *IX Hispana* in Britain for the deified emperor Vespasian Augustus, legate of the deified Titus Caesar Augustus and of the emperor Domitian Caesar Augustus in the province of Pamphylia and Lycia. Titus Caristanius Calpurnianus Rufus (set this up) to honour this deserving patron of our colony.

ILS 9485

Agricola now took *IX Hispana* north for his Scottish campaign. In AD 83/84, the legion was almost defeated by the Caledonian tribes, who deliberately targeted the legion as the weakest of Agricola's forces. According to Tacitus (*Agricola* 26), only the appearance of Agricola himself prevented a serious defeat. The legion had perhaps been weakened by sending a 1,000-man vexillation under its senatorial tribune, Lucius Roscius Aelianus (*CIL* 14, 3612), for Domitian's war against the Chatti. Tile stamps apparently referring to this vexillation were found at Mirebeau-sur-Bèze (near Dijon), in the Lingones' territory. After AD 83 a vexillation, with other vexillations from Britain and Upper Germany, was placed under the command of Gaius Velius Rufus (*ILS* 9100), perhaps for the occasion of Domitian's Dacian war.

Obscurity and Disappearance

Little is known of *IX Hispana* for the next 40 years. It is last attested in Britain in an inscription dated to AD 107–8 recording construction of a gateway at its Eboracum fortress (*RIB* 1, 665). The legion was not involved in construction of Hadrian's Wall, which suggests that it was no longer in Britain at that time. Some historians have claimed that *IX Hispana* was destroyed in a serious revolt in Britain in 119–20, or another in the later 120s. More recent scholarship has tended to reject this theory, since some of the legion's officers are attested elsewhere at later dates. For example, Aninius Sextius Florentinus, buried in an imposing tomb at Petra after 127, was legate of *IX Hispana* in 121 and went on to have a distinguished career as proconsul of Gallia Narbonenis and then governor of Arabia Petraea in 127 (*CIL* 3, 87).

There is also some possible epigraphic evidence for the legion's brief presence in Lower Germany, including at Noviomagus (Nijmegen) on the Lower Rhine. It is possible that the legion was transferred briefly to Germany and then to the East. It may have been destroyed in the Second Jewish Revolt of AD 132–35 or later at Elegeia in Armenia during Lucius Verus' campaign of AD 161–66. However, the details and exact date of this legion's demise remain uncertain and the theory of its destruction in Britain has been revived recently.

Soldiers of the Ninth

Inscriptions found at Lincoln (Lindum) and York (Eboracum) identify some of the legionaries of the Ninth and reveal where they came from.

Gaius Saufeius from Heraclea in Southern Italy died aged 40 after 22 years' service. He was buried at Lindum (*RIB* 1, 255).

Lucius Sempronius Flavinus from Clunia, Spain died aged 30, after only seven years' service and was buried at Lindum (*RIB* 1, 256).

Lucius Duccius Rufinus, an *aquilifer* (eagle-bearer) from Vienna (Vienne) in Gallia Narbonensis died aged 28, and was buried at Eboracum (*RIB* 1, 673).

Gaius Valerius from Italy died aged 35, after 13 years' service and was buried at Lindum (*RIB* 1, 257).

Quintus Cornelius died aged 40 after 19 years' service and was buried at Lindum (*RIB* 1, 254).

Lucius Celerinus Vitalis, a *cornicularis* (adjutant), made a dedication to Silvanus in Eboracum (*RIB* 1, 659). He may have been a Briton.

Two other soldiers (names unknown) came from Italy. One was from Novaria (modern Novara), and was commemorated by his freedmen at Eboracum (*RIB* 1, 680); the other came from Pisaurum (modern Pesaro) and was buried at Lindum (*RIB* 1, 260).

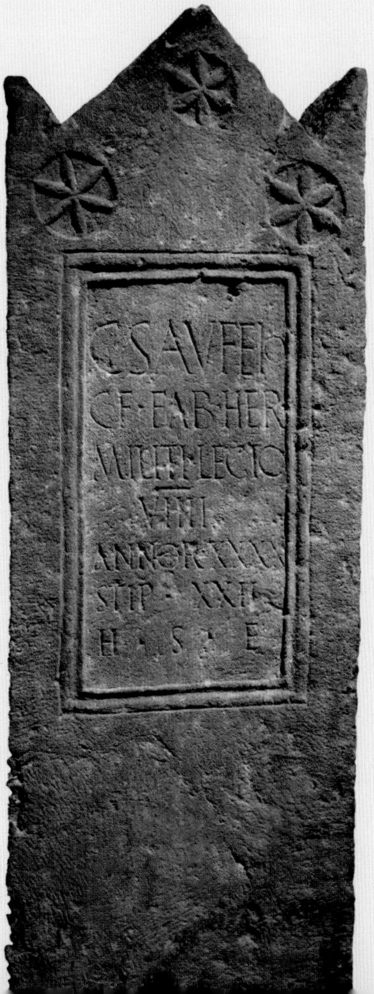

The tombstone of Gaius Saufeius from Lindum, now in the British Museum. Originally from Italy, he died in Britain after 22 years' service.

XX Valeria Victrix

XX Valeria Victrix

Cognomen	*Valeria Victrix*
Emblem	Boar
Main bases	Unknown
Major campaigns	Cantabrian wars (27–19 BC); Pannonian Revolt (AD 6–9); against the Marsi, Bructeri and Cherusci (AD 15); invasion of Britain? (AD 43); against Welsh tribes (AD 43–60); Boudican Revolt (AD 60–61); second battle of Bedriacum (AD 69); against Welsh tribes (AD 77); against northern British tribes (AD 77–84); battle of Lugdunum (196)

The history of *XX Valeria Victrix* before AD 6 is unclear. By the battle of Actium in 31 BC, Octavian and Antony had built up their armies and both probably had a Twentieth Legion in their army. One inscription (*AE* 1988, 396) suggests that veterans of a *XX Siciliana* may have been settled at Beneventum in the years after Actium (although the date of the inscription is uncertain). Veterans of a Twentieth Legion are also attested in the late 1st century BC in other parts of Italy, including Aquileia (*CIL* 5, 939 and 948), Tergeste (Trieste; *AE* 1977, 314) and Patavium (Padova; *CIL* 5, 2838). Inscriptions found in Spain, in and around Emerita Augusta (a colony founded by Augustus in 25 BC, modern Mérida), may be evidence that veterans from the Twentieth were among the new settlers there and thus, perhaps, the legion participated in Augustus' Spanish campaign of 27–19 BC. It is not known when the legion was moved north.

XX Valeria Victrix enters the historical record in AD 6 when it was transferred from Illyricum (the Balkans) to Carnuntum on the Danube, in preparation for Tiberius' campaign against the Marcomanni. Tiberius was forced to change his plans when Pannonia and Dalmatia revolted. Part of the legion was sent ahead to engage one group of rebels. Despite being outnumbered and suffering intial setbacks, the Twentieth was victorious and its commander, Valerius Messalinus, honoured with the *ornamenta triumphalia* ('triumphal honours'; Velleius Paterculus 2.112). During the Pannonian Revolt the legion was initially stationed at Siscia (Sisak, Croatia). In AD 9 Aemilius Lepidus was given command of the army at Siscia and transferred it to join Tiberius at Burnum in Dalmatia. Burnum probably become the legion's new base.

On the Rhine Frontier

In the aftermath of the Varian disaster of AD 9, the legion was transferred to the Rhine frontier where it was involved in securing the frontier against German incursions. Literary evidence suggest that the legion was initially stationed, along with *I Germanica*, in a double fortress at Oppidum Ubiorum (Cologne). Tacitus places it there in AD 14 (*Annals* 1.39), but there is no supporting archaeological evidence. It may be that the legions were based in nearby Köln–Alteburg. There is archaeological evidence of occupation of that site from the early 1st century AD, including tombstones belonging to members of the legion, but the remains of a fortress have not yet been found. Subsequently, the legion may have moved to Novaesium (Neuss).

The Twentieth was probably one of the legions that campaigned deep into German territory with Tiberius and Germanicus in AD 10–11, taking part in punitive activity across the Rhine against the tribes that had annihilated Varus' legions. These campaigns were short-lived and subsequently the Roman army assumed a defensive disposition, with four legions, *I*, *V*, *XX* and *XXI*, based on the left bank of the Rhine. When Augustus died in AD 14, the four Rhine legions mutinied in protest at their low pay and poor treatment, demanding that

A tile antefix found in Holt, Clwyd (Wales) and now in the British Museum. The inscription and wild boar emblem identify the Twentieth Legion. A similar antefix was found at Chester.

those who had served their time be discharged, among other things (see page 78). Eventually Germanicus shamed the soldiers into giving up their ringleaders, subjecting them to summary trial and execution (Tacitus, *Annals* 1.42).

After this revolt, Germanicus once again led the legions in a campaign across the Rhine, perhaps to distract them from further unrest. In AD 15 he crossed at Mainz with *II*, *XIII*, *XIV* and *XVI* to engage the Chatti. At the same time *I*, *V*, *XX* and *XXI* under Caecina Severus moved against the Marsi. The two Roman armies then linked up, raiding the territory of the Bructeri from whom they recovered the eagle of the *XIX*, and engaging the Cherusci in battle. Caecina and *XX* were sent to reconnoitre the Teutoburg Forest and ensure safe passage for the rest of the army. However, all the legions struggled to return to winter quarters. The Twentieth was part of the army that retreated via the *pontes longi*, the causeway built 16 years before through the vast swamp between the Ems and the Rhine; they were attacked along the way by the Cherusci. The following year Germanicus assembled his forces in the north, crossing the Ems and Weser and advancing successfully to the Elbe, defeating German tribes as they progressed. But, again, significant losses were inflicted on the Romans. Germanicus was recalled to Rome later that year, and the German wars were ended. From this time on, Tiberius relied on diplomacy to keep the German tribes in line.

There is little evidence for the activities of the Twentieth Legion in this period. An inscription reveals that a vexillation of this legion was part of a force commanded by the tribune Torquatus Novellius Atticus, but its date is uncertain (*CIL* 14, 3602). It may relate to Germanicus' German wars, the Gallic Revolt of AD 21 (suppressed by the German legions) or the Frisian Revolt of AD 28–47. Nor is it clear where the legion was based. After AD 16, legions were spread along the Rhine in individual bases. A series of fortifications built at Novaesium (Neuss) between AD 15 and the AD 30s, at the site of the later Claudian fortress, are generally thought to have been constructed by either *I* or *XX*, but the only real evidence for the presence of *XX* comes from a few tombstones at Neuss.

Opposite The tombstone of Marcus Favonius Facilis, found at Colchester. In the inscription (*RIB* 1, 200), the legion's later cognomen *Valeria Victrix* is missing, suggesting that Facilis died before this was awarded (after AD 61).

A digital reconstruction of the Balkerne Gate in Camulodunum (Colchester), where the Twentieth Legion is thought to have been based after the initial invasion of Britain in AD 43.

The Twentieth in Britain

In AD 40 the emperor Caligula gathered a large army, purportedly for the invasion of Britain, and *XX* may have been part of this force. According to the biographer Suetonius (*Gaius* 48), Caligula visited the fortress of the Twentieth Legion intent on slaughtering its men in revenge for their past mutiny against his father Germanicus. Suetonius claims he intended to decimate them (execute every tenth man), but abandoned the idea when they scented trouble and began to arm themselves.

The Twentieth was probably part of the Roman force that invaded Britain in AD 43, but we know little of its role. It is thought that the legion remained at Camulodunum (Colchester), the then capital of Roman Britain, established as a *colonia* in AD 49, while the other three legions headed southwest, northwest and north. However, the only archaeological evidence for the legion's presence there at this early date is the tombstone of Marcus Favonius Facilis (*RIB* 1, 200).

Our knowledge of the legion's movements from AD 49 until the Boudican Revolt is sketchy, based on limited archaeological and epigraphic evidence. It is likely that *XX* moved west, to conquer Welsh tribes who refused to submit to Roman domination. We know little about their actions against Welsh tribes, but they probably defeated Caratacus' Ordovices in mid-Wales in AD 51. Tacitus (*Annals* 12.37) describes how the Silures engaged in guerrilla warfare against the

The Legions at Glevum (Gloucester)

Excavations in 1972 and 1974 demonstrated that a fort was established at Kingsholm, Gloucester *c.* AD 49. This first base was built by a small vexillation of *XX Valeria Victrix*. During the AD 60s a fortress was built south of this site, either by the Twentieth or a vexillation of *II Augusta*. Within a few years the Twentieth was moved from Glevum to Viroconium, and the Second moved from Isca Dumnoniorum (Exeter) to Glevum. During the AD 70s, the Second Legion campaigned against the Welsh tribes, and a new base was established at Isca Silurum (Caerleon). It is unclear whether any troops remained at Glevum in this period. However, by the late AD 80s the fortress at Glevum was rebuilt (the legion responsible for the work is unknown). At the end of the 1st century AD, during the reign of Nerva (AD 96–98), Glevum became the *Colonia Nervia Glevensium*.

The Titles of *XX Valeria Victrix*

The cognomina *Valeria* and *Victrix*, along with the legion's boar emblem, appear on records of the Twentieth Legion from the late 1st century AD, but it is not known when or why it acquired them.

Valeria may have been acquired in AD 6, when, according to Velleius Paterculus (2.112), the legion was commanded by Marcus Valerius Messalla Messalinus. However, there are many objections to this theory. It has been pointed out that the legion is not known as *Valeria* this early, that legions were not named after their commanders, and that Valerius Messalinus was a rival of Augustus. It is possible that *Valeria* was never a formal cognomen. Another suggestion is that it relates to Claudius' conquest of Britain, with the legion named after Claudius' wife, Valeria Messalina. Messalina was related to Valerius Messalinus. Thus an informal cognomen from AD 6 may have been formalized by Claudius to honour his wife and her family.

Another possibility is that the legion was awarded the two titles together, to commemorate its role in suppressing the Boudican Revolt. Thus *Valeria Victrix* can be translated as 'Valiant and Victorious', and in support of this theory, the other legion involved in suppressing the Boudican Revolt, *XIV Gemina*, received the new title *Martia Victrix*. The fact that *Victrix* is only found in the records after AD 60 seems to support this. However, the Twentieth only contributed a vexillation to the army that destroyed the British rebels in AD 61, and it is unclear whether a vexillation could win such an honorific for the entire legion. Furthermore, it is *XIV Gemina* that became associated with this great victory in the literary sources, not the Twentieth.

An alternative theory is that the cognomen *Victrix* relates to the legion's leading role in Agricola's campaigns in the north.

Romans, inflicting heavy losses until the legionary troops were fully committed to the conflict.

The Silures seem to have been subdued finally by the AD 50s, and at about this time *XX Valeria Victrix* may have moved to a new fortress at Burrium (Usk). Campaigning now focused on the Ordovices of north Wales, and on capturing the Isle of Mona (Anglesey), which had become a rebel outpost. At this time Boudica's rebellion took place. A vexillation of *XX* joined *XIV* to defeat the rebels. The remainder of the legion probably remained in the west, in case the Welsh tribes attempted to take advantage of the situation.

It is likely that vexillations of *XX* were stationed at a number of bases through this period. Numerous forts throughout Britain may have been manned either by legionary vexillations or auxiliary troops, or a combination of both.

The Year of the Four Emperors, AD 69

At the time of Nero's death in AD 68 and the subsequent civil war, the Twentieth was commanded by Marcus Roscius Coelius. He was on bad terms with the governor of Britain, Trebellius Maximus, and in the unsettled conditions of the civil war, the army sided with Coelius, culminating in Trebellius fleeing his province, leaving it under the control of its legionary legates (Tacitus, *Histories* 1.60).

The legions of Britain all declared for Vitellius, and all sent vexillations to fight with him. They were defeated by Vespasian's forces at the second battle of Bedriacum (near Cremona, Italy) in October AD 69.

Agricola in Command

In AD 70 Gnaeus Julius Agricola was sent by Vespasian to replace Coelius as commander of the Twentieth Legion, taking with him new recruits to make up its numbers. Tacitus claims (*Agricola* 7) that the legion was disloyal and mutinous, a situation rectified by Agricola's disciplinary measures.

Agricola returned to Rome in AD 73–74, and it has been suggested – despite a lack of archaeological evidence – that Viroconium (Wroxeter) became the legion's new base at this time. The legion may have been based at Deva (Chester) by this point or shortly afterwards. Lead pipes that give Vespasian's titles for AD 79 and bear the names of Agricola and Vespasian reveal that the fortress here was being constructed in that year.

When Agricola returned to Britain as governor in AD 77 he moved quickly to capture Anglesey, and consolidate the conquest of Wales. He then took his forces to the north of Britain, probably including at least part of *XX* with him to spearhead his campaign. Agricola's army progressed north in AD 77, probably using Corbridge and Carlisle as bases for advances to the east and west respectively. The army's progress can be seen in the construction of camps and forts progressively further north over the next few years. By the end of the fifth year of campaigning, forts had been built on the Forth–Clyde isthmus. The seventh year culminated in the battle of Mons Graupius in Caledonia (AD 84).

The Twentieth Legion's participation in Agricola's northern campaigns is assumed on the basis of his past command of the legion, but it is not named specifically in the sources. We do not know whether Agricola fielded the entire legion or just part of it, or where its winter quarters were at the end of each campaigning season. One suggestion is that at least part of *XX* was quartered at Carlisle, where there is evidence for demolition and rebuilding over the winter of AD 83/84. A wooden tablet found there (*AE* 1992, 1139) records a loan of 100 *denarii* (one third of a year's pay) by C. Geminius Mansuetus in the century of Vettius Proculus, to Q. Cassius Secundus in the century of Calvius Priscus, on 7 November AD 83.

It is possible that the main body of the legion was stationed at Carlisle, while the fortress at Wroxeter became a base for administration, training and stores.There is archaeological evidence at Wroxeter for the demolition of barrack blocks to make way for a large, unidentified building in the final phase of the fortress. There may also be a connection with Newstead. Another tablet (*AE 1988, 843*) found in Carlisle was addressed to M. Iulius Martialis 'at Trimontium (Newstead) or Luguvalium (Carlisle)', which may imply that the main body of the legion was split between these two bases.

In the period AD 83 to 86, a line of forts was built along the southeast Highland front, including a new legionary fortress at Inchtuthil, generally assumed to have been built by the Twentieth. This was demolished and abandoned *c.* AD 88, before it was completed, and it is likely that it was never fully occupied by the legion. The abandonment of this line of forts and newly conquered territory can probably be explained by events elsewhere in the empire. Vexillations were taken from Britain to fight against the Chatti in AD 83 and then against the Dacians (AD 88), and eventually *II Adiutrix* was taken from Britain. The Romans no longer had the manpower to hold their new British conquests, and were forced to withdraw.

The Fortress at Deva

XX Valeria Victrix may now have transferred to Deva (Chester), although the date of its arrival there is unknown. Deva had been the base of *II Adiutrix*, which was transferred from Britain to Sirmium in the 80s. Thus the Twentieth inherited an established fortress, parts of which had already been constructed (or reconstructed) in stone. However, it appears that the majority of the legion did not occupy the fortress at Chester through the 2nd century and much of the base fell into disrepair. The legion was involved in campaigns further north, and does not appear to have wintered at Chester, although the location of its winter quarters is uncertain. Furthermore, *XX Valeria Victrix* may not have been up to full strength in this period, with vexillations on service elsewhere and soldiers divided between a number of bases.

Hadrian's Wall and the Antonine Wall

Inscriptions show vexillations of the Twentieth involved in the construction of Hadrian's Wall over the 15–20 years following the emperor's visit in 122, along with its forts and milecastles, and other forts in the north, such as Moresby. Eight slabs also record the legion's work on the Antonine Wall further to the north. From *c.* 161 there was a gradual withdrawal from the Antonine Wall, with consequent reuse of Hadrian's Wall. Inscriptions record the building activities of *XX* at Corbridge, and evidence of the legion at Carlisle is found again at the beginning of the 3rd century. More soldiers were taken from Britain to fight under Marcus Aurelius on the Danube frontier (166–80), which means that all the British legions were below their full strength.

The 3rd and 4th Centuries

The Twentieth Legion was part of the army of Clodius Albinus that fought Septimius Severus at Lugdunum (Lyon) in 196 and was defeated. Remnants of the defeated British legions were sent back to Britain, and *XX* probably returned to the north. After 210 building work resumed at Deva (Chester) and it is likely that the legion was brought back to full strength by recruitment of new soldiers or the drafting of replacements from other legions for Septimius Severus' northern campaigns. Tile stamps confirm that the legion was at Deva at this time.

In general, however, little is known about *XX Valeria Victrix*'s activities in the 3rd century AD. In 213 the province was divided into two, and the legion came under the command of the governor of Upper Britain, who was based in

London. There is subsequent evidence of combined vexillations of *XX Valeria Victrix* and *II Augusta* operating together in northern Britain, and possibly mainland Europe. A vexillation of the Twentieth was at Moguntiacum (Mainz) in 255 (*CIL* 13, 6780) and a few years later British troops were stationed in Lower Pannonia (during the reign of Gallienus, 260–68; *CIL* 3, 3228).

There is scattered inscriptional evidence of legionaries' activities in Britain in this period. The tribune Marcus Aurelius Syrio dedicated an altar to Jupiter Optimus Maximus, Juno, Mars, Minerva and Victory at Carlisle in the early 3rd century AD (*RIB* 3, 3460). Vexillations of the legion may later have been engaged in building at Netherby and Maryport (in both cases the inscriptions are fragmentary). An inscription from Chester (Deva; *AE* 1964, 201) records the legion's title as *XX VV D*. This has been expanded to *XX V(aleria) V(ictrix) D(eciana)*, which would date the inscription to the reign of Trajan Decius (249–51). Alternatively, the *D* could be read as *D(evensis)* ('of Deva'). Finally, *XX Valeria Victrix*

Left Inscriptions record the building activities of *XX Valeria Victrix* after its arrival at Deva, and numerous tombstones, such as this one (a reconstruction of the original) of an *optio* named Caecilius Avitus (*RIB* 1, 492) found in the North Wall of Chester, document the names of soldiers who lived at the base. Avitus was from Emerita Augusta (Mérida, Spain) and had served 15 years. He died aged 33.

is one of the legions commemorated in a series of gold coins issued by the Gallic emperor Victorinus (268–70), perhaps to reach out to legions beyond his control.

The last reference to *XX Valeria Victrix* comes on the legionary coinage of Carausius, minted between 286–93. Little is known of the legion after this, including when it ceased to exist. Archaeological evidence shows continued occupation of Deva into the 4th century AD, suggesting that the legion continued to exist in some form. However, it is not mentioned in the early-5th-century *Notitia Dignitatum*, perhaps implying it was disbanded at some time in the 4th century.

Above A hypothetical reconstruction of Deva (Chester). The Roman fortress and settlement lie beneath modern Chester today, but the remains of the fortress walls and the amphitheatre are still visible.

A plastercast of a distance slab (the original has been lost) that records that a vexillation of the Twentieth Legion constructed the Antonine Wall for a distance of 3,000 Roman feet (*RIB* 1, 2198). The slab was found at Hutcheson Hill in 1865.

The Legions of Roman Spain

VII Gemina

In the 3rd century BC, Spain was a zone of conflict between Rome (to the north) and Carthage, under the general Hannibal (to the south). Before the Second Punic War, the river Ebro formed the border between their spheres of influence, but the Romans had an alliance with Saguntum (modern Sagunto), south of the river. Hannibal's attack on that city in 219 BC triggered the second Punic war, and Hannibal attacked Italy.

While Hannibal campaigned in Italy, the Romans wrested Spain from the Carthaginians. After the end of the war, in 202 BC, they divided it into two provinces, Hispania Citerior (Nearer) and Hispania Ulterior (Further), and set about exploiting its rich mineral resources. However, both provinces were the scene of unrest and conflict with the local people for almost two centuries.

The northern part of Spain was occupied by the Cantabrians, famed for their warlike nature. Their aggression towards their neighbours gave excuse for Roman intervention in this last unconquered part of Spain in 29 BC. Initially the campaign was commanded by Statilius Taurus, Gaius Carisius Sabinus and Sextus Apuleius, but in 27–26 BC Augustus himself took charge. He deployed at least six legions against the Cantabrians and Astures. There is epigraphic and numismatic evidence for *I Germanica, II Augusta, IIII Macedonica, VI Victrix, IX Hispana* and *X Gemina*, but *V Alaudae* and *XX Valeria Victrix* also probably formed part of the army. Including auxiliary troops, the number of Roman soldiers must have exceeded 70,000, demonstrating the importance of Spain to the Romans.

Over the next two years the Romans campaigned in the mountains between Burgos and Santander (under Augustus himself) and then in Asturia. Cassius Dio (53.25) describes the guerrilla nature of the war, with the Romans suffering defeats in ambushes but winning open battles and reducing strongholds like the Astures' fortress of Lancia.

By 24 BC northwest Spain had been pacified and Augustus returned to Rome to celebrate a triumph. However, minor rebellions continued until, in 19 BC, Augustus'

The Los Milagros aqueduct of Emerita Augusta (Mérida), capital of Roman Lusitania and one of the most important Roman cities of Hispania. The city was founded at the conclusion of Augustus' Cantabrian wars and its earliest inhabitants were veterans of *X Gemina* and *V Alaudae*.

Map of Spain showing the legionary fortress at Legio and other places mentioned in the text.

general Agrippa put a brutal end to the unrest for good. Subsequently, Spain (including what is now Portugal) remained peaceful and the Romans exported its mineral and agricultural wealth. From the Flavian period, only a single legion was stationed there, charged with administrative duties and protection of Spain's gold mines.

Through the Julio-Claudian period, the province remained largely peaceful. By AD 43, at the latest, the legionary garrison was reduced when *IIII Macedonica* was sent to the Rhine frontier. In AD 63 *X Gemina* was transferred to Pannonia. *VI Victrix* remained in Spain with reduced numbers of auxiliary units and was the legion that proclaimed Galba emperor there in AD 68 (see page 93). However, the following year it was moved north by the emperor Vespasian and Spain was garrisoned by *VII Gemina* alone.

Augustus' Reorganization of Spain

Augustus returned to Spain between 16 and 13 BC, reorganizing the region into three provinces: Baetica, capital Corduba (Cordoba); Lusitania, capital the newly founded veteran colony of Augusta Emerita (modern Merida); and, the largest, Tarraconensis, capital Tarraco (Tarragona).

Veterans of the Fourth, Sixth and Tenth were settled at Caesaraugusta (Saragossa), probably at this time, and veterans of the First and Second at Acci (Guadix). Inscriptions show legions involved in road-building, improving the infrastructure of Spain as a whole during Augustus' reign.

After the Cantabrian wars, three legions remained, all based in the recently subdued northwest of Tarraconensis. Inscriptions suggest *IIII Macedonica* was based at Herrera de Pisuerga (*IRPPalencia* 193,0–10). *VI Victrix* and *X Gemina* initially shared a fortress in Asturia, exact location unknown. Later the Sixth may have been based at Legio (León) and the Tenth at Petavonium (Rosinos de Vidriales). Most legionaries were Italian in origin, but over the next three generations they increasingly came from *coloniae* and Romanized towns (*municipia*) in Spain itself.

VII Gemina

A fourth Spanish legion was raised by Servius Sulpicius Galba on 10 June AD 68 to support his claim to the throne (Cassius Dio 55.24.3). Galba already had *VI Victrix* under his command, so his new legion was numbered *VII*. At this stage it did not have an official *cognomen*, although Tacitus refers to it as *Galbiana* ('Raised by Galba') and *Hispana* ('from Spain').

After Nero's suicide, Galba marched on Rome with his newly formed Seventh Legion. Once established as emperor, Galba sent the legion to Pannonia, where it is thought it was based at Carnuntum (Petronell, Austria), charged with guarding the Danube. It replaced *X Gemina*, which was sent to Spain.

Early in the Year of the Four Emperors (AD 69), Galba was murdered (see page 59). The Seventh Legion sided with Otho and was summoned to Italy, but arrived too late to help him when he was defeated by Vitellius at the first battle of Bedriacum. Vitellius sent *I Adiutrix* to Spain, and the Seventh back to Pannonia. There its commander, Marcus Antonius Primus, declared his support for Vespasian, who had been acclaimed emperor by the eastern legions. Tacitus (*Histories* 2.86) describes Primus as 'a man who was energetic in action, a ready speaker, skilled in creating discord among others, powerful in times of unrest and rebellion, quick to rob or bribe, a man ill-suited to peace, but not to be despised in time of war'.

Primus played a crucial role through the civil war. Vespasian gave him command of the legions of Moesia (*III Gallica, VII Claudia, VIII Augusta*), Pannonia (*VII Galbiana, XIII Gemina*) and, later, Dalmatia (*XI Claudia*). Without waiting for Mucianus to arrive with troops from the East, Primus held a council of war at Poetovio (Ptuj on the river Drava), persuading the other Flavian commanders to march into Italy. They met Vitellius' forces at the decisive second battle of Bedriacum (October AD 69). Despite great losses, Primus' army was victorious.Tacitus records:

> The Seventh Legion, recently recruited by Galba, was particularly hard pressed. Six of the leading centurions were killed and some of its standards were captured. The *primus pilus* Atilius Verus had saved the legion's eagle by killing many of the enemy, only to die himself.
>
> Tacitus, *Histories* 3.22

VII Gemina

Cognomina	*Galbiana*; *Hispana*; *Gemina*; *Felix*; *Pia*
Emblem	Unknown
Main base	Legio (León)
Major campaign	Second battle of Bedriacum (AD 69)

This victory led the three legions in Hispania (*I Adiutrix, VI Victrix* and *X Gemina*) to defect to Vespasian, followed by those of Gaul and Britain.

Primus and the Seventh Legion marched on Rome, and fought their way in against Vitellian opposition. He then ruled the city in Vespasian's name, until Mucianus arrived and relieved him of power. The Seventh was sent back to Pannonia at the beginning of AD 70, because, according to Tacitus (*Histories* 4.39), it was thought to be loyal to Primus, whom Mucianus distrusted.

Flavian Reorganization

On his accession, Vespasian engaged in reorganization of the army. The depleted ranks of the Seventh were filled, perhaps with replacements from the disbanded *I Germanica*, accounting for *VII*'s new title *Gemina* ('Twin'). It may also have acquired its other title *Felix* ('Fortunate') at this time, in recognition of its role at Bedriacum. Otherwise it may have received this title while in Pannonia. During its stay there there, the legion perhaps took part in Gnaeus Pinarius Cornelius

Little can be seen today of the permanent fortress of *VII Gemina* at Legio (León, Hispania Tarraconensis). Remains of a water channel are shown here. Excavation has shown the fortress's outline and remains of barracks, baths and the *praetorium* (commander's house). Brick stamps of the legion have been found, along with military equipment and coins attesting occupation into the 3rd century AD.

Clemens' campaign in the Upper Neckar region east of the Rhine (AD 73–74). An inscription of AD 78 describes Titus Staberius Secundus as tribune of *VII Gemina Felix* in Germany (*CIL* 6, 3538). Secundus may have been tribune of the legion when it received the title *Felix*, if this title derives from the legion's role in Clemens' campaign.

For a brief period during the Batavian Revolt (AD 69–70), Spain was left without a legion, as *I Adiutrix* and *VI Victrix* had been transferred to the Rhine to suppress the uprising. Subsequently, Vespasian sent *VII Gemina* back to Hispania Tarraconensis from Pannonia. It has been argued that it was a deliberate Flavian policy to have a single legion in Spain. From this period the Roman legions became more territorial and less mobile, and were stationed permanently close to frontiers. It has also been suggested that one reason why the Seventh Legion was sent to Spain was that it would be able to move to Britain quickly if the legions there were threatened.

The next century or so was peaceful, with no major fighting in Spain. Soldiers of the legion seem mostly to have been engaged in administrative duties. An inscription from Aquae Flaviae (Chaves) (CIL 2, 2477), dated to early AD 79 records the participation of the legion and local *civitates* (communities without Roman status) in constructing a bridge. This demonstrates that soon after its arrival the legion had begun to develop close ties with the local communities near its base at Legio (León).

Although the legion was based permanently at Legio, it occasionally served on campaigns elsewhere. According to Pliny the Younger (*Panegyricus* 14.3), the future emperor Trajan commanded the legion between AD 86 and 89. In AD 89 Antonius Saturninus, governor of Upper

Las Medulas, the largest gold mine in the Roman empire. The base at Legio was deliberately located near to the gold and iron mines of Gallaecia, which were exploited on a large scale, using aqueducts to channel water from the surrounding mountains.

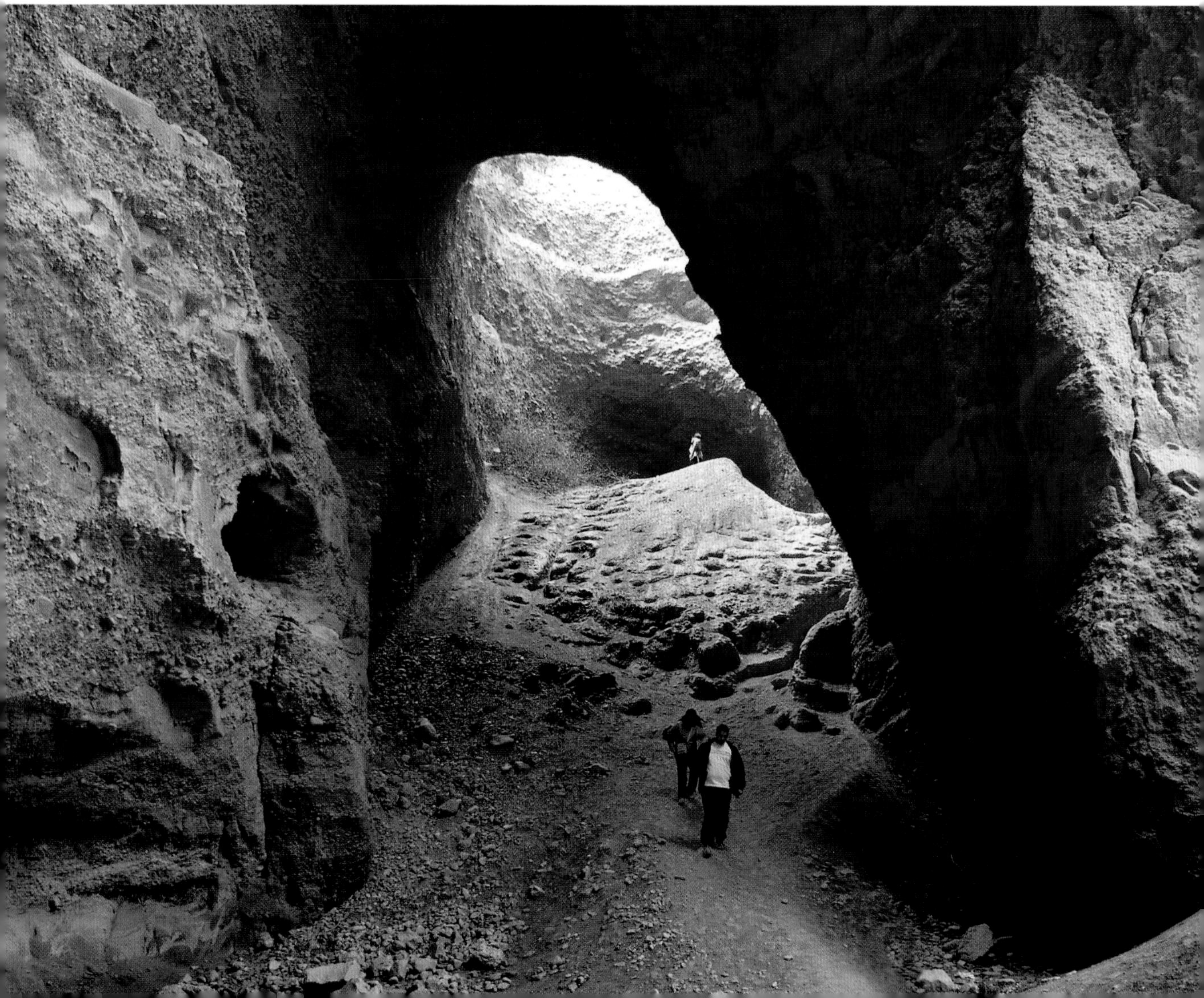

Germany, rebelled against Domitian. Trajan led the legion to the Rhine, but arrived after the rebellion had been crushed.

After this date there are no literary references to *VII Gemina*, but we can track its movements from inscriptions. For example, a vexillation seems to have been sent to Britain in the early 2nd century AD. A tombstone found in Ferentinum (Ferentino), Italy (*CIL* 10, 5829), records the career of Titus Pontius Sabinus, *primus pilus* of *III Augusta*. Earlier in his career he had commanded vexillations of *VII Gemina*, *VIII Augusta* and *XXII Primigenia* on the 'British expedition', apparently late in Trajan's reign or early in Hadrian's. This vexillation may have helped to build Hadrian's Wall.

Tombstones of soldiers of the Seventh have been found in Lambaesis (Algeria), the base of *III Augusta*. It is possible that a vexillation was sent to Lambaesis while part of *III Augusta* was engaged in the Second Jewish Revolt (AD 132–35).

Incursions and Disturbances in the 2nd and 3rd Centuries

During the reigns of Antoninus Pius (AD 138–61) and Marcus Aurelius (AD 161–80) there are references to incursions into Baetica by the Moors of North Africa, particularly in *c.* 172 according to the *Historia Augusta* (*Septimius Severus* 2.4), 'who caused devastation throughout Spain'. Publius Cornelius Anullinus served as governor of Baetica and as legate of the Seventh Legion, so it is possible that the legion was sent to fight the Moors. Alternatively troops from Africa may have been sent to deal with the problem, because the gold-producing regions of Gallaecia were too important to be left without the Seventh's protection. *VII Gemina* may also have helped to suppress unrest caused in northeast Spain in 186 by raids of deserters from Gaul led by Maternus (see page 73).

The Seventh's final title *Pia* ('Faithful') begins to appear on inscriptions in the Severan period, and may have been awarded because of its loyalty to Septimius Severus in 196, when the governor of Tarraconensis supported Clodius Albinus. In the aftermath of this civil war, Severus appointed Quintus Mamilius Capitolinus as legate of Asturia and Gallaecia and *dux* of *VII Gemina*, which is an unusual title and appears to have been a special commission. Perhaps the situation in Hispania was unstable in this period and Severus was not popular in all quarters.

Caracalla also seems to have had some problems in the Spanish provinces when he became emperor in 211. He attempted a major reorganization of the provinces (which did not last). A later inscription, dated to 244–49, also suggests difficulties in Hispania and within the legion. The inscription (*CIL* 3, 1464), from Sarmizegetusa in Dacia, records the career of Ulpius, an equestrian who was *praepositus* of *VII Gemina*. At this time, this command was usually held by a senatorial *legatus legionis*, and only unusual or difficult circumstances can explain it being held by an equestrian.

After this, there is very little evidence for the legion other than an inscription (*CIL* 13, 7564) from Wiesbaden that suggests a vexillation of *VII Gemina* fought in Severus Alexander's German war in 235.

Between 258 and 270 Spain, with Gaul, Germany and Britain, formed the breakaway Gallic empire. During this period, in 262, we hear of incursions into northeast Tarraconensis by Franks.

VII Gemina is still recorded as based at Legio in the *Notitia Dignitatum* compiled in the early 5th century AD.

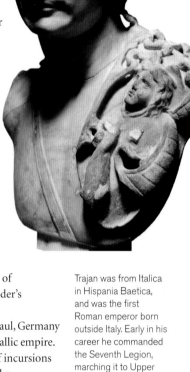

Trajan was from Italica in Hispania Baetica, and was the first Roman emperor born outside Italy. Early in his career he commanded the Seventh Legion, marching it to Upper Germany in AD 89 at the time of the revolt of Saturninus. This bust is in the Munich Glyptothek.

The Martyrdom of Marcellus

In 298 Marcellus, a Christian and centurion of *VII Gemina* was martyred (*The Passion of St Marcellus*, *BHL* 5255a). During a birthday celebration for Diocletian and Maximian he took off his soldier's belt and threw it to the ground, renouncing the emperors and their pagan gods. Fellow soldiers reported him to the governor and commander of the legion, who questioned him. Marcellus insisted that his Christian faith meant that he could no longer be a soldier. The governor sent him to Tingis (Tangiers) to be sentenced by the *vicarius* and he was executed.

The Legions of Roman Africa

III Augusta, I Macriana Liberatrix

The Roman province of Africa (modern Tunisia and Libya; later extended as far west as the borders of modern Morocco) was created after the destruction of Carthage in 146 BC. A century after its sack by Roman forces, Carthage was re-established as a colony of Roman settlers, to become one of the greatest cities of the Roman Mediterranean. Subsequently, wars against the Numidian king Jugurtha (112–105 BC) served as a catalyst for change in the organization and recruitment of the legions. Roman civil wars also impacted on the region, most notably Caesar's victory at Thapsus in 46 BC.

As an imperial province, Africa was important and wealthy, but rarely the focus of major wars. For most of the imperial period, it had one legion, *III Augusta*, that policed the region, took part in political unrest, and sent detachments abroad for foreign wars. It is a well-

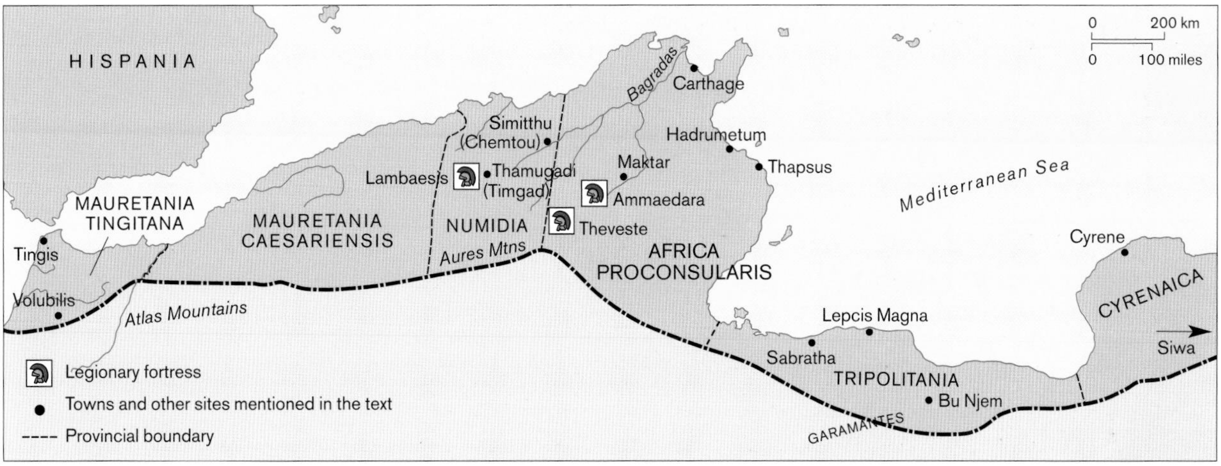

documented legion, however, thanks to the spectacular remains of its fortress at Lambaesis (in modern Algeria) and 3,000 or so inscriptions that relate to the legion and its men. The only other 'African' imperial legion was the short-lived (AD 68–69) *I Macriana Liberatrix*.

Map showing the fortresses of *III Augusta* in Africa, 1st–3rd centuries AD.

A relief depicting Septimius Severus celebrating a triumph (in the chariot, centre, flanked by his sons Caracalla and Geta). This comes from an arch in Severus' home city of Lepcis Magna in Tripolitania (the eastern part of Roman Africa; modern Libya).

III Augusta

We know very little about the origins of this principal imperial legion of Africa. It was probably raised in the triumviral period and its cognomen *Augusta* suggests later recognition of its loyalty to Augustus (Octavian), or a victory in his reign – perhaps that of Cornelius Balbus in 19 BC over the Libyan Garamantes, a Berber people from the Fezzan of south-central Libya. The earliest evidence that survives dates to the reign of Tiberius.

III Augusta

Cognomen	*Augusta*
Emblem	Pegasus?
Main base	Lambaesis in Numidia (modern Algeria) from *c.* AD 115–120 to *c.* 284; previously Ammaedara (Tunisia) and Theveste (Algeria)
Major campaigns	Cornelius Balbus' defeat of the Garamantes? (19 BC); Tacfarinas' Revolt in Numidia (AD 17–24) and other campaigns against indigenous peoples; Trajan's Dacian and Parthian wars? (vexillations; 101–6; 113–17); Marcus Aurelius' Marcomannic wars (vexillations, 166–80); Septimius Severus' Parthian wars? (vexillation, 195–97); Caracalla's eastern expedition (vexillation?, 216); suppression of the Gordians (238); German campaigns of Valerian and Gallienus (vexillation, 253)

Deployment

The earliest known fortress of *III Augusta* was probably at Ammaedara (modern Haïdra in Tunisia), but it had moved to Theveste (Tébessa, Algeria) by *c.* AD 75. An outpost was established at Lambaesis (Tazoult-Lambese, Algeria) and subsequently (*c.* 115–120) Lambaesis became the legion's main fortress.

Numerous inscriptions found at Lambaesis provide unparalleled information about *III Augusta* and the men who served in it. Of particular interest are the surviving fragments of a speech by the emperor Hadrian. In it, Hadrian, a man of great military experience, comments in great detail on military exercises carried out by the legion and supporting auxiliary units, confirming what Roman writers say about his deep personal engagement with military training and discipline as emperor.

One of the surviving fragments is addressed to *III Augusta*'s chief centurions:

> ... your commander, was very keen in arguing your cause and told me of many things that needed to be set out on your behalf. He told me that one cohort is sent away each year to the headquarters of the proconsul; that two years ago you gave up a cohort and five men from each century to support your comrades in that other Third Legion [Cyrenaica?]; that the many outposts your men garrison keep the legion split up; that, in my memory alone, you have not only moved fortress twice, but also built your new base yourselves each time. For these reasons, I would have excused you if the legion had been lax in performing these manoeuvres. But you did not seem lax at all, and there is absolutely no need for me to excuse you.

This reflects two important aspects of the legion's deployment and duties, namely its dispersed deployment for internal security duties (including a cohort at Carthage with the proconsul – the governor), and its provision of reinforcements to other legions elsewhere. Another fragment of the speech comments on the performance of the legion's cavalry detachment in their exercises.

Left Part of the inscription recording Hadrian's speech to the troops at Lambaesis, commemorating his visit in AD 128 (*ILS* 2487). These sections are addressed to auxiliary cavalry of the First *Ala* of Pannonians and the Sixth Cohort of Commagenians. Before becoming emperor, he had been a tribune in *II Adiutrix*, *V Macedonica* and *I Minervia*.

Command of the Legion

In the imperial period, most legions were based in provinces of the empire governed by men with the title of *legatus* (legate – of Augustus), direct appointees of the emperor with delegated military authority, who only commanded at the behest of the emperor as commander-in-chief.

For a while, Africa was an anomaly in this system, as it was the only province with a legionary garrison governed by a proconsul, a direct appointee of the Senate, who also commanded *III Augusta*. It was the last province of the empire where a senator could still exercise (nominally) independent military command as his predecessors had done. Thus in 19 BC, the proconsul Cornelius Balbus was the last private individual to hold a triumph, for his victory over the Garamantes of Libya, and in AD 23 the proconsul Junius Blaesus was saluted *imperator* ('victorious general') by his troops, the last time this honour was granted to a commander outside the imperial family.

This anomaly of command was corrected by Gaius Caligula in AD 37–39, who separated civilian administration of the province (by the proconsul) from command of the legion (by an imperial legate). Eventually the legate took on civilian responsibilities in the region around Lambaesis, which Septimius Severus finally made a separate province, Numidia.

III Augusta at War in Africa and Beyond

Roman Africa was never the scene of great external wars and, for the most part, *III Augusta* (with its auxiliary units) could secure the province by itself. This entailed internal policing and substantial conflicts with the Libyan and Berber peoples on the fringes of the province. *III Augusta* also sent reinforcements to wars elsewhere in the empire, including civil wars.

The best-documented war within Roman Africa is the guerrilla conflict of AD 17–24 against the indigenous leader Tacfarinas, a former Roman auxiliary officer, who relied on skirmishing and ambushing by his Numidian and Moorish light cavalry against the slower Roman legionary infantry. The historian Tacitus (*Annals* 3.20–21) describes one incident in which a Roman cohort was ordered out of its fort by its rash commander Decrius, to engage a larger enemy force. It was immediately driven back and Decrius himself was killed trying to stem the rout. The proconsul punished the cohort by having every tenth man beaten to death, something even Tacitus describes

The central hall of the legionary fortress headquarters (*principia*) at Lambasesis, where *III Augusta* remained until at least *c.* 284, with a hiatus in 238–53 when the legion was temporarily disbanded.

Moorish cavalry depicted on Trajan's Column, Rome. These men are fighting for the Romans in the Dacian wars, but Numidian and Moorish opponents of the Romans would have been equipped in a similar manner.

as old-fashioned and unusual – a practice documented in Polybius' account of the harsh discipline of the middle Republican legion. However, Roman defeats in open battle were rare and their strategy generally involved hemming in Tacfarinas' men and denying them access to resources by building forts and fortifications. Ultimately, in AD 24, *III Augusta* won the war with the assistance of *IX Hispana*, which had been sent on temporary detachment from Pannonia.

Similar low-intensity conflicts took place in subsequent decades. However, even low-intensity fighting caused Roman casualties, as shown by the epitaph of a soldier of *III Augusta* from Simitthu (Chemtou in Tunisia). This probably dates to the AD 50s, as Marcus Silanus was proconsul of Africa in AD 33–38.

> Lucius Flaminius, son of Decimus, of the voting tribe Arniensis, soldier of Legion *III Augusta*, in the century of Julius Longus. He was recruited in a levy conducted by Marcus Silanus, served 19 years, and was killed on active service in the Philomusian territory. He lived, dutifully, for 40 years. Here he lies.
>
> *EJ* 260

The emperor Claudius' annexation in AD 42 of Mauretania (Morocco) as a Roman province led *III Augusta* to assume similar responsibilities further west, with occasional help from detachments of other legions like *X Gemina* from Spain and even Balkan legions during unrest in the reign of Antoninus Pius (AD 138–61).

There is scattered evidence that vexillations of *III Augusta* participated in campaigns outside North Africa. Inscriptions from Lambaesis (*AE* 1895, 204; *CIL* 8, 2564) refer to troops returned from the Parthian war of Septimius Severus (AD 195–97) and Caracalla's eastern expedition (216). An officer buried at Maktar in Tunisia was commander of detachments of *III Augusta* 'among the Marcomanni' (*CIL* 8, 619), probably the wars of 166–80. Some of the inscriptions from Lambaesis show clusters of recruits to *III Augusta* from Syria (*CIL* 8, 18084) and the Danubian provinces (*CIL* 8, 18085) at times when they normally came from within Africa. These men seem to have been enlisted into vexillations to replace combat casualties while they were engaged in Trajan's Parthian and Dacian wars.

III Augusta in Civil Wars

In times of civil war, Africa was something of a backwater compared with the eastern frontier, the Rhine and the Danube. Nevertheless, AD 68–69 saw *III Augusta* support Clodius Macer (Tacitus *Histories* 1.11 – see page 119). In AD 238, a popular uprising in Africa upheld the claim of Gordian I and II (father and son) against the reigning emperor Maximinus. The legate of Numidia (commander of *III Augusta*), however, remained loyal to Maximinus and led the legion to Carthage to crush the revolt. The historian Herodian (7.9.6–8) described the slaughter when the disciplined legionaries and their supporting Numidian cavalry attacked the disorganized and ill-equipped rebels:

> The javelin-armed Numidian cavalry…easily routed the mob of Carthaginians, who didn't await the charge but fled, throwing away all their equipment. Shoving and trampling one another, more were killed by their own mass than by the enemy…. The remainder of the mob crowded around the city gates, as everyone rushed to get in. They were cut down by the cavalry and overwhelmed by the legionary infantry.

The younger Gordian was killed in battle, and the elder committed suicide. Subsequently, Maximinus also was overthrown (see page 208) and Gordian III (teenage grandson of Gordian I) became emperor, backed by the able praetorian prefect Timesitheus. *III Augusta* was punished by being disbanded, and it suffered *damnatio memoriae*, its name being chiselled out of some inscriptions, especially those describing it as *Maximiana* – 'of Maximian'. It was reconstituted in 253 as *III Augusta Valeriana Galliena* (after the father-and-son emperors of the day). We have little evidence for its later history, but it may have continued to exist down to the time of the Vandal conquest of Africa in 429, since a legion called *III Augustani* ('Augustans') appears in the *Notitia Dignitatum* that was compiled at about that time.

III Augusta **in Roman Africa**

The Third Legion was very active in the expansion of the Roman frontier to the Sahara and the development of Tripolitania to the east (Libya), a process that gathered pace in the Severan period (*c.* 193–235). The importance of internal security is emphasized by the outposts occupied by *III Augusta*'s detachments. One particularly well-studied example is the fort at Bu Njem in Tripolitania. This was a substantial (1.28 ha, 3.21 acres) rectangular stone fort with internal buildings including barracks sufficient for a cohort, a granary, a headquarters building and a bath complex.

The legions of Roman Africa supported the brief and unsuccessful claim to the throne of the proconsul Clodius Macer (AD 68–69). He issued *denarius* coins bearing *III Augusta's* title to show its loyalty.

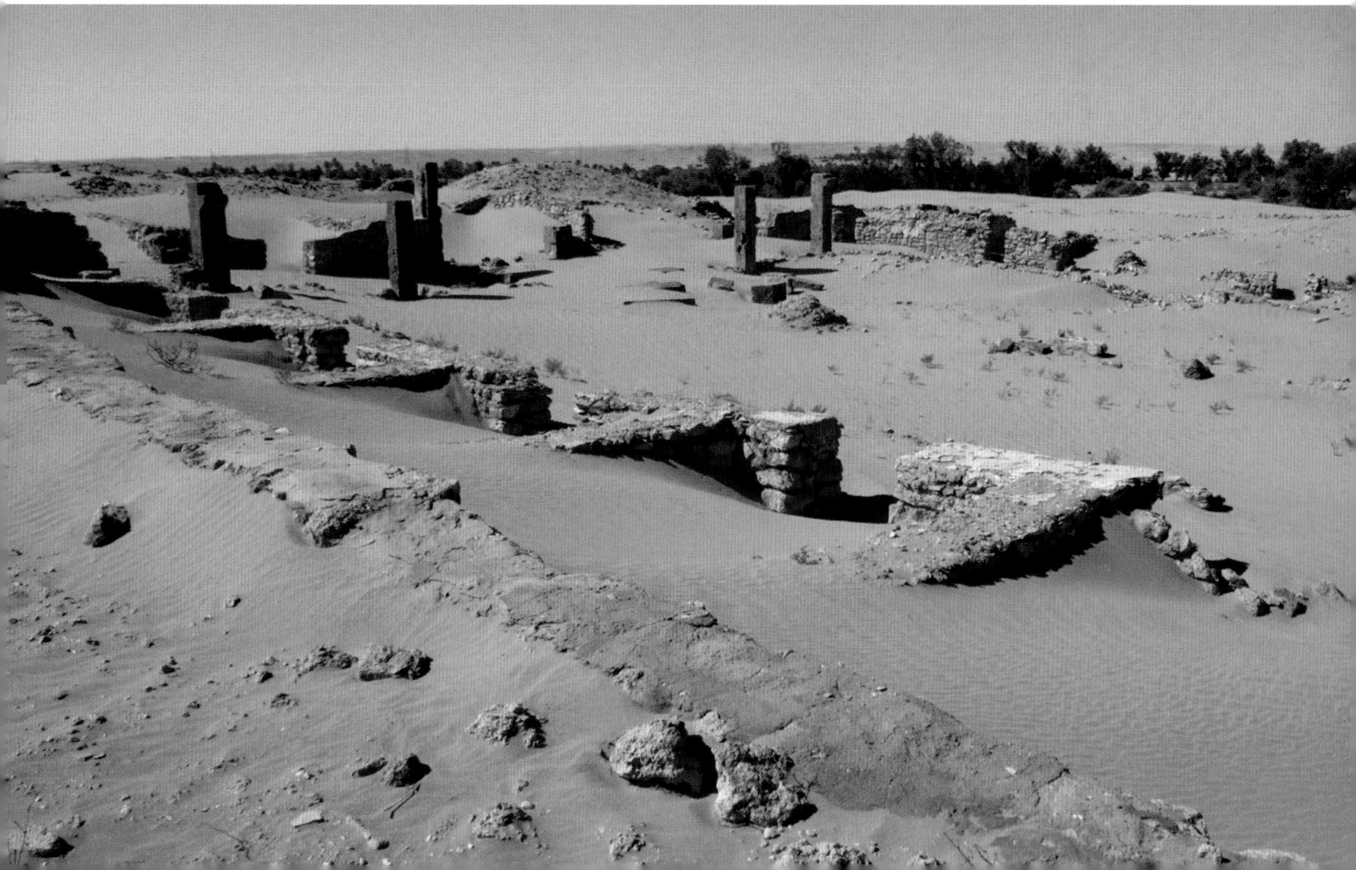

The Roman remains at Bu Njem. The fort was built by men of *III Augusta* in 201 and occupied by a vexillation until 238.

III Augusta and the *colonia* of Thamugadi

Thamugadi (modern Timgad, Algeria), a UNESCO World Heritage Site, is one of the most spectacular Roman sites. It was laid out and built in AD 100 by *III Augusta* as a *colonia*, a settlement of veterans retiring from the legion, and maintained close links with that legion at nearby Lambaesis. Its military origins are apparent from the fortress-like rectangular plan, divided into regular city blocks. It was settled by 400–900 military veterans, with their families. Many of Thamugadi's later inhabitants were also legionary veterans, and the commanders of *III Augusta* sometimes acted as patrons and benefactors of the colony.

Thamugadi flourished into Late Antiquity, but suffered from attacks by the Vandals who invaded North Africa in the 5th century AD. It was re-founded during the 6th-century Byzantine reconquest, but abandoned in the 7th century after Berber raids. The site is well preserved because it was unoccupied for 1,200 years until its excavation in the late 19th century.

Thamugadi was a civilian community, despite its connections with the army, and had public buildings such as a forum, a theatre (shown here) and baths, along with a civic constitution, magistrates and priests.

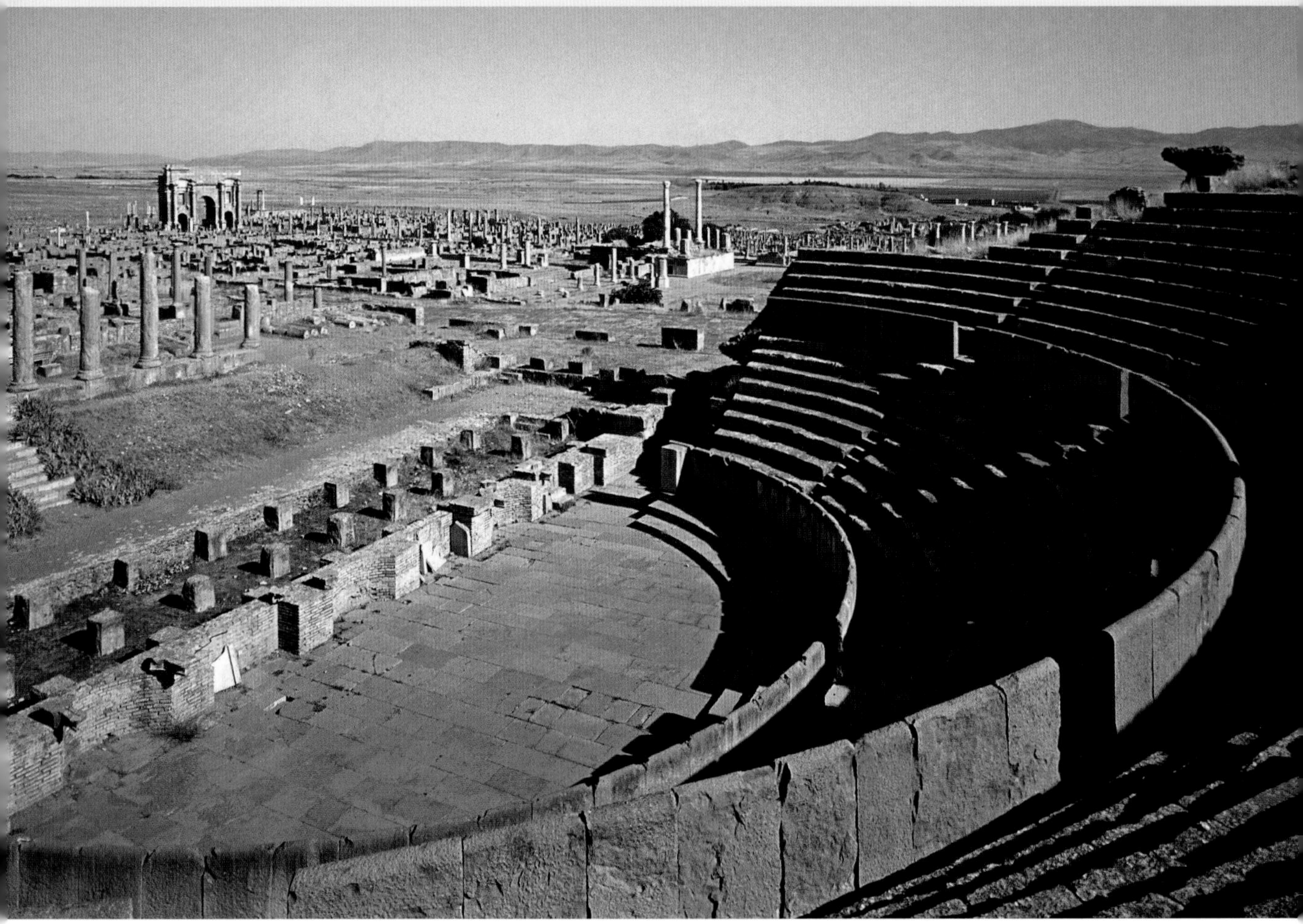

III Augusta also contributed to the construction of the province's infrastructure, providing technical specialists and skilled labour for activities like road-building. A series of Hadrianic inscribed milestones record the construction of a road from Carthage to Theveste. The 77th milestone, from near Guettar (Tunisia) reads:

Imperator Caesar Trajan Hadrian Augustus, grandson of the deified Nerva, son of the deified Trajan who conquered the Parthians, High Priest, holding tribunician power for the seventh time (AD 123), consul for the third time, paved the road from Carthage to Theveste through the agency of the Third Legion

> Augusta, when Publius Metilius Secundus was the pro-praetorian legate of the emperor. (Mile) 77. (*CIL* 8, 2204)

Other inscriptions show legionaries engaged in work to enhance the water supply of communities within the province.

A Soldier of *III Augusta* and his Brothers

'To the spirits of the departed, Marcus Silius Faustus, son of Marcus, of the voting tribe Quirina, from Ammaedara, soldier of the legion III Augusta, died in Parthia. He lived 41 years. Lucius Silius Rufinus, standard-bearer, and Silius Quietus, soldier of the same legion, (made this tomb) for their most dutiful brother.' (*CIL* 8, 2975)

This inscription from Lambaesis records the commemoration of a soldier of *III Augusta* by his two brothers, who served in the same legion. He was born at Ammaedara (modern Haïdra in Tunisia), which was the legion's fortress until c. AD 75. His father may well have been a legionary veteran who settled in the place he had served before having his sons, and the fact that three brothers served together in the legion strengthens the possibility that they came from a family with a military background. Marcus died in Parthia, no doubt a member of a vexillation sent to the eastern frontier for one of the 2nd-century Parthian wars.

The Soldiers of *III Augusta*

One of the most exciting features of the evidence for *III Augusta* is the light that it sheds on ordinary soldiers. Yann Le Bohec, a French historian, notes that its inscriptions record *c.* 3,000 individual soldiers, about 7 per cent of the *c.* 40,000–50,000 men who passed through its ranks between *c.* AD 115 and 238. We have nothing like this level of detail for any other legion. The inscriptions inform us about the origins of the legionaries, showing that they were originally a mix of Italians and men from culturally Roman towns, elsewhere, including towns in Africa like Carthage. By 120 there were no more Italians, and nearly all recruits were from Africa. Through the 2nd century AD, an increasing proportion of recruits were the sons of soldiers, whose origins were listed as *castris*, 'from the camp', probably brought up in the *canabae* ('civilian settlement') next to the fortress at Lambaesis. These general trends were true for the legions as a whole in the imperial period, but Africa was more self-sufficient in this regard than most.

These inscriptions also shed some light on the social and cultural backgrounds of legionaries and their officers. For example, centurions of the 2nd–3rd centuries AD were not, for the most part, battle-hardened veterans who rose from the ranks, but often seem to have been quite privileged individuals who joined the army with a higher status than ordinary soldiers. However, even legionary recruits of this period tended to come from the upper end of the 'working class', from backgrounds that were, in relative terms at least, more culturally Roman.

The tombstone of Q. Iulius Fortunatus (*CIL* 8, 3151) from Lambaesis, a legionary of *III Augusta*, who was recruited *castris* and died at the age of 28.

I Macriana Liberatrix

This legion was raised to back the claim to the throne of L. Clodius Macer, proconsul of Africa at the time of Nero's death in AD 68. We know of it primarily from *denarius* coins with the legend LEG I MACRIANA LIB 'of Macer the Liberator'. Macer was executed on the orders of Galba and this legion may have continued to serve briefly under Vitellius before being disbanded in AD 69.

I Macriana Liberatrix

Cognomen	*Macriana Liberatrix*
Emblem	Unknown
Main base	Unknown (perhaps Carthage)
Major campaigns	None

The Legions of Egypt

XXII Deiotariana, II Traiana Fortis

Egypt had a legionary garrison from the time of the province's creation in 30 BC, when Octavian (Augustus) took control of the kingdom after the defeat of Cleopatra VII and Mark Antony. Besides the usual forms of evidence, documents relating to the army written on papyrus survive from Egypt, providing a unique insight into the legions based there. In the reign of Augustus, Egypt had three legions (Strabo, *Geography* 17.1.12), stationed at Alexandria, Babylon (Old Cairo) and, probably, Luxor. They may have

included *III Cyrenaica* (later moved to Arabia; see page 156) and *XXII Deiotariana*, but the third is unknown. By AD 23 there were only two legions and, by the middle of the 2nd century only one, *II Traiana*. For political reasons, Egypt was governed by a member of the equestrian order (*equites* or 'knights'), rather than a senator, and so its legions were also commanded by *equites* rather than the usual senatorial legates.

The primary role of legions in Egypt was internal security, to prevent unrest that might disrupt the grain supply of Rome (much of it derived from Egypt). Alexandria, with its Greek and Jewish ethnic divisions, was particularly prone to rioting.

The temple of the Nubian sun god Mandulis, originally located at Kalabsha in Nubia, *c.* 31 miles (*c.* 50 km) south of Aswan. The temple was moved due to construction of the Aswan High Dam. Dedications inscribed by soldiers here and elsewhere provide a vivid record of the Roman garrison of Egypt itself and Nubia to the south.

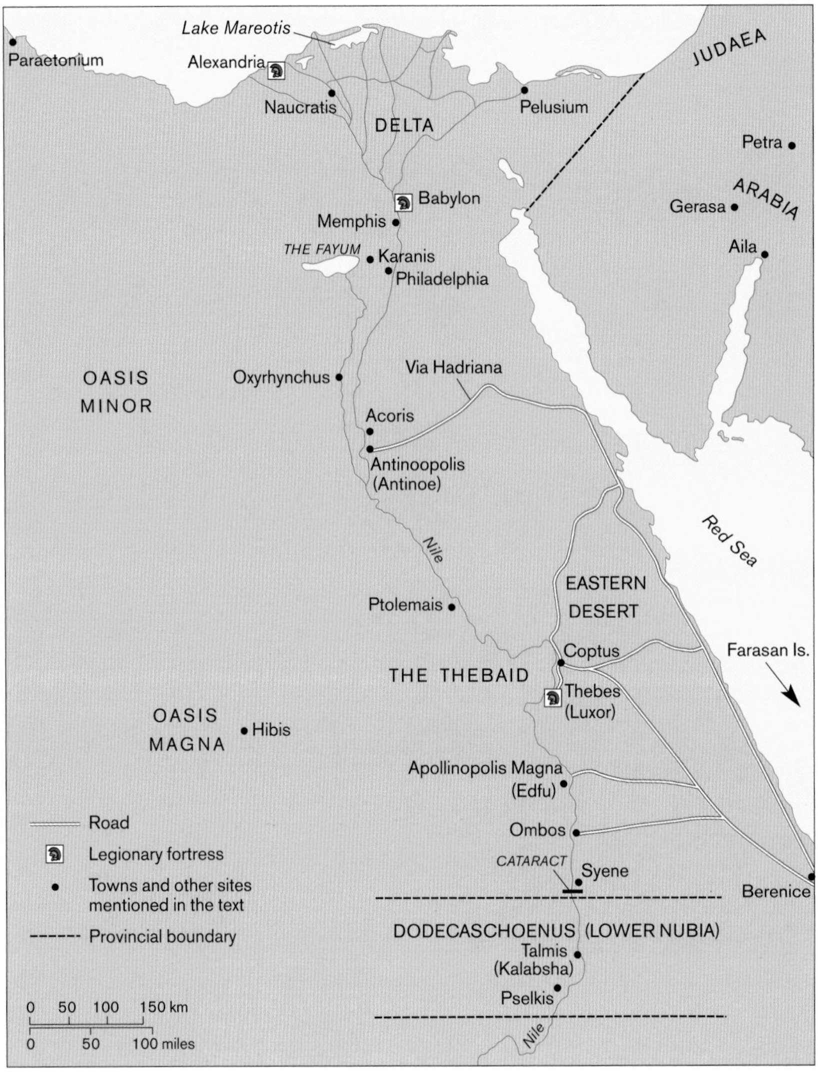

Map of Roman Egypt, showing the locations of legionary fortresses and other places mentioned in the text, along with major routes through the Eastern Desert to its quarries and the ports of the Red Sea coast.

External Wars and Internal Security

Egypt did not see great foreign wars except at the very beginning of the Roman occupation. An expedition of 10,000 men to the Arabian peninsula, led by the governor Aelius Gallus in 26–24 BC, was a failure, losing many men to disease and hunger (Strabo, *Geography* 16.4.24). In Gallus' absence the 'Ethiopians' of Nubia (modern Sudan) invaded the Thebaid (Upper/Southern Egypt), enslaving the people and pulling down statues of the emperor (*Geography* 17.1.54).

The next governor, P. Petronius, led a successful counter-attack against the poorly equipped 'Ethiopians', not only driving them from Egypt but also extending Roman power into Nubia, capturing important centres like Pselkis (Dakka) and Talmis (Kalabsha). Nero brought troops including *XV Apollinaris* to Egypt, apparently for a campaign against the 'Ethiopians', but this was abandoned because of the First Jewish Revolt in AD 66 (Josephus, *Jewish War* 3.8; see page 145). It was not until the mid-3rd century AD that another nomadic people, the Blemmyes, caused serious problems for Roman power in southern Egypt.

To maintain internal security, especially in Alexandria, the legions (two, then one) of Egypt were soon concentrated in a single fortress in the suburb of Nicopolis (Alexandria). In AD 66 the revolt in Judaea exacerbated tensions, leading to a threat by the Jewish population to burn down the city's amphitheatre while the Greek population was gathered there. In response, the governor, Tiberius Alexander, unleashed his two legions on the Jewish quarter:

> He realized that nothing short of a disastrous setback would stop the rebellion, so he sent the two legions stationed in the city to destroy the Jews. He ordered the soldiers not just to kill them but also to loot their property and burn their houses. The legions rushed to the quarter of the city called 'Delta' where the Jews lived, they and carried out their orders, but not without bloodshed on their side. For the Jews rallied and, with the best armed among them drawn up in the front, they resisted for a long time. But once they gave way, they were annihilated easily, overtaken by death of every kind.
>
> Josephus, *Jewish War* 2.494–96

Late in Trajan's reign there was a major challenge to Roman control of Egypt in the form of another Jewish revolt (AD 115–17). However, this uprising started in Cyrene (the part of modern Libya just to the west of Egypt) and spread to involve the Jewish populations of Egypt and Cyprus. Initial setbacks suffered by the Romans may have been due to the absence of elements of the regular garrison of Egypt, stationed abroad for Trajan's eastern wars. These absent elements may well have returned and formed part of the Romans' counter-attacking force under Q. Marcius Turbo.

A vivid letter of this period (Smallwood, *Nerva* no. 57), preserved on papyrus, describes fighting between Egyptian villagers and Jewish rebels, and refers to 'another legion' arriving at Memphis, perhaps *III Cyrenaica* on its way back from the East. Both *III Cyrenaica* and *XXII Deiotariana* were in Alexandria by the end of the revolt. *III Cyrenaica* soon moved to the new province of Arabia and within a few decades *XXII Deiotariana* disappeared from the historical record (see page 126). A relatively new legion, *II Traiana*, created, as the name suggests, by Trajan, was deployed to Egypt, where it remained, in one form or another, for at least three centuries.

XXII Deiotariana

Cognomen	*Deiotariana*
Emblem	Unknown
Main base	Nicopolis (Alexandria)
Major campaigns	Aelius Gallus' Arabian campaign? (26–24 BC); P. Petronius' invasion of Nubia? (24–22 BC); Corbulo's Parthian war? (vexillation, AD 63); First Jewish Revolt (vexillation, Judaea, AD 66–70); Jewish Revolt in Egypt (115–17); Second Jewish Revolt (Judaea, 132–35)?

XXII Deiotariana

This legion's name is unusual in that it was named after a non-Roman ruler, King Deiotarus of Galatia, in modern Turkey, who raised and trained Roman-style troops in the 1st century BC. In 48 BC, after Caesar's defeat of Pompey, the army of King Pharnaces of Pontus posed a threat to a number of Roman allies in Asia Minor, including Galatia. The Roman governor of Asia, Gnaeus Domitius Calvinus, was defeated by Pharnaces at Nicopolis in Lesser Armenia. Caesar's *Alexandrian War* (34) records that Domitius' army included two legions 'from Deiotarus, which he had for several years established according to our training system and equipped in our manner'. They fought badly, and suffered heavy casualties at Nicopolis. When Caesar arrived a few months later to confront Pharnaces at the battle of Zela in Pontus, Deiotarus' 'imitation legionaries' again formed part of the Roman army (*Alexandrian War* 69). This time, however, the Romans (with Deiotarus' 'legionaries') were victorious, despite Pharnaces' use of scythed chariots. The lightning speed and decisiveness with which the campaign was conducted gave rise to Caesar's famous tag 'I came, I saw, I conquered.' (Suetonius, *Caesar* 37).

By the time Galatia became a Roman province in 25 BC, some of these legionaries must have been serving in the regular Roman army. This explains the cognomen *Deiotariana* ('of Deiotarus') applied to the Twenty-Second legion, certainly by the Flavian period. However, there is every reason to assume that *XXII Deiotariana* was one of the three legions in Egypt mentioned by Strabo (writing at about the time it was created), and a papyrus document implies that it was based in the province by 8 BC. The vexillation of picked men from Egypt mentioned by Tacitus (*Annals* 15.26) as present with Corbulo in Syria for the Parthian war in AD 63 presumably included legionaries from *XXII Deiotariana* as well as *III Cyrenaica*. Men of the Egyptian legions participated in the First Jewish Revolt of AD 66–70, notably in the final siege and capture of Jerusalem in AD 70. The Roman historian Tacitus (*Histories* 5.1) specifies that vexillations from *XXII* and *III* were present with Titus in Judaea at the beginning of that year, and the Jewish writer Josephus (*Jewish War* 5.44) records their combined strength of 2,000 and the name of their commander, Eternius.

Internal Security and Policing

However, like other Egyptian legions, *XXII Deiotariana* spent most of its time in its home province, keeping the peace and supporting the Roman authorities there. A 1st-century AD inscription (*ILS* 2483) from the Nile valley town of Coptus (modern Qift) describes how work-parties of men from both legions and some auxiliary troops built cisterns for watering stations and fortifications along the route through the Eastern Desert of Egypt from the Nile valley to the ports on the Red Sea coast. This route was used by traders and travellers going from Egypt (and the wider Roman Mediterranean) to the Arabian coast and India. The Roman army was involved because Roman authorities were keen to monitor movements in frontier areas and also taxed goods moved into the empire at a high rate. Soldiers of *XXII Deiotariana* also served as guards for Nile river boats that shipped grain to Alexandria. Grain was collected as tax by the Roman authorities and shipped to feed the population of Rome. This evidence includes statements written on terracotta jars containing samples of grain from particular cargoes. Part of one such statement (from a text painted on a terracotta jar), dated 2 BC, reads as follows:

> From the Oxyrhynchite nome. Ammonios, son of Ammonios, helmsman of the public boat whose emblem is [...], through the agency of Lucius Oclatius, a soldier serving as a marine, from the Twenty-Second Legion, second cohort, century of Maximus Stoltius; and Hermias, son of Petalos, helmsman of another boat, whose emblem is 'Egypt', through the agency of Lucius Castricius, a soldier serving as a marine, from the Twenty-Second Legion, fourth cohort, century of Titus Pompeius. This is a specimen (of the wheat) that we put on board from the harvest of the 28th year of Caesar (2 BC).
>
> *SB* 6, 9223

Centurions of *XXII Deiotariana* also carved their names on the colossal statues of Amenhotep III (the 'Colossi of Memnon') across the Nile from modern Luxor. Most are undated, but some are from the reigns of Nero and Domitian.

Ethnicity and Recruitment

The inscription from Coptus also sheds light on the origins and status of legionaries in Egypt in the early imperial period. While most legionaries were Roman citizens when recruited, oddities in the names of these men suggest they were not. This is probably because fewer Roman citizens were available in the East than in the West in the early empire and Roman authorities had to supplement the legions by enlisting *peregrini*, free non-citizens (the sort of men normally recruited into auxiliary units), granting them citizenship on joining up.

Nearly all of the 36 Coptus legionaries were easterners, many from Galatia (central Anatolia), including ten from Ancyra (Ankara). This reflects *XXII Deiotariana*'s Galatian origins, but also the reputation of the region's men for toughness and the fact that Galatia had no legion of its own to maintain. Others were from Egypt itself (six from Alexandria) and two 'from the camp' (*castris*, probably the sons of soldiers). As in other provinces (see page 119 on the African legion *III Augusta*), the proportion of men recruited 'from the camp' increased over time, making recruitment hereditary in some respects. An inscription of *II Traiana* in Egypt (*CIL* 3, 6580) shows that 24 of a group of 41 men recruited in AD 168 were drawn from such sources.

From the reign of Augustus (13 BC) to the reign of Caracalla (AD 235) Roman soldiers, legionaries included, were not allowed to contract legitimate marriages. Of course, this didn't prevent many of them from developing informal relationships and having families – these were just not recognized

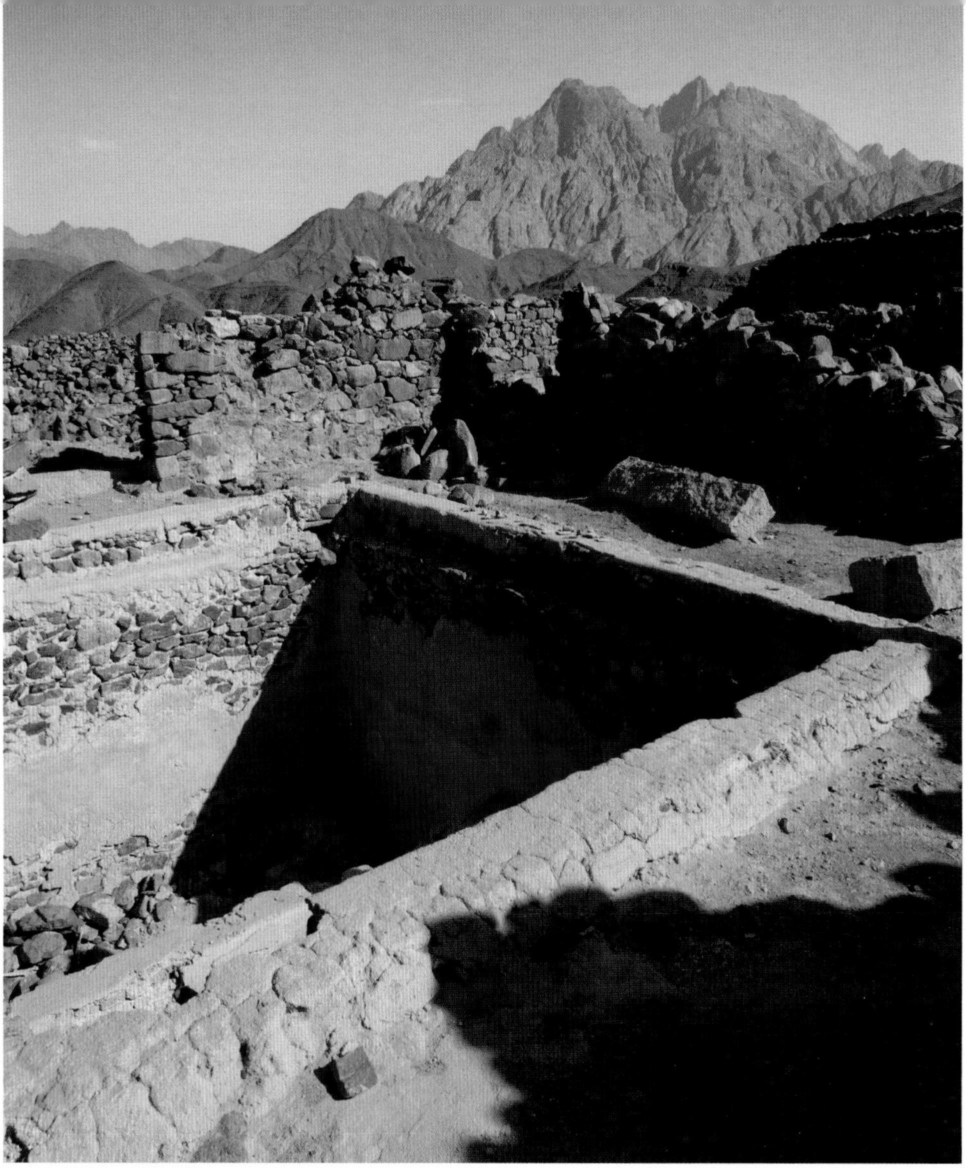

Cistern at the fort protecting quarries at Umm Balad. Legionary and auxiliary troops in the Eastern Desert guarded and supervised roads and facilities for stone quarrying and for long-distance trade with Arabia and India.

in law. This marriage ban had a number of important consequences: children born to the partners were considered illegitimate, and thus lacked the normal rights of citizenship and inheritance that belonged to the sons of most Romans. However, emperors, recognizing the importance of soldiers' loyalty to themselves and to the state, made legal pronouncements that diminished the harshest consequences of the ban. A vivid example of this can be seen in a papyrus letter of Hadrian to Quintus Rammius Martialis, prefect of Egypt AD 117–19, the original of which was set up in the fortress of *XXII Deiotariana* at Alexandria (*BGU* I 140). This extends the right of intestate inheritance (i.e., when no will was left) to the recognized but illegitimate children of deceased soldiers.

Copy of a letter of our lord Hadrian, translated and set up in [...] in the winter-quarters of Legions *III Cyrenaica* and *XXII Deiotariana*, in the headquarters building, in the third year of Hadrian's reign, when he was consul for the third time, along with Rusticus, on the 4th August, which is Mesore 11. 'I understand, my dear Rammius, that children whom parents registered during the fathers' military service have been prevented from succeeding to their inheritance and this isn't judged to be unfair, because their fathers had acted contrary to military regulations. It seems right to me to establish principles that allow me to interpret more generously the rather harsh rule put in place by my predecessors. For this reason, while it is true that children registered during their fathers' military service are not legitimate heirs, nevertheless I rule that they can make a claim for possession of the property on the basis of the part of the edict that also grants this right to relatives by birth.'

The End of *XXII Deiotariana*

In fact, this very same letter, showing *XXII Deiotariana* at Nicopolis (Alexandria) alongside *III Cyrenaica* on 4 August AD 119, is the last evidence for the existence of that legion. Subsequently it disappears completely. If it had remained in Egypt we would expect to find it mentioned somewhere, given the number of papyrus documents that survive and a move to another eastern province would probably be detected from surviving inscriptions.

It seems likely that the legion was disbanded or destroyed, and scholars have advanced theories that this happened in Judaea during the the Second Jewish Revolt (132–35; see pages 145–46), where Egyptian legions were certainly engaged. A series of inscriptions relating to the construction or reconstruction of the 'high-level aqueduct' at Caesarea may provide evidence for the legion's presence in Judaea at about the time of the Revolt. The legible examples refer to work in the reign of Hadrian (perhaps *c.* AD 130) by vexillations of *X Fretensis*, *VI Ferrata* and *II Traiana*. However, some scholars have recorded traces of a similar inscription, apparently erased in antiquity, leaving only faint indications of its letters. The historians Benjamin Isaac and Israel Roll proposed that the partially erased inscription referred to a disgraced legion, perhaps disbanded after a severe defeat, and existing hypotheses about the fate of *XXII Deiotariana* make its identification as the erased legion an attractive one. Another interesting but hardly conclusive piece of evidence is a claim by a later Christian writer, Sextus Julius Africanus, that the 'Pharisees' had destroyed a Roman 'phalanx' by poisoning its wine. While the details are clearly implausible, the story may reflect memories of the destruction of an entire legion such as *XXII Deiotariana*.

A relief of the god Anubis in military dress from the Roman-period catacombs of Kom esh-Shuqafa in Alexandria.

II Traiana Fortis

The name of this legion indicates that it was raised by the emperor Trajan, probably *c.* AD 105, and Cassius Dio (55.24.4) confirms its Trajanic origins. However, we know little about the circumstances of its establishment or its early career. It may have been recruited for the emperor's second Dacian war (105–6) or for the annexation of Nabataean Arabia (modern Jordan and southern Syria) in 106. It is likely that *II Traiana* participated in the emperor's invasion of the Parthian empire in 113–17, but there is no direct evidence.

Clearer proof of its location and activities dates to 120. A milestone of that year marked *II Traiana*'s construction of part of a road from the Roman colony at Ptolemais (Akko) to Diocaesarea (Sepphoris) and suggests that the legion was based in Judaea from *c.* 117 until it moved to Egypt by 127–28. Its base in Judaea may have been nearby Caparcotna (Lejjun, a name that derives from the Latin *legio*), later used by *VI Ferrata*. A vexillation of *II Traiana* was involved in construction (or reconstruction) of the 'high-level aqueduct' at Caesarea in the reign of Hadrian, either while based in Judaea or on its return for the Second Jewish Revolt. It may then have moved temporarily to the Euphrates frontier to deal with a developing crisis with Parthia in 123. An inscription found at Lyon (*CIL* 13, 1802) sets out the career of a senior senator Claudius Quartinus, who commanded a grouping of *II Traiana* and *III Cyrenaica* 'on the orders of the emperor Hadrian Augustus', and the crisis of 123, which subsided without recourse to war, seems the most likely time for this.

II Traiana was probably in Egypt by February AD 128, when a detachment set up an inscription at Pselkis (Dacca) in Nubia (*CIL* 3,14147). The main body of *II Traiana* may have been at Nicopolis (Alexandria) from the start of its posting, either alongside or in place of *XXII Deiotariana*. Certainly *II Traiana* was at Nicopolis by March AD 142, when an auxiliary cavalryman wrote his will 'at Alexandria in Egypt in the winter-quarters of the legion *II Traiana Fortis*' (*AE* 1948, 168). The *Notitia Dignitatum* shows part of the legion still at Alexandria at the end of the 4th century AD. The centuries that the legion spent in Alexandria are documented by a series of inscribed gravestones dedicated to the soldiers themselves and members of their families.

II Traiana Fortis

Cognomen	*Traiana Fortis*
Emblem	Hercules
Main base	Nicopolis (Alexandria)
Major campaigns	Trajan's second Dacian war? (AD 105–6); annexation of Arabia? (106); Trajan's Parthian war? (113–17); Second Jewish Revolt (132–35); Parthian wars of Lucius Verus and Septimius Severus? (161–66; vexillations?, 195–97); Pescennius Niger's civil war against Septimius Severus (193–94); Severus Alexander's Persian war (231–33)

***II Traiana* in Wartime**

If *II Traiana* came to Egypt from Judaea, it seems likely that part, at least, soon returned there. A senior centurion of the legion was decorated by Hadrian for his actions in the 'Jewish War' (*CIL* 10, 3733), probably the Second Jewish Revolt of 132–35. Another inscription from Alexandria (*AE* 1969/70, 633) shows that in *c.* 132–33, the

This funerary relief of a soldier from Alexandria (Graeco-Roman Museum) depicts a soldier in peacetime uniform, and another, togate, individual making an offering.

legion received recruits from unusual sources: 88 (of 130) from Africa, 19 from Syro-Palestine and 15 from Italy. None were from the legion's recruiting grounds in Egypt or *castris* 'from the camp'. The foreign recruits probably constituted an emergency measure to replace wartime casualties.

II Traiana may have contributed vexillations for later campaigns outside Egypt, such as the Parthian wars of Lucius Verus and Septimius Severus, but there is no positive evidence of this. It also took part in civil wars and attempted usurpations. Like much of the eastern army, *II Traiana* supported Avidius Cassius in his rebellion against Marcus Aurelius in 175 and Pescennius Niger against Septimius Severus in 193–94.

Later imperial biographies suggest that the Blemmyes on Egypt's southern frontier provided a more aggressive threat to Roman control of Lower Nubia and Upper Egypt by the mid-3rd century, and that the emperor Probus (276–82) defeated them after they had captured Coptus and Ptolemais. Undoubtedly *II Traiana* would have been heavily engaged in any such conflict (*SHA Probus* 17.2, 6). The legion may also have provided vexillations for wars in Syria and Mesopotamia. For example, Herodian (6.4.7) mentions a mutiny at Antioch of troops from Egypt preparing for Severus Alexander's Persian war in 231.

Internal Security and Policing

Despite occasional involvement in full-scale wars outside of Egypt, most of *II Traiana*'s duties related to internal security, local policing and administration. Probably the most serious internal challenge to Roman control during its time as the core of the Egyptian garrison came in *c.* 172, in the form of the poorly understood revolt of the Bucoli ('Herdsmen'), eventually suppressed by the same Avidius Cassius who later challenged Marcus Aurelius for the imperial throne.

Most of the internal security and policing duties were much less dramatic and violent, however. Papyrus documents show that centurions were stationed in communities throughout the province, where they served as the lowest level of Roman authority, receiving petitions concerning crime and public disorder from local residents and investigating and passing their complaints on to higher authorities. One example that has come down to us is a petition of 192, from a resident of the Fayum village of Karanis to the centurion Valerius Germanus:

> To Valerius Germanus (centurion) from [Sa]beinos, son of Sosimos, from the metropolis, living in the village of Karanis. On the night before the 12th, my threshing floor near to the village of Ptolemais Nea was set on fire by some people unknown to me. Thus I submit these petitions to be entered on the register, so that the individuals found guilty can be held accountable to me.
>
> *BGU* II 651

Soldiers themselves were sometimes in fact the cause of disorder in the Egyptian countryside. Egyptian papyri record complaints by civilians about drunken and violent behaviour by soldiers. Extortion is also documented in account books bearing blunt references to payments of *diaseismos* (extortion money – the Greek word literally means much the same as the American term 'shake-down') by civilians to soldiers. On the other hand, papyrus tax documents make it clear that retired soldiers settled down with their families in communities in the Egyptian countryside such as Karanis, and while they advertised and exploited their status as ex-soldiers when it was beneficial to do so (in legal matters, for example), in many ways they seem to have integrated quite well into local life.

II Traiana in the Red Sea

Perhaps the most remarkable recent discovery regarding *II Traiana* relates to the role played by the garrison of Egypt in trade with Arabia and India via the Red Sea. A Latin inscription (*AE* 2004, 1643; *AE* 2005 1638–39) was found on Farasan Kebir, one of a group of islands in the Red Sea off the western coast of Saudi Arabia, nearly 2,000 km (over 1,200 miles) south of Alexandria, and almost on the same latitude as modern Khartoum in Sudan. It records that in 144 a vexillation of *II Traiana* built and dedicated a structure under the authority of the 'prefect of the Port of Ferresan [i.e. Farasan]'. No doubt this very remote outpost of Roman military power was established to oversee long-distance trade, and perhaps protect it from pirates.

At the end of the 4th century AD, the *Notitia Dignitatum* shows an element of *II Traiana* still at Alexandria (specifically at Parembole, 'the Camp'), with another detachment at Apollinopolis Magna (Edfu), in Upper Egypt.

Mudbrick houses at the village of Karanis in the Fayum, home of Roman veterans and source of papyrus documents providing evidence for the Roman army.

Opposite above *Denarius* of Pescennius Niger, supported by Egypt and its legion in the civil war of AD 193–94.

Opposite below Part of a fragmentary inscription from Alexandria (*ILS* 2304), in which veterans of *II Traiana* honoured Septimius Severus. The remainder lists 45 individuals recruited in AD 168, most from Egypt or *castris*.

The Legions of the Eastern Frontier

Syria: *III Gallica, IIII Scythica, XVI Flavia Firma*
Judaea: *X Fretensis, VI Ferrata*
Arabia: *III Cyrenaica*
Cappadocia: *XII Fulminata, XV Apollinaris*
Mesopotamia: *I Parthica, III Parthica*

The eastern provinces of the Roman empire had an important legionary presence. Here, the Romans faced their only superpower neighbour, the Persian empire, ruled by the Parthian dynasty to AD 224, then by Sasanian kings. Roman legions fought a series of offensive and defensive wars against them throughout their history. They also faced ferocious revolts within the eastern empire, notably in Judaea in AD 66–70 and again

in 132–35 (see *X Fretensis*). The wealthy and turbulent cities of Syria and the other eastern provinces needed protection and local policing too. Finally, the great concentration of legions in the East gave it a crucial role in civil wars. Eastern legions were important in bringing Vespasian to the throne in AD 69 and Elagabalus in 193–94, and unsuccessfully championed Avidius Cassius against Marcus Aurelius, and Pescennius Niger against Septimius Severus in 193–94.

Syria became a Roman province in 64 BC, with a garrison of three to four legions throughout the imperial period. Further north, Cappadocia (in modern Turkey) was annexed as a province in AD 17, but only got a permanent garrison of two legions in AD 70. In the same year the existing province of Judaea received its first permanent legionary garrison, a second legion being added, probably, *c.* 117. Arabia (modern Jordan and southern Syria) became a Roman province in 106, garrisoned for most of its history by *III Cyrenaica*. Septimius Severus created three new legions in connection with the annexation of the new province of Mesopotamia in AD 197.

The colonnaded main street of the city of Apamea in Syria. Legions were based near Apamea from time to time in the late Republican and early imperial periods, but the legion best attested there is *II Parthica*, in the first half of the 3rd century AD.

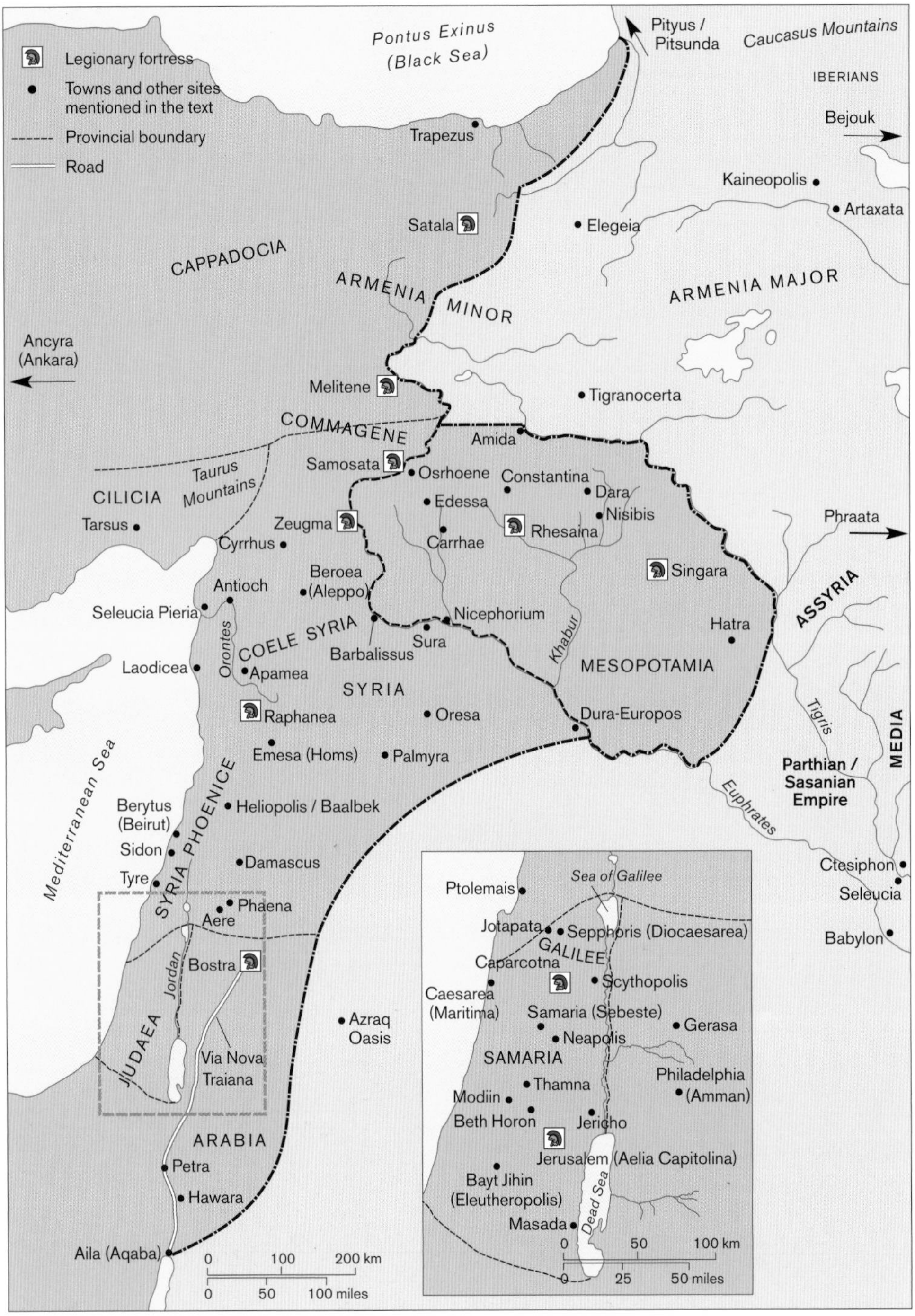

Map of the Roman East, showing legionary fortresses and other important sites in Cappadocia, Syria, Mesopotamia, Arabia and (inset) Judaea/Syria Palaestina.

The Legions of Syria

Through the 1st and 2nd centuries AD, Syria was a single province with a strong legionary garrison, reflecting its importance facing Parthian forces across the Euphrates and the desert frontier to the south. Septimius Severus divided the province in two: Coele (Narrow) Syria to the north, with two legions (*IIII Scythica* and *XVI Flavia Firma*) and Syria Phoenice (Phoenician Syria) to the south, with the single legion *III Gallica*.

III Gallica

	III Gallica
Cognomen	*Gallica*
Emblem	Bull (zodiac sign associated with Venus, divine ancestor of Julius Caesar)
Main base	Raphanaea, southern Syria
Major campaigns	Parthian wars of Mark Antony (40–33 BC); Actium? (31 BC); unrest in Judaea (4 BC); Corbulo's Parthian war (AD 58–63); First Jewish Revolt (Cestius Gallus' attack on Jerusalem, AD 66); civil war (AD 69); Jewish Revolt in Egypt? (115–17); Second Jewish Revolt (132–35)?; civil war between Elagabalus and Macrinus (218); other eastern civil wars and Persian wars of the 2nd and 3rd century, including Aurelian's recapture of Palmyra? (272–73)

III Gallica probably was the third of the legions raised by Julius Caesar as consul in 48 BC. Its name, 'Gallic', must reflect its recruitment and/or service in Gaul at this time. It continued to serve into the triumviral period, or was re-established then, forming part of Mark Antony's army in the East after Philippi (42 BC).

Probably *III Gallica* took part in the Parthian war of 40–39 BC, in defence of Asia Minor against the Parthian army led by Pacorus and his Roman ally Quintus Labienus (son of Caesar's legate and subsequent enemy, Titus Labienus), and the successful counter-attack by Publius Ventidius Bassus. It certainly took part in Antony's later invasion of the Parthian empire in 36 BC, and his subsequent retreat. Over a century later (AD 69), when *III Gallica* was fighting for Vespasian against the Vitellians, its general, M. Antonius Primus, reminded the men of past glories, including success against the Parthians 'when Mark Antony was your leader' (Tacitus, *Histories* 3.24).

War with the Parthians

In 36 BC, Antony led 16 legions, including the Third, with auxiliaries and allies, against the Parthians in a war of revenge. After their success in invading Roman Syria and Asia Minor four years earlier, the Parthians were in disarray caused by internal domestic struggles. After an initial feint into Mesopotamia and an alliance with the Armenians, Antony advanced into Media by way of Armenia, bringing the royal capital of Phraata, some 800 km (*c.* 500 miles) from friendly territory, under siege. However, Parthian cavalry destroyed the Roman siege-train, making an effective siege impossible. As supplies ran out and his Armenian allies deserted, Antony abandoned the siege and retreated. The Roman army was harassed by Parthian cavalry and threatened with destruction as it made the long journey back to safe territory.

Antony's biographer Plutarch (*Antony* 42) describes how he sought to ward off the enemy by marching his legionary infantry in a hollow square and using cavalry and light infantry to drive off Parthian attacks. One counter-attack got into difficulties until *III Gallica*, under Antony's personal command, relieved them and prevented the collapse of the Roman line of march. Nevertheless, the retreat through the wintry mountains of Armenia proved disastrous for the Roman army, which lost a third of its men.

III Gallica is attested on Antony's legionary coinage in the lead-up to Actium and it may well have taken part in that campaign. It formed part of the imperial standing army in the East after Octavian's victory, based in Syria from early on.

Left *Denarius* of Mark Antony's legionary series (*c.* 33–31 BC), depicting standards of *legio III*, the imperial *III Gallica*.

Right Antony saw his expedition as an opportunity to avenge Crassus' defeat at Carrhae in 53 BC and recover lost standards, but in fact it was only Augustus who managed to recapture the standards. This silver *denarius*, depicting a kneeling Parthian returning a standard, was produced to commemorate this diplomatic success in 20 BC.

Conflict in Judaea and Armenia

Along with other Syrian legions (like *VI Ferrata*), *III Gallica* was occasionally called on by the governor of Syria to suppress opposition to the Roman-backed kings of Judaea. One notable example came in 4 BC, when unrest broke out on the death of Herod the Great. Syria's governor, Quinctilius Varus, later infamous for his defeat in the German Teutoburg Forest (see pages 54–59), stationed a legion in Jerusalem to suppress the unrest, but mismanagement by Sabinus, procurator of Judaea, made the situation worse, and the rebels blockaded the Romans in the city.

Josephus describes fierce fighting within the Temple complex. Roman legionaries were trapped in a colonnaded courtyard, while their Jewish opponents threw missiles at them from the portico roofs. Eventually the Romans burned the colonnades, forcing the rebels to jump down into the courtyard and face the well-equipped legionaries, or die in the flames (Josephus, *Jewish War* 2.45–50). The Romans won the battle and looted the Temple treasury, but remained trapped in Jerusalem by growing numbers of rebels. Josephus describes how a century of Roman troops carrying supplies was surrounded at nearby Emmaus (probably modern Motza-Qaluniya – see *X Fretensis*). The rebels killed the centurion Arius and 40 of his men before the Romans were relieved by reinforcements. The situation was saved by Varus, who gathered his remaining two legions, auxiliaries and allied forces at the coastal town of Ptolemais (Akko). He advanced through Galilee and Samaria to Judaea, where the rebel force melted away. After executing the ringleaders, Varus returned to Syria, leaving a legion in Jerusalem as (temporary) garrison.

We know little of the legion's movements within Syria, although its number appears (along with *VI*, *X* and *XII*) on coins of the town of Ptolemais, re-established under Claudius as a *colonia* of retired soldiers from Syrian legions. However, *III Gallica* played an important and well-documented role in the wars against the Parthians in the reign of Nero (see page 152). It formed part of the army that Corbulo led into Armenia in AD 59 to capture Artaxata and Tigranocerta. Subsequently *III Gallica* also was in the force assembled by Corbulo in AD 62, to relieve Caesennius Paetus' demoralized army. Its presence east of the Euphrates around this time is documented by inscriptions (*CIL* 3, 6741–42; 6742a) from Ziata (northeast of the Euphrates crossing and the site of the later legionary fortress at Melitene) probably reflecting the construction of a fort there in AD 64.

Moesia to Rome – Civil War in AD 68–69

When the Great Revolt broke out in Judaea in AD 66 (see page 145), *III Gallica* provided a vexillation of 2,000 for Cestius Gallus' unsuccessful attempt to capture Jerusalem, but subsequently the legion remained in Syria while Vespasian mustered his army to invade Galilee in AD 67. However, in AD 68 *III Gallica* set out on a journey that took it from Syria to the Danube, on to Rome and then back to Syria in just two years: initially to suppress the Roxolani, Sarmatian nomads migrating from the steppes of the Ukraine, who now, as the civil war of AD 68–69 (see page 59) distracted the Roman world, launched incursions across the Danube.

Meanwhile on 1st July AD 69, Vespasian was proclaimed emperor by the army of Egypt, quickly followed by Judaea and Syria, the latter commanded by Licinius Mucianus, an ambitious partisan of the new emperor (see page 152). The other focus of pro-Flavian sympathy lay in the Balkan provinces, and *III Gallica* was instrumental in gaining Vespasian the support of the other legions in Moesia (Tacitus, *Histories* 2.85). Perhaps officers of *III Gallica* had encountered Vespasian in Syria, and been impressed by him. Thus the Balkan legions also declared for the Flavians, under Marcus Antonius Primus, legate of *VII Gemina* (see page 109). Primus' army was large enough, experienced enough and, unlike the armies of the East, which had first declared for Vespasian, close enough to Italy to take on Vitellius' army, drawn primarily from the Rhine legions.

Primus invaded Italy from the northeast, without waiting for Mucianus' army, and advanced into the Po valley, encountering the Vitellian army on 24 October on the road between Bedriacum and Cremona (Tacitus, *Histories* 3.21–22). This strategically important area commanded road and river routes crucial for invaders and defenders of northern Italy. Close by, Vitellius' forces had defeated Otho's army six months earlier. Primus' army comprised *XIII Gemina*, *VII Gemina/Galbiana*, *VII Claudia* on the left and, on the right, *III Gallica* and *VIII Augusta*. Auxiliary infantry and cavalry were deployed on the flanks. Vitellius' army consisted of *IIII Macedonica*, *V Alaudae* and *XV Primigenia* and veterans of the British legions on the right, with *I Italica*, *XVI Gallica* and *XXII Primigenia* on the left.

There was sporadic fighting throughout the night. The battle remained evenly balanced until morning, when, according to Tacitus (*Histories* 3.24–5), Primus encouraged his troops, reminding the men of *III Gallica* of their past successes. Then, as dawn broke, they saluted the sun 'as is the custom in Syria'. Primus' other legions thought this was Mucianus' eastern army arriving to reinforce them and, taking heart, attacked confidently, breaking the Vitellian battle-line. The Flavian army then advanced on the Vitellian camp and Cremona itself. Tacitus (*Histories* 3.29) records that men of *III Gallica* cut down the city gate with swords and axes, and one of them, Gaius Volusius, was the first man into Cremona. They then sacked the town, burning and killing for four days in what Tacitus describes as 'an atrocious crime.'

Meanwhile Vespasian's supporters in Rome itself, including his younger son, the future emperor Domitian, were beseiged on the Capitoline Hill by their opponents. In the fighting, the Capitoline temple of Jupiter, the most sacred building in Rome, was burned down, a shocking act of impiety described by Tacitus as 'the most deplorable and disgraceful event that had happened to Rome'. Romans regarded civil war as inherently impious, and this made it doubly so. The Flavians were defeated, and many of them killed, including Vespasian's brother. Domitian escaped, and went into hiding. Eventually Primus' army reached Rome and fought its way into the city, as the population looked on. Tacitus (*Histories* 3.83) records the incongruity of open warfare in Rome itself, juxtaposed with business as usual in the city's baths and taverns. Primus' army gained the upper hand and Vitellius and many of his supporters were killed. Vespasian was declared emperor by the Senate on 21 December AD 69.

III Gallica was sent into winter quarters in the Campanian city of Capua. Tacitus' view (*Histories* 4.3) that this was a punishment inflicted on Capua for its support of Vitellius, reminds us how traumatic the arrival of a Roman army might be for a civilian community even in peacetime, with soldiers billeted in civilian houses, engaging in theft, drunkenness and violence. When Mucianus reached Rome at the end of the year, he sought to undermine Primus' support, and so *III Gallica* was sent back to Syria, where it had started out some two years earlier.

A relief from Kerch in Ukraine depicting a Sarmatian cavalryman. During its brief period in Moesia (AD 68–69), *III Gallica* defeated an incursion by 9,000 Sarmatian Roxolani (Tacitus, *Annals* 1.79). The wet and snowy conditions and their heavy burden of booty prevented the Roxolani from exploiting their usual impetuous charge with lance-armed cavalry, and made them vulnerable to the Roman legionaries.

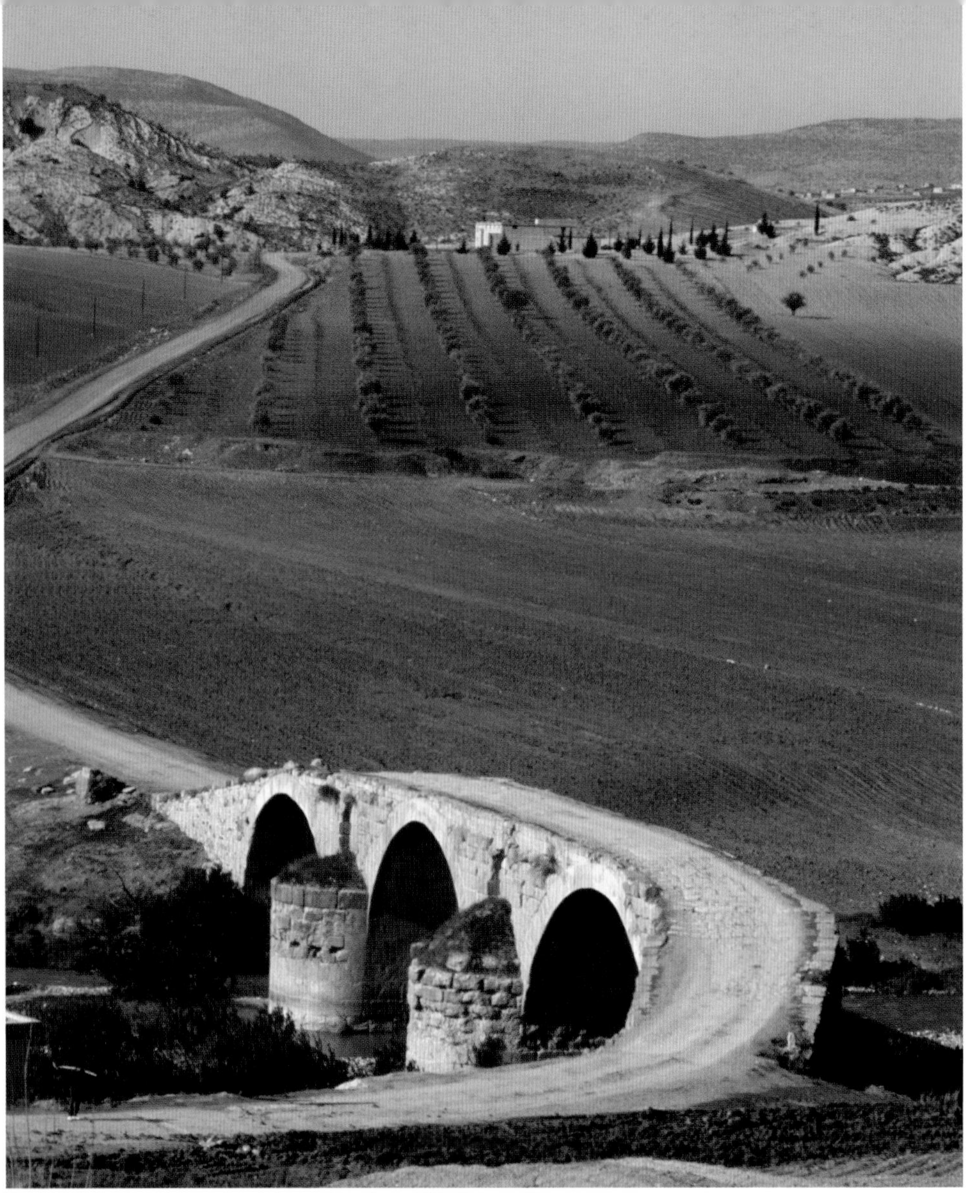

A Roman bridge crosses the Afrin river in northern Syria, near the ancient city of Cyrrhus. Construction of infrastructure was a regular activity of the legions. Like other Syrian legions, *III Gallica* contributed a vexillation to construct a canal and bridges near Antioch in AD 75 (see *XVI Flavia Firma*), and helped men of *IIII Scythica* construct a water-lifting device at Aini near Zeugma in AD 73. In Caracalla's reign, the legion reconstructed a road near Beirut damaged by a rock-fall caused by the river Lykos (*CIL* 3, 206).

III Gallica in Syria

The main fortress of *III Gallica* in Syria was Raphanaea (modern Rafniye) in west-central Syria. It probably moved there on its return from Italy, replacing *XII Fulminata*, which had besieged Jerusalem in AD 70 and then had been sent to Cappadocia by Titus. There is little evidence for the legionary base from the site, although Ptolemy's *Geography* (mid-2nd century AD), states that it was the Third's base and a marble altar has been found depicting an eagle and a Victory flying over a bull, with a dedication (*AE* 1951, 148) by the legion *III Gallica* to the safety and the victory 'of the emperors', either Marcus Aurelius (with Lucius Verus or Commodus) or Septimius Severus (with Caracalla). One famous member of *III Gallica* who must have served at Raphanaea was the writer and politician Pliny the Younger, who was one of its equestrian tribunes *c.* AD 82 (*CIL* 5, 5262).

There is more evidence for working parties and policing detachments of the legion dispersed throughout Syria. The Third Legion is also well-attested in the small towns and villages of southern Syria, where centurions (presumably with detachments of legionaries under their command) policed the region's roads, which were threatened by bandits. Other legions are attested here (see page 145), but *III Gallica* was the local legion and appears in more inscriptions, mostly of the later 2nd century AD. Centurions could exercise considerable power and influence in small communities like Phaena and Aera, and be the recipients of lavish local honours and titles. Julius Germanus, a centurion of *III Gallica*, was called benefactor and founder (honorific rather than literal) of Aera in an inscription (*IGR* 3, 1128) thanking him for his gifts to the village.

III Gallica also contributed troops to the garrison of Dura-Europos, in the middle Euphrates valley. When Septimius Severus divided Syria into two provinces, *III Gallica* became the sole legion of Syria Phoenice. The legion's number appears on 3rd century coins of Phoenician cities such as Tyre and Sidon, and a funerary inscription from Sidon (*CIL* 3, 152; probably 2nd century AD) names a soldier of the Third Legion. This evidence may indicate that legionary garrisons were posted in these cities, or that veterans settled there on their retirement.

We know little about the legion's history after the mid-3rd century AD. It remained in Syria, however, and the *Notitia Dignitatum* lists *III Gallica* at Danaba in the late 4th century AD, just south of its earlier fortress at Raphanaea.

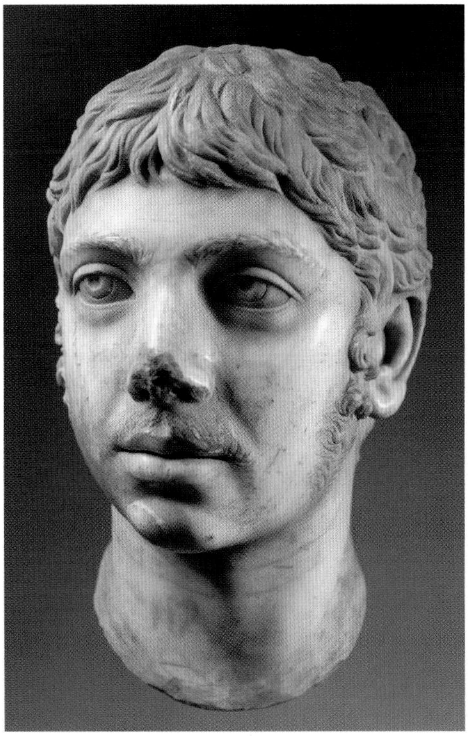

Elagabalus. Herodian describes how local soldiers (probably of *III Gallica* at nearby Raphanaea) admired the handsome young priest when they visited the temple at Emesa. The historian likens his appearance to that of the god Bacchus.

III Gallica at War on the Eastern Frontier

Like other eastern legions, *III Gallica* probably took part in wars against Parthia and the new Sasanian Persian dynasty in the 2nd and 3rd centuries AD, and perhaps the Jewish revolts of 115–17 and 132–35 (see page 145). Marcus Statius Priscus, commemorated in an inscription from Rome (*CIL* 6, 1523) served in a number of units during his career, but it was probably when a tribune of *III Gallica* that he was decorated by Hadrian for his actions in 'the Jewish expedition', the Second Jewish Revolt of 132–35.

It is very likely that elements, at least, of *III Gallica* were present when Shapur I defeated the emperor Valerian near Edessa in 260 and that the legion was caught up in subsequent events that led to Palmyra establishing itself as an independent power. However, when Roman rule over Palmyra was re-established in 272–73, according to a late biography of the emperor Aurelian (*SHA Aurelian* 31.7) standard-bearers and trumpeters of the 'Third Legion' sacked the Temple of the Sun at Palmyra. These may have been men of *III Cyrenaica* (see page 161), but *III Gallica*, based even closer to Palmyra, may in fact have been the legion responsible.

III Gallica and Elagabalus

The Third Legion was crucial to the accession of an emperor who was unusual even by the standards of Nero, Caligula and Commodus. He was Bassianus, generally known to us as Elagabalus, after the Syrian sun god worshipped as a conical black stone whose priest he was. Elagabalus was Syrian in origin, from Emesa (Homs), close to Raphanaea. The local legion was crucial in supporting his claim to the throne in May–June 218. Herodian (5.3–4) tells us that Bassianus' grandmother Julia Maesa claimed he was the son of Caracalla (recently assassinated in Syria by the praetorian prefect Macrinus), and thus a member of the Severan dynasty. She won over the troops with promises of money, they took Elagabalus into the fortress and proclaimed him emperor. Macrinus sent a force to suppress the revolt, but his men deserted to Elagabalus, cutting off their commander's head and sending it to Macrinus. A final battle, in which *II Parthica* fought alongside *III Gallica*, took place at the village of Imma near Antioch. Macrinus fled, was captured and put to death, and Elagabalus assumed the throne.

IIII Scythica

The Fourth Legion *Scythica* (typically written *IIII* rather than *IV* in Roman inscriptions) was a long-serving legion of Roman Syria, although its cognomen *Scythica*, reflects earlier service in the Balkans and victories over the 'Scythians'. The capricorn emblem suggests an association with Octavian (Augustus) as it was his zodiacal conception sign and thus probably reflects his reconstitution of the legion, but another legion (the imperial *IIII Macedonica*) bore that number in the sequence of Octavian's legions. Thus *IIII Scythica* may have been an Antonian legion reconstituted for the imperial army by Octavian/Augustus. Alternatively, it may originally have been the legion *IIII Sorana* in the consul Pansa's army at Mutina in 43 BC, subsequently incorporated into Octavian's forces. The earliest clear reference to *IIII Scythica* by name is an inscription (*CIL* 10, 680) from Sorrento mentioning an officer of the legion in the reign of Augustus.

The Fourth Legion probably spent its early life in Macedonia (modern Greece and Bulgaria), then, with the expansion of the Roman frontier to the lower Danube under Augustus, in the new (AD 6) province of Moesia. However, we know relatively little about its activities there. Probably it took part in campaigns in 29–27 BC, when the governor of Macedonia, Marcus Licinius Crassus (a son of the triumvir defeated at Carrhae in 53 BC) led his army to conquer the territory between his province and the Danube that subsequently became Moesia. He celebrated a triumph over the Dacians and Bastarnae, the latter described by Cassius Dio as 'Scythians', a vague term applied to nomadic peoples who lived in the region. It is probably from this victory that *IIII* derived its title *Scythica* – 'victorious over the Scythians'. Crassus' triumph was one of the last celebrated by a commander outside the imperial family.

IIII Scythica undoubtedly participated in other campaigns in the Balkans. These included the Pannonian Revolt of AD 6–9 that threatened Roman control of new territories along the Danube and encroached on older possessions such as Macedonia, and the savage suppression of Thracian tribes in AD 26 described by Tacitus (*Annals* 4.46–51). Part of the legion was in Pannonia in AD 33, as a road-building detachment of *IIII Scythica* (alongside men of *V Macedonica*) inscribed a dedication to the emperor Tiberius into the rock of the Iron Gates gorge (bordering modern Romania and Serbia – *ILS* 2281).

IIII Scythica

Cognomen	*Scythica*
Emblem	Capricorn
Main base	Zeugma (Seleucia on the Euphrates)
Major campaigns	Conquest of Moesia (29–27 BC)?; Pannonian Revolt (AD 6–9) and other early imperial Balkan campaigns?; Corbulo and Caesennius Paetus' Armenian campaigns (AD 58–63); First Jewish Revolt (Cestius Gallus' attack on Jerusalem, AD 66; siege of Jerusalem, AD 70); civil war? (vexillation, AD 69); Trajan's Parthian war (113–17); Niger's civil war against Severus (193–94); Severus' Parthian wars? (195–97); Caracalla's Parthian campaign? (216–17); Severus Alexander's Persian campaign (231–33); campaigns against Shapur I of Persia, including Roman defeats in 252 and 260?

IIII Scythica in the East

How *IIII Scythica* joined the garrison of Syria is somewhat obscure, although most scholars agree it is the legion described by Tacitus (*Annals* 13.35.4) as 'a legion added from Germany' that reinforced Corbulo in AD 56–57, the Roman historian apparently confusing Moesia with Germany. If this was *IIII Scythica*, then it participated in Corbulo's first, successful, invasion of Armenia (see page 152). Later Tacitus refers (*Annals* 15.6.5) to the Fourth Legion in winter quarters in Cappadocia under Caesennius Paetus (along with its former comrades of *V Macedonica* from Moesia and *XII Fulminata*) and its subsequent employment (with *XII*) in Paetus' disastrous expedition of AD 62 to relieve Tigranocerta from a Parthian siege. The Roman forces were cut off and forced to withdraw – Tacitus (*Annals* 15.14–16) paints the withdrawal as a humiliating Roman defeat, with rumours that the legions had 'passed under the yoke', the traditional ritual of submission. He describes how the retreat turned into a panic-stricken rout, until the Romans reached the safety of the Euphrates and Corbulo's relief force.

Corbulo sent Paetus' demoralized and defeated legions back to Syria. *IIII Scythica* remained based in Syria at least until the early 3rd century AD, for the most part in the north of the province. At first it probably remained close to the provincial capital, Antioch, since its commander acted as deputy to the provincial governor whenever he had to leave Syria, notably in 132 for the Second Jewish Revolt (*IGR* 3, 174). In AD 75, work parties of *IIII Scythica* and other local legions (*III Gallica*, *XVI Flavia Firma* and *VI Ferrata*), under the governor Marcus Ulpius Traianus (father of the emperor Trajan), constructed three Roman miles of canal, with bridges, to improve water transportation just east of the city. The work was recorded in an inscription (*AE* 1983, 927). Probably this was done to improve supply, from the Mediterranean through Antioch and its port (Seleucia Pieria), of armies campaigning on the eastern frontier. Scholars have also noted that many aristocratic young senators served as tribunes in the Fourth Legion, explaining their attraction to the legion by its proximity to the notorious luxuries of Antioch.

IIII Scythica played a minor role in the First Jewish Revolt. Some 2,000 men participated in Cestius Gallus' unsuccessful attack on Jerusalem in AD 66, but the legion took no part in Vespasian's advance into Galilee, remaining in Syria, where it perhaps replaced *X Fretensis* at Zeugma, subsequently its long-term base. The legion declared allegiance to Vespasian when he was proclaimed emperor in AD 69 and probably sent a vexillation west under Mucianus to support the Flavian claim. Elements of *IIII Scythica* (with detachments of other Syrian legions) joined Titus for the siege of Jerusalem in AD 70, since Josephus (*Jewish War* 5.44) records his army as including 3,000 'men who guarded the Euphrates'.

A tribune of *IIII Scythica* decorated by Trajan (*CIL* 3, 10336) probably distinguished himself during the emperor's Parthian war of 113–17. Additionally, an inscription (*AE* 1968, 510) documents a construction party of the legion at the Armenian capital of Artaxata (modern Artashat) in 116. *IIII Scythica* was probably in the invasion force for Armenia, and was intended as the garrison for the new province until revolts forced Trajan to abandon his eastern conquests. There is no specific evidence of the legion's involvement in other 2nd-century Parthian wars, but its participation is likely, given the location of its base at Zeugma and its detachments at the Middle Euphrates fortress of Dura-Europos. In

The main ('Palmyrene') gate of the city of Dura-Europos. This walled city in the Euphrates valley was an important outpost of power against the Persians from its capture by the Romans in AD 165 to its loss to the Sasanians in 256. It was garrisoned by a mixed contingent of legionaries (including men of *IIII Scythica*) and auxiliaries.

Zeugma: The 'Yoke' of the Euphrates

Seleucia on the Euphrates was a Greek city generally known as Zeugma, 'the Yoke', due to its important bridge across the Euphrates. For several centuries the river formed the border between Roman and Parthian empires, and Zeugma was a place of great strategic importance. It was the starting point for campaigns, a focal point for road and river supply of Roman armies, and even in peacetime, soldiers based at Zeugma monitored travellers and oversaw collection of customs duties from traders crossing the frontier. It was an obvious location for a legionary base even before *IIII Scythica* established its fortress there in the later 1st century AD.

There is little evidence of the fortress from the site itself, and it was only in the 1970s, with the discovery of tiles stamped by the unit and a single inscription referring to a soldier of *IIII Scythica*, that it was generally accepted that the site of Zeugma was modern Belkis in Turkey. Subsequently the site became famous due to rescue excavations conducted there in the 1990s, before the site was largely submerged by flooding caused by the Birecik Dam. Fieldwork in the area revealed some military installations nearby, reflecting the general strategic importance of the location, but nothing as substantial as a legionary fortress. The base of *IIII Scythica* must have been located in an unexplored part of the site. The most dramatic finds from the excavation were the mosaics discovered in the city's luxurious villas.

The city produced coins with a capricorn emblem, probably alluding to its association with the legion.

No long-term legionary fortress was located during the excavations at Zeugma, but the results were otherwise impressive, particularly the discoveries of mosaics in the city's luxurious houses.

about 180, *IIII Scythica*'s commander was the future emperor Septimius Severus, but even so, the legion supported Severus' rival Pescennius Niger in the civil war of 193–94. Subsequently, the legion participated in Severus' wars against the Parthians and other eastern enemies.

Bases and Outposts of *IIII Scythica* – Zeugma and Beyond

IIII Scythica was almost certainly based at Zeugma, but is also seen elsewhere in the Euphrates valley and northern Syria, engaged in building and engineering activities. In the 2nd and 3rd centuries AD its men cut inscriptions into a quarry at Arulis (modern Ehnes), about 12 km (7.5 miles) upstream from Zeugma itself, where they cut stone or supervised quarrying. One such inscription (*AE* 2001, 1956) gives *IIII Scythica* the titles *Operosa Felix* 'Over-worked, Lucky', perhaps a sarcastic soldier's reflection on this work.

An inscription from nearby Aini (*ILS* 8903), dated to AD 73, refers to the construction of an *opus cochli[s] (sic)*, probably a water-lifting screw, by detachments of two legions whose names were deliberately erased. Undoubtedly they were *IIII Scythica* (from nearby Zeugma) and *III Gallica*, their names erased due to activities in the reign of Elagabalus. Further north, a vexillation of *IIII Scythica* built a fort at modern Eski Hisar on the east bank of the Euphrates in 197, at the time of Severus' Parthian war (*AE* 1984, 917 and 918).

Downstream from Zeugma, men of *IIII Scythica* were prominent in the Romans' Middle Euphrates outpost of Dura-Europos in the first half of the 3rd century AD, with a senior centurion of the legion commanding a mixed garrison in the fortified city. Its soldiers, with men of *III Cyrenaica*, helped to build a small amphitheatre in 216 (*AE* 1937, 239), probably used for entertainment and training of the soldiers there. With men of *XVI Flavia Firma*, they also built a Mithraeum (*AE* 1956, 222), whose inscriptions and graffiti suggest the congregation was largely, or entirely, composed of soldiers. Graffiti from Dura suggest some soldiers of *IIII Scythica* were billeted in the homes of private citizens, a practice widely attested in legal and other sources.

Above Reliefs from the Mithraeum at Dura-Europos, depicting Mithras slaying the bull, the central image of Mithraism (Yale University Art Gallery). The religion's masculine character and emphasis on service and progression appealed to soldiers, and membership of a Mithraic community perhaps enhanced the local and private solidarity of army units.

Below A soldier's graffito inscription from inside the Palmyrene gate at Dura-Europos. It commemorates Euphratas, one of the *beneficiarii* who policed the main entrance to the city.

Rock-cut relief (Naqs-i-Rustam, Iran) with Shapur I victorious over Valerian (standing), captured after his defeat near Edessa, AD 260. The kneeling figure may be Philip the Arab, who came to terms with Shapur after Gordian III's death in AD 244.

The Later History of *IIII Scythica*

Like *III Gallica*, *IIII Scythica* was involved in unrest in the reign of Elagabalus (218–22). After Macrinus was defeated, his son Diadumenianus attempted to escape to the Parthians, but was captured by a centurion at Zeugma, presumably a member of *IIII Scythica*, and killed (Cassius Dio 79.40). Dio (80.7) relates rather cryptically that Gellius Maximus, legate of the Fourth, was executed for conspiracy against Elagalabus in 219. The legion's name was erased in disgrace from a few inscriptions at this time, but not to the same extent as those of *III Gallica*.

Participation of *IIII Scythica* in Caracalla's Parthian war of 216–17 seems probable, and, like other legions at this time, it bore the title *Antoniniana*, derived from the emperor's full name. Its involvement in Severus Alexander's Persian war in 231–33, against the newly established Sasanian dynasty, is better documented: the legion's commander was killed at Dura-Europos (*AE* 1956, 222) in the course of that conflict. The outcome of this campaign, against King Ardashir I, is unclear. However, Ardashir's son Shapur I won a decisive victory over the Romans at Barbalissus in Syria in 252. *IIII Scythica* undoubtedly fought in this battle, and its base, on whose coins its emblem appears as late as 249, is listed among the cities captured by the Persians in their rock-cut victory inscription at Naqs-i-Rustam in Iran.

IIII Scythica probably also formed part of the emperor Valerian's army, defeated near Edessa in 260. We know little about *IIII Scythica*'s subsequent history until the later 4th century AD, when it was listed in the *Notitia Dignitatum* at a new base at Oresa (Tayibeh), further southeast in Syria.

XVI Flavia Firma

XVI Flavia Firma was established in AD 70 by the emperor Vespasian to replace the disloyal *XVI Gallica*, disbanded after Civilis' revolt of AD 69 (see *XVI Gallica* whose lion symbol, associated with Jupiter, *XVI Flavia Firma* may have inherited). The new Flavian legion spent its entire lifetime on the eastern frontier of the Roman empire, initially at Satala in Cappadocia (Sadak, Turkey – see page 168) and then at Samosata (Samsat, Turkey) in Commagene on the Euphrates. Originally Commagene was an allied kingdom, annexed to the province of Syria initially by Tiberius in AD 17, and again by Vespasian in AD 72 (see pages 152–53), after Caligula had restored the local monarchy. *XVI Flavia Firma* was the northernmost of the Syrian legions and, like *IIII Scythica* and the Cappadocian legions, it guarded an important crossing of the Euphrates. Its activities, however, are less well documented than those of other eastern legions.

XVI Flavia Firma served in the East from soon after its establishment. Important evidence for this is provided by an inscription from near Antioch (*AE* 1983, 927). It lists work parties of the eastern legions and other military units from the region engaged in construction of a canal. Imperial titles date it securely to AD 75 and it shows *XVI Flavia Firma* was an established part of the eastern frontier garrison within five years of its creation. The Sixteenth Legion was initially sent to Satala in Cappadocia along with *XII Fulminata* when Vespasian established its legionary garrison in the AD 70s (Suetonius, *Vespasian* 8). It probably moved to Samosata in the reign of Hadrian.

XVI Flavia Firma

Cognomen	*Flavia Firma*
Emblem	Lion?
Main base	Samosata (Samsat in Turkey)
Major campaigns	Trajan's Parthian war (AD 113–17); most or all eastern civil wars and Parthian/Sasanian wars of the 2nd and 3rd centuries

***XVI Flavia Firma* in War and Peace**

The legion probably participated, in full strength or as a vexillation, in some or all of the Persian wars of the 2nd and 3rd centuries. However, the only one for which firm evidence survives is Trajan's (113–17), since a centurion of the legion was decorated by the emperor for bravery at that time (*ILS* 2660). A vexillation of the Sixteenth Legion reconstructed (with men of *IIII Scythica*) the Mithraeum at Dura-Europos in *c.* 210 (*AE* 1940, 220), and so probably fought in Caracalla's Parthian campaign (216–17). Like other Syrian

Roman road at Tall 'Aqibrin, Syria, between Antioch and Cyrrhus. Inscriptions emphasize the work of the eastern legions in construction and maintenance of infrastructure like roads, bridges, canals and port facilities.

legions, *XVI Flavia Firma* must have participated in all or most of the eastern civil wars and foreign wars of the 2nd and 3rd centuries, particularly the dramatic events of the mid-3rd century, but little evidence survives. However, the legion remained in Syria, as the *Notitia Dignitatum* lists its fortress as Sura, in the Euphrates valley in the late 4th century AD.

Most of what we know of the Sixteenth's activities relate to construction and policing duties. Besides its work at Antioch in AD 75, the legion participated in sporadic harbour maintainance and improvement work at Seleucia Pieria, the port of Antioch – a joint detachment with *IIII Scythica* is attested in the reign of Antoninus Pius, for example (*ILS* 9115). Inscriptions also show that Volusius Maximus, a centurion of the legion, oversaw reconstruction of a road through the Barada gorge, northwest of Damascus, during the joint reign of Marcus Aurelius and Lucius Verus. One text (*CIL* 3, 199; the legion is identified in 200 and 201) recounts that the road had been torn up by the force of the river, and the reconstruction entailed quarrying into the mountainside. Closer to the legion's base at Samosata, its commander oversaw reconstruction of a bridge over the river Chabinas (pictured below).

Samosata was the royal capital of Commagene, and its once-prominent tell (an artificial mound of debris created by long-term habitation; pictured here, but flooded in 1989) attested to centuries of earlier occupation.

The Fortress at Samosata

Samosata was already a substantial urban community when *XVI Flavia Firma* arrived there. Its importance was, in great part, brought about by its location at a crossing point on the Euphrates. Samosata was an important Roman and Byzantine city and was excavated in the 1970s prior to flooding caused by a dam construction project, but this shed little light on the Roman military presence beyond the few stamped tiles of the Sixteenth Legion and an inscribed dedication to Jupiter naming the legion (*CIL* 3, 13609) that were already known.

The fortress may have been on low ground below the tell. The earliest firmly dated evidence of *XVI Flavia Firma* there comes from the 2nd century AD, including Ptolemy's *Geography* (5.14.8) and an inscription from Rome (*CIL* 6, 1409) referring to Lucius Fabius Cilo as legate of that legion 'at Samosata'. Cilo was consul in 193 and probably commanded the Sixteenth Legion *c.* 180.

Like other Syrian legions (see *III Gallica*, pages 136–37), *XVI Flavia Firma* sent centurions to oversee movements and protect travellers and local communities in the border country of southern Syria and northern Arabia, where bandits were a regular problem. One such centurion, Petusius Eudemus, is attested in a series of inscriptions dating to 176–78. Two come from the village of Phaena in Trachonitis:

> The people of Phaena (honour) Petusius Eudemus, centurion of legion *XVI Flavia Firma*
> *IGR* 3, 1122

> Rusticus, son of Sopater, from Phaena, honours his friend and benefactor Petusius Eudemus centurion of legion *XVI Flavia Firma*
> *IGR* 3, 1123

These demonstrate how important and powerful Roman legionary centurions might be in a small community. They probably performed a similar function to village centurions in Roman Egypt (see *II Traiana*, pages 128–29).

Army personnel must have passed through this region regularly, since another inscription from Phaena (*IGR* 3, 1119) shows that the community had built a guest house for travellers to avoid the disruption of having soldiers and officials billeted in private houses. Inscriptions from Anatolia suggest that detachments of *XVI Flavia Firma* performed policing duties there too (with *XII Fulminata*, see page 164, and *XV Apollinaris*, see page 168).

We have little information about the legion's activities in following centuries, but undoubtedly it was involved in other wars on the eastern frontier like other Syrian legions. The *Notitia Dignitatum* shows it was based at Sura on the Euphrates by *c.* 395.

XVI Flavia Firma constructed a bridge 'from the ground up, restoring the crossing' of the Samosata to Melitene road. This project was completed in 204 (*CIL* 3, 6710) and the bridge, the Cendere Köprüsü, still stands in the Adiyaman province of Turkey.

The Legions of Judaea

Judaea came under Roman control in 63 BC, but was ruled by a sequence of 'client kings' who depended on Roman support until AD 6. Subsequently, it was the Roman province of Judaea, ruled directly by a Roman governor, until 135, when, after the Second Jewish Revolt, it became Syria-Palaestina. The governor was based in the coastal city of Caesarea, but Judaea did not have a regular legionary garrison until AD 70. The Syrian legions were used to support Roman authority and their royal appointees, as after the death of Herod the Great in 4 BC. *X Fretensis* was established at Jerusalem after the First Jewish Revolt, and a second legion was added *c.* 117. Initally, this was probably *II Traiana*, but *VI Ferrata* was soon established at Caparcotna (Lejjun) as the second long-term legion in the province.

The main challenges to Roman authority in Judaea were internal. Religion and a strong nationalist ideology motivated considerable resistance, most notably in the First Jewish Revolt ('The Great Revolt') of AD 66–70 and the Second ('Bar-Kochva') Revolt of 132–35. The first revolt arose from tensions between Roman authorities, Jewish elites and radical nationalists. The initial Roman response commanded by Cestius Gallus (governor of Syria) included *XII Fulminata* and vexillations of *IIII Scythica* and *VI Ferrata*. Cestius was replaced by Vespasian and his son Titus, who ended the revolt after his father's accession to the imperial throne in AD 69. The revolt culminated in the siege and destruction of Jerusalem and the establishment of a legionary base there.

This bronze *sestertius* coin (AD 71) of Vespasian, with the legend *IVDEA CAPTA* ('Judaea Captured') commemorates the defeat of the First Jewish Revolt. It depicts a bound male captive and a mourning female (symbolizing Judaea or Jerusalem) under a palm tree.

The causes and events of the Second Jewish Revolt are less well documented, but Roman writers suggest that this ferocious conflict was provoked by the emperor Hadrian. *X Fretensis*, as the garrison of Jerusalem, was surely involved, and no doubt *VI Ferrata* was already in Judaea at the time of the revolt. There is also evidence that legions, or vexillations, from outside Judaea were engaged, including *III Cyrenaica*, *II Traiana* and *III Gallica* from the east, and *X Gemina*, *V Macedonica* and *XI Claudia* from further west. Some scholars believe that *XXII Deiotariana* (from Egypt) and possibly even *IX Hispana* (last known in Britain) were destroyed or otherwise disbanded during this revolt. Its end marked the demise of Judaea as a substantially Jewish province and was an important turning point in the Jewish diaspora, as much of the surviving Jewish population dispersed into exile throughout the Roman and Parthian empires.

X Fretensis

The Tenth Legion came into being during Octavian's rise to power, over a century before it was stationed in Jerusalem. Its title *Fretensis* (from *fretum*, 'strait') clearly commemorates a victory in the Strait of Messina during Octavian's campaigns of 42–36 BC to unseat Sextus Pompey, son of Pompey the Great, who had established an independent power base in Sicily after his father's defeat by Julius Caesar. After Octavian and Antony defeated Caesar's assassins at Philippi in 42 BC, Sextus' fleet raided the coast of Italy and blockaded the grain supply of Rome, causing political unrest. Initially failing to capture the island, in 36 BC Octavian, with Lepidus and Agrippa, launched a three-pronged amphibious assault. Agrippa's fleet defeated Sextus at Naulochus and Sextus fled to Asia Minor, where he was killed by one of Mark Antony's lieutenants.

The legion's title and the galley used as a symbol of the legion suggests its men served on board ship as marines, probably at Naulochus. Appian (*Civil War* 5.118; 120) describes how Agrippa countered the faster ships and skilful sailors of Sextus' fleet by inventing a new device to grapple the ships and hold them together, so marines could board and capture the enemy vessels. The use of a dolphin emblem may relate to the Actium campaign in which men of *X Fretensis* may again have served as marines. Dolphins were associated with Apollo, to whose help Octavian credited his victory. A little later and a little further east, an inscription from the Strymon valley in Macedonia shows the legion building a bridge there in Augustus' reign and *X Fretensis* may have fought against the Scordisci (on the borders of Macedonia) and the Sarmatians (from Ukraine) whom Cassius Dio (54.20) describes as threats to Roman power in Macedonia and Thrace *c.* 15 BC.

In AD 17–18 *X Fretensis* was in winter quarters at Cyrrhus in Syria (Tacitus, *Annals* 2.57.2).

X Fretensis

Cognomen	*Fretensis*
Emblems	Boar; bull; dolphin; ship
Main base	Jerusalem
Major campaigns	Octavian's campaign in Sicily against Sextus Pompey, including Naulochus (36 BC); Actium? (Octavian's side, 31 BC); Macedonia/Thrace? (*c.* 15 BC); Corbulo's Parthian war (including sack of Artaxata, vexillation, AD 59); First Jewish Revolt (Judaea, AD 66–70: vexillation with Cestius Gallus, AD 66; Galilee campaign, AD 67; siege of Jerusalem, AD 70; Masada, AD 72–73); Trajan's Parthian war (vexillation?, 113–17); Second Jewish Revolt (132–35); Marcus Aurelius' Marcommanic wars (vexillation, 166–80); Niger's civil war against Severus (193–94); Valerian's campaign against Shapur I? (260)

Subsequently, it may have guarded the Euphrates crossing point at Zeugma (see page 140). Minucius Rufus, commander of *X Fretensis*, set up an inscription (*AE* 1933, 204) at the oasis city of Palmyra, honouring the imperial family, including Tiberius' nephew Germanicus – who was on a diplomatic mission in AD 18–19 and visited Palmyra, so the legate may have been in his entourage, with an escort provided by the legion. *X Fretensis* later served in Corbulo's campaigns, defending Syria against the Parthians in AD 55–60, and a contingent was present when Corbulo sacked the Armenian capital of Artaxata (*Annals* 13.40.3 refers to 'picked men of the Tenth') in AD 59. During the latter part of the war, *X Fretensis* remained in Syria to defend the province against Parthian attack (*Annals* 15.6.5).

The First Jewish Revolt

X Fretensis contributed a vexillation of 2,000 men to the disastrous expedition of Cestius Gallus in AD 66 (see page 163), then the whole legion joined the army assembled by Vespasian at the coastal city of Ptolemais (Akko/Acre) in winter AD 66–67 (Josephus, *Jewish War* 3.65). It served in his invasion force for Galilee in the following year. There was a lull in the fighting between AD 67 and 70 as the Romans prepared for an attack on Jerusalem itself, and Vespasian was distracted by his bid for the imperial throne in AD 69. Road construction formed part of the logistical build-up, and a milestone of AD 69/70 (*AE* 1977, 829) shows men of *X Fretensis* building a road between Caesarea and the important town of Scythopolis (Beit She'an). This also reveals that the legion's commander was Marcus Ulpius Traianus, father of the future emperor Trajan.

X Fretensis participated in the siege of Jerusalem that formed the climax to the revolt in AD 70. Josephus describes how the legion advanced from Jericho, encamping on the Mount of Olives, northeast of the city. An early sortie by the city's defenders nearly routed *X Fretensis* and even Titus' personal intervention initially failed to halt their flight – but eventually they rallied and defeated the sortie.

The Romans constructed siege towers and attacked the walls on the north side of the city, but again the defenders sortied to destroy the siege machines of *X Fretensis* and *XV Apollinaris.* They set fire to them and held off Roman troops who attempted to put out the blaze. Many Roman troops panicked and ran, only stopping when they reached their camps (Josephus, *Jewish War* 5.473–90).

Once more, Titus rallied the shaky troops and the situation stabilized. After these setbacks, he decided to enclose and blockade Jerusalem completely within a wall. Josephus describes how the legions and their individual cohorts competed to complete their stretch of this circuit. They stripped the area of timber to construct new siege towers, renewed their attack on the walls and eventually (in mid-May, AD 70) breached the outer wall. Even then they faced inner walls, and ferocious fighting continued for nearly four months, before they captured and destroyed the fortress of Antonia, then the Temple, located in its own strongly fortified enclosure. Even then, the Romans were forced to assault another, final, refuge for the rebels in the Upper City, while most of what the Romans already occupied burned, and its population was massacred or enslaved.

Reconstruction of the culmination of the siege of Jerusalem in AD 70: the assault on the Temple complex. Contemporary sources claim that Titus wished to preserve the Temple, but fires spread during the Roman assault and it was destroyed.

The Siege of Masada

X Fretensis also played a central role in the final act of the Revolt. Even after the fall of Jerusalem, the fortress of Masada, by the Dead Sea some 30 miles (48 km) to the south, remained occupied by violently anti-Roman Zealot *sicarii* ('knife-men') commanded by Eleazar ben Yair. Masada is a spectacular natural fortress on a hilltop some 1,200 ft (366 m) high, surrounded on all sides by steep cliffs. The natural defences were reinforced by Herod the Great in the 30s BC as a refuge in case of rebellion against his rule. The new Roman governor of Judaea, Lucius Flavius Silva, led an army of *X Fretensis* and auxiliary troops against Masada in AD 72.

As Josephus (*Jewish War* 7.275; 304–7) records, the Romans encircled the site with an enclosing wall backed up by a series of camps. Then, continuing its remarkable feat of engineering, the Roman army constructed a huge ramp on the west side of the hill, apparently using a natural rocky spur as a base, until it was high enough to bring a siege tower up to the level of the fortress wall to clear it of defenders while it was breached with a battering ram. Even then the Romans could not capture Masada immediately, as the defenders constructed a shock-absorbing earth and wood rampart behind the wall, and the Romans had to destroy it by fire. When they finally captured the fortress (in April AD 73 according to Josephus, although archaeological evidence suggests it may have been the following year), they found that the defenders had killed their families and committed suicide.

> The Romans, expecting further combat, armed themselves before dawn and, bridging the approaches from their earthworks with gangways, they launched an assault. But they saw not a single enemy and there was a terrible solitude everywhere, and flames, and silence.
>
> Josephus, *Jewish War* 7.402–3

Eight Roman camps around Masada have been identified from the air and on the ground, including this example. Probably *X Fretensis* was divided between the two larger examples, while the smaller ones were occupied by auxiliaries.

X Fretensis Policing Jerusalem and Judaea

Besides a detachment left to occupy Masada, *X Fretensis* returned to Jerusalem to become its legionary garrison. The exact location of its fortress within Jerusalem is still unknown, although remains of a brick and tile production facility operated by the legion, producing material stamped with the legion's number, were excavated on Giv'at Ram Hill. Clearly the primary role of *X Fretensis* during this period was internal security. Besides garrisoning Jerusalem itself (the religious and symbolic centre of resistance to Roman occupation), inscriptions show that it policed road routes and communications centres throughout the province. Soldiers of the legion may have been based at Caesarea and vexillations contributed to construction or repair of an aqueduct (the 'high level aqueduct') there in the reign of Hadrian. Five short inscriptions attest to the participation of *X Fretensis* (along with other legions) in this work. In one of them (*Inscriptions of Caesarea* no. 51), the written text is surrounded by a frame depicting a dolphin and a galley, both symbols of the legion.

Judaea is unusual in that literature produced by the conquered has survived to shed light on attitudes to Roman policing. Roman-period Jewish commentaries on biblical texts often relate them to contemporary circumstances, and these and the Christian New Testament often characterize Roman soldiers as disruptive and brutal oppressors, a useful corrective to the presentation of the army as a relatively benign force promoting urban and economic development. Among the soldiers described in negative terms are *beneficiarii*, legionary soldiers detached for special duties, often policing. A funerary epitaph from Jerusalem (*CIL* 3, 14155) commemorates such a soldier:

> To the spirits of the departed. Lucius Magnius Felix, soldier of *Legion X Fretensis*, *beneficiarius* of the tribune. He served 19 years, lived for 39 years.

The Second Jewish Revolt

The Second ('Bar-Kochva') Revolt of 132–35 is much less well documented than the First Revolt, as we lack detailed narrative accounts like those of Josephus and Tacitus. *X Fretensis*, the primary legion of Judaea, must have been involved and confirmation is provided by an inscription (*CIL* 3, 7334) recording a centurion of the legion decorated by Hadrian 'on account of the Jewish War'. Ancient writers imply that Jerusalem was besieged by the Romans and, in some sense, 'destroyed' at this time. Some scholars have interpreted this to indicate that *X Fretensis* was driven out of the city, but the Romans then recaptured it, undoubtedly more easily than in AD 70, as the city's fortifications had been wrecked in the earlier revolt.

However, the emphasis in our limited ancient accounts of the war is on steady blockade and reduction of the rebels' rural strongholds. Cassius Dio (69.12–13) describes how the rebels fortified these positions, using tunnels as places of refuge. The Roman commander Julius Severus defeated the rebels above ground, then blockaded their refuges. Dio says 50 major settlements and 985

An inscription from Abu Ghosh, 13.5 km (*c.* 8 miles) from Jerusalem. It refers to a vexillation of *X Fretensis* and a road station may have been situated there to guard the nearby springs.

Veterans of *X Fretensis*

In the reign of Claudius, veterans of *X Fretensis* were settled in the colony of Ptolemais (Akko) in the very south of Roman Syria. Their presence, along with men from the other Syrian legions, is attested by legionary numbers on coins minted there. After the First Jewish Revolt, Vespasian settled 800 veterans on newly conquered territory at Emmaus, just outside Jerusalem (Josephus, *Jewish War* 7.216–17, probably modern Motza-Qaluniya; the second part of the name derives from the Latin *colonia*, 'colony').

The Colony at Aelia Capitolina

One of the causes of the Second Jewish Revolt was Hadrian's intention to establish a Roman *colonia*, a settlement of veterans, at Jerusalem, called *Colonia Aelia Capitolina*, after the emperor's family name (Aelius) and Jupiter's epithet 'Capitoline'. There are also suggestions that a temple to Jupiter was to be founded on the site of the Jewish Temple, an obvious (and perhaps intentional) slight to Judaism.

This project was advanced in the aftermath of the Second Revolt. Remaining Jews were expelled, and forbidden from entering the city. Veterans of *X Fretensis*, living alongside their legion's fortress, were the principal settlers of the new colony. This is emphasized by early coins of the colony depicting a legionary eagle and a ploughing scene symbolizing foundation of the colony, with a *vexillum* in the background. Other coins depicting two *vexilla* may imply participation in the colony by *VI Ferrata*, based at Caparcotna (Lejjun).

villages were destroyed, 580,000 people killed in battle, and many more died of hunger, disease and fire. 'Thus nearly all of Judaea was made desolate…' Dio's account of the Roman tactics seems to be borne out by discoveries in the 1950s in the 'Cave of Horrors', near the Dead Sea, containing the remains of individuals apparently blockaded in the cave by a Roman camp above.

Spoils from Jerusalem, including a menorah, depicted in a sculpted relief of the triumphal procession of AD 71, on the inner passageway of the Arch of Titus in Rome.

Sandal preserved by the dry conditions in the 'Cave of Horrors' near the Dead Sea. Its owner may have been a victim of the Roman blockade of that cave.

The Later History of *X Fretensis*

Like other legions, *X Fretensis* participated, often with vexillations, in campaigns beyond its own province. For example, a tribune called Aulus Atinius Paternus was decorated by Trajan on his Parthian expedition (113–17; *CIL* 6, 1838), implying a significant contingent of *X Fretensis* was engaged in that campaign. Probably elements of the legion participated in Lucius Verus' and Septimius Severus' Parthian wars, but there is no clear evidence. Like other eastern legions, *X Fretensis* supported Pescennius Niger in the civil war against Severus in 193 (see pages 154–55). There is some indication that some men served further afield in the 2nd–3rd centuries AD, as an inscription from Rome (*CIL* 6, 41278) shows that a senior centurion commanded a vexillation of *VI Ferrata* and *X Fretensis* in Marcus Aurelius' Marcomannic wars of 166–80. Finally, gold coins of the Gallic usurper Victorinus minted in 269 carry the legion's name. Perhaps a vexillation was sent to the West by the emperor Gallienus and had switched its allegiance (for reasons unknown) to Victorinus.

X Fretensis (like all legions) gained additional titles in the 3rd century, mostly reflecting loyalty to a particular emperor. These included *Antoniniana* (probably Caracalla, 212–17), *Severiana* (Severus Alexander, 222–35) and *Gordiana* (the Gordians, 238–44) and *Pia Felix* ('Dutiful and Fortunate'). Coins of Neapolis (modern Nablus, on the West Bank), issued in 251–53 indicate it had the status of a *colonia* and some carry emblems of *X Fretensis*, so veterans may have settled there. The rock-cut inscription at Naqs-i-Rustam (Iran) commemorating the Roman defeat near Edessa by Shapur I in 260, lists Judaea among the origins of the defeated Roman troops and *X Fretensis*, *VI Ferrata*, or both, probably provided vexillations for Valerian's army. The legion would have been caught up in the political and military chaos that followed, as well as Aurelian's reconquest in 270–72. *X Fretensis* remained at Jerusalem at least until the mid-3rd century and probably until the reign of Diocletian (284–305). Subsequently it moved south to Aila (modern Aqaba in Jordan), where it was certainly based when the *Notitia Dignitatum* was drawn up at the end of the 4th century.

VI Ferrata

Cognomen	*Ferrata*
Emblem	Romulus and Remus with the she-wolf
Main base	Caparcotna (Lejjun, near Megiddo)
Major campaigns	Caesar's Gallic and civil wars (58–45 BC); Antony's Parthian war (40–33 BC); Actium (31 BC, Antony's side); Corbulo's Parthian war (including sack of Artaxata and capture of Tigranocerta; AD 58–63); First Jewish Revolt (Judaea; vexillation with Cestius Gallus, AD 66); civil war (AD 69); campaign in Moesia (AD 69); annexation of Commagene (AD 72); Trajan's second Dacian war (vexillation, 105–6); Trajan's Parthian war (113–17); Jewish Revolt in Egypt? (115–17); Second Jewish Revolt? (Judaea, 132–35); Lucius Verus' Parthian war? (163–66); Marcus Aurelius' Marcommanic wars (vexillation, 166–80); Severus' civil war against Niger (193–94); Severus' Parthian wars? (195–97); Valerian's campaign against Shapur I (260)?

VI Ferrata

The Sixth Legion served under Julius Caesar in Gaul and the civil wars against Pompey and his supporters (see Part I). Its bravery at the battle of Dyrrhacium (modern Durrës, in Albania) in the summer of 48 BC was recorded by Caesar's later biographer, Suetonius:

> A single cohort of the Sixth Legion deployed in an advanced fort held off four of Pompey's legions for several hours, with almost every man wounded by the clouds of enemy arrows. 130,000 of these were later found within the fort's ramparts.
>
> Suetonius, *Caesar* 68

Later that year the Sixth fought at Pharsalus and, after Pompey's death, was besieged with Caesar in Alexandria (48–47 BC). Subsequently it followed Caesar to Pontus (modern northwestern Turkey), where, despite having been reduced to just 1,000 men, it contributed to Caesar's victory at Zela, fighting against Pharnaces, alongside 'imitation legionaries' of King Deiotarus of Galatia, possible antecedents of *XXII Deiotariana* (see page 123). After the battle, Caesar sent the Sixth back to Italy to receive honours and rewards.

After Caesar's assassination, the Sixth was reconstituted and undoubtedly formed part of the triumvirs' army at Philippi in 42 BC. After that battle, veterans retired and were resettled at Beneventum (Benevento) in Italy, as documented by veterans' funerary inscriptions, one with the first known use of the title *Ferrata*, 'Iron', perhaps metaphorical, or perhaps a reference to a distinctive kind of armour. *VI Ferrata* was part of Mark Antony's army in 42–31 BC, taking part in his Parthian war, and undoubtedly the Actium campaign of 31 BC. A legion described as *VI Macedonica* in a Greek inscription found at Ephesus (*ILS* 8862) may be *VI Ferrata* during its time in Antony's army, its (otherwise unknown) title perhaps a temporary one, reflecting the victory at Philippi.

War in Armenia

After Octavian's defeat of Antony, *VI Ferrata* remained in the East, in the legionary garrison of Syria. We know little about its early activities and movements, besides Tacitus' report (*Annals* 2.79.3), that it was in winter quarters near Laodicaea in AD 19, perhaps at Apamea, whose important strategic location on the Orontes and Seleucid military heritage made it an obvious site for an early Roman legionary base. *VI Ferrata* participated in Corbulo's Parthian campaigns, initially in Corbulo's own army stationed in Cappadocia, opposite Armenia.

After the winter, the army advanced into Armenia, harassed by Tiridates (the Parthian appointee to the Armenian throne) and his predominantly cavalry army. The Romans continued deep into the mountains, and destroyed the distant northern Armenian capital of Artaxata (Artashat, in the Ararat valley of in modern Armenia). Corbulo led the army back some 300 miles (480 km) to the southwest, suffering considerable hardship from lack of food, exhaustion and blazing hot summer weather (Tacitus, *Annals* 14.24). Eventually they reached the Armenian southern capital of Tigranocerta, which surrendered.

Corbulo installed the Roman appointee Tigranes VI as king, bringing the first phase of the war to a successful conclusion. However, in AD 62, war resumed, as the Parthians beseiged Tigranocerta. *VI Ferrata* stood on the defensive in Syria with Corbulo while Caesennius Paetus, the new governor of Cappadocia, advanced into Armenia with *IIII Scythica* and *XII Fulminata*, to rescue Tigranes. However, Paetus was cut off and forced to agree terms, while Corbulo led his troops, including *VI Ferrata*, north to threaten a crossing of the Euphrates at Melitene in Cappadocia. However, an armistice was signed and a compromise reached whereby Tiridates, the Parthian choice for king of Armenia, was restored on condition he swore allegiance to Nero. Thus the war ended with success and failure on both sides, but largely to the credit of *VI Ferrata*.

Revolt in Judaea and March on Rome

In the First Jewish Revolt, *VI Ferrata* provided a detachment of 2,000 men for Cestius Gallus' disastrous expedition to Jerusalem in AD 66 (see page 163). Josephus (*Jewish War* 2.19.6) records that its commander, Priscus, was killed in the retreat. Subsequently the legion remained in Syria under the new provincial governor Mucianus, while Vespasian and Titus concentrated forces at Ptolemais and then led them into Judaea.

When the eastern legions acclaimed Vespasian emperor in July AD 69, *VI Ferrata* took a leading role in the civil war that followed. While the pro-Flavian legions closest to Italy were in the Balkans, commanded by Marcus Antonius Primus, Mucianus led a force westwards from Syria consisting of *VI Ferrata* and 13,000 men drawn from other units. The Balkan legions reached Italy first and defeated Vitellius' forces at the second battle of Bedriacum, near Cremona, on 24 October AD 69, opening the road to Rome (see pages 134–35). *VI Ferrata* was delayed in Moesia on its march to Italy as it countered raiders from beyond the Danube (Tacitus, *Histories* 3.46), but Mucianus reached Rome at the very end of AD 69, a few days after Primus, and took control of the city until Vespasian arrived.

Return to the East

VI Ferrata had returned to the East by AD 72, when there were claims that Antiochus, king of Commagene (an allied kingdom in modern Turkey, north of Roman Syria,) was conspiring with the Parthians against Rome and planning a revolt. In response to these rumours (which, Josephus – *Jewish War* 7.220–21 – alleges, he started), Caesennius Paetus, now governor of

View across the Armenian plain towards Mount Ararat. Corbulo spent some time hardening and training his allegedly unwarlike force before he led it into Armenia in AD 19. Tacitus (*Annals* 13.35) records that he kept the army under canvas in a bitter cold winter, and men froze to death on sentry duty.

Syria, invaded the kingdom with *VI Ferrata* and auxiliary and allied contingents. Antiochus and his sons fled. Their kingdom was incorporated into the Roman province of Syria. Its leading city of Samosata was probably initially garrisoned by *VI Ferrata* but *XVI Flavia Firma* was stationed there in the 2nd century AD.

We know little about the legion's movements in Syria. It may have spent some time at Raphanaea (Rafniye) in the south, later the fortress of *III Gallica*, as an undated inscription (*CIL* 3, 14165) shows that Claudia, wife of a tribune of *VI Ferrata*, was buried there. A vexillation of the legion contributed to the construction of the canal near Antioch in AD 75 (*AE* 1983, 927 – see page 143).

Nor is it much easier to track *VI Ferrata* after it left Syria. It participated in Trajan's Parthian war of 113–17, apparently in full strength, as its legate was decorated for his conduct in that campaign (*AE* 1950, 66), as were a tribune (*CIL* 10, 5829) and a centurion (*CIL* 5, 955). The legion must have seen some fighting, as the tribune, Titus Pontius Sabinus, received the awards of an untipped spear and a mural crown. These were awards that were appropriate for his rank, but substantial nevertheless. Returning from that war, *VI Ferrata*, for a brief period apparently provided a legionary garrison for the new Roman province of Arabia, annexed by Trajan in 106. A fragmentary inscription of 119 from Gerasa (modern Jerash in Jordan; *AE* 1983, 937, as revised by David Kennedy and Hannah Cotton) and undated vexillation inscriptions from sites such as Gadara (modern Umm Qais in Jordan; *AE* 1995, 1577) suggest that *VI Ferrata* was dispersed throughout the province. The heavily damaged inscription from Gerasa suggests that soldiers had come from Alexandria, so they may have deployed from the eastern frontier to help suppress the Jewish Revolt in Egypt in 115–17, then sent to Arabia.

Eventually *VI Ferrata* moved to Judaea, to a fortress at Caparcotna (modern Lejjun, whose name comes from '*legio*'). When it arrived is unclear and depends on the poorly understood movements of other legions like *II Traiana*. All or part of *VI Ferrata* was already in Judaea during

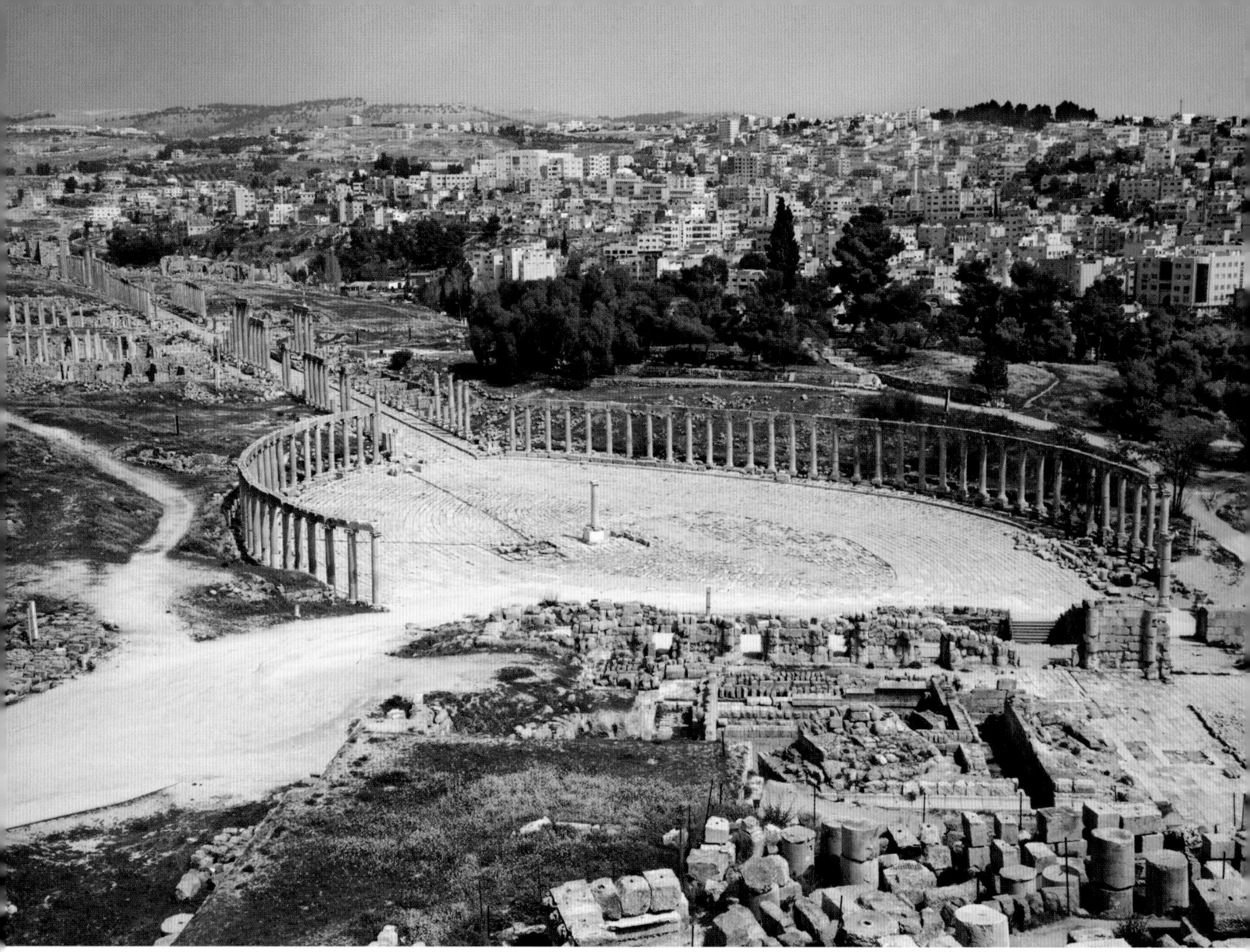

Hadrian's reign, as (like *X Fretensis*, *II Traiana* and, perhaps, *XXII Deiotariana*), it helped construct or reconstruct the 'high-level aqueduct' at Caesarea. The entire legion perhaps moved to Arabia from Judaea at about the time of the Second Jewish Revolt (132–35), but we cannot be sure exactly when, or even if, it participated in that war.

Caparcotna and *VI Ferrata* in Syria-Palaestina

The base of *VI Ferrata* at Caparcotna (Lejjun) lay in southern Galilee, close to the tell of ancient Megiddo, overlooking the Jezreel valley and important ancient routes linking the coast (and Caesarea) with important sites such as Diocaesarea (Sepphoris) and Scythopolis (Beit She'an). The legionary fortress itself has not been studied intensively archaeologically, but a recent survey by Israeli archaeologist Yotam Tepper has provided some information about its topography. Like other eastern legions, *VI Ferrata* deployed detachments to outposts within the province. Besides evidence from Caesarea, an inscription from Eleutheropolis (Bayt Jibrin; *AE* 1933, 158) near Hebron, far to the south of Caparcotna, refers to a vexillation of the legion. A brick stamp of the legion was found at Horwath Hazon, north of its base. Coins suggest that veterans of *VI Ferrata* participated in the foundation of the Claudian *colonia* of Ptolemais (Akko) and also settled at Aelia Capitolina (Jerusalem).

It seems likely that *VI Ferrata* was loyal to Severus rather than (as most eastern legions) Niger in the civil war of 193–94. A slightly later inscription (*AE* 1948, AD 145) gives it the appropriate titles *F(idelis)* and *C(onstans)* 'Loyal and Reliable'. Samaria-Sebaste, which had a vexillation of *VI Ferrata*, was promoted in status for its loyalty to Severus, while its neighbour Neapolis (modern Nablus, later, at least, associated with *X Fretensis*) was punished for supporting Niger. Possibly the civil war of

The distinctive oval forum of Gerasa in Roman Arabia (modern Jerash, Jordan). An inscription from this city suggests that a detachment of *VI Ferrata* was stationed at Gerasa in 119.

193–94 took place in microcosm in Syria-Palaestina, involving the province's two legions on different sides.

VI Ferrata Abroad

We have already seen that *VI Ferrata* fought in Trajan's Parthian war, and even earlier a detachment served under that emperor in Dacia, probably in the second Dacian war of 105–6. Inscriptions mentioning a vexillation of *VI Ferrata* have been found at the Roman colony of Sarmizegetusa (modern Gradiste), established after that war, perhaps reflecting involvement by the eastern legionaries in construction of fortifications at the new settlement. Other inscriptions (such as *CIL* 8, 10230, 145) attest to construction work by elements of the legion in the African province of Numidia.

A coin of Lucius Verus and Marcus Aurelius as joint emperors depicts the eagle and numeral of *VI Ferrata*, along with Mark Antony's name and title as triumvir. This probably commemorates the legion's participation both in Lucius Verus' Parthian war (163–66) and Antony's Parthian war almost two centuries earlier. An inscription from Rome (*CIL* 6, 41278) shows a senior centurion commanding a vexillation of *VI Ferrata* and *X Fretensis* in Marcus Aurelius' Marcomannic wars of 166–80. There is no direct evidence for the participation of *VI Ferrata* in Severus' Parthian war, although given its loyalty to Severus in the civil war of 193–94, it seems likely that a vexillation was engaged in the conflict.

VI Ferrata's most distant deployment is documented by an inscription from Farasan Island off the Red Sea coast of Saudi Arabia, referring to a vexillation of the legion (*AE* 2005, 1640), probably stationed there in connection with trade from the Roman world to Arabia and India (see pages 124, 129). The undated inscription perhaps relates to the period when elements of the legion were based in Arabia, since the Nabataean kingdom formed an important link between the Mediterranean and Arabia/India.

VI Ferrata was almost certainly engaged in the eastern frontier wars of the 3rd and perhaps 4th centuries AD. However, it is not listed in the *Notitia Dignitatum* (*c.* 395) and so probably had ceased to exist by then.

The Legion of Arabia

In 106 the Nabataean kingdom was annexed to create the Roman province of Arabia Petraea. The invasion was carried out by the Roman governor of Syria, apparently with little or no resistance. While Romans used the term 'Arabia' in a very general sense to refer to desert regions to the east, the province of Arabia was essentially modern Jordan and southern Syria, with military outposts further afield, such as in the Hejaz (in modern Saudi Arabia). The province included cities like Bostra (Bosra in modern Syria, the Roman provincial capital and legionary base), Gerasa (Jerash) and Petra (both in Jordan).

There were no major threats to its frontiers, the main security issue being relations with nomads on the eastern desert fringes. It was a wealthy area, as it played an important role in long-distance trade with the Arabian peninsula and India.

It is clear now that *III Cyrenaica*, previously based in Egypt, played an important role in its annexation, as papyrus documents show its men there in 107. When *III Cyrenaica* moved back to Egypt, it was replaced temporarily by *VI Ferrata*, part of which was at Gerasa in 119, with detachments at other locations such as Gadara. However, *VI Ferrata* moved to Judaea (Syria-Palaestina) and *III Cyrenaica* returned to Arabia, perhaps in the 130s, and remained the sole legion there for nearly two centuries.

Aerial view of *Via Nova Traiana* ('Trajan's New Road'), which was constructed linking Bostra in the north to Aqaba in the south. A Roman governor and garrison were installed in Arabia in 106.

III Cyrenaica

The name of *III Cyrenaica* suggests it originated as a legion commanded by Lucius Pinarius Scarpus, an ally of Mark Antony appointed to govern Cyrenaica (eastern Libya), at the time of the battle of Actium. After Antony was defeated, he attempted to flee to Pinarius, who refused to receive him, and killed Antony's messengers and any of his own troops reluctant to defect to Octavian (Cassius Dio 51.5.6). Pinarius' troops then came under the command of Cornelius Gallus, Octavian's subordinate, and future first prefect of Egypt. He led them to Paraetonium (Marsa Matruh) in western Egypt, where Antony unsuccessfully tried to regain their loyalty. Presumably *III Cyrenaica* was one of these legions that Gallus subsequently used to subdue Egypt, remaining there in its garrison.

III Cyrenaica

Cognomen	*Cyrenaica*
Emblem	Unknown
Main bases	Nicopolis (Alexandria, Egypt); Bostra (Roman Arabia, Bosra in modern Syria)
Major campaigns	Aelius Gallus' Arabian campaign (26–24 BC)?; P. Petronius' invasion of Nubia (*c.* 24 BC)?; Corbulo's Parthian war (vexillation, AD 63)?; First Jewish Revolt (Judaea, vexillation, AD 66–70); annexation of Arabia (106); Trajan's Parthian war (113–17); Jewish Revolt in Egypt (117); Second Jewish Revolt (Judaea, 132–35); Parthian wars of Lucius Verus and Severus? (161–66; 195–97); Niger's civil war against Severus (193–94); Gallienus' campaign against the Alamanni and Franks (vexillation?, 258–60); Valerian's campaign against Shapur I? (260); Aurelian's campaign against Palmyra (270–72)

The earliest secure reference to the legion is a Greek inscription of AD 11 (*AE* 1910, 207) referring to a tribune of the Third who was prefect of *Mons Berenice*, the mountainous areas and quarries in the Eastern Desert of Egypt. The earliest reference to it as *Cyrenaica* comes in another, slightly later, inscription (*EJ* 368) of Gaius Fabricius Tuscus, a military tribune of the legion. Undoubtedly it was one of the three legions recorded by Strabo in Egypt under Augustus, although a hypothesis that it was initially based in Upper Egypt (perhaps Thebes, modern Luxor) cannot be proved.

The early history of *III Cyrenaica* in Egypt must have paralleled that of *XXII Deiotariana* in its recruitment, duties and participation in early campaigns in the Arabian peninsula and Nubia. Both legions were stationed in the Nicopolis fortress at Alexandria. *III Cyrenaica* must have been the other legion recorded in the Coptus inscription (see page 124), and, while Gaius Sossius is a fairly common name, it is tempting to identify the legionary from Pompeiopolis (Paphlagonia, Turkey) in that inscription with the Gaius Sossius attested as an *optio* of the Third Legion in Alexandria (*CIL* 3, 659). Besides Alexandria, centurions and soldiers of *III Cyrenaica* were stationed throughout Egypt, policing rural communities, overseeing and protecting the movement of goods and people, and supervising quarrying. For example, Titus Egnatius Tiberianus set up an inscription at Acoris (Tehna, Middle Egypt), dedicated to Zeus for the wellbeing of an emperor (probably Domitian – the name was erased), describing himself as 'the man in charge of the quarry for the paving stones of Alexandria' (*IGR* 1, 1138). Another inscription with Domitian's name erased (*CIL* 3, 13580) records the centurion Gaius Iulius Magnus supervising construction of a bridge at Coptus (Qift, Upper Egypt). Like the other legions in Egypt, *III Cyrenaica* provided detachments for Roman-controlled Nubia, some of whom set up inscriptions at the temples of Pselkis (Dakka) and Talmis (Kalabsha).

***III Cyrenaica* Moves to Arabia**

The date of the legion's move to Arabia has been debated extensively, but evidence suggests it was involved in the initial annexation in 106, moving back to Egypt temporarily (it is attested there in 119) only to return to Arabia, and specifically its long-term base at Bostra, by *c.* 140. It was still at Bostra when the *Notitia Dignitatum* was compiled at the end of the 4th century AD.

The legion's first stay in Arabia is attested by a letter (*P. Mich.* 8.466) written on papyrus on 26 March 107 by a legionary *librarius* (clerk) of *III Cyrenaica* called Iulius Apollinaris. He wrote from Petra (towards the south of modern Jordan) to his father in Karanis, Egypt. His letter shows that the legion was in Arabia, part of it engaged in stone-cutting at Petra, with another cohort at Bostra, probably after helping to annex the kingdom in the previous year. It fought in Trajan's Parthian war of 113–17 and returned to Egypt, perhaps in 117 to suppress the Jewish revolt there (see page 123). At the very latest, *III Cyrenaica* was back at Nicopolis (Alexandria) on 4 August 119, alongside *XXII Deiotariana* (*BGU* I 140; see pages 125–26). The final redeployment to Arabia took place before *c.* 140–44, when coins bearing the legend *LEG III CYR* and depicting the god Jupiter Ammon, associated with *III Cyrenaica* (see box overleaf), were minted in Bostra. Ptolemy, who wrote his *Geography* at about this time, also records Bostra as a legionary base.

The Fortress at Bostra

Colonia Nova Traiana Bostra in Arabia Petraea (modern Bosra in Syria) was the base of *III Cyrenaica* from before *c.* 140 to at least 395. The only substantial known structures on the ground are the north and south gates of the fortress and a bath building on the west side. Bostra was a Nabataean town at the time of annexation, and developed into a Roman city that served as provincial capital. Today Bosra is a UNESCO World Heritage Site, best known for its spectacular Roman theatre.

Much of what we know about the legion and legionaries based at Bostra derives from inscriptions, a number of which survive from the site. Most legionaries were recruited in the eastern provinces, and increasingly from Arabia itself the longer the legion was based at Bostra.

> To the Spirits of the Departed. To Lucius Valerius Bessus, Bithynian by nation, a soldier of Legion *III Cyrenaica*. He lived for 38 years and served for 21 years. His heir made this monument for him.
>
> *CIL* 3, 104

As always, centurions came from a wider geographical area, and had a career structure that saw them move from legion to legion across the empire:

> Titus Quintius Petrullus, a centurion of Legion *III Cyrenaica*, whose homeland was Britannia. He lived for 30 years.
>
> *IGLS* 13.1, 9188

As we have seen (pages 124–26), ordinary serving soldiers could not contract legal marriages (before Severus, at least), but created informal marriages and family networks, undoubtedly one reason for the development of the civilian community of Bostra alongside the fortress. Centurions and other officers, however, could marry even while they were serving.

The Roman theatre at Bostra. The legionary fortress has not been excavated, but aerial photographs show a rectangular enclosure of 16.8 ha (41.5 acres) on the north side of the Roman town, and brick stamps and inscriptions of the legion have been found in the area.

> Sacred to the Spirits of the Departed. To Marcus Ulpius Propinquus, centurion of *Legion III Cyrenaica, hastatus prior* of the 7th cohort. He lived for 42 years. Rufonia Avitilla made [this monument] for her most dutiful husband.
>
> *IGLS* 13.1, 9198

Besides serving soldiers, retired veterans of *III Cyrenaica* were also at Bostra, reflecting their local origins and desire to maintain social networks created during their service. Collective inscriptions were set up by groups of veterans on discharge from the army, like these men who were recruited in 136 and discharged in 161, the first year of the joint reign of Lucius Verus and Marcus Aurelius:

> (Dedicated) to the Emperor Caesar Lucius Aurelius Verus Augustus by the veterans of the Legion *III Cyrenaica* who began their military service in the consulship of Commodus and Pompeianus and Lucius Aelius Caesar (for the second time).
>
> *AE* 1973, 533

Some veterans died at Bostra, commemorated by inscribed funerary monuments. Others settled in the small towns and villages of Arabia and southern Syria. In addition, coins of Neapolis (modern Nablus, on the West Bank), minted in 251–53 describe it as a *colonia* at that time, some bearing emblems of *III Cyrenaica*. Veterans of the legion may have settled there too, alongside men from *X Fretensis*, also named on the coins.

Policing Arabia

As in Egypt, *III Cyrenaica* performed internal security functions in Arabia, in its urban centres and desert fringes. We see evidence of legionary detachments in the core towns of Petra and Gerasa (Jerash), and inscriptions naming soldiers of *III Cyrenaica* from those places, as well as from Philadelphia (Amman in Jordan), suggest that this practice continued. We also find outposts established in two principal directions, to the east and to the south. The south was important because of trade routes leading to the Red Sea ports and towards the interior of modern Saudi Arabia and Yemen, a source of luxury goods such as myrrh. There was a Roman fort of Trajanic date at the Nabataean settlement of Hawara (Humayma) between Petra and Aqaba, and an inscription records a vexillation of *III Cyrenaica* there, probably towards the middle of the 3rd century AD:

***III Cyrenaica*, Bostra and Jupiter Ammon**

'Ulpius Taurinus, Chief Clerk to the Legate, discharged his vow to Jupiter, the Best and Greatest, (in his guise as) Holy Ammon, Divine Spirit ('*Genius*' of the Legion).' (*IGLS* 13.1, 9010)

This inscription from Bostra highlights the close ties between the town, its legion and Jupiter (Zeus) identified with Ammon, a manifestation of the Egyptian sun god Amun-Ra, whose sanctuary at Siwa on the Libyan–Egyptian border was an important oracular centre. Ammon was identified with the Greek god Zeus (and Roman Jupiter) by Greek colonists from nearby Cyrene. Given the Third Legion's origins in Cyrenaica (the territory of Cyrene) and its long service in Egypt, it is unsurprising that it became linked with the god. When *III Cyrenaica* moved to Arabia, it continued an association with Jupiter Ammon.

The legion's importance to Bostra is demonstrated by its adoption of Ammon as a patron and symbol, and the fact that he had an important temple there. We know little about the temple, but we do know that when the Palmyrenes captured the town in 268–70 they sacked it, since an inscription (*AE* 1947, 165) records the subsequent restoration of its silver statues and iron doors.

Denarius *(31 BC) of L. Pinarius Scarpus, Mark Antony's subordinate in Cyrenaica. Besides a winged victory, it depicts Ammon as a bearded man with ram's horns.*

> For the wellbeing of the emperors. The vexillation of Legion *III Cyrenaica*, Fortunate, made an offering to Jupiter Ammon (here) at Hawara with Julius Priscus.
>
> *AE* 2002, 1572

We have seen other evidence of Roman interest in the Red Sea and its trade routes, including installations built by legionaries in Egypt's Eastern Desert, linking the Nile to ports on the Egyptian (eastern) shore of that sea, and also legionary vexillations on Farasan Island (see pages 124, 129 and 155), far to the south, off the west coast of Saudi Arabia.

A Roman-period manual for merchants in the Red Sea records a centurion and soldiers collecting 25 per cent tax on incoming goods at a Nabataean Red Sea port called Leuke Kome ('the White Village'). Scholars have disputed whether these were Roman troops or Nabataeans borrowing Roman military terminology. We have some evidence of *III Cyrenaica* from the mouth of the Gulf of Aqaba (Eilat) that connects into the Red Sea proper (an inscription naming a legionary and his centurion, for example – *AE* 1972, 671), and perhaps there was a regular legionary presence there. However, the activities of *III Cyrenaica* also extended inland and much further (nearly 400 km, *c.* 249 miles) to the southeast, into the part of Saudi Arabia known as the Hejaz. In antiquity, this was occupied by the Thamudic Arab confederation, who recognized Roman authority after the creation of the province of Arabia. A Roman military presence can be seen, for example, at the Nabataean town of Hegra (modern Madā'in Ṣāliḥ in Saudi Arabia). A Latin inscription found there records personnel of *III Cyrenaica* rebuilding the town walls in 175–77 (*AE* 2004, 1620) and another (AE 1974, 662) is a dedication to the *Tyche* ('Good Fortune') of Bostra by a man called Hadrian, describing himself as a 'painter with the Legion *III Cyrenaica*'.

Roman military presence also extended out into the Arabian desert to the east, particularly from the Severan period, echoing the similar expansion undertaken by *III Augusta* and its auxiliaries in Africa. The focus of the army's activity in this area was the Azraq Oasis, about 90 km (56 miles) east of Amman, in eastern Jordan. Besides a Roman fort at Azraq itself, and Roman milestones from the area, inscriptions from nearby Qasr el'Uweinid record that a vexillation of *III Cyrenaica* built a fort with headquarters building and a bath there in 201 (*AE* 2001, 1978). Again, the military

Nabataean rock-cut tombs at the town of Hegra (modern Madā'in Ṣāliḥ in Saudi Arabia). Probably soldiers deployed to this area were responsible for observing the activities of nomads and maintaining the security of the settled population (like the people of Hegra) and of travellers and traders.

The fort at Qasr el'Uweinid near the Azraq Oasis, an outpost of *III Cyrenaica*.

presence was in great part intended to watch over and police nomadic populations in the area and protect the settled population. However, the Azraq Oasis lies at the north end of the Wadi Sirhan, another overland route for trade and travel to the centre of the Arabian peninsula. Roman observation and policing of travellers on this route is attested by an inscription from Jauf/Al Jawf at the south end of the Wadi Sirhan, some 370 km (230 miles) to the southeast. There, Flavius Dionysius, a centurion of *III Cyrenaica*, probably commanding a detachment policing the southern end of the wadi, set up an inscription for the wellbeing of 'our emperors' (presumably Septimius Severus and Caracalla) to the gods Jupiter Ammon and Sulmus Sanctus (*AE* 2001, 1979).

***III Cyrenaica* Abroad**

Most activities of *III Cyrenaica* beyond Egypt and Arabia were focused in the East. Vexillations from Egypt were in Corbulo's army in AD 63 (Tacitus, *Annals* 15.26), and *III Cyrenaica* provided men for the 2,000-man detachment of the Egyptian legions that served in Judaea under Titus in AD 70 (Tacitus, *Histories* 5.1; Josephus, *Jewish War* 5.44; 6.236). The legion moved around a great deal between 106 and *c.* 140. Besides its transfer to Arabia, back to Egypt and then back to Arabia. It participated in Trajan's Parthian war of 113–17, during which (115–16) it set up a victory arch at Dura-Europos in the Middle Euphrates valley. Vexillations of *III Cyrenaica* were deployed to Dura later too, and one built the amphitheatre there in 216, with *IIII Scythica.*

After Trajan's Parthian war, a vexillation was stationed in Jerusalem, where it made a dedication to Jupiter Serapis in thanks for the wellbeing and victory of Trajan (*ILS* 4393). These men may have been returning from the Euphrates to Egypt when the Jewish revolt in Cyrene and Egypt broke out. It made sense to leave men in Jerusalem to ensure the revolt did not spread to Judaea itself, while the rest returned to suppress the uprising in Egypt. In (probably) 123, elements of *III Cyrenaica* joined men of *II Traiana* for a temporary deployment on the Euphrates under the senior centurion Claudius Quartinus (*CIL* 13, 1802), to deal with a threat from the Parthians that, ultimately, came to nothing.

Gaius Popilius, a senatorial tribune of *III Cyrenaica*, was decorated by Hadrian for his conduct in the Second Jewish Revolt of 132–35, and the whole legion may have been engaged in that campaign. There is also evidence (*ILS* 1058) that Haterius Nepos, probably its commander at the time, was

awarded triumphal *ornamenta*, an honour in place of a triumph (which was reserved for the emperor) implying his involvement in a major victory. We don't know very much about the legion's involvement in other foreign and civil wars of the 2nd century, but it probably took part in some or all of those conflicts. Given the continuing presence of detachments of *III Cyrenaica* at Dura-Europos, it is likely to have sent vexillations for Lucius Verus' and Severus' Parthian wars (161–66 and 195–97), and also to have supported Avidius Cassius and Pescennius Niger in their bids for the imperial throne.

The inscription at Naqs-i-Rustam (Iran) commemorating Shapur I's victory over Valerian near Edessa in 260, lists Arabia among the origins of the defeated troops, perhaps a reference to men of *III Cyrenaica*. After Shapur I's victory, the kingdom of Palmyra initially defended the Roman eastern provinces, driving the Persians back. Subsequently the rulers of Palmyra carved out an empire for themselves in the East, and, as we have seen sacked Bostra and its temple to Jupiter Ammon. However, *III Cyrenaica* may have got its revenge: in 272–73 the emperor Aurelian reconquered the territories overrun by the Palmyrenes and captured Palmyra itself. A letter quoted in his later (rather unreliable) biography (*SHA Aurelian* 31.7) refers to the sacking of the Temple of the Sun at Palmyra by standard-bearers and trumpeters of the 'Third Legion'. This may have been *III Gallica*, based close to Palmyra, but it would have been particularly appropriate for *III Cyrenaica* to avenge the sack of their god's temple by sacking that of Palmyra's equivalent deity.

Like most legions, we know little of the history of *III Cyrenaica* from the 3rd century AD onwards. Besides the evidence of the legion's involvement in the wars against Shapur and Zenobia of Palmyra, an inscription from Iversheim (near Bonn; *AE* 1968, 392) in Lower Germany, naming a soldier of *III Cyrenaica*, may attest to the presence of a vexillation for Gallienus' campaign in 258–60 against the Alamanni and Franks. However, the *Notitia Dignitatum* indicates that Bostra was still the legion's fortress in the late 4th century AD.

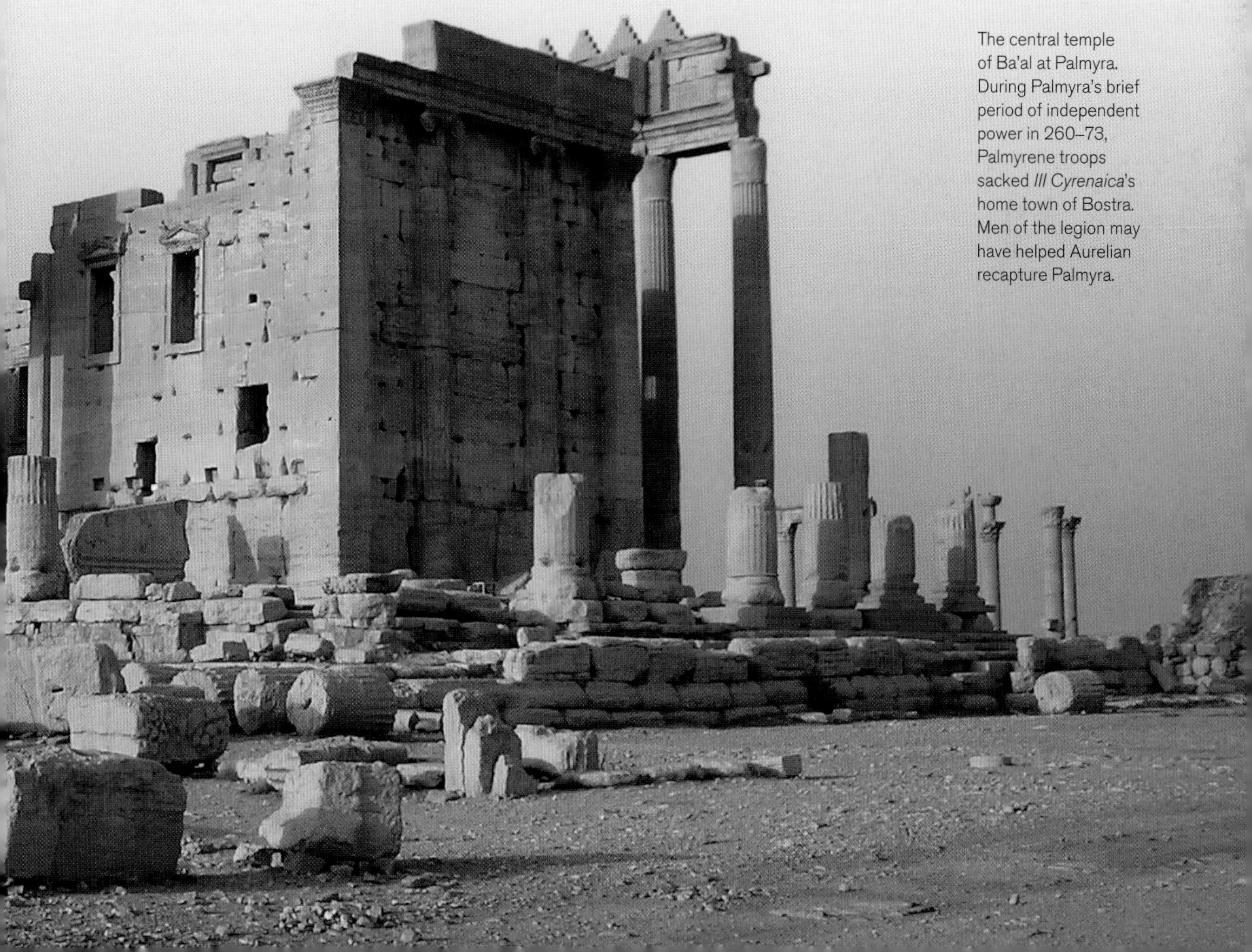

The central temple of Ba'al at Palmyra. During Palmyra's brief period of independent power in 260–73, Palmyrene troops sacked *III Cyrenaica*'s home town of Bostra. Men of the legion may have helped Aurelian recapture Palmyra.

The Legions of Cappadocia

Cappadocia lies in modern Turkey, in east-central Anatolia, and contains important crossing points over the Euphrates river to the east. It was an independent kingdom, ruled by the Roman appointee Archelaus, whose place was established by Mark Antony and confirmed by Augustus. He was deposed in AD 17 by Tiberius, who made the region a Roman province governed, initially, by an equestrian prefect. Corbulo's Armenian and Parthian wars of AD 58–63 emphasized the importance of the province as a Roman base for influencing and even invading Armenia. For example, Corbulo concentrated his army at Melitene, later the base of *XII Fulminata*, in preparation for an advance into Armenia after the defeat of Caesennius Paetus in AD 62.

Subsequently, Vespasian established a legionary garrison (probably of *XII Fulminata* and *XVI Flavia Firma*) and installed a high-status imperial legate of consular rank. The 2nd-century legionary garrison consisted of *XII Fulminata* at Melitene on the Euphrates and *XV Apollinaris* in its fortress at Satala. The province's importance lay not only in its proximity to Armenia and zones of Parthian control, but also to the Black Sea and Caucasus, where there was Roman military interest and activity.

XII Fulminata

Cognomen	*Fulminata* (Greek *Keraunophoros*, 'Lightning-Bearer')
Emblem	Thunderbolt
Main bases	Melitene on the Euphrates (Malatya, Turkey)
Major campaigns	Perusia (41 BC – as *XII Victrix*?); Caesennius Paetus' Armenian campaign (AD 62); First Jewish Revolt (Gallus' attack on Jerusalem, AD 66; siege of Jerusalem, AD 70); Second Jewish Revolt (vexillation?, 132–35); Arrian's campaign aganist the Alans? (vexillation, 135); Parthian wars of 2nd–3rd centuries, including Lucius Verus'? (Armenia, 161–66); Marcus Aurelius' Marcomannic wars? (vexillation, 166–80); against Shapur I's invasion? (252)

XII Fulminata

XII Fulminata probably originated as Julius Caesar's Twelfth Legion, recruited in 58 BC for his campaign against the Helvetii, a Celtic tribe that attempted to migrate west from their homeland in modern Switzerland. Legions numbered *XII* are attested sporadically before Augustus' reign, with a variety of *cognomina* – *Victrix*, *Paterna* and *Antiqua*. However, these may all have their origins in the same Caesarian legion. A Twelfth Legion fought in Octavian's army at the siege of Perusia (modern Perugia) in Italy in 41 BC, its numeral appearing on sling bullets from the battle. One includes the title *victrix*, 'victorious', implying an older legion with a successful past: it seems likely that the Twelfth was re-established by Octavian from a cadre of Caesar's veterans. Mark Antony's legionary coin series includes a *XII Antiqua* 'the Old Twelfth', implying a legion with a long history, perhaps Caesar's Twelfth, reconstituted by Antony or, perhaps, by Lepidus, with a cadre of Caesarian veterans, and passed to Antony. *Paterna*, attested in an early Augustan inscription of a veteran of *XII* settled at Parma (*ILS* 2242), probably derives from Caesar's title *pater patriae* – 'Father of his Country' (Suetonius, *Caesar* 76.1; Augustus also held this title but not before 2 BC).

Fulminata is first attested as the title of a Twelfth Legion in inscriptions from Patras in Greece (*CIL* 3, 504; 507; 509) commemorating veterans settled in the early Augustan colony established there in 16 BC. It has been suggested that *XII Fulminata* was the third legion (with *III Cyrenaica* and *XXII Deiotariana*) recorded by Strabo (17.1.12) in Augustan Egypt, but if so it had moved, probably to Syria, by AD 23, since Tacitus (*Annals* 4.5) records only two legions in Egypt by then. It was based in Syria by Claudius' reign, since coins show its veterans helped to found the colony of Ptolemais (Akko in modern Israel), with men from the other Syrian legions.

Disasters in Armenia and Judaea

XII Fulminata had the misfortune to be involved in two major Roman defeats in the East in a decade: Caesennius Paetus' surrender in Armenia in AD 62 and Cestius Gallus' disastrous retreat from Jerusalem in AD 66. During the first part of the Armenian/Parthian war of AD 58–63, *XII Fulminata* remained on the defensive in Syria. However, when the Parthians invaded Armenia and beseiged Tigranocerta in AD 62, the Twelfth joined *IIII Scythica* in the relief expedition led by Caesennius Paetus. As we have seen (page 152), that expedition resulted in a humiliating Roman surrender and retreat, and Corbulo sent the disgraced Twelfth Legion back to Syria, where it was based at Raphanaea, in the south of the province, until the end of the Jewish Revolt in AD 70 (Josephus, *Jewish War* 7.17–18).

In response to the uprising in Judaea in AD 66, Cestius Gallus, governor of Syria, gathered at Antioch an army including all of *XII Fulminata*, 2,000-man vexillations of the other Syrian legions, six (infantry) cohorts and four (cavalry) *alae* of auxiliary troops and some 16,000 allied troops. The army advanced into Galilee, where Caesennius Gallus, legate of *XII Fulminata*, led his men to Sepphoris and skirmished with the enemy beyond. Josephus (*Jewish War* 2.512) notes that the lightly armed rebels were able to inflict heavy casualties on the Romans with javelins when they were able to hold them at a distance in hilly terrain, but could not stand up to the heavily armoured Roman legionaries at close quarters. The army regrouped at Caesarea, then advanced on Jerusalem. The rebels resisted the advance fiercely, inflicting numerous casualties on the Romans, but were forced to withdraw into the city.

The Romans established a camp on Mount Scopas, then advanced into and burned the suburb of Bezetha. However, for several days they failed to break into the inner city. Just as it appeared the Romans might break in and dissidents within the city were willing to surrender it, Cestius Gallus and his army withdrew. He may have been surprised by the rebels' resistance, and felt the need to assemble more siege equipment. However, what should have been an orderly withdrawal degenerated into a rout: the rebels ambushed the Romans with missiles from high ground as they struggled along narrow roads and passes below (Josephus *Jewish War* 2.547–49). By the time the Romans escaped the ambush, they had lost 5,300 infantry and 380 cavalry and, according to Suetonius (*Vespasian* 4), *XII Fulminata* had lost its eagle. The legion was lucky to avoid disbandment – but presumably the need for troops to suppress the revolt and garrison the other eastern provinces was so great that it survived.

XII Fulminata advanced on Jerusalem again, in AD 70, and participated in Titus' siege of the city, but apparently did not do well enough to atone for its earlier disgrace. Josephus (*Jewish War* 7.18) records that at the end of the siege, Titus 'remembering that the Twelfth Legion had given way to the Jews when it had been under the command of Cestius, sent it…to a place called Melitene, on the banks of the Euphrates on the borders of Armenia and Cappadocia.' The legion was still based there at the end of the 4th century, when the *Notitia Dignitatum* was compiled.

XII Fulminata in Cappadocia and Beyond

Melitene (modern Malatya in Turkey) was located on the Euphrates crossing of an important east–west route between Roman Anatolia and southern Armenia (with its capital of Tigranocerta) and northern Mesopotamia. It does not seem to have been an urban site of much significance before AD 70, though there was an important Bronze Age site at Arslantepe nearby, and the much later (6th-century AD) writer Procopius (*Buildings* 3.4.15–19) attributes its development as a city to the presence of the legion. He describes a classic model of urban development seen in some parts of the Roman empire that lacked pre-Roman cities. A Roman legionary fortress, of familiar regular-rectangular form, is established in an undeveloped site. This

A bust traditionally (but probably incorrectly) identified as a portrait of Corbulo, commander in the war against the Parthians in AD 58–63. Rome, Centrale Montemartini.

attracts civilians – soldiers' families, traders, and so on – who form a community adjacent to the fortress. The growth of the community is recognized by Roman authorities (in this case Trajan) with a grant of formal city status and administrative responsibilities, and this in turn leads to increased wealth and population.

However, we have little clear evidence for the early fortress from the site itself. The fortifications visible at Eski Malatya probably date to the 6th century AD and the original legionary fortress may have been at Karamildan, 8 km (5 miles) east of modern Malatya.

A scattering of inscriptions east and west of the legion's base suggest that detachments carried out construction, policing and surveillance duties over a wide area. Some of these come from Anatolia, and probably reflect recruitment and veteran settlement in that region. Others relate to serving soldiers. A milestone (*AE* 1976, 658) from Eumeneia in Phrygia (central Anatolia) records men of *XII Fulminata* constructing a stretch of road to Phrygian Apamea. An inscription from Amorium (*CIL* 3, 353), also in Phrygia, shows that Gaius Salvius Calpurnianus, an Italian legionary of the Twelfth, was buried there by comrades in a vexillation of the legion. Another soldier of the legion was buried at Smyrna (modern Izmir), on the Aegean coast of Roman Asia (*CIL* 3, 414). That he was buried by a *signifer* (standard-bearer), presumably of the same legion, suggests that he was there on duty with other soldiers. The Roman provinces of Asia, Galatia and Bithynia-Pontus in Anatolia did not have full legionary garrisons in the imperial period. Letters written by Pliny the Younger (as governor of Bithynia-Pontus in 110) show small legionary garrisons stationed at important locations and men of *XII Fulminata* were probably detached to perform policing and surveillance duties, several hundred miles west of their base. These inscriptions appear to be largely or entirely of 2nd-century date.

Below left An altar dedicated at Caesarea to the Cappadocian god Turmasgada by Julius Magnus, a centurion of *XII Fulminata* (*Inscriptions of Caesarea*, no. 119). The eagle and winged victory perhaps reflect a victory over Jewish rebels in the Second Revolt.

Judaea, far to the south, sometimes required more active suppression. It is likely that a detachment of *XII Fulminata* was employed in suppressing the Second Jewish Revolt (132–35), since an incomplete inscription from Jerusalem (*AE* 1904, 91) refers to a vexillation of the legion alongside men of *X Fretensis* and *II Traiana*. Julius Magnus, a centurion of *XII Fulminata* set up an altar at Caesarea (in Judaea) and this too may reflect the presence of a detachment of *XII Fulminata* at the time of the Second Revolt. Likewise countermarks of *XII Fulminata*, on coins of Neapolis (modern Nablus in Palestine), dating to between AD 86/87 and 156/57, probably relate to a deployment there during the Second Revolt, or a temporary strengthening of the garrison of Judaea during the unrest of 115–17.

The location of *XII Fulminata*'s base made it very likely that it participated in any 2nd–3rd-century Persian war entailing an advance into Armenia or northern Mesopotamia, as most did. A vexillation of *XII*, along with one of *XV Apollinaris*, is attested in the reign of Marcus Aurelius (*ILS* 9117, AD 177) at modern Echmiadzin, deep in Armenia, over 400 km (250 miles) east of the Euphrates. In 163, the northern element of Lucius Verus' counter-attack against the Parthians (*I Minervia* and *V Macedonica*, deployed for the campaign) had entered Armenia, captured Artaxata, and deposed Pacorus, the Parthian nominee to the throne. He was replaced by a Roman nominee, and Roman coins proclaimed *rex Armeniis datus*, 'a king given to

Opposite A remarkable Domitianic inscription attests the presence of a centurion of *XII Fulminata* at Bejouk Dagh, near the Caspian Sea, south of Baku in Azerbaijan (*AE* 1951, 263). This is about 900 km (560 miles) from the legion's fortress at Melitene. Certainly Roman emperors (like Nero) planned ambitious campaigns to the Caucasus, but this inscription perhaps shows the temporary presence of an advanced outpost under the centurion's command rather than a permanent base. The detachment may have been there to support allied Iberian and Albanian rulers.

the Armenians'. The Romans established a new capital for the kingdom, Kaineopolis (Greek for 'New City'), with a garrison of Roman troops. The inscriptions from Echmiadzin may provide evidence for the location of this new capital and elements of the Cappadocian legions probably performed construction and policing duties.

There were also Roman bases and interests north of Melitene and Satala (base of *XV Apollinaris*) on the coast of the Black Sea. *XII Fulminata*'s involvement in this area is demonstrated by an inscription from Trapezus (modern Trabzon) showing a vexillation of the legion under one of its centurions in the 2nd century AD (*CIL* 3, 6745). The Alans, a nomadic steppe people, threatened Roman control of this area, and, perhaps, Cappadocia itself when Arrian (better known as a historian of Alexander the Great) governed the province in 135. Arrian's account of how he intended to deploy his army to meet this threat has survived and refers to the Twelfth Legion (see page 168).

When Avidius Cassius, supported by most eastern legions, attempted to usurp Marcus Aurelius' imperial throne in 175, Martius Verus, legate of Cappadocia, along with his army (including *XII Fulminata*) remained loyal and played an important part in regaining control. This probably explains the legion's additional titles *Certa Constans* ('Sure and Reliable') in a few late-2nd-century inscriptions. Alternatively these may have been awarded by Septimius Severus, if *XII Fulminata* sided with him rather than Pescennius Niger in 193–94.

The depiction of the 'rain miracle' on the Column of Marcus Aurelius in Rome, with the rain storm personified as a god trailing streams of water from his arms.

The Lightning Hurlers

XII Fulminata appears in an amusing but implausible anecdote relating to Marcus Aurelius' campaign against the Quadi on the Danube frontier in 172. Cassius Dio (72.8) relates how a body of Roman soldiers was cut off by the enemy in intolerably hot conditions, and an Egyptian magician conjured up a rain storm that relieved their thirst. Xiphilinus, the 11th-century Byzantine excerptor of Dio's text claims that the 'rain miracle' was actually brought about by the prayers of Christian soldiers from Melitene, and that the legion there was granted its cognomen (*keraunobolos*, 'lightning-hurling', rather than *keraunophoros,* 'lightning-bearing', in Xiphilinus' version) by Marcus Aurelius for this reason.

Of course, the cognomen is attested much earlier than Marcus Aurelius' reign, and there is no reason to believe Xiphilinus' elaborate etymological gloss, even as evidence that part of the legion participated in that campaign (but see page 169).

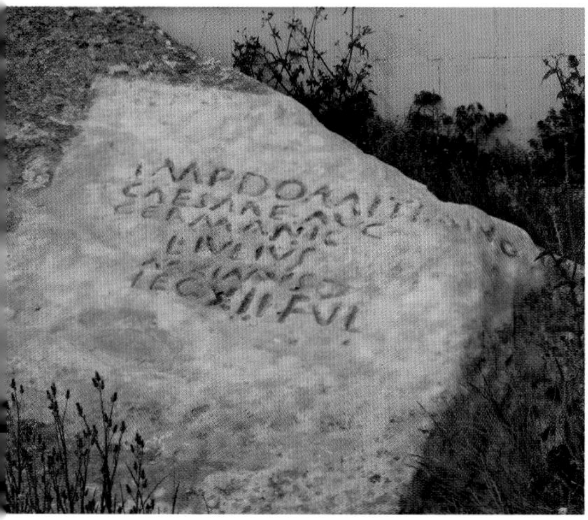

We know very little about the legion in the 3rd century AD, although it probably provided vexillations, at least to campaigns against the Persians that entailed activity in Armenia, and perhaps beyond. Shapur I's invasion in 252 captured Satala, but not, apparently, Melitene, although *XII Fulminata* must have taken part in the fighting. The legion remained at Melitene until at least the late 4th century, as recorded in the *Notitia Dignitatum*.

XV Apollinaris

The cognomen of *XV Apollinaris* suggests it was established by Octavian, whose patron deity was Apollo. Scholars have debated the exact date and circumstances of its origin, and the possibility that it derived from a Caesarian Fifteenth Legion, either the original one that Caesar transferred to Pompey before the civil war, or a replacement *XV* raised subsequently. L. Valerius, a veteran, is attested in an inscription (*CIL* 5, 2516) at the colony of Ateste (Este) in northeast Italy, established after Actium. Given the role Octavian attributed to Apollo in his victory, it is reasonable to assume that the legion got its cognomen then. However, another inscription (*AE* 1975, 442) commemorating Naevius, a veteran of *XV Apollinaris*, has been found at Cremona, a colony of mostly Antonian veterans established after Philippi (42 BC). If the inscription was contemporary with the early years of the colony, it suggests the legion was established very early in Octavian's career, or was of Caesarian origin, and was associated with Apollo even before Actium.

At the start of the imperial period, *XV Apollinaris* was stationed in Illyricum (subsequently Pannonia), probably close to the Italian border, since a number of inscriptions relating to the legion were found around Aquileia. Undoubtedly it fought in the Pannonian war of 14 to 9 BC, and the Pannonian Revolt of AD 6–9, but we have no specific evidence of its activities in these campaigns. In AD 14, *XV Apollinaris* was sharing a summer marching-camp with *VIII Augusta* and *IX Hispana* when the three legions mutinied over their terms of service (Tacitus, *Annals* 1.16-30). The mutiny was suppressed by Tiberius' son, Drusus, and the legions dispersed to their winter quarters. The legion's principal fortress in Pannonia was at Carnuntum, an important crossing point on the Danube (modern Petronell-Carnuntum, Austria). It is uncertain when *XV Apollinaris* first moved to this fortress. There is little evidence that the known site was developed much before the mid-1st century AD, and the move may have taken place during the reign of Claudius, since Tacitus (*Annals* 12.29.2) refers to legions moved up to the river then in response to disturbances among the Germanic Suevi.

XV Apollinaris

Cognomen	*Apollinaris*
Emblem	Griffin?
Main bases	Carnuntum in Pannonia (Petronell-Carnuntum, Austria); Satala (modern Sadak in Turkey)
Major campaigns	Pannonian war (14–9 BC); Pannonian Revolt (AD 6–9)?; Corbulo's Parthian war (AD 62–63); First Jewish Revolt (Galilee campaign AD 67; siege of Jerusalem, AD 70); civil war? (vexillation, AD 69); Trajan's Parthian war (114–17)?; Jewish Revolt in Egypt? (117); Arrian's campaign aganist the Alans? (135); Parthian wars of 2nd–3rd centuries, including Lucius Verus'? (161–66); Marcus Aurelius' Marcomannic wars? (vexillation, 166–80); against Shapur I's invasion? (252)

First Deployment to the East

In AD 62–63 *XV Apollinaris* was transferred across the empire in response to another border problem, namely the defeat of Caesennius Paetus in Armenia. *XV* was in the army mustered at Melitene by Corbulo and sent across the Euphrates to bring Tiridates to terms.

XV Apollinaris was still in the East at the outbreak of the First Jewish Revolt in AD 66, this time in Egypt, perhaps preparing a campaign against the Ethiopians. Titus travelled to Alexandria to take command of the legion, leading it to the colony of Ptolemais on the border between Syria and Judaea, where it joined an army including *V Macedonica* and *X Fretensis* (Josephus, *Jewish War* 3.64–65). The following spring and summer (AD 67), *XV Apollinaris* played an important role in the Roman invasion of Galilee, including the attack on Jotapata, defended by Josephus. Titus himself led a surprise assault with men of the legion to secure control of the town (*Jewish War* 3.324). Some 40,000 of the defenders and population are said to have died in the slaughter that followed and 1,200 prisoners taken, including Josephus himself.

When Vespasian was acclaimed emperor in July AD 69, a vexillation of *XV Apollinaris* probably joined Mucianus' march on Italy in the Flavian cause. The main body of the legion remained in Judaea, participating in the siege of Jerusalem in AD 70. Josephus details its siege-engineering activities in vivid terms. After the fall of Jerusalem,

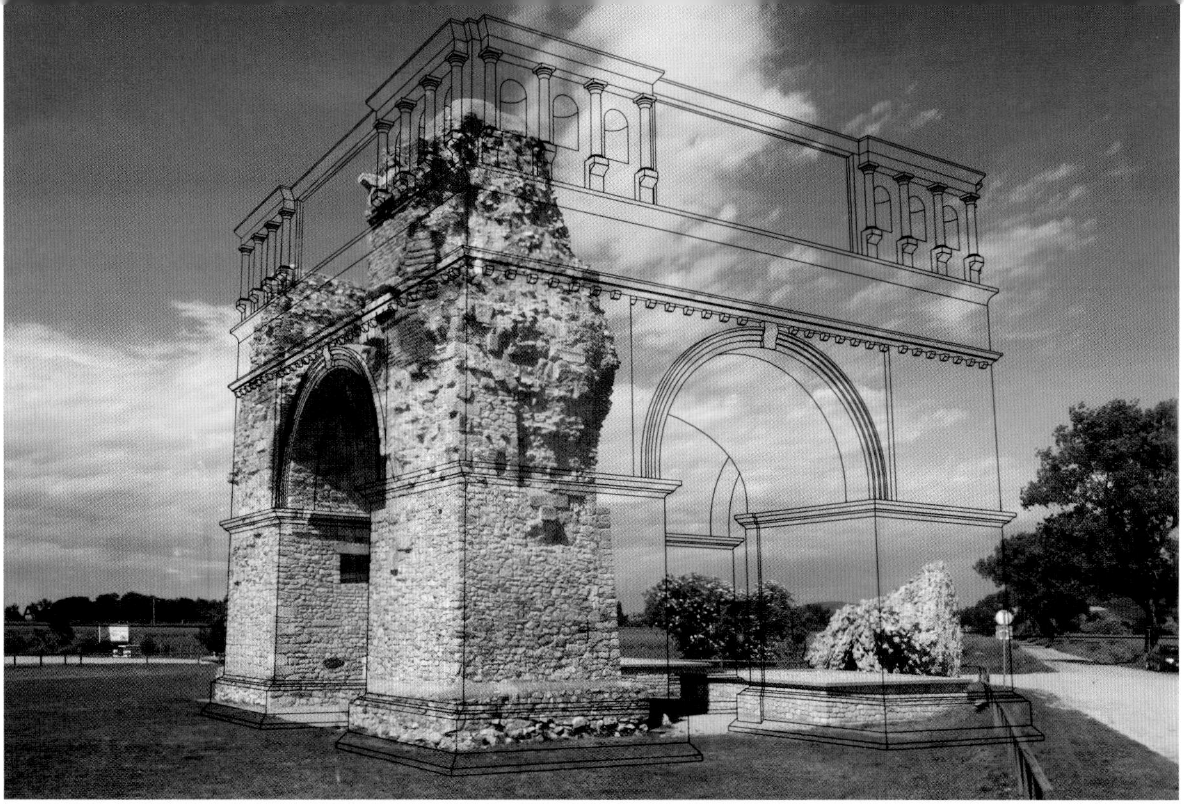

Carnuntum continued as a legionary fortress and civilian community long after the departure of *XV Apollinaris*. The so-called Heidentor, depicted here, is a triumphal arch from the reign of Constantius II (AD 337–61).

XV Apollinaris (with *V Macedonica*) accompanied Titus back to Alexandria, from where it returned to Pannonia. Tomb inscriptions from Carnuntum show that men recruited in Syria during the legion's stay in the East, accompanied it back to its old fortress, where eventually they were commemorated on their deaths.

Return to Pannonia and Second Deployment to the East

An inscription of AD 73 shows reconstruction of the Carnuntum fortress by the legion under its legate, Q. Egnatius Catus (*CIL* 3, 11194). It remained there until at least 106, and the whole legion or vexillations must have fought in the sequence of Domitian's and Trajan's wars in the area, but the period is poorly documented. The dates of its departure from Pannonia and arrival in Cappadocia equally lack clear evidence. It must have arrived at Satala by 135 to be mentioned in Arrian's treatise on the Alans (see box overleaf) but scholars have disputed its movements between *c.* 106 and that date. The most recent overview (that of Everett Wheeler) has *XV Apollinaris* in Egypt *c.* 106–119, participating in Trajan's Parthian war and the subsequent Jewish uprising in Egypt, all on the basis of very limited evidence.

Funerary monument of Titus Calidius Severus from Carnuntum (*ILS* 2596). After service in an auxiliary cohort, *I Alpinorum*, he became a centurion of *XV Apollinaris*. His gravestone shows his helmet with centurion's transverse crest, greaves and a mail or scale armour cuirass; mid-1st century AD.

Just as the legion took Syrian recruits back with it to Pannonia, so Pannonian recruits were still with it (or subsequently joined it) when it arrived at Satala:

> To the spirits of the departed. Tiberius Julius Martialis, son of Tiberius, of the tribe Claudia, from Savaria, a soldier of the legion *XV Apollinaris*. He lived 30 years and served 13 years. Tiberius Buccio, cavalry *optio*, set up this monument to his brother.
>
> *AE* 1988, 1043

Wheeler argues that this man was recruited in Pannonia (he came from Savaria, the provincial capital of Upper Pannonia, modern Szombathely in Hungary) shortly before *XV Apollinaris* left Carnuntum in 106 and died at Satala (after 13 years service) in *c.* 118–19. Alternatively, the inscription may show that the legion continued to receive recruits from Pannonia even after it had moved overseas. Other scholars have placed the legion's arrival in Cappadocia immediately after Trajan's Parthian war, in 117 or at the time of disturbances on the Parthian frontier in 123 (see page 160).

Arrian on *XV Apollinaris* and the Alans

As noted, *XV Apollinaris* was certainly at Satala by 135, when the politican and writer Lucius Flavius Arrianus (known to us as Arrian) was governor of Cappadocia, since it is included in his treatise *Battle Formation Against the Alans.* At this time his province was threatened by incursions of a nomadic Sarmatian people, the Alans, but it is unclear whether Arrian actually fought them, and whether this work describes a hypothetical or real situation. Nevertheless, it is unique as a document and grounded in reality, naming real Roman military units.

Arrian (*Battle Formation* 15) describes how his heavy infantry (*XV Apollinaris*, with *XII Fulminata* providing a vexillation) was supported by auxiliary infantry and cavalry units. Arrian describes the legionary infantry drawn up in an unusually deep (eight-rank) and close-ordered phalanx formation to receive the cavalry charge that was the primary tactic of the Alans. Their equipment is also unusual. The first four ranks are described as *kontos*-bearers, deployed to hold off the Alan cavalry, *kontos* being a Greek term for a long thrusting spear like a cavalry lance. The remaining four ranks are *lonchophoroi*, *lonchos*-bearers, throwing javelins (either light *lanceae*, whose Latin name derived from the Greek *lonchos*; or ordinary *pila*) over the heads of the front ranks.

Given Arrian's historical interests in the Macedonian army of Alexander the Great, this novel formation and equipment may be antiquarian and/or theoretical rather than real. Nevertheless, the basic tactics seem sound, with catapults and auxiliary archers shooting over the heads of the legionaries as their deep formation receives the Alan charge, with the numerically inferior Roman cavalry held back behind the main formation – to pursue the enemy if repulsed and guard against outflanking.

Satala and Beyond

Little is known about the legionary fortress at Satala and the excavated fort there is Byzantine, although stamped tiles of *XV Apollinaris* have been found. However, like *XII Fulminata*, the Fifteenth performed 'internal security' and garrison duties at a number of outposts. To the west, 2nd-century inscriptions show centurions of the legion at Ancyra (Ankara), some probably on policing duties (*CIL* 3, 268; see page 164). As the most northerly legion on the eastern frontier, it is hardly surprising that *XV Apollinaris* contributed to the garrison of Trapezus (Trabzon), an important supply port and naval base on the Black Sea: an inscription from the site mentions a doctor (*medicus*) of the legion (*CIL* 3, 6747).

The epitaph of Titus Aurelius Apolinarius (*AE* 1993, 1562), a legionary of *XV Apollinaris*, provides evidence for the presence of a vexillation of that legion at Trapezus (Trabzon), where it was found. He came from Caesarea, undoubtedly the one in Cappadocia (Kayseri).

Much further from the legion's base, at Pityus (modern Pitsunda in Georgia) on the northeast shore of the Black Sea, stamped tiles of *XV Apollinaris* associated with the remains of a mid-2nd-century Roman military installation suggest a garrison of the legion there, perhaps the one destroyed in 258 by raiding Scythian Borani (Zosimus 1.32.3–33.1).

Like *XII Fulminata*, elements of *XV Apollinaris* were perhaps caught up in the initial Roman defeat by the Parthian king Vologeses IV at Elegeia in Armenia in 161 (Cassius Dio 72.2.1), but the legion Dio says was destroyed was certainly not one of the Cappadocian legions. However, *XV Apollinaris* was definitely involved in the aftermath of the Roman counter-attack of 163, since inscriptions (*ILS* 9117, AD 177; *ILS* 394, AD 184) attest a detachment alongside elements of *XII* at the new Roman-established capital of Kaineopolis (modern Echmiadzin). It also seems that *XV Apollinaris* provided a vexillation for Marcus Aurelius' Danubian wars, since an inscription of that period (*AE* 1956, 227) found near Plovdiv in Bulgaria records that Aurelius Dizes, a Thracian soldier of the legion, made a dedication 'for the success of the campaign'. Probably he was recruited locally to supplement the existing strength of the vexillation transferred from Cappadocia.

Everett Wheeler has argued that a soldier with a griffin on his helmet in panel XV of the sculptured frieze of the Column of Marcus Aurelius in Rome represents a legionary of the Fifteenth Legion. This panel appears immediately before that depicting the 'rain miracle', itself associated (rather tenuously) with *XII Fulminata* (see above).

XV Apollinaris remained loyal to Marcus Aurelius during Avidius Cassius' revolt of 175 (see page 165), but we know nothing of its allegiance in the war between Niger and Severus.

We have very little evidence for *XV Apollinaris* from the 3rd century AD onwards. The Naqs-i-Rustam inscription of Shapur I states he captured Satala in his campaign of 252, and part or all of the legion must have been caught up in the fighting of that campaign. However, it continued to be based there, as it is listed at Satala in the *Notitia Dignitatum* at the end of the 4th century, while a new legion, *I Pontica*, occupied the former outpost of Trapezus.

This panel of the Arch of Septimius Severus in the Roman Forum depicts the Roman attack on the Parthian city of Seleucia on the Tigris, and its surrender. The arch was set up in 203 to commemorate Severus' victories in the East.

The Legions of Mesopotamia

The Roman province of Mesopotamia (and Osrhoene) was the northern part of the 'land between two rivers' (the Euphrates and the Tigris), now mostly within Kurdish eastern Turkey and northern Iraq. For much of the Principate, this area lay under Parthian control, and the border lay on the Euphrates. It came under definitive Roman control and was annexed as provincial territory by 198, after Septimius Severus' Parthian wars. Cassius Dio, a contemporary, was sceptical of Severus' motives in conquering this territory, and of its value:

> Severus said that he had conquered a huge territory that served as a forward defence for Syria. However, the reality of the situation refutes his claim, since it has caused us numerous wars and great expense. For it gives us very little and drains us completely of resources.
>
> Cassius Dio 75.3.2–3

In some respects Dio's statement is unfair, since the new provinces contained substantial and wealthy cities like Edessa (Urfa), Carrhae (Harran) and Nisibis (Nusaybin). However, he was right to characterize it as a cause of 'numerous wars and great expense'. Conquest and defence of the new territory required recruitment of new legions, called *Parthica*, 'Parthian', with two of them (*I* and *III Parthica*) based in Mesopotamia throughout its history. *II Parthica* had its permanent fortress at Albanum, just south of Rome, but spent much of its history engaged in wars on the frontiers of the empire (see *II Parthica*). In the longer term, Mesopotamia became a focus of conflict between Rome and Persia, as Sasanian armies battled the Romans and, later, Byzantines for control of fortress cities like Amida (Diyarbekir), Nisibis and Dara.

We know little about *I* and *III Parthica*, as they were created in a period when our literary evidence and inscriptions begin to dry up, and served in a region that has not been studied intensively. They were probably raised in the East, and the few known soldiers of these legions are nearly all easterners. They were commanded by equestrian officers with the title of *praefectus legionis* ('prefect of the legion'), rather than by senatorial legates. This was because, like Roman Egypt, the governor of Mesopotamia was appointed by the emperor from the equestrian order rather than the Senate.

I Parthica

Cognomen *Parthica*
Emblem Centaur
Main bases Singara (modern Sinjar, Iraq); later Nisibis (Nusaybin) and Constantia/Constantina (Viransehir in Turkey)
Major campaigns Wars against Persia from the reign of Caracalla (AD 216) through the 4th century and beyond

III Parthica

Cognomen *Parthica*
Emblem Centaur
Main bases Singara (modern Sinjar, Iraq); later Nisibis (Nusaybin) and Constantia/Constantina (Viransehir in Turkey)
Major campaigns Wars against Persia from the reign of Caracalla (AD 216) through the 4th century and beyond

I Parthica

I Parthica was based at Singara (modern Sinjar) soon after the legion was created and an inscription by a veteran of the legion found at Aphrodisias in Caria (western Turkey; *ILS* 9477) refers to it being stationed at Singara. This fortified city was in the front line against Sasanian incursions into Roman Mesopotamia until its loss to the Persians in 360 and the late Roman historian Ammianus Marcellinus (20.6.8) lists *I Parthica* in the city's garrison (with *I Flavia* and auxiliaries) even then. Ammianus also notes that Singara had been captured by the Persians with the loss of its garrison on numerous past occasions. Undoubtedly *I Parthica* was involved in such campaigns, including Shapur I's second successful invasion of the Roman empire, in 260, culminating in Valerian's defeat near Edessa, as well as an indecisive night battle near Singara itself in 344 (Libanius *Oration* 59.99–120; Julian *Oration* I; Ammianus Marcellinus 18.5.7).

The site of ancient Singara preserves a substantial wall circuit with towers, enclosing *c.* 20 ha (*c.* 50 acres), probably representing the defences in the 4th century, rather than the original Severan legionary fortress. Singara was finally surrendered to the Persians in 363 by the emperor Jovian as part of the peace settlement following the death of his predecessor Julian (Ammianus Marcellinus 25.7.9).

The late-4th-century *Notitia Dignitatum* gives *I Parthica* the additional title *Nisibena*, 'of Nisibis', referring to another great fortress city of Mesopotamia surrendered to the Persians in 363. This suggests that the legion was based at Nisibis when Singara was under Persian control, or that a detachment was based there. The fortress of *I Parthica* when the *Notitia Dignitatum* was compiled was Constantia or Constantina (modern Viransehir), another Mesopotamian city developed as a fortress in the 4th century.

The handful of inscriptions relating to veterans of *I Parthica* suggest that its soldiers were largely recruited in the eastern empire, from places like Aphrodisias, Ankara and Balboura (Lycia) in Anatolia. The scattering of inscriptions from elsewhere mostly relate to centurions and higher officers who had moved on or were on detached duty. A funerary epitaph from Svalenik in Bulgaria (the Roman province of Lower Moesia; *AE* 1954, 34) commemorates Publius Aurelius Sirus, perhaps an ordinary soldier. He may have served there in a detachment deployed to the Danube, but no date is given. His name, *Sirus* ('Syrian') shows he was another eastern recruit.

Rock-cut relief from the site of Bishapur in Iran, showing Shapur I riding over the corpse of Gordian III, while Philip the Arab kneels before him. After his victory near Rhesaina in 243, the praetorian prefect Timesitheus died of uncertain causes and was replaced by Philip. Persian sources indicate that Gordian was defeated and killed by Shapur at Misiche in Iraq early in 244, as depicted in this relief. Roman sources suggest Gordian was murdered by Philip (who succeeded him) instead.

I Parthica also bore, at various times, the titles *Severiana*, *Severiana Antoniniana* (Caracalla, 198–217, and Elagabalus 218–22), *Severiana Alexandriana* (Severus Alexander, 222–35) and *Philippiana* (Philip the Arab, 244–49).

III Parthica

Even less is known about *III Parthica*. It is widely assumed that its long-term fortress was the fortified city of Rhesaina (Ras-el-Ain) on the river Khabur (northeast Syria, near the Turkish border). This identification is based on coins minted there depicting a vexillum standard and the (disputed) legend *LEG(io) III P(arthica) S(everiana)*. Even if these coins (dating from the reign of Caracalla to Severus Alexander) have been read correctly, the allusion may be to a veteran settlement or a vexillation and the archaeologist David Kennedy argues that the legion's regular base in the Severan period was at Nisibis.

Excavations at Rhesaina (Tell Fakhariyah) have revealed substantial late-Roman fortifications, although much less is known of the ancient site of Nisibis, an important Roman fortress city until its surrender to the Persians in 363. Like *I Parthica*, *III Parthica* must have been involved heavily in wars between Rome and Persia in the 3rd and 4th centuries. We know, for example, that Macrinus stalemated the Parthians in a bloody battle near Nisibis in 217 (Herodian 4.14–15) and Gordian III's praetorian prefect Timesitheus won a battle near Rhesaina in 243 (Ammianus Marcellinus 23.5.17), but we have no specific details of *III Parthica*'s role in these or any other wars.

A gold *aureus* coin of Victorinus, minted at Cologne in 271, bears the legend LEG III PARTHICA and depicts a centaur (the emblem of all the Parthian legions). This belongs to a series depicting other legions (including eastern ones), and may reflect the presence of a vexillation in the West at that time.

A corrupted section of the manuscript of the *Notitia Dignitatum* probably allows us to identify the late-4th-century base of *III Parthica* as Apatna, in the province of Osrhoene.

The Legions of the Balkan Provinces

Moesia: *VII Claudia, XI Claudia, I Italica, IIII Flavia Felix*
Pannonia: *X Gemina, XIV Gemina, I Adiutrix, II Adiutrix*
Noricum: *II Italica*
Raetia: *III Italica*
Dacia: *V Macedonica, XIII Gemina*

The Balkan provinces were a focus of Roman military activity throughout the imperial period. Augustus' reign saw Roman control advanced from the Dalmatian coast and Macedonia to the Danube and Pannonia (the area south and west of the Danube) was conquered. Roman control was extended beyond the Danube to encompass a new province of Dacia (part of modern Romania) after Trajan's victory in AD 106. On the other hand, Marcus Aurelius' Marcomannic wars (166–80) marked the beginning of a bitter defensive struggle on the Danube that lasted through much of Rome's history, against Marcomanni, Alamanni, Sarmatians, Goths and other Germanic peoples. The Balkan garrison doubled from 6 to 12 legions between the reign of Tiberius and the Severan period.

The size of the army on the Danube also made it an important player in civil wars, from AD 69 (when Balkan legions were crucial in bringing Vespasian to the throne), to the mid-3rd century and beyond, when Balkan military leaders (starting with Maximinus I Thrax, 'The Thracian', in 238) came to the throne and were overthrown with bewildering rapidity. Unfortunately our evidence for the activities of individual legions largely dries up at this period, but most or all of the Balkan legions must have been heavily engaged not just in these civil wars, but also in the frontier struggles of the 3rd century.

Illyricum (a region within the modern Balkans) had become a province around 32 BC. Moesia, bordering Macedonia, was subdued in 29 BC and Noricum and Raetia, the Balkan provinces closest to Italy, were conquered by Tiberius and Drusus in 16–15 BC. Roman Illyricum was expanded eastward in the Pannonian war of 12–9 BC, but after the great Pannonian Revolt of AD 6–9, this area was divided into two provinces: Pannonia to the north and Dalmatia to the south. Dacia became a province in 106.

VII Claudia was involved in the construction at Drobeta of a bridge across the lower Danube, designed by Apollodorus of Damascus to enable the Roman army to cross into Dacia and commemorated on Trajan's Column in Rome.

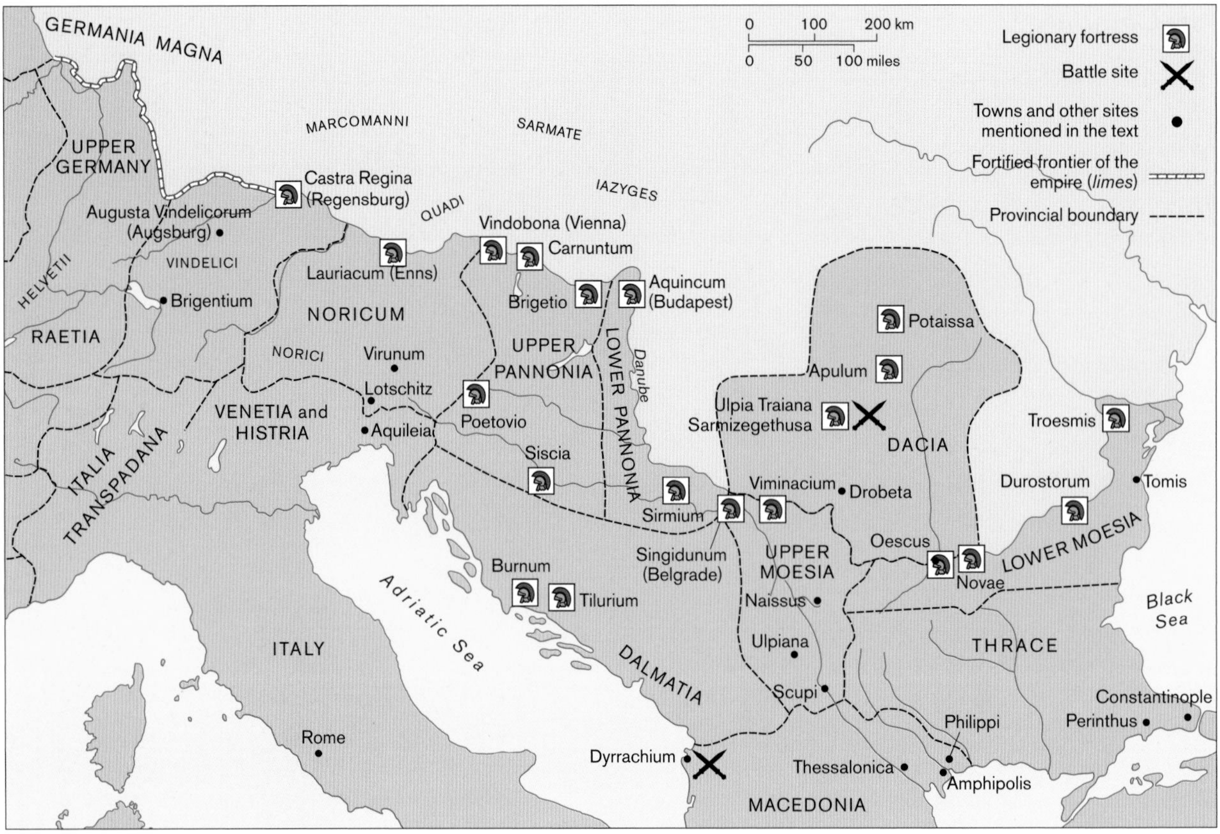

Map of the Balkan provinces showing the legionary fortresses and other places mentioned in the text.

The Legions of Moesia

Moesia was an agriculturally fertile area on the lower Danube, rich in minerals. In modern terms, it includes parts of Serbia, Bulgaria, Romania and Macedonia. The Moesi, a Thracian tribe, were defeated by the Romans in 29 BC and their lands assigned to the Roman province of Macedonia. The poet Ovid was banished to Tomis in Moesia during the reign of Augustus, describing it as violent and uncivilized (*Tristia* 5.10).

Initially Macedonia and the Balkans formed a single military command, divided in AD 45–46, when Moesia became a separate province. This province stretched along the lower Danube from the river Drinus to the west coast of the Black Sea. There, legions protected the border with Dacia, and a Roman fleet, the *classis Moesica*, patrolled the northern shores of the Black Sea. Moesian legions were also responsible for protecting allied Greek cities in the Crimea, as shown by inscriptions naming *XI Claudia*, *I Italica* and *V Macedonica*. Later, in Domitian's reign, Moesia was split in two, Inferior (Lower) and Superior (Upper). The province was invaded repeatedly by Goths during the 3rd and 4th centuries AD.

Denarius of Septimius Severus with eagle of *VII Claudia* (AD 193). The legion participated in Severus' civil war against Pescennius Niger and Clodius Albinus and its name appears on legionary coinage he minted after his victory.

VII Claudia

Like other legions that served with Julius Caesar in Gaul, the Seventh's emblem was a bull. Its first cognomen, *Paterna* probably derives from Caesar's title *pater patriae* ('father of his country'). The legion fought with him against the Helvetii in Gaul in 58 BC. It accompanied Caesar on his invasion of Britain and fought for him through the civil war against Pompey.

VII Claudia

Cognomina	*Paterna*; *Macedonica*; *Pia Fidelis*
Emblem	Bull
Main bases	Viminacium
Major campaigns	Caesar's Gallic and civil wars, 58–46 BC; Mutina (43 BC); Philippi (42 BC); Perusia (41 BC); AD 69 civil war; Domitian and Trajan's Dacian wars (AD 89 and 101–6); Lucius Verus' Parthian war (161–66); Marcus Aurelius' Marcomannic wars (165–80); 3rd-century wars on the Danube frontier.

The Augustan Period

By 45 BC, *VII Claudia* had been sent back to Italy to be pensioned off and its veterans had received land near Capua and Luca. But when Caesar was murdered a year later, Octavian quickly reconstituted the Seventh Legion along with the Eighth to bolster his political position. These legions played a crucial role in the victory against Mark Antony at Mutina (Modena) in 43 BC, at Philippi (42 BC) and at the siege of Perusia (Perugia, 41 BC). By 36 BC some veterans had settled in southern Gaul and others were later given land in Mauretania. It is unclear whether the Seventh fought for Octavian at Actium.

In the reorganization after Actium, the Seventh was probably transferred to Galatia (central Turkey), where inscriptions suggest that the legion served early in Augustus' reign, drawing on local recruits. If so, it probably formed part of the army of Lucius Calpurnius Piso, governor of Pamphylia in 13–11 BC. He was sent to fight in Thrace in 11 BC, perhaps taking the Seventh with him. The cognomen *Macedonica* may date to this period, or otherwise to the battle of Philippi.

Information about the legion remains limited into the 1st century AD. At some point, perhaps after the Pannonian Revolt (AD 6–9) or the Varian disaster of AD 9, the legion was sent to Dalmatia.

VII Claudia in Moesia

The Seventh Legion was transferred to Moesia in AD 56–57 (probably to Viminacium, its later base, near Kostolac, in eastern Serbia), replacing *IIII Scythica*, which had been sent to the Euphrates.

Reconstructed ruins at Tilurium (Gardun, Croatia). In the first half of the 1st century AD, *VII Claudia* was sent to Dalmatia and was based at Tilurium to guard the southern approach to the city of Salona.

In AD 69, the legion sided with Otho and sent a large detachment to Italy to support the fight against his challenger Vitellius. However, by the time the troops arrived at Bedriacum, near Cremona, where the two sides met, Otho's army had been defeated. Vitellius sent them back to Moesia, where – with the other Danube legions – they promptly declared for Vespasian. Without waiting for eastern reinforcements, the Danubian legions under Marcus Primus marched on Italy and defeated Vitellius at the second battle of Bedriacum (see pages 134–35).

VII Claudia must now have returned to Moesia, settling permanently in the fortress at Viminacium, which it rebuilt in stone. Evidence of the legion's activities have also been found elsewhere in Moesia, at Timacum Minus (Ravna; *AE* 1952, 193), Naissus (Nis; *AE* 1980, 791, *CIL* 3, 8252) and Scupi (near Skopje; *CIL* 3, 8196, 8201, 8237). Members of the legion served in Dalmatia, Macedonia, Pannonia and, later, Dacia.

Fighting the Dacians

VII Claudia was in the front line in wars against the Dacians. They first invaded Moesia in AD 86, impelling the emperor Domitian to reorganize his forces there. He divided Moesia in two, Superior (Upper) and Inferior (Lower), and in AD 88 invaded Dacia. A year later, the Seventh Legion was in the army that defeated the Dacian king Decebalus at Tapae. The army was soon recalled, however, (as Lucius Antonius Saturninus, governor of Upper Germany, revolted against Domitian in AD 89) and peace was negotiated.

Trajan's reign saw a full-scale invasion of Dacia. Moesia was the staging area for Trajan's army and the Seventh's base at Viminacium was his headquarters. *VII Claudia* was heavily involved in Trajan's Dacian wars (101–6) and inscriptions attesting its presence have been found north of the Danube at Contra Margum (Kovin; *IDR* 3.1, 1b–d), Banatska Palanka (*IDR* 3.1, 8–9), Pojejana (*IDR* 3.1, 21b–c, 22, 22a), Gornea (*IDR* 3.1, 30b–e, 31) and Vrsåc (*IDR* 3.1, 107b–c, e).

The 2nd Century AD

The Seventh Legion perhaps fought in Trajan's Parthian war, since many legions that fought in the Dacian wars were subsequently used in the East. When the Jewish revolt broke out in Egypt, Cyrenaica and Cyprus during the reign of Hadrian, a vexillation of the legion was sent to Cyprus (*AE* 1912, 179), and it may have been

Plot to Overthrow the Emperor Claudius

The Seventh Legion was still in Dalmatia in Claudius' reign and was caught up in an attempt to overthrow him in AD 42. According to the biographer Suetonius (*Claudius* 13), Furius Camillus Scribonianus, governor of Dalmatia, supported by the Dalmatian legions (*VII* and *XI*), rebelled against Claudius. The civil war was short-lived, ending within five days when 'the legions' intentions were changed by a religious omen. For ... by some divinely inspired chance, their eagle could not be adorned and their standards could not be pulled up and moved.'

Cassius Dio (60.15) gives a different version of the story: Scribonius was encouraged to rebel by senators at Rome who hoped to restore the Republic. However, the soldiers changed their minds when this was announced to them, preferring continued imperial rule. Scribonius committed suicide and Claudius rewarded the soldiers with the titles *Claudia Pia Fidelis* ('Claudian, Dutiful and Loyal').

This scene from Trajan's Column in Rome depicts the suicide of the Dacian leader, Decebalus. Decebalus cut his own throat rather than be captured by the Romans.

Aerial photographs and geophysical surveys of the surrounding area have identified the walls, towers and the barracks at Viminacium, enabling reconstructions such as this one. The imposing remains of the north gate of the fortress, seen to the left, were excavated in the early 2000s.

The Fortress at Viminacium

Viminacium was located in a strategically important position in the rich agricultural lands of northern Moesia. From here, a network of roads spread throughout the Balkans, connecting Moesia to the surrounding provinces and providing swift communication with Macedonia, Greece and the Black Sea.

The Roman fortress here may have been built in the early 1st century AD by *IIII Scythica* and *V Macedonica*, but its first stone fortifications were constructed by *VII Claudia* in the second half of the century. Various brick stamps and inscriptions of that legion attest to its long stay there: until the 5th century AD. The impressive architectural remains include an entrance gate, sewer and massive paving slabs.

transferred there from the East rather than from Moesia. One centurion of the legion was decorated by Trajan for his actions in the Parthian war (*CIL* 10, 3733), but during his career he was also a centurion of *III Cyrenaica*, *primus pilus* of *II Traiana* and a member of the Praetorian Guard. He may have served in Parthia with any of these. The same centurion was also decorated by Hadrian during the Jewish War.

A vexillation may have taken part in Lucius Verus' Parthian war (161–66), but the main part of the legion was caught up in Marcus Aurelius' Marcomannic wars from 165. The Marcomanni, Sarmatians and Quadi were threatening the Danube regions and, once Marcus Aurelius had concentrated a huge army in the region, the Seventh spent the next ten years fighting the barbarian invaders. In 178–80 hostilities were renewed. Marcus Aurelius died at Vindobona (Vienna) in 180 and Commodus made peace with the Marcomanni, bringing the war to an end.

The 3rd Century AD

Septimius Severus was proclaimed emperor by the Balkan legions at Carnuntum in 193. The Seventh Legion supported Severus in the subsequent civil war against Pescennius Niger and Clodius Albinus, but its role in these conflicts is uncertain.

During the reign of Philip I, the Danube region was threatened by the Goths and the ancient historian Zosimus (1.20.2) mentions unrest among the legions stationed there. This culminated in a rebellion and usurpation by Pacatian, datable to 248 from coins he minted at Viminacium, the Seventh's fortress. His reign was short-lived and he was murdered before the year was out. This incident gives an indication of the turmoil in the region during this period.

In the next few years the legions of Moesia and Pannonia suffered a series of defeats at the hands of invading barbarians, but succeeded in driving back the Goths in 269. During this period the legion supported the emperor Gallienus against the pretender Postumus and like many other legions was rewarded with the title *Pia VI Fidelis VI* ('Six times Dutiful and Loyal' also with *VII*).

According to the *Notitia Dignitatum*, the Seventh Legion was still stationed at Viminacium at the end of the 4th century.

XI Claudia

Like its sister-legion *VII Claudia*, *XI Claudia* was raised by Julius Caesar (see pages 24–25) and fought for him in 58 BC against the Helvetii and throughout the subsequent Gallic war and the civil war against Pompey. It was disbanded in 45 BC and its veterans given land at Bovianum in central Italy. Along with *VII Claudia* it was reconstituted by Octavian in 42 BC and fought at Philippi and at the siege of Perusia (Perugia). Funerary inscriptions (*CIL* 5, 2501) show that the legion was present at the battle of Actium.

XI Claudia

Cognomina	*Claudia*; *Pia Fidelis*; *Alexandriana*
Emblems	Neptune; possibly also a bull
Main bases	Durostorum (Silistra, Bulgaria)
Major campaigns	Caesar's Gallic and civil wars (58–45 BC); Philippi (42 BC); Perusia (41 BC); civil war (AD 69); Batavian Revolt (AD 69–70); Clemens' campaign east of the Rhine (AD 74); Domitian's war against the Chatti (AD 83); Second Jewish Revolt (132–35); Severus' civil war against Niger (193–94); 3rd-century wars on the Danube frontier

Early Deployment

After Actium, *XI Claudia* apparently moved to the Balkans, but it is unclear where it was first stationed. After the Varian disaster of AD 9, the legion was moved to Burnum (Kistanje) in Dalmatia. A vexillation seems to have been based at Tilurium (Gardun), with its sister-legion. Like *VII Claudia*, the Eleventh supported the governor of Dalmatia in his short-lived rebellion against Claudius in AD 42, but when it put an end to the rebellion (see page 176) was awarded the cognomen *Pia Fidelis*.

During the Year of the Four Emperors (AD 69; see page 59), the legion supported Otho (Tacitus, *Histories* 2.11), but the large vexillation it sent arrived too late to help at the first battle of Bedriacum. The victorious Vitellius sent the legion back to Dalmatia (*Histories* 2.67), where it then declared for his rival Vespasian. The legion was with the other Danubian legions that ignored Vespasian's orders to wait and marched on Italy, defeating Vitellius at the second battle of Bedriacum (see pages 109; 134–35).

Tacitus (*Histories* 4.68) tells us the legion was sent north a year later as part of the expeditionary force led by Petillius Cerialis that put down the Batavian Revolt. It remained in Upper Germany after the revolt, and – on the basis of inscriptions (e.g. *AE* 1991, 1260; *AE* 1946, 258 and 260) recording both soldiers and veterans found there and in the surrounding region – was based at Vindonissa (Windisch) where it remained until AD 101. It was also in the army that campaigned on the east bank of the Rhine in AD 74, under Gnaeus Cornelius Pinarius Clemens, governor of Upper Germany. In AD 83 it took part in Domitian's campaign against the Chatti.

Lucius Sertorius Firmus was *signifer* and *aquilifer* of the Eleventh Legion during Claudius' reign. He is depicted here holding a legionary eagle, on the tomb that he set up in Verona for himself and his wife Domitia Prisca (*CIL* 5, 3375).

XI Claudia at Durostorum

Durostorum lay on the Danube river, and was an important port and customs post in Lower Moesia. Originally garrisoned by an auxiliary unit, it became the fortress of *XI Claudia* after Trajan's Dacian wars (101–6). Many inscriptions and sculptural fragments have been found in excavations on the site, but few architectural remains survive (a bath building and parts of the fortifications) since the fortress and surrounding settlement lie under the modern town of Silistra. There is little information about the earliest phases of the fortress, but excavations show it was rebuilt in the 3rd century, and the thickness of the walls was increased at this time. This probably relates to barbarian attacks (by the Costoboci, Carpi, Goths and Sarmatians), which occurred with increasing frequency from the late 2nd century.

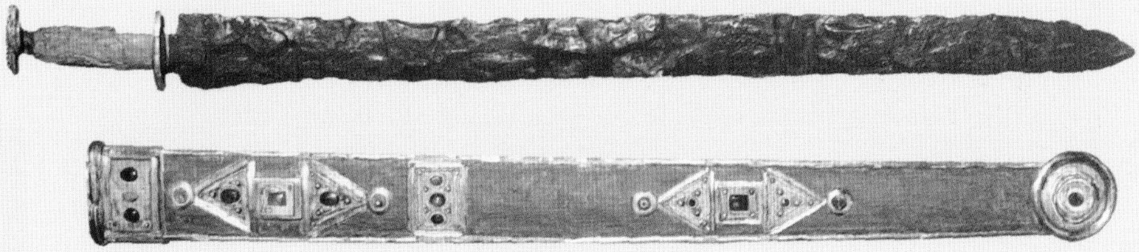

The wooden scabbard of this large sword (left) was set with semi-precious stones and must have belonged to a high-ranking military officer. The sword has been dated to the 4th or 5th century AD *and was found in a tomb near Durostorum (below, with the Danube in the background), where the Eleventh Legion was based for several hundred years.*

In 101 *XI Claudia* was sent back to the Balkans. It was stationed first at Brigetio (Szöny) in Lower Pannonia where it helped complete the reconstruction of the fortress in stone. It took part in Trajan's Dacian wars (101–6), but little is known of its role. Within a few years, the legion was transferred to Durostorum (Silistra) in Lower Moesia, where it would remain for the next 300 years. While there it provided detachments, along with other legions of the province, to guard the Greek towns of the Crimea. Inscriptions relating to soldiers of the legion have been found at Charax (*CBI* 661 and *AE* 1997, 1332).

Other Activities

XI Claudia is known to have participated in campaigns outside its province, but the details are limited. A vexillation may have been sent to Judaea during the reign of Hadrian to help put down the Second Jewish Revolt of 132–35 (*CIL* 3, 13586). From the same period another vexillation was stationed in Regio Montanensium (modern Montana) in Lower Moesia to guard mining facilities and members of the legion are attested here on inscriptions into the 3rd century. One (*AE* 1967, 867) reveals that an activity of the soldiers' was to capture wild animals for the *venationes* (beast hunts in the arena).

Due to its location in Lower Moesia, the Eleventh must have fought in Marcus Aurelius' Marcomannic wars, but there is no direct evidence of this. In 193 the Eleventh supported Septimius Severus' claim to the throne, but did not join his march on Rome. However, it fought in his eastern campaign against Pescennius Niger in 193–94 (Herodian 2.14.6), at the siege of Byzantium and the subsequent battle of Issus, and it probably also joined Severus on his Parthian wars. It bore the cognomina *Antoniniana* during the reign of Caracalla and *Alexandriana* in the reign of Severus Alexander, and the title *Pia V Fidelis V* ('Five times Dutiful and Loyal'; also with *VI*) reveals that the legion supported Gallienus against the usurper Postumus in the 260s.

While there is little specific evidence, *XI Claudia* undoubtedly participated in the wars to defend the Danube frontier against external enemies as well as the civil wars of the 3rd century AD. The *Notitia Dignitatum* records that *XI Claudia* was still at Durostorum in the early 5th century.

Remains of the North Gate of the legionary fortress at Vindonissa. Inscriptions reveal the presence of three legions here: *XIII Gemina*, which built the first wooden fortress in *c.* AD 15, *XXI Rapax*, which rebuilt the fortress in stone in AD 47, and *XI Claudia* which was sent here for about 30 years after the Batavian Revolt (AD 69–70). When the Eleventh Legion was sent back to the Balkans in 101, the fortress was abandoned.

I Italica

'Nero recruited the First Legion that is named *Italica*, with its winter quarters in Lower Moesia' (Cassius Dio 55.24.2). *I Italica* was probably raised in Italy in AD 66 or 67, the later years of Nero's reign, because, according to Suetonius (*Nero* 19), the emperor planned an expedition to the Caspian Gates, to build on the successes of Corbulo in the East. Recruits to the legion were six Roman feet (*c.* 1.8 m) tall, and Nero called them 'the Phalanx of Alexander the Great'. An inscription (*CIL* 3, 7591) found in Moesia records that the legion was given its *aquila* and *signa* on 20th September, but the year is debated.

In AD 68 the legion had still not left for the Caucasus, but was instead sent to Gaul because Gaius Julius Vindex, governor of Gallia Lugdunensis, had rebelled against Rome. The legion arrived in Gaul in March or April AD 68, but was too late to engage Vindex, who had already been defeated by Lucius Verginius Rufus, governor of Upper Germany.

Civil War

In June that same year the Senate proclaimed Galba emperor and Nero committed suicide. Verginius Rufus' legions then rebelled against Galba and joined forces with Vitellius, governor of Lower Germany. In AD 69 *I Italica* joined *V Alaudae*, *XXI Rapax* and *XXII Primigenia* in their march on Rome. It helped to defeat the forces of Otho (who had replaced Galba in Rome by this time) at the first battle of Bedriacum, near Cremona (see page 59) and, according to Tacitus, it was the bravest of the legions. Its eagle was one of the four displayed when Vitellius entered Rome (Tacitus, *Histories* 2. 89) after this battle.

The Danube legions chose to support Vespasian and met Vitellius' army at the second battle of Bedriacum. Tacitus (*Histories* 2.100) records that *I Italica* was part of the Vitellian army sent to Bedriacum under Aulus Caecina Alienus, bringing up the rear of the column with *XXI Rapax* and vexillations of the British legions. Caecina attempted to defect to Vespasian, however, and so his advance troops mutinied. Taking advantage of the confusion, Vespasian's army attacked and defeated Vitellius' men. Lacking leadership and discipline, *I Italica* was defeated.

I Italica

Cognomina	*Italica*; *Moesiaca*; *Alexandriana*; *Antoninana*; *Gordiana*; *Felix Victirx Pia Semper*; *Severiana*
Emblem	Boar
Main base	Novae
Major campaigns	Civil war (AD 69); campaign against the Sarmatians (AD 69–70); Domitian and Trajan's Dacian wars (AD 86–89; 101–6); Trajan's Parthian war (vexillation?, 115–117); Second Jewish Revolt (vexillation?, 132–35); Mauretania (vexillation, *c.* 150); Marcus Aurelius' Marcomannic wars (166–80); Severus' civil war against Niger (193–94); 3rd-century wars on the Danube frontier

I Italica in Moesia

Vitellius' defeated legions were dispersed across Illyricum (the modern Balkans). *I Italica* must have been one of the legions stationed in Moesia, under the governor Fonteius Agrippa, along with *V Alaudae*, *VII Claudia* and *V Macedonia*. Tacitus (*Histories* 3.46) claims that, in the interests of peace, the intention was to distract them with foreign wars and almost immediately, in winter AD 69–70, the legions had to deal with a Sarmatian invasion of Moesia. The First Legion was heavily defeated and Agrippa was killed (Josephus, *Jewish War* 7.89–91). After this defeat, the new governor, Rubrius Gallus, reorganized the army of Moesia. From this time, *I Italica*'s main base was at Novae (near modern Svištov).

The legion apparently garrisoned a number of small outposts in militarily important parts to the west of the province. An inscription (*CIL* 3, 14409,1) referring to the *principales* of the garrison at Almus (modern Lom), the last major city on the Danube before Upper Moesia, suggests this was one of these outposts.

Like the other Balkan legions, *I Italica* took part in the Dacian campaigns under Domitian and Trajan (see page 176). Inscriptions have been found that record members of the legion, such as the tribune Gaius Nummius Verus (*CIL* 11, 3100), decorated for their acts during these wars.

All the legions of Moesia, or their vexillations, were probably involved in Trajan's Parthian campaign, as shown by an inscription found in Rome (*CIL* 6, 32933) which records that Lucius Paconius Proculus led vexillations of the Moesian

I Italica at Novae

Novae is located on the Danube, near Svištov in northern Bulgaria. Having briefly served as the base of *VIII Augusta* (AD 46–69) until that legion moved to Upper Germany, it was the main fortress of *I Italica* from AD 70 to the end of the Roman period. The legion's presence is documented in literary sources and by extensive archaeological evidence, including tombstones naming soldiers of the legion and brick stamps with its *cognomen*.

The site has been excavated partially, over several decades, and is one of the best-known archaeological sites in Bulgaria. The excavations revealed that the original wooden fortress was rebuilt in stone during the reign of Trajan. Extensive sections of the late antique defensive wall have been uncovered, along with the foundations of buildings such as baths, a basilica, *principia* and a hospital, in which medical instruments were found.

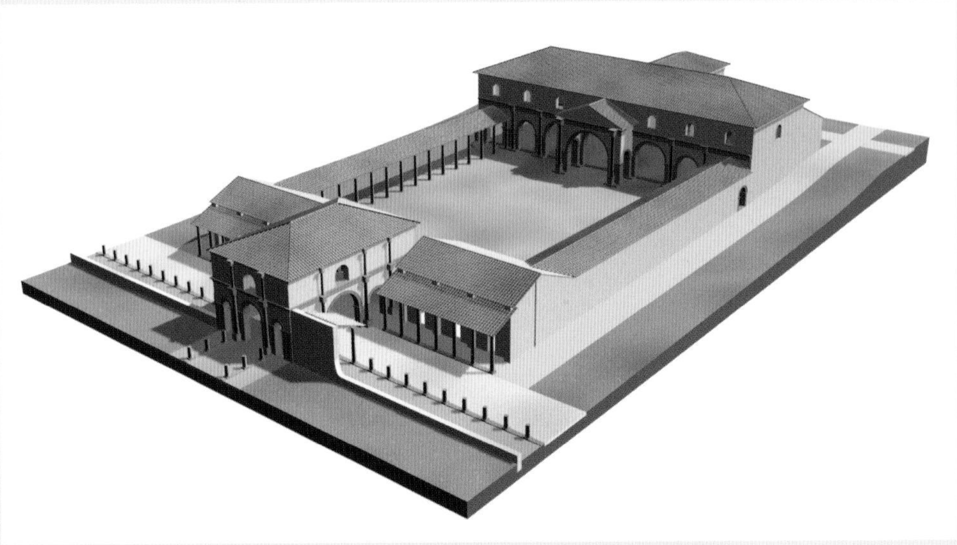

Right *Reconstruction of the central* principia *(headquarters) of the fortress at Novae. This comprised a monumental entrance to the enclosed courtyard with a basilica and administrative rooms. Smaller entrances led to a bath building and barracks.*

Left *Hypothetical reconstruction of the legionary fortress at Novae, constructed in the 1st century* AD*; by the 4th century it had become a fortress-town and was an important urban and religious centre.*

and Dacian legions on a Parthian expedition. A vexillation may have been sent to help put down the Second Jewish Revolt (*CIL* 3, 13586).

During the reign of Antoninus Pius, the situation in Moesia was calm and vexillations of the Moesian legions may have been sent to Mauretania to campaign against the Moors (a barely legible inscription found in Numidia, *CIL* 8, 10474, 13, seems to name *I Italica*). In 139–42, another vexillation may have been in Britain, where an inscription (*AE* 1983, 642) found at Old Kilpatrick at the western end of the Antonine Wall records a centurion of the legion.

The First Legion was part of Marcus Aurelius' army on the Dacian and Danubian frontier from 166 to 175, and again, some of its soldiers were decorated for their bravery. An inscription (*CIL* 8, 2582) records that at this time Aulus Iulius Pompilius Piso was placed in charge of *I Italica* and *IIII Flavia Felix*. By 178 the Romans were again fighting on this northern border, but the conflict ended with the death of Marcus Aurelius in 180, and the succession of Commodus. The next few years were quiet in Moesia. Clodius Albinus, a future claimant to the imperial throne, was an officer of the legion in this period.

Although *I Italica* was based primarily in Lower Moesia, there is evidence that it sent officers and a vexillation to protect Greek towns on the Taurian Chersonese (Crimea). By the 2nd century AD, vexillations from other legions (*V Macedonica* and *XI Claudia*) had joined *I Italica* there. Some of the commanders of the combined force were tribunes of *I Italica*, including Tiberius Plautus Felix Ferruntianus, who, in a late-2nd-century inscription (*CIL* 8, 619), bears the title *praepositus vexillationibus Ponticis apud Scythia(m) et Tauriam* ('Commander of the Pontic detachments in Scythia and Tauria'). Tile stamps from a small fort at Charax (modern Ai Todor) provide further

Excavation of the *principia* at Novae (shown here) revealed inscribed statue bases of at least six emperors from Marcus Aurelius to Severus Alexander, dedicated by the *primi pili* of the legion. There were also statues of Jupiter, Victory, Mars and the *Genius* (divine spirit) of the legion. The *principia* was destroyed by the Huns in the 5th century.

evidence for this vexillation. The stamps (*CIL* 3, 14215–4) record that the tiles were produced under supervision of a centurion of the legion.

Activities in the 3rd Century AD

Our evidence for the activities of *I Italica* is patchier in the 3rd century AD. Memorials to soldiers of *I Italica* of that period have been found at Salona (modern Split) in Dalmatia, suggesting that the legion, or part of it, was based there (e.g. *CIL* 3, 2009). This may have been during the reign of Severus Alexander, when the legion was awarded the cognomen *Alexandriana* (*AE* 1991, 1378). Moesia was invaded repeatedly by Goths in the middle years of the 3rd century and during this period *I Italica* was active in the field and known for its ferocity, bearing the title *Felix Victrix Pia Semper Ubique* ('Fortunate, Victorious and Dutiful Always and Everywhere'; *ZPE* 95, 1993, 197–203), which was found on a statue base at the legion's fortress at Novae).

The *Notitia Dignitatum* shows the legion still guarding the Danube frontier at Novae in the early 5th century, with a detachment based at Sexaginta Prista (modern Ruse, Bulgaria), a small garrison to the east.

Denarius coins naming *I Italica* show the legion supported Septimius Severus in April AD 193. Its legate was Lucius Marius Maximus (*CIL* 3,1450). His legion participated in the lengthy siege of Byzantium against Pescennius Niger and fought against its former legate Clodius Albinus in 196–97. Marius Maximus was Severus' senior commander in this war (and also a writer of history).

IIII Flavia Felix

Cognomen	*Flavia Felix*
Emblem	Lion
Main bases	Singidunum (Belgrade)
Major campaigns	Domitian and Trajan's Dacian wars (AD 86–89, 101–6); Hadrian's Sarmatian war (118); Mauretania (vexillation, *c.* 150); Marcus Aurelius' Marcomannic wars (166–80); Severus' civil war against Niger (vexillation?, 193–94); 3rd-century wars on the Danube frontier

IIII Flavia Felix

IIII Flavia Felix was reconstituted by Vespasian from soldiers of the disbanded *IIII Macedonica*, disgraced during the Batavian Revolt of AD 69–70 (see pages 65–66). It is not clear when the legion received the cognomen *Felix*.

The new legion was initially stationed at Burnum (Kistanje) in Dalmatia, where brick stamps and a few inscriptions attest to the legion's presence, replacing *XI Claudia* which was transferred to the Rhine. It soon moved to Upper Moesia in Domitian's reorganization of the Danube frontier after the Dacian invasions of AD 86 and was stationed at Singidunum (Belgrade). Although Singidunum was the legion's main base, epigraphic traces of its presence have been found throughout the province, at Viminiacum, Horreum Margi (Margum), Timacum Minus and Naissus and elsewhere. In AD 88 the legion was part of Domitian's army that invaded Dacia, defeating Decebalus at Tapae.

Trajan's Dacian Wars

As one of the legions of Moesia, where Trajan gathered forces for his invasions of Dacia, *IIII Flavia Felix* undoubtedly took part in the Dacian wars of 101–6. At the end of the war there is evidence that the legion was stationed briefly at Sarmizegetusa, the capital of the new Roman province of Dacia (*AE* 1933, 242; *AE* 1996, 1279a–e). A number of inscriptions also place the legion at Berzobis (Berzogia), closer to the Sarmatian border, from where it would have guarded the Iron Gates pass on the Danube river. Brick stamps of the legion have been found elsewhere in Dacia, at Sucidava (*AE* 1966, 325) and Drobeta (*AE* 1977, 713).

The Site at Singidunum

Singidunum was originally a Celtic settlement overlooking the confluence of the Sava and the Danube. The Roman fortress was built by *IIII Flavia Felix* in the late 1st century AD, along with the bridge that crossed the Sava connecting Singidunum to Taurunum. Singidunum was the start of the *Via Militaris*, the military road that ran to Constantinople via Viminacium, Naissus, Serdica and Adrianopolis, linking the provinces of Moesia, Dacia and Thrace. The *Notitia Dignitatum* shows the Fourth Legion stationed at Singidunum until at least *c.* 400. The town and fortress were attacked repeatedly by Goths and Huns in the 4th and 5th centuries, and eventually fell from Roman control in the 6th century.

Although the Roman fortress itself was later built over, elements of its walls can still be seen in the west wall of the Kalemegdan (the later fortress of Belgrade). Excavations have revealed cemeteries and a temple of the Roman period nearby, with other Roman material from the vicinity of modern Belgrade. The names of soldiers and veterans of *IIII Flavia Felix* are recorded in numerous inscriptions, mainly funerary, but also some religious dedications.

Fortress walls of Singidunum (in Kalemegdan, Belgrade). After trans-Danubian Dacia was abandoned in AD 271, Singidunum was an important stronghold against Sarmatians and Huns, to whom it fell in the 5th century.

Subsequently, the Fourth Legion returned to Singidunum, where it was responsible for guarding important road routes. Inscriptions tell us about military control posts along the *Via Militaris* at Naissus (modern Niš on the Morava) (*CIL* 3, 8249) and Ulpiana (*CIL* 3, 8173), at a junction of the roads from the Aegean and the Adriatic.

The 2nd and 3rd Centuries AD

The Danube regions were relatively quiet after Trajan's conquests, and like other Balkan legions, *IIII Flavia Felix* probably sent a vexillation to Mauretania to fight the Moors during the reign of Antoninus Pius. A monument and numerous inscriptions of the 2nd century AD have also been found at Aquincum (Budapest) which suggest that a vexillation may have been based there while that fortress's normal legion, *II Adiutrix*, campaigned in Parthia with Lucius Verus. With the other legions of Moesia, *IIII Flavia Felix* must have played an important part in Marcus Aurelius' Marcomannic wars after 166.

In the 180s Clodius Albinus was an officer of *IIII Flavia Felix* (*SHA Clodius Albinus* 6.2). Nevertheless, when civil war broke out in 193, along with the other Danube legions, the Fourth supported Septimius Severus, the governor of Upper Pannonia. An inscription (*CIL* 3, 387) from Alexandria Troas in northwestern Turkey suggest that part of the legion followed Severus east for the civil war and subsequent Parthian wars. Its legate at this time was Gaius Julius Avitus Alexianus, Severus' Syrian brother-in-law (*AE* 1963, 42).

A selection of undated inscriptions from throughout the empire emphasize the importance of the experienced Danube legions as a source of vexillations for campaigns beyond the Balkans in the late 2nd–early 3rd centuries, but include little specific information about their contexts. One is a soldier's tombstone from Cyrrhus in Syria (*CIL* 3, 195) attesting to the legion's participation in a Persian war of this period. Similarly undatable evidence from Speyer, Germany, (*CIL* 13, 6104) records involvement in a campaign against the Alamanni. According to the *Notitia Dignitatum*, the Fourth was still stationed at Singidunum in the early 5th century.

The Legions of Pannonia

Pannonia lay to the south and west of the Danube, and came under Roman control in 12–9 BC, after a long history of conflict with the Roman empire starting in the late 2nd century BC. In AD 6, the region rebelled against Roman rule and it took three years to crush the revolt. Afterwards, the province of Pannonia was created. It was divided in two in AD 106, Superior (Upper) to the west and Inferior (Lower) to the east. Both provinces were further subdivided under Diocletian. During the 4th century, Pannonia suffered a series of Gothic invasions.

The Pannonian Revolt

The historian Velleius Paterculus was prefect of a cavalry unit of Tiberius' army in Germany, part of a huge force mustered for an attack on the Marcomanni in AD 6, when news arrived of events in Pannonia:

> ...all Pannonia, arrogant from the benefits of a long period of peace and mature in its power, suddenly took up arms, bringing with it in alliance Dalmatia and all the other peoples who lived in that region.... Roman citizens were oppressed, traders were slaughtered and a large formation of recalled veterans, stationed in the region farthest from their commander, was exterminated. Macedonia was seized by armed enemies and the whole region was completely devastated by fire and the sword.
> Velleius Paterculus, *Roman History* 2.110

It took Tiberius three years to pacify Pannonia and Dalmatia.

The reliefs on the Column of Marcus Aurelius tell the story of the Marcomannic wars, which broke out in 166. The Column was dedicated in 193, after the emperor's death, to commemorate his victories.

X Gemina

X Gemina originated as Caesar's famous Tenth Legion (see page 26), serving with him in Gaul and in the civil war against Pompey the Great and his senatorial supporters in battles such as Pharsalus (in Greece, 48 BC), and Thapsus (Tunisia, 46 BC). After Munda, the last battle of the civil war in 45 BC, the legion's veterans were settled on land in southern Gaul, at Narbo (Narbonne).

After Caesar's death, the legion was almost immediately reconstituted and fought against Caesar's assassins at Philippi in 42 BC. Some veterans were settled at Cremona in north Italy after this battle. The rest of the legion went east with Mark Antony, taking part in his Parthian war (40–33 BC). At Actium in 31 BC, when Octavian defeated Mark Antony, the Tenth was one of the legions forced to surrender, albeit reluctantly. Suetonius (*Augustus* 24) comments that Octavian 'discharged with dishonour the entire Tenth Legion, because they obeyed him in an insolent manner'.

Soldiers from other legions were transferred into its ranks, leading to a new title, *Gemina* ('Twin'). The chastened legion was then sent to Spain, where it took part in Augustus' Cantabrian campaigns of 25–13 BC. Evidence of the legion has been found in Astorga in the northwest (*AE* 1928, 163 and *AE* 1904, 160) and also further south, where it would have policed the Astures and the Callaeci. Epigraphic evidence suggests that its main base at this time was at Petavonium (modern Rosinos de Vidriales), in Hispania Tarraconensis (*CIRPZamora* 133, 135, 136, 145; *AE* 1976, 289), but other smaller outposts have been identified on the basis of inscriptions. Early coins reveal that its veterans were among the first settlers of Augusta Emerita (Merida) and Caesaraugusta (Saragossa).

After about a century in Spain, *X Gemina* was transferred to Carnuntum in Pannonia, where a number of inscriptions attest to its presence. The exact date is unknown, but it was not before AD 62–63, since Carnuntum was garrisoned by *XV Apollinaris* until then. Within a couple of years Galba had sent the legion back to Spain and it is thought that Carnuntum was handed over to the newly raised *VII Galbiana*.

X Gemina

Cognomina	*Equestris*; *Gemina*; *Domitiana*; *Antoniniana*; *Severiana*; *Gordiana*; *Deciana*; *Floriana*; *Cariniana*
Emblem	Bull
Main bases	Vindobona (Vienna)
Major campaigns	Caesar's Gallic and civil wars (58–45 BC), Philippi (42 BC), Mark Antony's Parthian war (40–33 BC); Actium (31 BC); Augustus' Cantabrian war (27–19 BC); Batavian Revolt (AD 69–70); Saturninus' Revolt (AD 89); Trajan's second Dacian war? (105–6); Second Jewish Revolt (132–35); Mauretania (vexillation, *c.* 150); Lucius Verus' Parthian war (vexillation, 161–66); Marcus Aurelius' Marcomannic wars (166–80); Severus' civil war against Niger? (vexillation, 193–94); 3rd-century wars on the Danube frontier, perhaps including those of Caracalla, Decius and Carinus

Transfer to Germania

During the Year of the Four Emperors (AD 69; see page 59), the legion declared for Vitellius, but otherwise played no part in the events. It was one of the legions sent to Germany with Petillius Cerialis to put down the Batavian Revolt (AD 69–70). Almost immediately it came under attack by the Batavians:

> The troops who had been assigned the task of attacking the camp of the Tenth Legion thought it would be difficult to assault a legion, but managed to rout a group of soldiers who had left the camp for fatigue duties, to cut timber. Their camp prefect was killed, along with five of the leading centurions and a few soldiers. The rest defended themselves behind the ramparts.
>
> Tacitus, *Histories* 5. 20

After the revolt, *X Gemina* (or part of it) was stationed at Hunerberg, east of Noviomagus (Nijmegen) where they could keep watch over the defeated Batavians. One inscription here commemorates two soldiers born in Spain (*CIL* 13, 8732). Other inscriptions relating to members of the legion have also been found at Novaesium (Neuss; *AE* 1905, 139), and Vetera (Xanten; *AE* 1899, 8; *AE* 1905, 234; *CIL* 13, 8646).

In AD 89 the Tenth Legion was in the army that defeated Lucius Antoninus Saturninus, who had led *XIV Gemina* and *XXI Rapax* in revolt against

Domitian (see page 80). For its loyalty to the emperor, the legion was awarded the title *Pia Fidelis Domitiana* ('Dutiful and Loyal, of Domitian'; *CIL* 13, 7717). When Domitian was murdered in AD 96, *Domitiana* was dropped from the title.

Back to Pannonia

The Tenth Legion now moved to Aquincum (Budapest) to help defend the Danube frontier. It probably took part in Trajan's second Dacian war (105–6), but the evidence is not conclusive. It has also been suggested that Trajan used the legion in his Parthian campaign, but again the evidence is contested. Inscriptions relating to the legion have been found in Greece, Asia Minor and Syria, but only one can be dated with certainty (*AE* 1941, 166, to the late 2nd century AD). A few years later during the reign of Hadrian another vexillation was sent to help suppress the Second Jewish Revolt (132–35; *CIL* 6, 3505).

Within a few years the legion had moved again, this time to Vindobona (Vienna). From here, it is possible that a vexillation was sent to Mauretania during Antoninus Pius' reign (based on an inscription found in North Africa, *CIL* 8, 21669). A vexillation was sent to support Lucius Verus' Parthian war (*CIL* 8, 7050). The whole legion must have fought with Marcus Aurelius against the Marcomanni and other Germanic tribes from 166–80. Vindobona was the emperor's base and he died there in 180.

The 3rd Century AD

During the civil wars that followed the death of Commodus in 192, *X Gemina* supported Septimius Severus and may have sent a vexillation to the East to take part in his war against Pescennius Niger (*AE* 1941, 166).

During the 3rd century, the legion received a series of new titles advertising its loyalty to a succession of emperors: *Antoniniana* (Caracalla or Elagabalus; *CIL* 3, 4030), *Gordiana* (Gordian III; *CIL* 11, 6338), *Deciana* (Decius; *CIL* 3, 4558), *Floriana* (Florian; *CIL* 3, 11354) and *Cariniana* (Carinus; *AE* 1987, 821e). Caracalla, Decius and Carinus all campaigned against German tribes, and it is likely that the Tenth Legion took part in these campaigns. Gordian III and Florian both fought in the East, but there is no evidence that the legion was part of their armies. The legion's final titles date to the conflict between Gallienus and his rival emperor Postumus from 260. *X Gemina* supported Gallienus and like many other legions received the title *Pia VI Fidelis VI* ('Six times Dutiful and Loyal').

According to the *Notitia Dignitatum*, the legion was still at Vindobona in the early 5th century. There was also a field-army legion of the same name, probably a vexillation that had taken on its own identity.

This inscription found in Noviomagus (Nijmegen) records a soldier of the Tenth who was born in Amphipolis. It reads: 'Marcus Scanius Maximus, son of Marcus, of the voting tribe Voltinia, from Amphipolis, soldier of the legion *X Gemina Pia Fidelis*, lived 51 years' (*AE* 1979, 415).

The Site at Vindobona

During the reign of Augustus, the Romans built a series of timber fortifications along the Danube frontier, including one at Vindobona (Vienna), which became part of Pannonia. The fortress itself was rebuilt in stone at the beginning of the 2nd century AD, sacked by the Marcomanni in 166 and rebuilt by Marcus Aurelius, but once more rebuilt in the early 3rd century AD. A civilian town grew up around the legionary base. Today the remains of the fortress and town are buried beneath modern Vienna and only small parts have been excavated, including houses with hypocaust heating and an elaborate bath building.

Before the arrival of the Tenth Legion at Vindobona, the fortress housed first *XIII Gemina*, then *XIV Gemina*. All three legions are recorded on brick stamps, inscriptions and monuments found in Vienna.

Reconstruction view of Vindobona, which was situated on the Danube. The fortress was built in the 80s AD by XIII Gemina *and later occupied briefly by* XIV Gemina *before becoming the permanent base of the Tenth Legion in the 2nd century.*

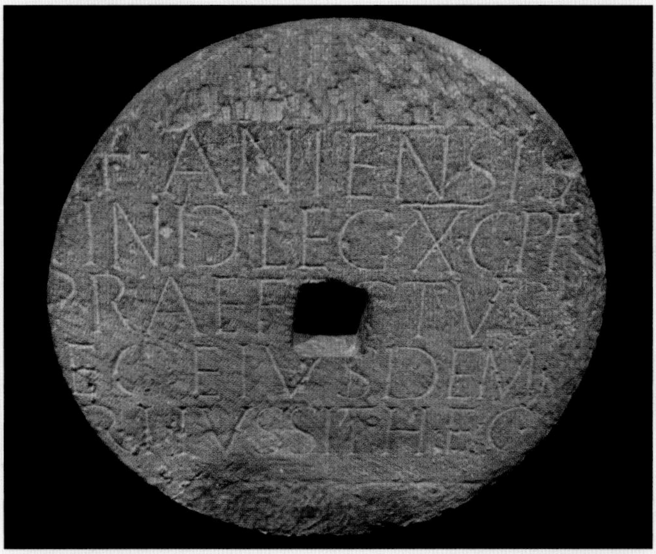

This stone epitaph commemorating an officer of the Tenth Legion was later reused as a quernstone. It was found in Vienna.

XIV Gemina

Julius Caesar raised a Fourteenth Legion before his Belgic campaign in 57 BC. It was effectively destroyed by the Gallic Eburones in the winter of 54/53 BC and then re-established, serving in the subsequent civil war, notably in the Thapsus campaign in Africa in 46 BC. Octavian had a Fourteenth Legion after 41 BC, either descended from Caesar's or newly raised. It must have fought against Antony at Actium and afterwards been reinforced with soldiers from Antony's disbanded legions, explaining its cognomen *Gemina* ('Twin'). A single inscription (*CIL* 5, 2497) suggests that Octavian settled veterans of the legion at the colony of Ateste in Gallia Cisalpina.

In AD 6 *XIV Gemina* was one of at least eight legions assembled by Tiberius to campaign against King Maroboduus of the Marcomanni. However, the outbreak of the Pannonian Revolt meant that the Romans were forced to conclude a treaty with Maroboduus to deal with the troubles in Illyricum (the Balkans). After Varus' disastrous defeat in the Teutoburg Forest in AD 9 (see pages 54–59), *XIV Gemina* was transferred to Moguntiacum (Mainz) in Upper Germany, where it shared a base with *XVI Gallica.*

A number of tombstones attest to the presence of these legions. In AD 21 *XIV Gemina* (or a vexillation), was sent to suppress a revolt by the Turoni in Gaul, who had rebelled against heavy taxation. The legion is next found in the army that campaigned against the Chatti during Caligula's reign. The Chatti were finally defeated near *XIV Gemina*'s Moguntiacum base in the winter of AD 40/41.

XIV Gemina

Cognomina	*Gemina*; *Martia Victrix*; *Pia VI Fidelis VI*
Emblems	Capricorn; eagle
Main base	Carnuntum (Petronell)
Major campaigns	Dyrrhacium (48 BC); Pharsalus (48 BC); Actium (31 BC); against the Turoni (AD 21); against the Chatti? (AD 40/41); invasion of Britain (AD 43); against the Silures, Ordovices and Deceangi (AD 47–52); Boudican Revolt (AD 60–61); first battle of Bedriacum (AD 69); against the Batavian Revolt (AD 69–70); Domitian's war against the Chatti (AD 83); against the Suebians and Sarmatians (AD 92–93); Trajan's Dacian wars (101–6); against the Moors (144–52); Lucius Verus' Parthian war (161–66); Marcus Aurelius' Marcomannic wars (166–80); against the Parthians (194–99)

The Legion in Britain

The Fourteenth Legion was probably one of the legions Claudius sent to invade Britain in AD 43, although is not firmly attested in Britain until the Boudican Revolt (AD 60–61; see page 97) when it defeated Boudica's forces, earning itself the title *Martia Victrix* ('Warlike and Victorious') from Nero. Before the revolt it must have campaigned in Wales (Gaius Suetonius Paullinus marched the legion from Anglesey to meet Boudica's forces) against the Silures, Ordovices and Deceangi. Inscriptions suggest that the legion was based at Viroconium (Wroxeter).

Transfer to the Balkans

XIV Gemina was transferred from Britain in AD 68 for eastern campaigns planned by Nero. These were prevented by the Jewish Revolt, and the legion was in the Balkans when Nero committed suicide (summer AD 68). In the civil war of AD 69, it supported Otho, along with the other Balkan legions, and marched to Bedriacum (Cremona) to fight for Otho against Vitellius, though the main body of the legion failed to arrive in time for the defeat:

> The Fourteenth Legion was particularly famous, as it had put down the revolt in Britain. Nero had added to its glory by singling out its men as his mightiest soldiers, which was why it had been loyal to him for so long, and enthusiastic in its support for Otho. But the stronger and more loyal they were, the slower their advance.
>
> Tacitus, *Histories* 2.11

The legion claimed it had not been defeated, and Vitellius sent it back to Britain to reduce any threat it might pose to his power. It marched north with a cohort of Batavian auxiliaries, old rivals, their rivalry breaking out into violence on a number of occasions on the way (Tacitus, *Histories* 2.66). The legion remained in Britain for the remainder of the civil war between Vitellius and Vespasian, even though they received letters exhorting them to support Vespasian.

Opposite Tombstone of Gnaeus Musius, found in Mainz. Musius was *aquilifer* of the Fourteenth Legion, and died at the age of 32 after 15 years' service. His tombstone was set up by his brother, Marcus Musius, a centurion (*CIL* 13, 6901).

Back to the Continent

In AD 70 *XIV Gemina* was summoned back to mainland Europe as part of the army commanded by Petillius Cerialis to suppress the Batavian Revolt. It took part in the decisive battle at Vetera (Xanten), where, acccording to Tacitus (*Histories* 5.16), the legionaries were incited by Cerialis calling them 'Conquerors of Britain'. It was then sent back to Moguntiacum (Mainz), a base it now shared with *XXI Rapax*. Its first task was to rebuild the fortress, destroyed in the revolt. It was also responsible for building a bridge over the Rhine.

In AD 89 *XIV Gemina* and *XXI Rapax* supported Antonius Saturninus, governor of Upper Germany, in his revolt against Domitian (see page 80). This was put down quickly by the legions of Lower Germany. *XXI Rapax* was sent to Pannonia where, in AD 92, it was destroyed by the Dacians. *XIV Gemina* was subsequently sent to Pannonia to replace it, based firstly at Osijek and later at Vindobona (Vienna). From Vindobona it campaigned against the Suebians and Sarmatians in AD 92–93, and then took part in Trajan's Dacian wars (101–6). Veterans of *XIV* settled at Colonia Ulpia Traiana Augusta Dacica (Sarmizegetusa), capital of the new province of Dacia (modern Romania).

The legion was now based at Carnuntum (Petronell, Austria), on the Danube, and remained there for the next three centuries. Vexillations were sent to North Africa to support *III Augusta* in its campaign against the Moors during the reign of Antoninus Pius (144–52), and to the eastern frontier for Lucius Verus' Parthian war (161–66). Marcus Aurelius used Carnuntum as his headquarters during the Marcomannic wars (166–80), suggesting that the Fourteenth was involved in this conflict.

It was in Carnuntum that Lucius Septimius Severus was proclaimed emperor in 193, granting 1,000 sesterces to each soldier. He took a large part of *XIV Gemina* with him on his march to Rome, and vexillations fought in the civil war against Pescennius Niger.

There is little evidence of the legion's activities after this period. It supported a usurper called Regalianus in 260–1, and Gallienus (260–68) against the usurper Postumus, receiving the titles *Pia VI Fidelis VI.* ('Six times Dutiful and Loyal'). When Gallienus died, *XIV* supported the Gallic emperor Victorinus (269–71). The *Notitia Dignitatum* records that the legion was still at Carnuntum at the start of the 5th century AD.

I Adiutrix

I Adiutrix was formed in AD 67 or 68 from sailors of the Misenum fleet (*CIL* 16, 7–9), either by Nero or, if after his suicide in AD 68, by Galba (Cassius Dio 55.24.2). A year later it fought for Otho alongside *XIII Gemina*, but was defeated at the first battle of Bedriacum. Vitellius then sent it to Spain, but by AD 70 it was in Germany, fighting the Batavians under the command of Petillius Cerialis.

Brick stamps and tiles reveal that *I Adiutrix*'s first legionary base was at Moguntiacum (Mainz), which it shared with *XIV Gemina*. From there the legion was transferred to Pannonia (where it would remain into the 5th century), taking over the legionary fortress there at Brigetio (modern Szöny, in Hungary) after 118.

In AD 86 the Roman legions of Moesia suffered a defeat at the hands of the Dacians. *I Adiutrix* participated in Domitian's retaliatory expedition and two years later fought at the Dacian capital Tapae when the Romans defeated Decebalus. An inscription (*ILS* 9200) reveals that a year later a vexillation of *I Adiutrix*, along with vexillations of other legions, was commanded by Gaius Velius Rufus, probably during this campaign.

In AD 97 the legion took part in Nerva's Suebian war, along the Danube between Brigetio and Vindobona. One of its tribunes, Quintus Attius Priscus, was decorated for actions in this campaign. It has been argued that the legion received the title *Pia Fidelis* for its actions during this war, but the epithet might equally have been awarded for service in Trajan's second Dacian war.

I Adiutrix

Cognomina	*Adiutrix; Pia Fidelis Bis; Constans*
Emblems	Capricorn; Pegasus
Main base	Brigetio (Szöny, Hungary).
Major campaigns	Civil war (AD 69); Batavian Revolt (AD 70), Domitian's wars in Germany and Dacia (AD 83; AD 86–89); Nerva's Suebian war (AD 97); Trajan's Dacian and Parthian wars (101–6; 115–17); Second Jewish Revolt (vexillation?, 132–35); Marcus Aurelius' Marcomannic wars (166–80); Severus' civil war against Niger and Parthian wars (vexillation?, 193–94; 195–97); Caracalla's Parthian war (vexillation?, 215–17); Gordian III's Parthian war (vexillation, 244); 3rd-century wars on the Danube frontier

The 2nd Century AD

I Adiutrix was used by Trajan in his conquest of Dacia (101–6), and was in the subsequent occupying force, with a vexillation stationed at Apulum (Alba Iulia, Romania), where a handful of inscriptions relating to the legion have been found. An inscription found in Syria (*CIL* 3, 6706) suggests that the legion also took part in his Parthian war (115–17), but returned to Brigetio at its conclusion. Subsequently, parts of the legion were sent to wars in other regions. For example, a Bar Kochva coin was found at Brigetio, suggesting that some soldiers were sent to Judaea for the Second Jewish Revolt (132–35). Another vexillation formed part of the force commanded by Pertinax (who would be emperor briefly in

The Fortress at Brigetio

The Romans established an auxiliary fort at Brigetio in the reign of Claudius, when numerous roads were being constructed throughout Pannonia. It was converted into a stone legionary fortress under Domitian and completed in AD 97 by the future emperor Trajan. Occupied initially by *XI Claudia* and *XXX Ulpia Victrix*, it became the permanent base of *I Adiutrix* after Hadrian's Sarmatian war (118).

Today the legionary fortress of Brigetio lies in the vicinity of Szöny. Excavations have uncovered its walls, towers and gates, a necropolis, baths, several temples and an amphitheatre, as well as the forum and some housing from the civilian settlement that grew up around it.

One of the many bricks stamped with *LEG I AD* found at Mainz.

193), campaigning against the Marcomanni in Bohemia in the 170s (*SHA Pertinax* 2.6). The legion also engaged in construction work throughout Upper Pannonia, for example at Scarbantia and Carnuntum.

After Pertinax's assassination in 193, *I Adiutrix* declared for Septimius Severus, as shown by the coins minted by the emperor at the end of the civil war to honour and pay the legions that supported him. Severus employed the legion against Pescennius Niger and in his two Parthian campaigns. In 244 the legion fought against the Persians for Gordian III (*CIL* 3, 196).

Closer to its home base, *I Adiutrix* fought for Maximinius in the civil war of 238, taking part in the siege of Aquileia in northern Italy (*CIL* 5, 954). Its titles in that period, *Severiana, Maximiniana* and *Pupiena Balbina Gordiana*, show how the legion switched allegiance from Severus Alexander, to Maximinus and then to Gordian III and his co-emperors Pupienus and Balbinus. Also in the course of the 3rd century, the legion earned the titles *Pia Fidelis Bis* ('Twice Dutiful and Loyal') and *Constans* ('Reliable'). Undoubtedly it also participated in the regular and ferocious wars against foreign enemies that took place on the Danube frontier through the 3rd century. According to the *Notitia Dignitatum*, the legion was still at Brigetio in the early 5th century AD.

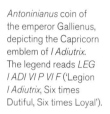

Antoninianus coin of the emperor Gallienus, depicting the Capricorn emblem of *I Adiutrix*. The legend reads *LEG I ADI VI P VI F* ('Legion *I Adiutrix*, Six times Dutiful, Six times Loyal').

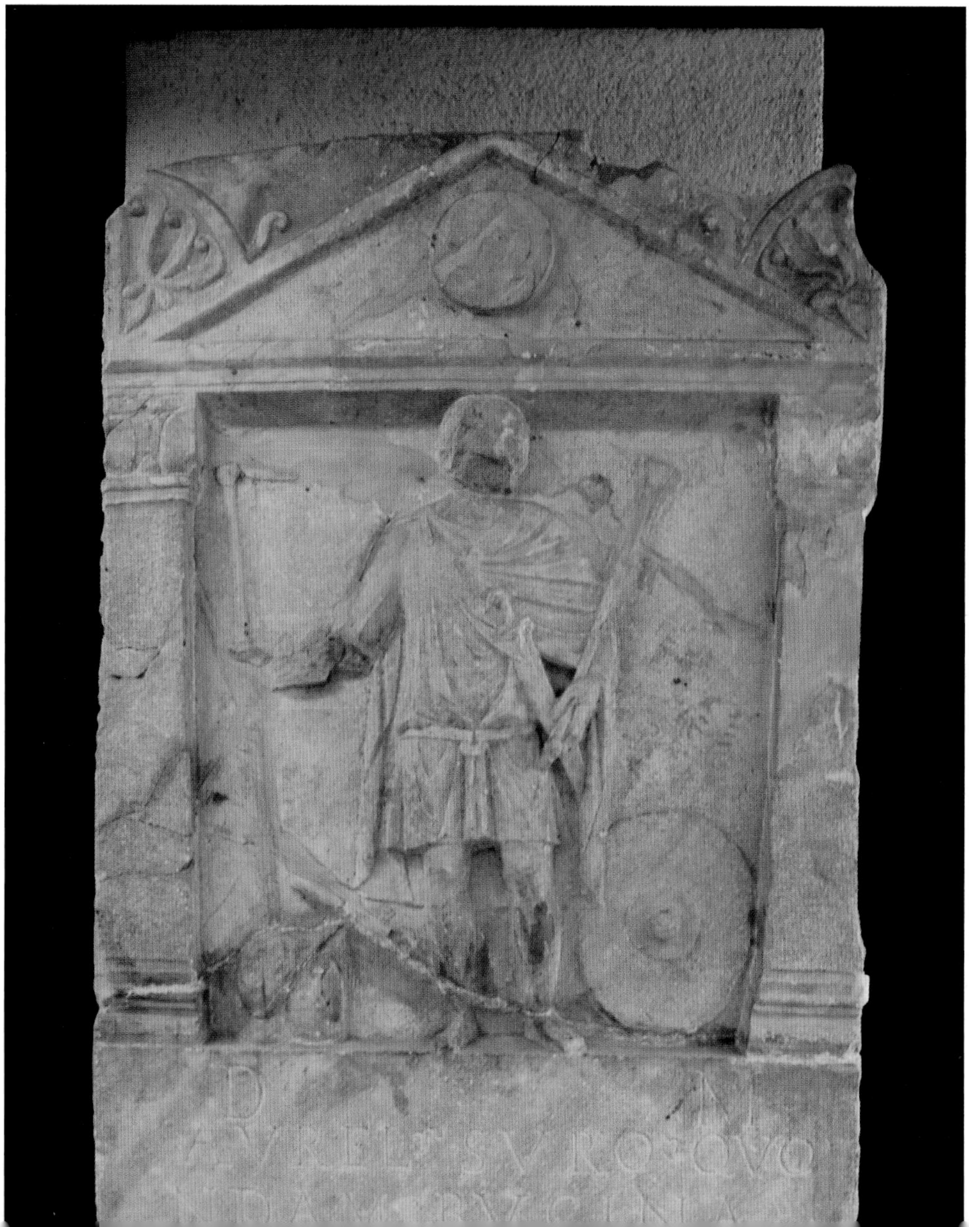

In the late 2nd century, Aurelius Surus was a trumpeter of *I Adiutrix*. His gravestone (*AE* 1976, 642) was found in Constantinople and depicts him holding his trumpet. Tombstones of two other soldiers from the legion have been found at Perinthus (*CIL* 3, 7396) and Zeugma (*AE* 2003, 1791b); all three may relate to Severus' Parthian campaigns, or those of his son Caracalla (215–17).

II Adiutrix

A military diploma reveals that *II Adiutrix* was formed in AD 70 by Vespasian, from marines of the Ravenna fleet who had supported him against Vitellius (*CIL* 16, 9; 11). The title *Adiutrix* or 'Helper' perhaps relates to its original role 'helping' the Flavian cause: the legion saw its first action in the year of its creation, when it was sent with Quintus Petillius Cerialis to suppress the Batavian Revolt. Together with *VI Victrix*, *XIV Gemina* and *XXI Rapax*, it defeated Julius Civilis' rebels besieging Vetera (Xanten). It remained at Vetera for a year, before being replaced by *XXII Primigenia*.

Cerialis then took the legion to Britain in AD 71, where it saw action against the Brigantes, who had revolted under Venutius. Inscriptions suggest it may have been stationed at Deva (Chester; *RIB* 1, 483) and Lindum (Lincoln; *RIB* 1, 253, 258).

II Adiutrix

Cognomina	*Adiutrix*; *Pia Fidelis*
Emblems	Boar; Pegasus
Main base	Aquincum (Budapest)
Major campaigns	Batavian Revolt (AD 70); campaigns in Britain against the Brigantes and Ordovices (AD 71–77); Domitian's Dacian war (AD 86–89), Trajan's Dacian and Parthian wars (101–5; 115–17), Hadrian's Sarmatian war (118); Second Jewish Revolt (vexillation, 132–35); Mauretania (vexillation, 150); Lucius Verus' Parthian war (vexillation?, 161–66), Marcus Aurelius' Marcomannic wars (166–80); Severus civil war against Niger and his Parthian wars? (193–94; 195–97); Caracalla's war against the Alamanni and Parthian wars (213; 216–17); 3rd-century wars on the Danube frontier

Under the governorship of Agricola (AD 77–84) it campaigned against the Ordovices in Wales and occupied the Isle of Mona (Anglesey).

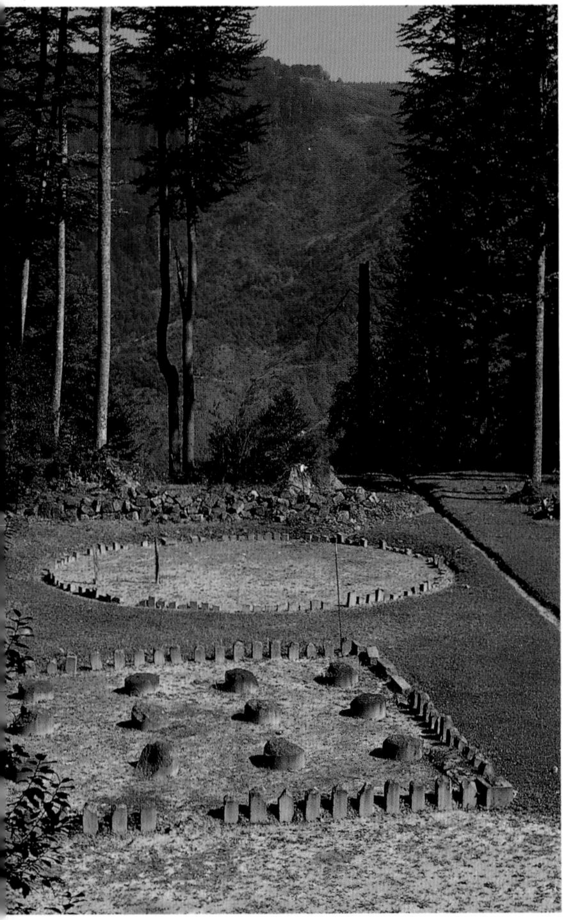

The site of Sarmizegetusa Regia, the Dacian capital. This site was destroyed during Trajan's Dacian wars (101–6) and the Romans established a new capital, Ulpia Traiana Sarmizegetusa, 40 miles away. Veterans of the Dacian wars settled here.

War in Dacia and the East

A vexillation was sent to the continent where it was commanded by Velius Rufus, probably taking part in Domitian's Dacian war of AD 85 (*ILS* 9200). The rest of the legion followed this vexillation to the Lower Danube region shortly afterwards. Its base was at Sirmium (modern Sremska Mitrovica), where numerous inscriptions relating to the legion have been found. In AD 88 it was part of the army of nine legions that defeated the Dacian king Decebalus at Tapae. The future emperor Hadrian was a tribune of the legion in AD 95 (*ILS* 308).

During Trajan's Dacian campaigns, *II Adiutrix* was based at Singidunum (Belgrade) along with *IIII Flavia Felix*. An inscription at Sarmizegetusa reveals it was in the army that took the Dacian capital. It also took part in Trajan's Parthian campaigns. Then, in 106, it was transferred to Aquincum (Budapest), where it remained for many centuries.

II Adiutrix participated in several wars east of the Danube in the 2nd century AD. In 118, Quintus Marcius Turbo led the legion against the Sarmatians (*AE* 1933, 31) and, based on inscriptions of the legion's soldiers found in Thessaloniki (*CIL* 3, 3528), Pelagonia (*CIL* 3, 3530) and Ancyra (*CIL* 3, 10497), a vexillation

Tombstone of a soldier of II Adiutrix, *Gaius Castricius Victor, who served 38 years (CIL 3, 14349 – 2). The tombstone was found at Aquincum, the legion's fortress from 106 until the 5th century.*

*The ruins of the fortress at Aquincum lie beneath modern Budapest. Parts of the city walls still stand, however, and excavations have revealed parts of the civilian settlement (*above*), including an amphitheatre (*below*), houses, an aqueduct, baths and two* mithraea.

The Fort at Aquincum

Aquincum (modern Budapest) lay at an important crossing-point of the Danube. A Roman auxiliary fort was located here from the reign of Tiberius and a legionary fortress from the reign of Domitian. In AD 106 Aquincum became the capital of Lower Pannonia and *II Adiutrix* took over the fortress. Numerous inscriptions, including dedications and epitaphs, have been found naming individual members of the legion. In the 4th century AD, Aquincum came under frequent attack by the Sarmatians, and in the 5th century it was overrun by Germans.

may have helped to put down the Second Jewish Revolt (132–35). During the reign of Antoninus Pius a vexillation may have been sent to Mauretania to fight against the Moors. *II Adiutrix* then fought against the Parthians (161–66) under Lucius Verus (*AE* 1893, 88). By 171 the legion was back on the Danube, fighting against the Marcomanni.

In the civil war of 193, *II Adiutrix* supported Septimius Severus, governor of Upper Pannonia. It accompanied him to Rome, probably fought against Pescennius Niger, and perhaps took part in Severus' Parthian wars. There is some epigraphic evidence that vexillations were involved in Caracalla's campaign against the Alamanni (213) and his Parthian war of 216–17. Our later knowledge of the legion is sketchy, although it must have taken part in foreign and domestic wars through the turbulent 3rd century. According to the *Notitia Dignitatum*, *II Adiutrix* was still based at Aquincum in the early 5th century AD.

Below left Aurelius Bitus, trumpeter of *II Adiutrix*, set up this tombstone in Aquincum for his son, who died at the age of 4 years, 11 months and 17 days (*CIL* 3, 15160).

Below Scenes from the Dacian wars (101–6) are depicted on Trajan's Column in Rome. At the end of the wars Dacia became a Roman province.

The Legions of Noricum

The province of Noricum (modern Austria) encompassed the eastern Alps to the south of the Danube. It was incorporated into the Roman empire in 16 BC, but only during Marcus Aurelius' Marcomannic wars was a legion, *II Italica*, based permanently in the province. The emperor Diocletian divided the province into two: Noricum Ripense on the Danube and Noricum Mediterraneum to the south. In the 5th century Germanic tribes overran Noricum.

II Italica	
Cognomina	*Pia*; *Italica*; *Fidelis*; *Antoniniana*; *Severiana*; *Gordiana*
Emblems	Capricorn; she-wolf and twins
Main base	Lauriacum
Major campaigns	Marcus Aurelius' Marcomannic wars (166–80); Severus' civil wars against Niger and Clodius Albinus (193–94; 197); Maximinus' war against the Dacians (235–36); 3rd-century wars in the region, including against the Goths

II Italica

According to Cassius Dio (55.24), *II Italica* was raised by Marcus Aurelius. It was recruited in Italy *c.* AD 165 to fight in Noricum at the same time that *III Italica* was raised to fight in Raetia. Both new legions were created to combat the Marcomanni and protect Italy from incursions while other legions were engaged in the Parthian campaigns of Marcus Aurelius' co-emperor Lucius Verus. The single cognomen, *Pia*, is found on the earliest inscription naming it (*CIL* 3, 1980), but *Italica* soon appears and was used as the legion's main title.

Transfer to Noricum

The legion's first base is unknown, and it may have lacked a permanent fortress in its early years, serving as a mobile reserve in the Marcomannic wars. *II Italica* may have been based temporarily in a fortress at Lotschitz (Ločica), constructed *c.* 168–69 and occupied only briefly. Brick stamps from the site name the legion and individual soldiers, such as Quintianus (*CIL* 3, 5757, 4), Auspicatus (*CIL* 3, 14369,2l), and Fabianus (*CIL* 3, 14369, 2n). From this location the legion could guard the route from Pannonia to Aquileia in Italy. We know that the future emperor Publius Helvius Pertinax campaigned successfully in Raetia and Noricum. It seems likely that *II Italica* and *III Italica* formed part of his army.

A few brick stamps of the legion have been found at Albing (an island in the Danube) in Noricum, which may mean that part of the legion was based there briefly after 172. However, *II Italica* soon established its permanent base at Lauriacum (Enns-Lorch), just 5 km (3.1 miles) away. The construction of the legionary fortress (on the site of an auxiliary fort) took place in the last years of Marcus Aurelius' reign.

Lauriacum was located at the confluence of the Danube and its tributary the Enns and was the base of the governor of Noricum. *II Italica* remained there until Noricum fell from Roman control in the 5th century AD. Besides the numerous brick stamps there is little epigraphic evidence of its presence besides a few tombstones, and few visible archaeological remains have been found beneath the city of Enns-Lorch. Numerous inscriptions reveal that

The emblem of *II Italica*, the wolf and twins, is found on *antoninianus* coins dating to the reign of Gallienus.

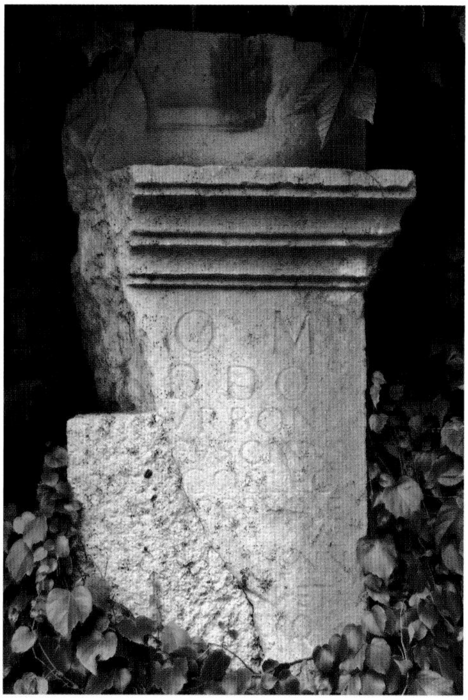

This fragmentary inscription (*AE* 1968, 411, AD 202) found at Grödig in Austria is a dedication to Jupiter Optimus Maximus 'and all the gods and goddesses' by Turbonius Fuscinus, *beneficiarius* of the Second Legion.

Close-up view of the Arch of Constantine, constructed in 315 to commemorate the emperor Constantine's victory over Maxentius at the battle of the Milvian Bridge in 312. The battle is illustrated in the frieze beneath the two roundels (which depict a boar hunt and a sacrifice).

members of the legion were posted to the provincial capital at Virunum (near Magdalensberg) to serve the governor (who was also the legionary legate) and inscriptions relating to individual soldiers have been found throughout the province.

During the civil wars of 193–97, *II Italica* supported Septimius Severus. The emperor later employed the legion against Pescennius Niger and Clodius Albinus, and some men from the legion joined Severus' reorganized Praetorian Guard in Rome.

The 3rd Century and Beyond

II Italica probably took part in Maximinus' Dacian war (235–36), as shown by a fragmentary inscription found at Virunum recording that Veponius Avitus, a legionary of *II Italica*, died 'in the Dacian war' (*CIL* 3, 4857). It supported Gallienus against the pretender Postumus and was given the cognomen *Pia V Fidelis V* ('Five times Dutiful and Loyal'; also *VI* and *VII*, found on coins of the period.

According to the *Notitia Dignitatum*, the Second Legion was still there in the early 5th century, commanded by the *dux Pannoniae Primae et Norici Ripensis*. The legion protected the Danube in western Noricum, and detachments were based at Lentia (Linz; *CIL* 3, 5688; 11853a) and Ioviacum, as well as other locations.

In the late 3rd century, a vexillation was transferred to Divitia (Deutz), near Colonia Claudia Ara Agrippinensis (Cologne), and eventually became a unit in its own right, *II Italica Divitensium*, fighting for Constantine on his way to Rome and at the battle of the Milvian Bridge in 312.

The Legions of Raetia

The province of Raetia was formed in 15 BC and included the modern Tyrol and parts of Bavaria and Switzerland, guarding routes into Italy. Although troops were stationed in the province, it was only during the 2nd-century Marcomannic wars that a full legion, the newly formed *III Italica*, was based there, commanded by the provincial governor.

III Italica

Cognomina	*Italica*; *Concors*; *Gordiana*
Emblem	Stork (the symbol of *Concordia*)
Main base	Castra Regina (Regensburg)
Major campaigns	Marcus Aurelius' Marcomannic wars (AD 166–80); Severus' civil wars? (193–97); Caracalla's Parthian war (vexillation?, 216–17); Gordian III's Persian war (vexillation?, 244)

III Italica

Cassius Dio (55.24.4) tells us that *III Italica* was raised by the emperor Marcus Aurelius, along with *II Italica*. This probably dates to *c.* AD 166, at the time of the emperor's Marcomannic campaigns, in which the legion took part. An inscription (*AE* 1980, 959) records that Gaius Annius Flavius, a tribune of the Third, was awarded *dona militaria* for his role in 'the German war'. The title *Italica* suggests that both legions were initially recruited in Italy. At first the legion also had another cognomen, *Concors* ('Harmonious'; seen on *CIL* 3, 11989a).

The legion's first base is unknown, but an inscription reveals that its earliest legate was Gaius Vettius Sabinianus Iulius Hospes (*AE* 1920, 45). Early on, the legion must have been part of the mobile reserve that also included *II Italica*, commanded by Quintus Antistius Adventus (*ILS* 8977) during the Marcomannic wars. Both legions may have been in the army of the future emperor Pertinax that finally drove back the Marcomanni.

For a time after this victory (*c.* 172–79), *III Italica* may have been based at Eining in Noricum, where brick stamps have been found with the legend *Leg III Ital Con* (*CIL* 3, 11989a–c, *IBR* 496a–b). Late in Marcus Aurelius' reign, the legion's fortress at Castra Regina (modern Regensburg) was built. The fortress itself had imposing fortification walls, unusual at this date. Milestones from the reign of Septimius Severus reveal that the base and the settlement around it became known collectively as 'Legio'. The legion remained there until the 5th century AD, but its legate, the provincial governor, was based at Augusta Vindelicorum (Augsburg), the provincial capital and epitaphs reveal that some members of the legion served him there (e.g. *CIL* 3, 58140).

The 3rd and 4th Centuries AD

Coins minted by Septimius Severus reveal that he enjoyed the legion's support after Pertinax' death in 193. The epitaph (*AE* 1898, 122) of a member of the legion (with the cognomen *Antoniniana*) found at Perinthus (Turkey) suggests that a vexillation took part in Caracalla's Parthian campaign of 216–17. Vexillations may also have fought with Gordian III against the Sasanians in 244, since an inscription (*CIL* 3, 5768) found at Brigentium (Bregenz) gives the legion the cognomen *Gordiana*. Gallienus (260–68) had previously awarded it the cognomen *VI Pia VI Fidelis* ('Six times Dutiful and Loyal' also found with *VII*), found on coins from the period for their service, against his rival, the pretender Postumus.

During the 3rd century the legion's permanent fortress at Regensburg was completely rebuilt.

The *Notitia Dignitatum* records that in the early 5th century AD the legion was commanded by the *dux Raetiae*, divided into five elements based in forts along the Danube, including Regensburg. A sixth vexillation was transferred to Illyricum.

Remains of the east tower of the *porta praetoria* of Castra Regina. Marcus Aurelius' titles in the building inscription (*CIL* 3, 11965) date it to AD 179. Other inscriptions (mainly funerary) and brick stamps found there also name *III Italica*.

The Legions of Dacia

Dacia was a region across the lower Danube (largely modern Romania). The tribes in this area occasionally banded together to threaten Roman territory, but it was not until Decebalus revived Dacian military power in AD 85 that Rome faced a real threat. Decebalus was defeated by the Romans at Tapae in AD 88 and Domitian made peace with him. Trajan later conquered Dacia, destroying Decebalus' capital Sarmizegetusa, making it a province and depicting his victories on Trajan's Column in Rome.

Dacia was invaded by the Goths in the mid-3rd century AD and Aurelian abandoned it in 271. In Late Antiquity there was still a Roman province of Dacia, but it lay on the near side of the Danube, not across the river as before.

V Macedonica

Cognomina	*Macedonica; Pia Fidelis* or *Constans*
Emblems	Bull; eagle (connection to Jupiter?)
Main bases	Potaissa
Major campaigns	Conquest of Moesia? (29–27 BC); other early imperial Balkan campaigns?; Caesennius Paetus' Armenian campaign (AD 62); First Jewish Revolt (Galilee, AD 67; siege of Jerusalem, AD 70); Domitian's Dacian wars (AD 86–89); Trajan's Dacian and Parthian wars (101–6; vexillation, 115–17); Second Jewish Revolt (vexillation, 132–35); Lucius Verus' Parthian war (vexillation, 161–66); Marcus Aurelius' Marcomannic wars (166–80); Pescennius Niger's campaign against the Sarmatians (183); Severus' civil war against Niger and Parthian war (193–94; 195–97); campaign against the Carpi (244–45); other 3rd-century Balkan wars

V Macedonica

This legion's early history is uncertain, although it may have served in the army commanded by Octavian and the consuls Hirtius and Pansa at Mutina in 43 BC. From 30 BC to AD 6 the legion served in Macedonia, hence its cognomen *Macedonica* ('Macedonian'). It may also have been known as *V Scythica* (see below), after Marcus Licinius Crassus' defeat of the 'Scythian' Dacians and Bastarnae in 29–27 BC. It fought subsequently in other Balkan wars and engaged in road-building in the region alongside *IIII Scythica* (see page 138).

Moesia, Dacia and Pontus

In AD 6 the legion was transferred to Oescus (Gigen) in Moesia. Forty years later, the army of Moesia was used by the emperor Claudius to annex Thrace, although the precise role of *V Macedonica* is unknown. In AD 62, *V Macedonica* was transferred to join Caesennius Paetus' army in Cappadocia, and (with *IIII Scythica* and *XII Fulminata*) participated in his disastrous retreat from Armenia (see page 152). Remaining in the East, *V Macedonica* later took part in suppressing the First Jewish Revolt, joining Vespasian's army concentrated at Ptolemais in the winter of AD 66–67 (Josephus, *Jewish War* 3.64–65) and campaigning in Galilee. Josephus describes its prominent role in Titus' siege of Jerusalem in AD 70, particularly in Roman attempts to capture the Antonia Fortress.

The legion's time in Judaea is further attested by a funerary inscription (*Atiqot* 1976, 89) from Abu Ghosh near Jerusalem and a few examples of coins counter-marked LVS, recently interpreted as *L(egio) V S(cythica)*, perhaps attesting another cognomen for *V Macedonica* rather than an error for *IV* (i.e. *IIII*) *Scythica*. After the fall of

Imposing traces of the fortress at Roman Potaissa, located in modern Turda, Romania, can still be seen, including the *principia*. The fortress was built after the conquest of Dacia by Trajan in AD 106, and may have been shared with *XIII Gemina* since the two legions often operated together from the 2nd century onwards.

Jerusalem, *V Macedonica* and *XV Apollinaris* accompanied Titus to Alexandria, from where the former returned to Oescus in Moesia.

As a Moesian legion, *V Macedonica* undoubtedly took part in Domitian's Dacian wars, but nothing specific is known about its participation. The future emperor Hadrian was a military tribune in the legion in AD 96 (*ILS* 308), and by 101 he was its legate for Trajan's Dacian wars. Afterwards, *V Macedonica* garrisoned Troesmis, near the Danube delta, and part of Lower Moesia. Here it guarded the northwest coast of the Black Sea and the Greek cities of the Crimea. Its location there also explains the deployment of detachments for campaigns further east. For example, Hadrian possibly sent a vexillation to Judaea during the Second Jewish Revolt (132–35; *CIL* 3, 13586). Vexillations also took part in Lucius Verus' Parthian campaign in the 160s (*CIL* 3, 7505). During this period some soldiers are also known to have served the provincial governor at Tomis (as shown by *CIL* 3, 7550) and undertook construction activities in the province.

At an unknown date (perhaps after Verus' Parthian campaign) the legion moved again, this time to Potaissa (Turda) in Dacia Porolissensis. Numerous inscriptions reflect the legion's long stay here, until the late 3rd century AD. From here the legion must have taken part in Marcus Aurelius' Marcomannic wars (166–80). The *Historia Augusta* claims that the Dacians were conquered during the reign of Commodus, so it is reasonable to assume that the legion received the cognomen *Pia Fidelis* or *Pia Constans* ('Dutiful and Loyal' or 'Reliable') for their actions in this period.

During the civil war of 193-94, *V Macedonica* sided with Septimius Severus and a vexillation accompanied him to Rome. It later fought with him in Parthia. The legion must have been engaged in fighting in Dacia throughout the 3rd century. Valerian and Gallienus awarded the legion the cognomina *III Pia III Fidelis* and *VII Pia VII Fidelis* respectively.

The emperor Aurelian eventually gave up Trans-Danubian Dacia in 271 and *V Macedonica* returned to its old base at Oescus. Here it remained until at least the early 5th century AD, as shown by the *Notitia Dignitatum*.

XIII Gemina

Cognomina	*Gemina*; *Pia Fidelis*
Emblem	Lion
Main base	Apulum (Alba Iulia, Romania)
Major campaigns	Caesar's Gallic and civil wars (57–45 BC); Octavian's campaigns against Sextus Pompey (38–36 BC); conquest of the Alps (15 BC); Pannonian Revolt (AD 6–9); civil war (first and second battles of Bedriacum, AD 69); Batavian Revolt (AD 69–70); Domitian's Dacian wars and against the Suebi and Sarmatians (AD 86–88; 92–93); Trajan's Dacian wars (101–6); Hadrian's Sarmatian war (118); against the Dacians and Sarmatian Iazyges (158); Marcus Aurelius' Marcomannic wars (166–80); Commodus' Dacian war (183); Severus' civil war against Niger and Parthian wars (193–94; 195–97); against the Alamanni (vexillation, 260s or 270s); other 3rd-century Balkan wars

XIII Gemina

The Thirteenth Legion was raised by Julius Caesar for his campaign against the Belgae in 57 BC and fought throughout his Gallic war. After accompanying him across the river Rubicon in 49 BC, it took part in the subsequent civil war until its soldiers were pensioned off with land in a new colony at Hispellum (Spello) in Italy.

The legion was reconstituted by Octavian in 41 BC – or Octavian raised a new one with the same number – to be used against Sextus Pompey who had occupied Sicily and was preventing grain from reaching Rome (see page 146). Octavian suffered several setbacks in this campaign, including a shipwreck off the coast of Calabria, from which the legion rescued him:

> The Thirteenth Legion was approaching by the mountainous overland route and, having found out about the disaster, they made their way there guided by the signal fires, passing through the rocky outcrops. They discovered their commander and his fellow survivors, exhausted and hungry.
>
> Appian, *Civil War* 5.87

We do not know whether the Thirteenth Legion fought at Actium, but after the battle the legion may have been reinforced with soldiers from disgraced legions, explaining its cognomen *Gemina* ('Twin'), first attested in the Augustan period. It then moved to the Balkans, where it remained until AD 9. During this period it participated in Tiberius' conquest of the Alps in 15 BC (at which time it constructed the first wooden fortress at Vindonissa). It was then based at Ljubljana in Pannonia, where a small number of inscriptions relating to its soldiers have been found (e.g. *CIL* 3, 3844 and 14354,10). It also formed part of the army that Tiberius gathered to use against the Marcomanni in AD 6, but instead employed in suppressing the Pannonian Revolt.

Germania and Civil War

After the Varian disaster of AD 9, the Thirteenth Legion was transferred to Moguntiacum (Mainz) for several years before moving to Vindonissa in Upper Germany. Its stay there has been dated from AD 16/17 to 43/45 on the basis of inscriptions.

Further evidence of the legion's movements in the 1st century AD exists, but is difficult to date. For example, a helmet found at Buggeneem suggests the legion spent some time in Lower Germany, and brick stamps with the legion's name have been discovered at Stupava in Upper Pannonia (e.g. *AE* 1987, 822d). The legion is known to have been sent to Poetovio (Ptuj) in Pannonia during the reign of Claudius, to replace *VIII Augusta*, so the legion's presence at Stupava probably dates to after AD 43.

In AD 69 *XIII Gemina* sided with Otho. It fought for him against Vitellius at the first battle of Bedriacum, but was routed by *V Alaudae*. The legion was set to building amphitheatres at Cremona and Bononia before being transferred back to Pannonia. Once there it went over to Vespasian. Tacitus reports (*Histories* 3.1) that Vespasian's generals met to discuss their strategy against Vitellius at the Thirteenth Legion's winter quarters at Poetovio and were persuaded by Marcus Antonius Primus, commander of *VII Gemina*, to march on Italy without waiting for reinforcements from Vespasian. The Thirteenth was in the army that defeated Vitellius at the second battle of Bedriacum (see pages 134–35). It was then sent to the Rhine under the command of Petillius Cerialis to suppress the Batavian Revolt.

In the Balkans

At some time in the AD 80s, the Thirteenth Legion moved to a new base at Vindobona (Vienna), where they constructed a new fortress. The legion was part of the army that Domitian used against the Dacian incursion of AD 86, and helped to defeat the Dacians at Tapae in AD 88. It also took part in Domitian's wars against the Suebi and Sarmatians in AD 92–93.

The Thirteenth Legion was used by Trajan in his Dacian wars (101–6). Between these two wars, it was part of the occupation force under the command of Pompeius Longinus. Its main base was at Apulum (Alba Iulia, Romania), where brick stamps with the legion's name have been found. Vexillations were probably also stationed at Sarmizegetusa and auxiliary forts at strategic

The tombstone of Gaius Allius, centurion of *XIII Gemina*, found at Vindonissa (Windisch), is decorated with three *coronae* (crowns), two torques, two *armillae* (bracelets) and nine *phalerae* (gold discs) (*CIL* 13, 5206).

points such as at Tihău in northern Dacia (*AE* 1994, 1484). There is evidence that *I Adiutrix* was also stationed briefly at Apulum, possibly to make up for soldiers sent to serve at Sarmizegetusa and elsewhere in the province (e.g. *AE* 1997, 1290d and *CIL* 3, 981).

In 117 the legion was involved in the emperor's Sarmatian war, commanded by Marcius Turbo, Hadrian's great friend, who had been appointed prefect of Dacia and Pannonia (*SHA Hadrian* 6). At this time Dacia was split into three provinces and *XIII Gemina* became the only legion of the newly formed Upper Dacia. Nevertheless, evidence of the legion has been found in Lower Dacia too, where, during Hadrian's reign, it was responsible for rebuilding the fortress at Hoghiz in stone (*CIL* 3, 953).

The legion was involved in another war against the free Dacians and Sarmatian Iazyges in 158. An inscription (*CIL* 6, 1523) from Rome suggests that Marcus Statius Priscus commanded *XIII Gemina* at this time. In *c.* 168 *V Macedonica* was sent to Dacia and from this period the two legions often served together. Both took part in Marcus Aurelius' Marcomannic wars (166–80) and fought against the Dacians in the reign of Commodus. *V Macedonica* was awarded the cognomen *Pia Constans* ('Dutiful and Reliable') for its actions during this second war, and *XIII Gemina* was perhaps awarded the title *Pia Fidelis* ('Dutiful and Loyal') the same time, since *PF* has been found on a single undated inscription at Apulum (*AE* 1997, 1290c). Both legions supported Septimius Severus in 193 and a mixed vexillation accompanied him to Rome and fought for him against Pescennius Niger, breaking through the Cilician Gates (one of the passes through the Taurus Mountains from Anatolia to Syria) and storming the city of Issus. From here it is likely that the vexillation also took part in Severus' Parthian campaign.

Little more is known of *XIII Gemina*. Mixed vexillations of the Thirteenth and Fifth fought the Alamanni in the 260s or 270s. The Thirteenth remained in Trans-Danubian Dacia until the province was abandoned by the Romans in 271, during the reign of Aurelian. It then transferred to Ratiaria (Arçar in northern Bulgaria) in the newly created province of Dacia Ripensis and was still there in the 5th century AD, as shown by the *Notitia Dignitatum*.

The main gate to the fortress of Apulum (after reconstruction). Apulum was a strategically important location, from which communications between the Dacian interior and the neighbouring province of Pannonia could be controlled.

A Legion in Italy

II Parthica

Throughout most of the early and middle imperial period, Rome itself was garrisoned by the Praetorian Guard and the paramilitary urban cohorts, but legions only entered Italy during civil wars and at times of crisis, such as when the Dacians' penetration of the Danube frontier threatened northern Italy in AD 170. However, *II Parthica*, one of the three

legions that Septimius Severus created in 193–97 for his Parthian wars (see page 170), was established in a fortress at Albanum, in the Alban Hills south of Rome.

Severus' reasons for deploying a legion in Italy were partly military – *II Parthica* effectively served as a central reserve, deployed for imperial campaigns across the empire throughout his reign and his successors' – but it could also be a political instrument. The contemporary writer and senator Cassius Dio makes much of Severus' militarization of the state and use of intimidation as a political ploy, and the emperor may have intended *II Parthica* to supplement the Praetorian Guard to maintain his regime in power. However, after Severus' death and throughout the following century, *II Parthica* was heavily involved in political intrigue, and contributed to the rise and fall of several emperors.

The Arch of Septimius Severus in the Roman Forum, built in AD 203 to commemorate his eastern victories. Some ancient writers criticized Severus for excessive dependence on the army, a view perhaps supported by his stationing of *II Parthica* near Rome.

II Parthica

The three legions *Parthica* were created by
Septimius Severus nominally, at least, for his
Parthian wars and to garrison the new province
of Mesopotamia. *II Parthica* existed by AD 197 at
the latest, since an inscription from Rome (*CIL* 6,
3409) relates to a recruit of that year. Whether or
not *II Parthica* actually served in the East, it was
soon established at a new fortress at Albanum,
just south of Rome. The historian Anthony Birley
suggests that it was left there while Severus was in
the East to ensure the loyalty of the capital in his
absence. It is possible that the legion accompanied
Severus on campaign, in Britain in 208–11, where
he fought against the Caledonians until his death
(at Eboracum, York) in 211. Severus was
accompanied by his sons Geta and Caracalla, who
succeeded him as joint rulers. However, Caracalla
soon murdered his younger brother and assumed
sole power. An ancient biography of Caracalla
(*SHA Caracalla* 2.7–8) records that the men of
II Parthica, now back in their fortress at Albanum,
were angry at Geta's assassination, citing their
allegiance to both brothers. They shut the gates
against the emperor and he had to harangue them
in person – and promise them money – before
they relented.

Caracalla to Elagabalus

II Parthica accompanied Caracalla on campaign
to the eastern frontier in AD 216–17, and
inscriptions of his reign from Apamea in Syria
give it the title *Antoniniana* (part of Caracalla's
name). One of these (*AE* 1993, 1572) records that
a legionary died in the night at Aegeae in Cilicia,
on the Mediterranean coast of modern southeast
Turkey. He was buried at nearby Catabolum and
commemorated with an epitaph at Apamea.
This suggests that the legion was shipped to
Aegeae and then marched overland into
Syria. Situated on the Orontes, Apamea
was an important military centre for
the Seleucid kings of Syria who had
succeeded Alexander the Great five
centuries before *II Parthica* was
formed. Its strategic location also led to
its use from time to time as a legionary
fortress and base in earlier periods of
Roman history.

II Parthica

Cognomen	*Parthica*
Emblem	Centaur
Main base	Albanum (modern Albano Laziale), Italy
Major campaigns	Septimius Severus' British campaigns? (AD 208–211); Caracalla's Parthian war (216–17); civil war between Macrinus and Elagabalus (218); Severus Alexander's Persian war (231–33); Severus Alexander and Maximinus' German and Dacian campaigns (235–38); civil war between Maximinus and Pupienus and Balbinus (238); Gordian III's Persian war (242–44); other imperial campaigns? (250–360); campaign against Shapur II's invasion of Mesopotamia (359–60)

Both Cassius Dio (78.7.1–2; 78.18.1) and
Herodian (4.8.1–2) make the rather bizarre claim
that Caracalla trained a phalanx of men equipped
with pikes, emulating the army of Alexander the
Great. A recently discovered inscription from
Apamea refers to a member of *II Parthica* as a
'trainee (*discens*) phalanx soldier', suggesting the
phalanx legion may not have been fantasy, nor, as
with similar accounts from the reign of Severus

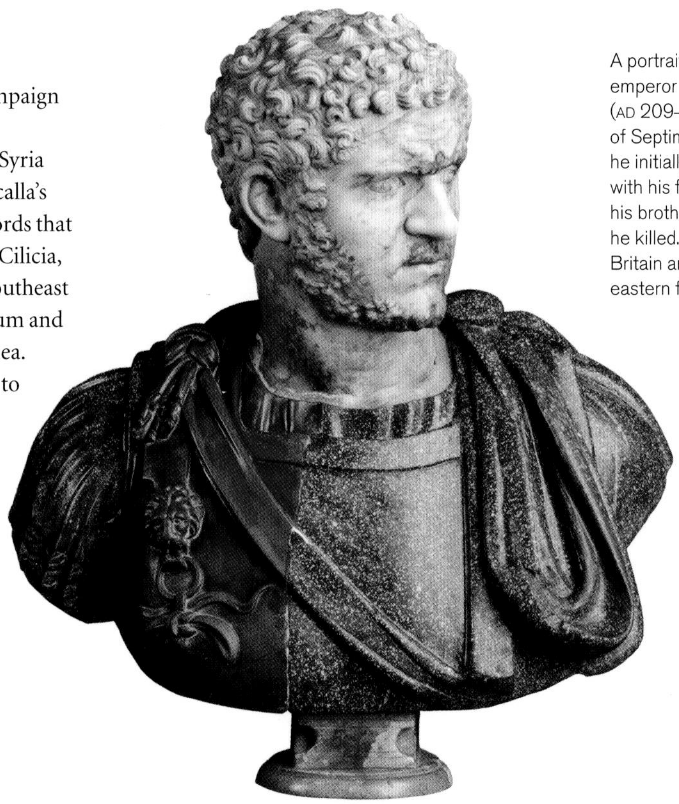

A portrait bust of the
emperor Caracalla
(AD 209–17). The son
of Septimius Severus,
he initially ruled jointly
with his father and then
his brother Geta, whom
he killed. He fought in
Britain and on the
eastern frontier.

The Fortress of *II Parthica* at Albanum

The permanent fortress of *II Parthica* at Albanum, the *Castra Albana*, in the Alban Hills just south of Rome, provides us with archaeological evidence and inscriptions illustrating the legion's presence from Septimius Severus to at least AD 249. The base lies adjacent to the Via Appia, the main road from Rome to the southeast of Italy and thence (by sea) to the empire's eastern provinces. It has a slightly irregular rectangular enclosure wall constructed from large blocks of tufa stone, with one grand fortified gateway and a few towers preserved. The area enclosed is about 10 ha (*c.* 25 acres), half the size of earlier fortresses like Inchtuthil. Little is known of the interior, which is covered by more recent buildings. However, the modern streets and buildings partly follow the ancient plan. An early Severan bath building inside the fortress has been excavated and there is also a large cistern complex for storing water.

The remains of the porta praetoria *(praetorian gate) of the fortress of* II Parthica *at Albanum (modern Albano Laziale).*

An *antoninianus* coin of Gallienus, minted in AD 260, with the titles of *II Parthica* and its centaur symbol.

Alexander (*SHA Severus Alexander* 50.4–5), just anachronistic terminology applied to men equipped in normal legionary fashion.

In the course of Caracalla's Parthian campaign, *II Parthica* became embroiled, not for the last time, in politics. Triccianus, its commander, conspired with Macrinus, the praetorian prefect, to assassinate Caracalla. Macrinus became emperor, winning over the 'Alban legion' and other troops at Apamea with promises of money (Cassius Dio 79.34). Shortly afterwards the Roman army fought a battle against the Parthians near the Mesopotamian fortress city of Nisibis. The historian Herodian (4.15.1–3) describes how the Roman infantry used caltrops (spiked iron devices) spread on the ground to defeat the Parthian cavalry and their tender-footed camels. Nevertheless, the battle was indecisive, and both sides lost heavily.

Elements of the army grew discontented with Macrinus, and another claimant to the throne emerged in the form of the rather exotic Elagabalus (see *III Gallica*). *II Parthica* defected to Elagabalus and joined his supporters (including *III Gallica*) in a battle against the Praetorian Guard and other forces supporting Macrinus at the village of Imma near Antioch in June 218. Initially Elagabalus' army fought poorly, but it was rallied by the young claimant and Macrinus fled, to be captured and killed later. The battle, and Atinius Ianuarius, a soldier of *II Parthica* who died in it, were commemorated in an inscription found at Apamea. Subsequently, the legion took the titles *Pia Fidelis Felix Aeterna* ('Dutiful, Loyal, Fortunate, Eternal').

Severus Alexander and Maximinus

The legion returned to Italy when Elagabalus took the imperial throne, but was back in the East in the reign of his successor Severus Alexander, in 231–33. He campaigned against the rising power of the new Sasanian Persian empire. Ancient accounts of this war are rather confused, and there were victories and defeats on both sides, but *II Parthica* (with the new title *Severiana*) is well documented at Apamea in this period.

Herodian (6.5.4–10) claims that the Romans launched a three-pronged attack into the Persian heartland, and that initially this was successful. However, the emperor was afraid to advance with his army, and the other Roman forces were forced to withdraw, suffering heavy casualties. Alexander was forced to return to the West with his army because the Germanic Alamanni had crossed the Rhine and Danube, and there were fears for the security of Italy itself. The emperor took his troops to Moguntiacum (Mainz) in Germany in 235 (a few inscriptions from Germany name the legion), but, when he sought to buy off the Germans instead of attacking them, they deserted and killed him, proclaiming a Balkan military man, Maximinus, emperor instead.

Subsequently, *II Parthica* served under Maximinus, who spent his entire reign fighting on the frontiers. A handful of inscriptions from Germany and the Balkan provinces may relate to the deployment of the legion or its vexillations to those regions during his reign as well as those of Severus Alexander and others. Maximinus finally set out for Rome at the head of an army in 238 to suppress an uprising supporting Pupienus and Balbinus, senatorial candidates to the imperial throne. Maximinus besieged Aquileia in northeastern Italy, but as the besiegers' supplies began to run short and disease took hold, his support began to unravel. *II Parthica* turned on Maximinus, killed him and his son, and mutilated their bodies, sending their heads to Rome (Herodian 8.5.8). The soldiers may have been motivated by fears for the safety of their families back in Albanum if they continued to support Maximinus.

Inscriptions show that *II Parthica* spent part of the following decade back in Albanum and part of it in Apamea, where its use of the title *Gordiana* suggests that it participated in Gordian III's campaign against the Sasanians in 242–44. The legion returned to Italy, and clearly won the favour of the emperor Gallienus (253–68) for its support against his rivals, since he struck *antoninianus* coins depicting the legion's centaur emblem and bearing the legend *LEG(io) II PART(hica) V P(ia) V F(idelis)* – 'Five times Dutiful and Loyal', along with another issue with *VI P VI F*.

After this time *II Parthica* disappears from view for over a century. It is likely that it participated in campaigns led by other emperors, although there is no specific evidence. When it does appear again, the legion is back in the East. Ammianus Marcellinus (20.7.1) names it as part of the garrison that unsuccessfully defended Bezabde in Mesopotamia against Shapur II's Sasanian army in 360. A few decades later, the *Notitia Dignitatum* lists *II Parthica*'s base as Cefa in Mesopotamia.

The Soldiers of *II Parthica*

About 90 inscriptions naming *II Parthica* at Apamea (most found in the 1980s) shed light on the organization of the legion. They provide information on most individuals' cohort and century, as well as their occupations and ranks. One contains the earliest evidence for *lanciarii* (legionary light infantrymen) as specialist troops within a legion's organization. A *lanciarius* is depicted in sculpted relief on his funerary monument, carrying a bundle of light javelins and a small shield, appropriate to his military function.

Numerous inscriptions from Albanum and Rome relating to soldiers of *II Parthica* remind us that Septimius Severus granted soldiers the right to legally recognized marriage during their service, something previously forbidden:

> For Gypsania Lepida, a wife without compare, who lived 19 years, four months and 14 days. Publius Septimius Proculus, a soldier on double pay of *II Parthica Severiana*, her husband, made this monument to his wife who well deserved it.
>
> *ILS* 2433

Inscriptions from Italy and Apamea also provide information on the origins of the men of *II Parthica*. Of 52 men with a recorded place of origin, 37 were from Balkan provinces (Thrace 24, Pannonia 9, Illyricum 3, Dacia 1), 10 from Italy, 2 from Syria, 2 from Africa and 1 from Egypt. Many more have names that are probably Thracian, reflecting the long-term importance of Thrace as a Roman recruiting ground, the importance of that region as a focus of military activity from the later 2nd century AD and the prominence of Balkan recruits in the Praetorian Guard and the *equites singulares* (imperial horse guards) from the reign of Septimius Severus.

The tombstone of L. Septimius Viator, a Pannonian soldier of *II Parthica*, from Apamea (*AE* 1993, 1574). He is described as a *lanciarius* and carries a bundle of javelins and a round shield appropriate for a legionary skirmisher.

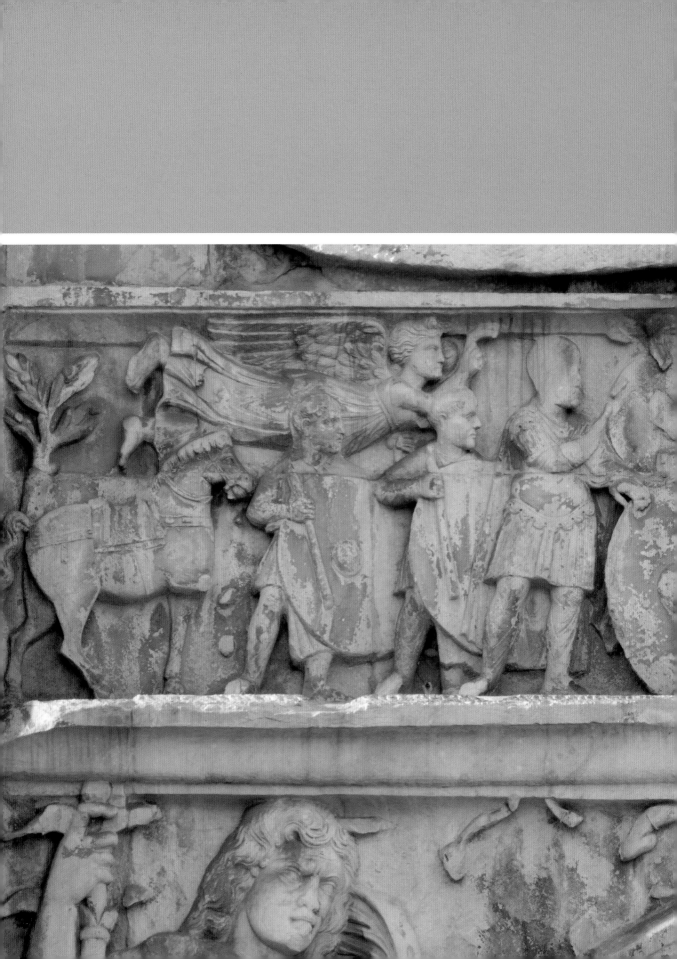

PART III

The Legions in Late Antiquity

The Crisis of the 3rd Century

The period AD 235 to 293 was one of upheaval, caused by interlinked crises, both within the Roman empire and on its frontiers. The latter comprised conflicts on the Rhine, Danube and eastern frontiers, against Franks, Alamanni, Goths and Sasanian Persians. Roman legions suffered disastrous defeats, notably at Abritus (Bulgaria, in 251) and Edessa (Turkey, in 260). These external crises caused internal problems such as the temporary breakaway of regions of the empire to form semi-autonomous entities, notably the Gallic empire in the West and the kingdom of Palmyra in the East.

Emperors of this period were typically brought to power by the army, ruled briefly and died violent deaths. There were often multiple emperors in power at the same time, or at least usurpers who never consolidated their power. It took the accession of Diocletian (284–305) and his establishment of the Tetrarchy (a coalition of four emperors, two senior Augusti and two junior Caesars) in 293 to bring about consolidation and re-birth of the empire. This formalized the political and military division of the empire that by necessity had characterized much of the second half of the 3rd century. Division remained normal for the rest of Rome's history, particularly with the establishment of other imperial capitals such as Constantinople. Thus, in many respects, the Roman empire we see after 293, a period generally referred to as 'Late Antiquity', was very different from that of the 2nd century AD, as were its legions.

The legions of Late Antiquity cannot be presented in the same way as the legions of the Principate: their sheer number and the lack of evidence for them makes it impossible to use individual 'biographies'. Civil wars and external conflicts in the 3rd century AD and later led to existing legions being split up, moved around and disbanded. Many new legions were created, too. We have far less written evidence, with fewer detailed narrative accounts of Roman wars and fewer inscriptions. The best approach to studying the legions in Late Antiquity is a broader one, with less focus on individual legions.

Previous pages
Detail of a frieze from the Arch of Constantine in Rome, depicting Constantine's siege of Verona in north Italy in the war against his rival Maxentius (AD 312).

This porphyry statue group (taken to Venice from Constantinople after the sack of 1204) depicts the Tetrarchy established by Diocletian in AD 293. He and his senior colleague ('Augustus') Maximian ruled the eastern and western halves of the empire respectively, along with their subordinate 'Caesars', Galerius and Constantius Chlorus. This system broke down after AD 306.

The Roman Army in 293–476

Legionary heavy infantry remained the core of Roman armies, although some aspects of their equipment and organization changed.

The status distinction between legions and auxiliary units was eclipsed by new distinctions between field armies (*comitatus*) and frontier troops (*limitanei*), with legions in each: some cavalry units were elevated in status to set them on a par with the legions. New elite infantry units, both legions and auxiliaries, bore the title 'Palatine', meaning 'Imperial' (from the Palatine Hill and its imperial palace in Rome).

The fortress of *IV Martia* at El-Lejjun ('Legion', ancient Betthorus) in Arabia covers an area of 4.6 ha (11.4 acres), about a quarter of the size of an early–middle imperial fortress like Inchtuthil, and probably only large enough for about 1,500 men.

The Size of Legionary Units

By the end of the 4th century, there were far more legions. A document cataloguing the Roman army in the late 4th–early 5th centuries AD, the *Notitia Dignitatum* (see page 215), lists about 180 units described as legions, compared with 25 to 33 in the Principate. However, a Roman army with 180 or so legions the same size as those of the Principate would have been implausibly large, with nearly a million men in the legions, let alone the other parts of the army. There is archaeological and documentary evidence that late antique legions were typically smaller than their earlier counterparts. Surviving identifiable late antique legionary fortresses are also smaller than their imperial counterparts. Papyrus documents from Egypt (such as Diocletianic papyri from Panopolis) have been interpreted as showing small units in Late Antiquity, including legionary vexillations of *c.* 500 men. Legionary units of 1,000–1,500 men may have been the norm from as early as the reign of Diocletian (284–305).

Recruitment, Barbarization and Terms of Service

In contrast with those during the Principate, most late Roman legionary recruits seem to have been conscripts, and legal texts give one the impression that the late Roman army had problems recruiting enough men, and that military service often was unpopular. An obligation to serve particularly applied to soldiers' sons (*Theodosian Code* 7.23.1), making military service (like much else in late antiquity) effectively hereditary.

In the 4th and (particularly) 5th centuries AD many 'barbarians', notably men of Germanic origin, served in the Roman army. Some formed

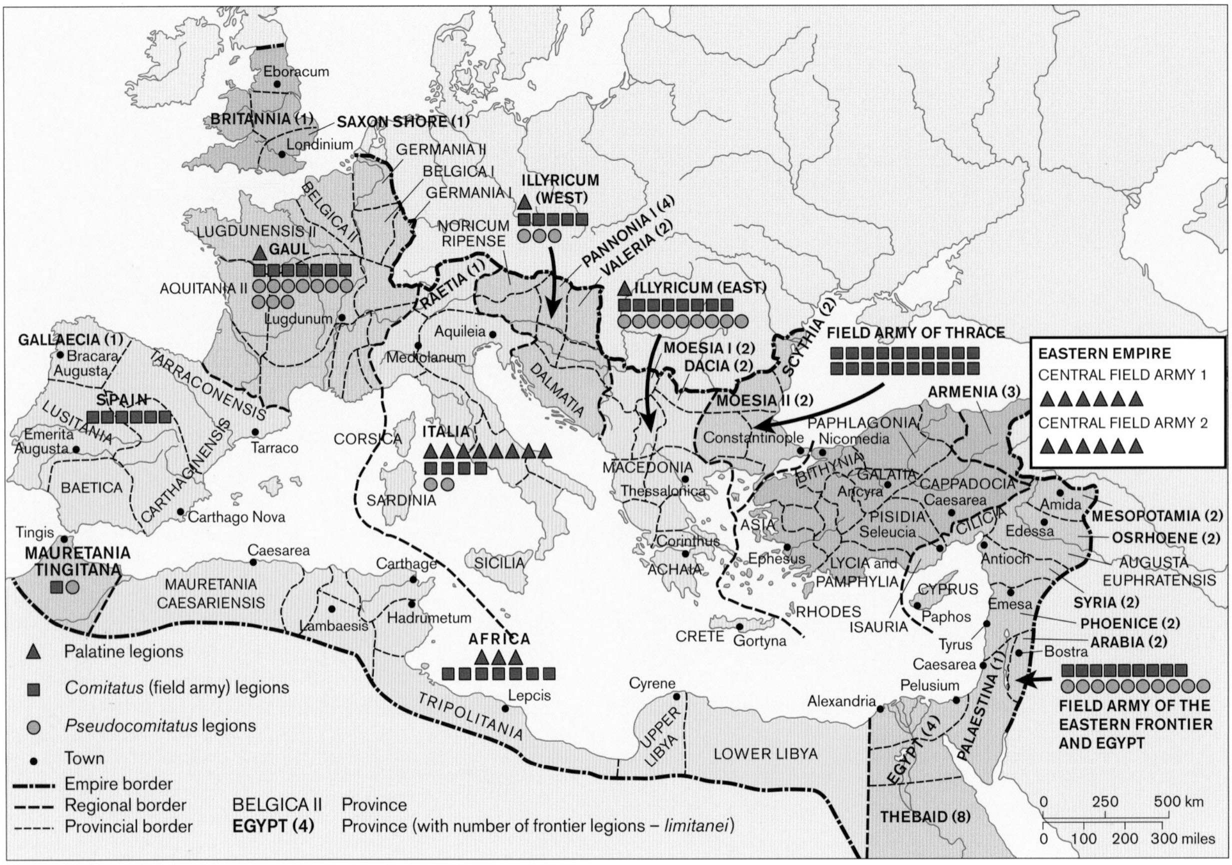

Map showing the disposition of the legions of the frontier armies (*limitanei*) and field armies (*comitatus*) as recorded in the *Notitia Dignitatum* (c. AD 395–420).

auxiliary units with ethnic titles, just as auxiliary cohorts and *alae* in earlier periods were drawn from less 'Romanized' fringes of the empire like Gaul and Thrace. Others served in separate units of *laeti* and *gentiles*, under their own or Roman officers. It is clear that barbarian recruits were accepted into the legions too. This is shown to a limited extent by the ethnic names borne by a minority of legions (see page 221), but more clearly in descriptions by the late Roman historian Ammianus Marcellinus. Recounting the siege of Amida in Mesopotamia in 359, he refers to two 'Magnentian' legions, raised by the usurper Magnentius (350–53), 'recently brought from Gaul'. They are described as brave but reckless, undertaking heroic but futile sorties against the enemy outside the city, like caged wild beasts, all of which is characterized by Ammianus (19.5–6) as symptomatic of their Gallic 'great-heartedness'.

Despite the importance of conscription, basic terms of service seem to have been broadly similar to those of earlier periods. Legal sources suggest legionaries and other troops served for 20 to 24 years before retirement (depending on the status of their unit), and veterans received a cash bonus or land on discharge, as well as privileges such as exemption from taxation and onerous duties required by the state or their community. However, while legionaries and other soldiers continued to receive cash payment, and bonuses on imperial accessions and anniversaries (the bonuses often given in multiples of *solidi*, gold coins) the most important element of their income was calculated in kind, typically as rations of grain (*annona*).

The *Notitia Dignitatum* and the Legions in Late Antiquity

While we lack much of the evidence that exists for the earlier Roman legions we do have a unique source for Late Antiquity: the *Notitia Dignitatum.* This is a document, preserved in medieval manuscripts, listing all the major offices of the Roman empire by region and province. It preserves titles of military units, including legions, and, sometimes, the location of their base. Although not without problems, it provides, in effect, an order of battle for the late Roman army. Current scholarly opinion is that the *Notitia Dignitatum* as a whole was compiled in the form in which we have it in *c.* AD 420. The first half of the document covers the eastern half of the empire (*Oriens*, abbreviated to *Or.*), containing information that probably was put together *c.* 395. The second half covers the western empire (*Occidens*, abbreviated to *Oc.*), and its information dates to the first decades of the 5th century, shortly before the compilation of the whole document.

The Roman army of the *Notitia Dignitatum* was divided into frontier garrisons (composed of troops called *limitanei* or *ripenses*) and the regional and central field armies, the *comitatus*, commanded by senior generals (whose soldiers were called *comitatenses*). This distinction existed by 325, when the emperor Constantine confirmed both it and the different privileges of troops and veterans in the different armies (*Theodosian Code* 7.20.4). However, the origins of the *comitatus* may go back much further, to central reserves created by Diocletian (284–305), Gallienus (253–68), or even the Severan legion *II Parthica.*

The *Notitia Dignitatum* also lists new, higher-status cavalry units called vexillations (the same title as the legionary detachments of earlier periods, but not to be confused wth them). These new cavalry vexillations had the same status as legions and their troopers the same privileges as legionaries, as shown by a rescript (imperial letter) from the reign of Diocletian (*Codex of Justinian* 10.54.3).

Legions of the Frontier Garrisons (*limitanei*)

Frontier garrisons of *limitanei* and *ripenses* provided border security and policing in the provinces and served as the first line of defence against external attack. Typically they were a mix of legions and cavalry vexillations, with cavalry *alae* and infantry cohorts that were descendents of past auxiliary units. For example, the *Notitia Dignitatum* records (*Or.* 32) that the province of Phoenice (Phoenicia, southern Syria) had two legions, *I Illyricorum* ('of Illyrians') at Palmyra, and *III Gallica* at Danaba. There were also 12

Page from a coloured medieval manuscript of the *Notitia Dignitatum.* It depicts the shield emblems of *comitatenses* and *pseudocomitatenses* legions from the field armies of the West (*Notitia Dignitatum Oc.* 5.254–74) including (l.–r., top line) the (*III*) *Augustani, Fortenses,* (*I*) *Alpini* and *II Iulia Alpina.*

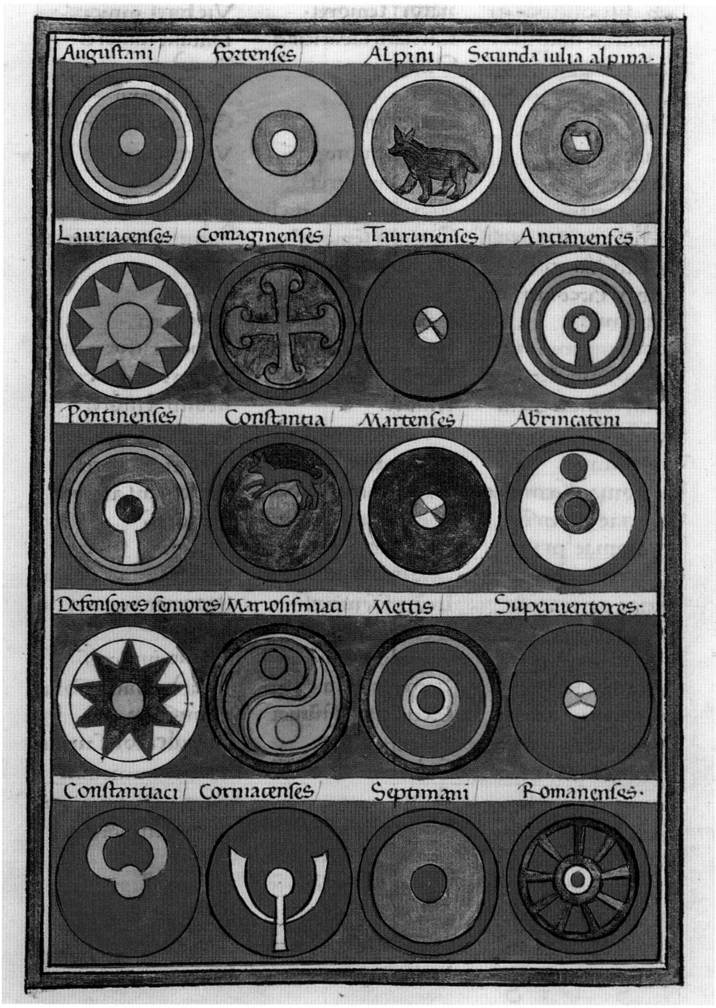

Legions of the Frontier Garrisons (*limitanei*)

Legions marked * existed at the time of Cassius Dio (early 3rd century AD)

Egypt (*Notitia Dignitatum Or.* 28)

*V Macedonica**	Memphis
*XIII Gemina**	Babylon (Old Cairo)
III Diocletiana 'of the Thebaid'	Andropolis
*II Traiana**	Parembole ('the Camp' in Alexandria)

Thebaid (Upper Egypt, *Or.* 31)

III Diocletiana	Ombos
II Flavia Constantia Thebaeorum	Cusae
III Diocletiana	Praesentia (Ombos)
*II Traiana**	Apollinopolis Magna (Edfu)
I Valentiniana	Coptus
I Maximiana	Philae
III Diocletiana	Thebes
II Valentiniana	Hermonthis

Isauria (southeast of Mediterranean Turkey, *Or.* 29)

II Isaura	(not recorded)
III Isaura	(not recorded)

Phoenice (southern Syria, *Or.* 32)

I Illyricorum	Palmyra
*III Gallica**	Danaba

Syria (*Or.* 33)

*IV Scythica**	Oresa
*XVI Flavia Firma**	Sura

Palestina (*Or.* 34)

*X Fretensis**	Aila (modern Aqaba)

Osrhoene (southeast Turkey, *Or.* 35)

IV Parthica	Circesium
[*III Parthica* – there is a gap in the manuscript, but *III Parthica* probably belongs in this place]	[Apatna – not listed due to a gap in the text, but recorded on a map with the manuscript]

Mesopotamia (Roman Mesopotamia, southeast Turkey and north Iraq, *Or.* 36)

*I Parthica Nisibena**	Constantina
*II Parthica**	Cefa

Arabia (southern Syria–Jordan, *Or.* 37)

*III Cyrenaica**	Bostra
IV Martia	Betthorus (modern El-Lejjun)

Armenia (including what had been Roman Cappadocia and the Black Sea area, *Or.* 38)

*XV Apollinaris**	Satala
*XII Fulminata**	Melitene
I Pontica	Trapezus (modern Trabzon)

Scythia (eastern Danube, *Or.* 39)

II Herculia	Trosmis, Axiopolis
I Iovia	Noviodunum, Aegyssus, Inplateypegae

Moesia Secunda (*Or.* 40)

*I Italica**	Novae, Sexaginta Prista
*XI Claudia**	Durostorum, Transmarisca

Moesia Prima (*Or.* 41)

*IV Flavia**	Singidunum (modern Belgrade)
*VII Claudia**	Viminacium; Cuppae

Dacia (not the 2nd century AD province, but south and west of the Danube, *Or.* 42)

*V Macedonica**	Variniana, Cebrus, Oescus, Sucidava
*XIII Gemina**	Egeta, Transdrobeta, Burgus Novus, Zernis, Ratiaria

Britannia, Saxon Shore (*Oc.* 28)

*II Augusta**	Rutupiae (modern Richborough)

Pannonia (*Oc.* 32)

V Iovia	Bononia, Burgenae, Castellum Onagrinum
VI Herculea	Mons Aureus, Teutoburgium, Castellum Onagrinum

Valeria (*Oc.* 33)

*I Adiutrix**	Brigetio
*II Adiutrix**	Aliscae, Florentia, Aquincum (modern Budapest), Castellum contra Tautantum, Cirpi, Lussonium

Pannonia Prima (*Oc.* 34)

*X Gemina**	Vindobona (modern Vienna)
*XIV Gemina**	Carnuntum
*II Italica**	Lauriacum
I Noricorum	Faviana

Raetia (*Oc.* 35)

*III Italica**	Castra Regina (modern Regensburg), Vallatum

Britannia (*Oc.* 40)

*VI (Victrix)**	(not recorded)

Hispania Callaecia (*Oc.* 42)

*VII Gemina**	Legio (modern León)

cavalry vexillations, 7 cavalry *alae*, and 5 auxiliary infantry cohorts, probably none of them more than a few hundred men strong.

Continuity and Change in the Frontier Legions

The legions of the *Notitia Dignitatum*'s frontier armies (*limitanei*) show, superficially at least, substantial continuity with the Principate. Many bear the names of legions familiar to us from Cassius Dio's list of those in his day (see pages 48–49). Some are even based at the same place as before, for example *II Traiana* at Alexandria, *III Cyrenaica* at Bostra, *XV Apollinaris* at Satala, *XII Fulminata* at Melitene, *I Italica* at Novae, *XI Claudia* at Durostorum, *IV Flavia* at Singidunum, *VII Claudia* at Viminacium and *VII Gemina* at Legio. Others are in the same province or region, including *X Fretensis*, previously in Jerusalem, now at Aila (Aqaba, in Jordan), and most of the Syrian legions.

However, some legions appear in multiple locations. For example, Cassius Dio listed *V Macedonica* in the Trans-Danubian province of Dacia and the *Notitia Dignitatum* also records it in Dacia – though this shows the creation of a new province west of the Danube (as Trajan had abandoned Trans-Danubian Dacia). However, a *V Macedonica* also appears in Egypt, at Memphis. A legionary vexillation was perhaps sent from the legion's base to Egypt at some point (probably by Diocletian in 297–98, to suppress a revolt, and campaign on the southern frontier), only to settle there, far from its original base. Another unit named *V Macedonica* is listed in the field army of *Oriens* (the eastern frontier and Egypt).

Likewise, *II Traiana* is not just in its old base at Alexandria, but also at Apollinopolis Magna (Edfu) in the Thebaid (Upper/Southern Egypt). *III Diocletiana* appears in three locations in the Thebaid as well as at Andropolis in Lower Egypt and in the field army of Thrace: it was clearly sent from Egypt for a campaign, only to remain in its new location. So at least some of the units listed as legions are dispersed detachments rather than complete legions.

Despite this continuity, the list of legions in the frontier garrisons also reveals new units. Some have geographical titles denoting the locations of their base, for example *I Pontica* (at Trapezus-Trabzon in Pontus), two legions *Isaurae* (Isauria, the southeast corner of Anatolia) and *IV Parthica* (in Mesopotamia, like Septimius Severus' *I–III Parthica*, created by him to garrison that province on the Persian border). *I Illyricorum* at Palmyra in Syria was recruited in Illyricum in the Balkans, probably by the emperor Aurelian when he gathered an army to return the breakaway kingdom of Palmyra to central authority in 273.

Other legions are named after emperors who recruited them and give us some idea of the expansion of the legions over the previous century or so. *III Diocletiana* was named after Diocletian and *I Maximiana* after Maximian, Diocletian's colleague in the Tetrarchy. Other legions are named after Valentinian (364–75). *Flavia* in *II Flavia Constantia Thebaeorum* reflects the use of the title *Flavius* by emperors of Constantine's family, rather than the old Flavian dynasty – in contrast with the Moesian legion *IV Flavia*, which really was an Flavian in origin.

Some legions derive their names from gods: *IV Martia* was appropriately named for Mars, the war god. *I Iovia* ('of Jupiter') and *II Herculia* ('of Hercules'), both in Scythia (at the mouth of the Danube) were actually named for emperors, specifically Diocletian (whose patron god was Jupiter) and Maximian (Hercules), so, again, their titles help us to date their creation.

The deployment of the frontier legions in the *Notitia Dignitatum* also shows strategic changes

The Missing Legions

The *Notitia Dignitatum* lists at least 25 (probably 27) of the 33 legions recorded by Cassius Dio nearly two centuries earlier, mostly in frontier armies, but some in field armies. The following legions, however, did not survive as late as the *Notitia Dignitatum*:

I Minervia	*XX Victrix*
VI Ferrata	*XXII Primigenia*
VIII Augusta	*XXX Ulpia Victrix*

Most of these six legions are last attested in the 3rd century, and may have been destroyed or disbanded during that century's internal and external conflicts. Some may have survived into the 4th century and our ignorance of their later careers is due to a lack of evidence rather than their early and total disappearance. Ammianus Marcellinus (18.9.3) mentions a Thirtieth Legion at Amida in AD 359, perhaps *XXX Ulpia Victrix*, lost along with that fortress city.

when compared with Cassius Dio's early-3rd-century account. As well as the creation of a new Dacia (see above), the high concentration of legionary units in Egypt (especially the Thebaid, Upper Egypt) is also new. For much of the middle imperial period, Egypt was garrisoned by a single legion stationed at Alexandria (see page 122), but in Late Antiquity there was serious external threat from peoples such as the Blemmyes, a nomadic people from the south who attacked and raided Upper Egypt and the Eastern Desert, and forced the Roman army to evacuate Nubia at the end of the 3rd century AD.

Legions of the Field Armies

In contrast to the continuity of legions in the frontier armies, those of the field armies (*comitatus*) are strikingly new in their titles, most of which provide evidence for the establishment of new units. *Comitatus* were organized at different levels. In the eastern half of the empire there were two *comitatus* with the emperor, each commanded by a general called a *magister militum* ('master of the soldiers'). There were also three regional field armies, for the East ('*Oriens*'), Thrace (the eastern Balkans) and Illyricum (the western Balkans) respectively.

Legionary units of the field armies were also more numerous than those of the frontier armies, a total of about 120 compared to the 50 or so of the frontier provinces. The *Notitia Dignitatum* (*Or.* 5–9) lists units of different status: Palatine (imperial; 24 in number), *Comitatenses* ('companions', members of the *comitatus*; 69 legions) and *Pseudocomitatenses* (former frontier legions elevated to the *comitatus*; 37).

Alongside the field armies' legions were *auxilia Palatina* and cavalry vexillations of Palatine and field-army status. Modern scholars often characterize these field armies as central reserves, and certainly they were used for major offensive operations and to support the *limitanei* against major enemy incursions into the provinces. However, defining them as 'central' and 'mobile' is problematic. Some were stationed regularly in provinces to bolster *limitanei*, and the mobility of field armies was limited by the numerous infantry (including legions) they contained.

The Eastern Empire

The *Notitia Dignitatum* concerning *Oriens*, the eastern part of the Roman empire, does not list the bases of field army legions, perhaps because they moved around more than those of the frontier garrisons. At any given time a legion may have been deployed in a particular province to bolster its *limitanei*, or concentrated at a regional centre like Antioch, or even the eastern capital, Constantinople.

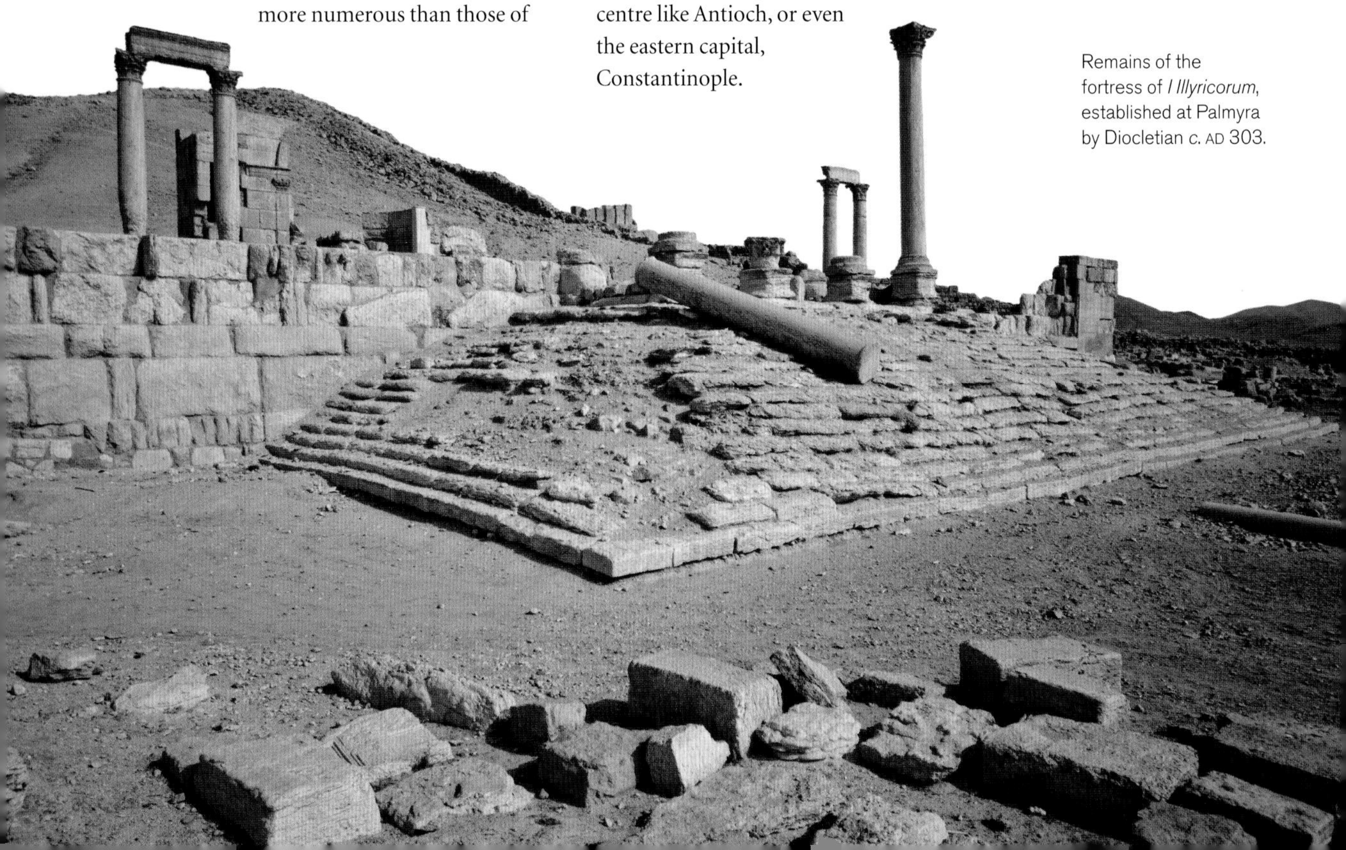

Remains of the fortress of *I Illyricorum*, established at Palmyra by Diocletian *c.* AD 303.

Field Armies of the East (*Oriens*)

Units marked * are legions that existed at the time of Cassius Dio (early 3rd century AD)

Central field army 1 (commanded by the first *magister militum praesentalis*, 'master of the soldiers in the imperial presence')

6 Palatine legions:

Lanciarii seniores	*Fortenses*
Ioviani iuniores	*Nervii*
Herculiani iuniores	*Matiarii iuniores*

Central field army 2 (commanded by the second *magister militum praesentalis*, 'master of the soldiers in the imperial presence')

6 Palatine legions:

Matiarii seniores	*Primani*
Daci	*Undecimani*
Scythae	*Lanciarii iuniores*

The field army of the eastern frontier and Egypt (commanded by the *magister militum per Orientem*, 'master of the soldiers for the East')

9 legions of *comitatenses*:

*V Macedonica**	*Ballistarii seniores*
Martenses seniores	*I Flavia Constantia*
*VII Gemina**	*II Flavia Constantia Thebaeorum*
*X Gemina**	*II Felix Valentis Thebaeorum*
I Flavia Theodosiana	

10 legions of *pseudocomitatenses*:

I Armeniaca	*I Italica**
II Armeniaca	*IV Italica*
Fortenses auxiliarii	*VI Parthica*
Funditores	*I Isaura sagittaria*
Ballistarii Theodosiaci	*Transtigritani*

The field army of Thrace (commanded by the *magister militum per Thraciam*, 'master of the soldiers for Thrace')

20 legions of *comitatenses*:

Solenses seniores	*Tertiodecimani*
Menapii	*Quartodecimani*
I Maximiana Thebaeorum	*I Flavia Gemina*
III Diocletiana Thebaeorum	*II Flavia Gemina*
Constantini Seniores	*Taanni / Tsaanni / Tzanni*
Divitenses Gallicani	*Solenses Gallicani*
Lanciarii Stobenses	*Iulia Alexandria*
Constantini Dafnenses	*Augustenses*
Ballistarii Dafnenses	*Valentinienses*
Ballistarii Iuniores	*Pannoniciani iuniores*

The field army of Illyricum (commanded by the *magister militum per Illyricum*, 'master of the soldiers for Illyricum')

1 Palatine legion:

Britones Seniores

8 legions of *comitatenses*:

Matiarii constantes	*Secundani*
Martii	*Lanciarii Augustenses*
Dianenses	*Minervii*
Germaniciani seniores	*Lanciarii iuniores*

9 legions of *pseudocomitatenses*:

Timacenses auxiliarii	*Merenses*
Felices Theodosiani iuniores	*Secundi Theodosiani*
Bugaracenses	*Ballistarii Theodosiani iuniores*
Scupenses	*Scampenses*
Ulpianenses	

The Western Empire

The lists in this part of the *Notitia Dignitatum* – *Occidens* – typically indicate where, in general terms, a legion was located, showing some concentrated centrally in Italy, with others deployed in provinces. Some provinces (like Gaul, Spain and Africa) were active war zones – or were about to become such. Some no longer had a full regular establishment of frontier troops to defend them, although the *Notitia Dignitatum* also records units of barbarian *laeti* and *gentiles* that fought alongside the more familiar regular units. Even Italy was a potential battleground in this period, since Rome was sacked by Goths, led by the king of the Visigoths, Alaric, in 410, shortly before the compilation of the western *Notitia Dignitatum*.

The *magister peditum* ('master of the infantry') in the western empire also commanded elite *auxilia Palatina* as well as legions. The cavalry vexillations of the field army are listed under a separate commander, the *magister equitum*, 'master of the horse'. Of course, this does not mean that the infantry and cavalry were deployed and fought as separate forces, merely that they belonged to different branches of the military organization.

The Identities of the Field-Army Legions

Few units of the field armies are recognizable from Cassius Dio's account of the legions. Any familiar names are almost all in the field army of *Oriens* (the eastern frontier and Egypt) and consist of *V Macedonica* (also listed in Egypt and

Field Armies of the West (*Occidens*)

Field army legions commanded by the *Magister Peditum Praesentalis*, the 'Master of Infantry in the Imperial Presence'

12 Palatine legions:

Ioviani seniores – Italy	*Moesiaci seniores* – Italy
Herculiani seniores – Italy	*Armigeri propugnatores seniores* – Africa
Diuitenses seniores – Italy	*Lanciarii Sabarienses* – Gaul
Tongrecani seniores – Italy	*Octavani* – Italy
Pannoniciani seniores – Italy	*Thebaei* – Italy
Cimbriani – Africa	*Armigeri propugnatores juniores* – Africa

32 legions of *comitatenses*:

Menapii seniores – Gaul	*Propugnatores Iuniores* – Illyricum
Fortenses – Spain	*II Britannica* or *Secundani Britones* – Gaul or Britain?
Propugnatores seniores – Spain	*Septimani iuniores* – Italy, Mauretania Tingitana or Gaul?
Armigeri defensores seniores – Spain	*Praesichantes* – Gaul
Septimani seniores – Spain	*Ursarienses* – Gaul
Regii – Italy	*Cortoriacenses* – Gaul
Pacatianenses – Illyricum	*Geminiacenses* – Gaul
Uesontes – Spain	*Honoriani felices Gallicani* – Gaul
Mattiarii Iuniores – Italy	*III Iulia Alpina* – Italy
Mauri cetrati – Illyricum	*I Flavia Pacis* – Africa
Undecimani – Spain	*II Flavia Virtutis* – Africa
Secundani Italiciani – Africa	*III Flavia Salutis* – Africa
Germaniciani iuniores – Italy	*Flavia victrix Constantina / Constantici* – Africa
Tertiani, 'otherwise known as *III Italica*' – Illyricum	*II Flavia Constantiniana* – Mauretania Tingitana
III Herculea – Illyricum	*III Augustani* – Africa?
Lanciarii Gallicani Honoriani – Gaul	*Fortenses* – Africa

18 legions of *pseudocomitatenses*:

I Alpina – Italy	*Abrincateni* – Gaul
II Iulia Alpina – Illyricum	*Defensores seniores* – Gaul
Lanciarii Lauriacenses – Illyricum	*Mauri Osismiaci* – Gaul
Lanciarii Comaginenses – Illyricum	*I Flavia Metis* – Gaul
Taurunenses	*Superventores iuniores* – Gaul
Antianenses	*Constantiaci* – Mauretania Tingitana or Africa
Pontinenses – Italy	*Corniacenses* – Gaul
I Flavia Gallicana Constantia – Gaul	*Septimani* – Gaul
Martenses – Gaul	*Romanenses* – Gaul

Region or province	**Palatine legions**	***Comitatenses* legions**	***Pseudo-comitatenses* legions**	**Total**
Italy	8	4	2	14
Gaul	1	7	10	18
Spain		6		6
Africa	3	7		10
Mauretania Tingitana		1		1
Illyricum		5	3	8

The locations of some legions are either uncertain or unstated

its former province of Dacia), *VII Gemina* (also listed in its former province of Spain), *X Gemina* (in Upper Pannonia in Cassius Dio's day, not otherwise attested in the *Notitia Dignitatum*) and *I Italica* (also listed at its original base of Novae in Lower Moesia). The *III Augustani* listed as a legion of the western *comitatus* may be a survival of *III Augusta*.

The majority of field army legions bear unfamiliar names, were created after the 3rd century and we typically know little (if anything) about them besides their names. However, unit names can provide us with information about their origins and nature, organized, roughly, into four groups.

NUMERALS

Some of the legions' titles are just numbers, which tell us virtually nothing, unless they are the same as the numbers of older legions. Other numbers probably record new series of legions raised by particular emperors or for particular campaigns. Such titles include the *Undecimani* ('Men of the Eleventh'), *Tertiani* ('Men of the Third') and *Quartodecimani* ('Men of the Fourteenth').

IMPERIAL NAMES

Many late antique legions' names derived from an emperor's name, presumably denoting when they were raised, providing some evidence for the growth of the army. These emperors include

Diocletian (284–305), Maximian (285–305), Constantine (306–7), Constantius (probably II, 337–61), Valentinian (364–75), Valens (364–78), Theodosius I (379–95), and Honorius (395–423).

As seen above for the names of the legions of the frontier garrisons, the *Ioviani* were named for Jupiter, associated with Diocletian, and *Herculiani* for Maximian. *Flavia* is a title associated with the family of Constantine.

ETHNIC AND GEOGRAPHICAL NAMES

Some of the names are traditional in form, with a number and an adjective describing the legions' origin or location, such as *I Alpina* (from or in the Alps), *II Armeniaca* (Armenia) and *VI Parthica* (the Persian frontier/Mesopotamia). Many are simpler, meaning 'Men from...' or similar, describing the barbarian peoples incorporated into the army at this time. They may denote peoples or regions within the empire that produced notably warlike troops or particular types of soldiers. Such names include *Nervii, Dacii, Transtigritani, Pannoniciani, Menapii, Mauri, Thebaei, Cimbriani* and *Scythae.* The *Nervii*, for example, were a Germanic people, while the *Transtigritani* were presumably recruited in areas beyond the Tigris, a region conquered in 298, but abandoned in 363.

FUNCTION AND STATUS

Other names denote the legions' equipment or manner of fighting. Originally *lanciarii* formed light-infantry detachments within legions such as *II Parthica.* By the time of the *Notitia Dignitatum*, we find legion-sized units composed entirely of *lanciarii. Sagittaria* means 'of archers', and *ballistarii* 'equipped with catapults'. In earlier periods, of course, archers were not found in the legions (they were provided by auxiliary units), but Vegetius (writing between 383 and 450) advocates training a proportion of legionaries as bowmen. The title here, however, may just indicate a unit composed entirely of archers. The *ballistarii* may have been armed with hand-held crossbow-like *manuballistae* and/or heavier weapons.

Some scholars have suggested that these units provided concentrated firepower, perhaps created by brigading integral artillery elements of individual legions. *Armigeri* means 'Armoured', but it is unclear if they wore special armour (or just more of it) compared with other troops. *Propugnatores* are 'Front-Rank Fighters', perhaps denoting elite troops. *Superventores* means something like 'Skirmishers', while *defensores* were 'Defenders' or 'Protectors'.

Seniores are 'senior' and *iuniores* 'junior', probably indicating when, in relative terms, they were recruited.

Late Antique Weapons and Tactics

Despite the improvement in status of cavalry and the increase in the number of cavalry units, the core of the late Roman army remained its heavy infantry. These legionaries certainly looked very different from their predecessors, but in technological terms they were similar.

Equipment

The distinctive *lorica segmentata* of early-middle imperial legionaries had disappeared, but late imperial legionaries still wore armour, including mail and scale. The late antique author Vegetius' claim (1.20) that armour had largely been abandoned after Gratian (375–83) is not borne out by archaeological evidence – and is in fact contradicted by some artistic depictions and literary descriptions.

As for the nature of such late armour, there are depictions (from 3rd-century Dura-Europos in Syria, for example) of men wearing a long mail garment (like the medieval hauberk) including sleeves and a hood (like the medieval coif). Other late imperial legionaries wore helmets, such as the 'Intercisa' type, named for a group found in a deposit in Hungary. Other helmets were of *spangenhelm* type, the bowl made up of four to six segments held together by metal strips. Like their predecessors, late Roman legionaries also carried shields. Those depicted in late antique art typically are large and oval or round in shape.

Offensive weapons continue the trends of the 3rd century AD. Archaeological evidence and terminology employed by late antique writers show that later Roman infantry used a variety of spears and javelins with names like *spiculum*, *verutum* and *lancea*. Vegetius (1.17) also indicates that lead-weighted darts he calls *mattiobarbuli* were introduced by Diocletian and used by the elite Palatine *Ioviani* and *Herculiani* legions. He states that that each man carried five, slotted behind his shield, to throw at the enemy probably at short range before hand-to-hand combat, the lead weighting of the weapons enhancing their armour-piercing qualities. As in the 3rd century, the main sword of Roman infantry was the long-bladed *spatha*, used primarily for cutting rather than stabbing. Vegetius (1.12) contrasts the technique used in his day with the stabbing technique emphasized in earlier training, advocating a return to past practice and equipment.

Vegetius also recommends (1.15; 3.14) training a proportion of recruits in archery and integrating them into the rear ranks of the main heavy-infantry battle line, along with light infantry using javelins called *veruta* and also *plumbatae* (also lead-weighted darts). While his account of battle-formations and organization is rather confused and clearly anachronistic in places, he also mentions cart-mounted catapults, *manuballistae*, slings and staff-slings (slings mounted on a pole to increase leverage, and thus both range and velocity). All such weapons are attested in Late Antiquity by other literary and archaeological evidence.

Late Antique Legions in Battle

Despite the increased prestige of cavalry, disciplined armoured infantry remained crucial to the success of late Roman armies. For example, the historian Ammianus Marcellinus (16.12.36–7) describes the mutual support of cavalry and infantry, and the role of the legions in rallying defeated cavalry, at the battle of Strasbourg (ancient Argentoratum), a victory won by the Caesar (junior emperor) Julian against the Germanic Alamanni in 357.

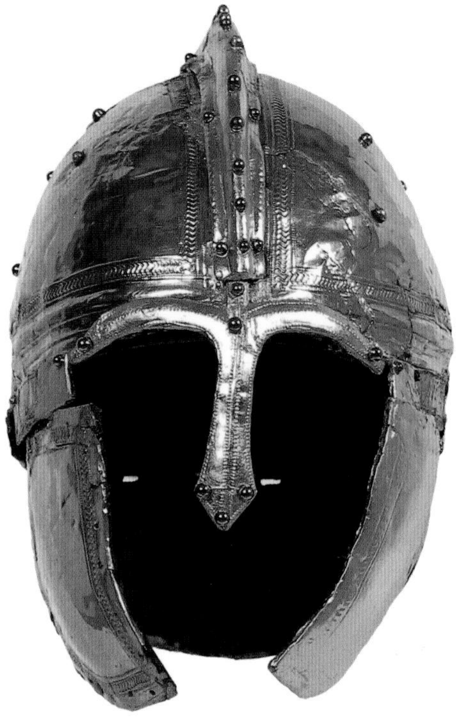

This 'ridge' helmet (early 4th century AD) was found at Berkasovo in Serbia. The 'Intercisa' type is another subtype of ridge helmet. These were made of an iron bowl made in two parts, fixed together with a prominent ridge, rather than the one-piece bowl of earlier helmets. They had large cheek pieces, with cut-outs to allow hearing and neck guards. This example is coated with silver, while others were even more highly decorated, with settings for semi-precious and imitation paste gem stones.

Sieges and defence of fortified cities form an important theme in late Roman warfare, as the Romans relied upon impregnable bases against German incursions in the West and sought to defend them against sophisticated Sasanian Persian siege techniques in the East. Many late Roman legions were based in such cities and in wartime other legions would be brought up to increase their garrisons. Ammianus provides us with information on the composition of some wartime garrisons during the Persian invasion of Mesopotamia in 359, including Amida (18.9.3),whose regular garrison, *V Parthica*, was supplemented by six other legions force-marched as reinforcements. These included the 'barbarian' Magnentian and Decentian legions (see above page 214), subsequently lost with the city, and 'also the soldiers of the Thirtieth, and the Tenth, also called *Fortenses*, and the *Superventores* and *Praeventores*'.

X Fortenses may be a corruption of *X Fretensis*, which still existed at this time in the garrison of Palestina, but the *Notitia Dignitatum* also lists a field army legion called *Fortenses* (probably deriving its name from *fortis*, 'brave'), based in Spain. The *Notitia Dignitatum* also records a legion called *Superventores* ('Skirmishers'), but not *Praeventores* (a similar meaning) nor a Thirtieth (perhaps the old *XXX Ulpia Victrix*?). *V Parthica* does not appear in the *Notitia Dignitatum* about half a century later, so must have been destroyed with the fall of Amida. Presumably it had been raised by Septimius Severus to garrison Mesopotamia continuing his sequence *I–III Parthica*.

The End of the Legions

While Late Antiquity has often been seen as a time of decline and fall, many aspects of Roman institutions and culture survived for centuries both in the East (as the Byzantine empire) and in the Germanic kingdoms of the West, and many scholars emphasize themes of continuity.

Though it is tempting to see, for example, the defeat of the Roman infantry at the hands of the Goths at the battle of Adrianople in 371 as symbolizing the twilight of the legions that we have now followed for a millennium of Roman history, in reality, Roman military and political power survived for a century even in the West – and revived and flourished for centuries in the East.

The individual identity of some legions continued to exist as late as the early 7th century AD, when the Byzantine historian Theophylact Simocatta (2.6.9) referred to a soldier of the *Quartoparthoi* (*Koartoparthoi* in Greek) at Beroea (Aleppo) in Syria. This is clearly the title of *IV Parthica*, part of the garrison of Syria in the *Notitia Dignitatum*. Its title provides a link to Septimius Severus' legions *I–III Parthica*, and thence to the legions of the middle and early imperial period.

However, even today, when the identities of individual legions are mere history, the term 'legion' survives and remains synonymous with military prowess.

These huntsmen or bodyguards depicted in a mosaic at a late antique Roman villa near Piazza Armerina (Sicily) carry large round shields similar to those carried by some legionaries of the period.

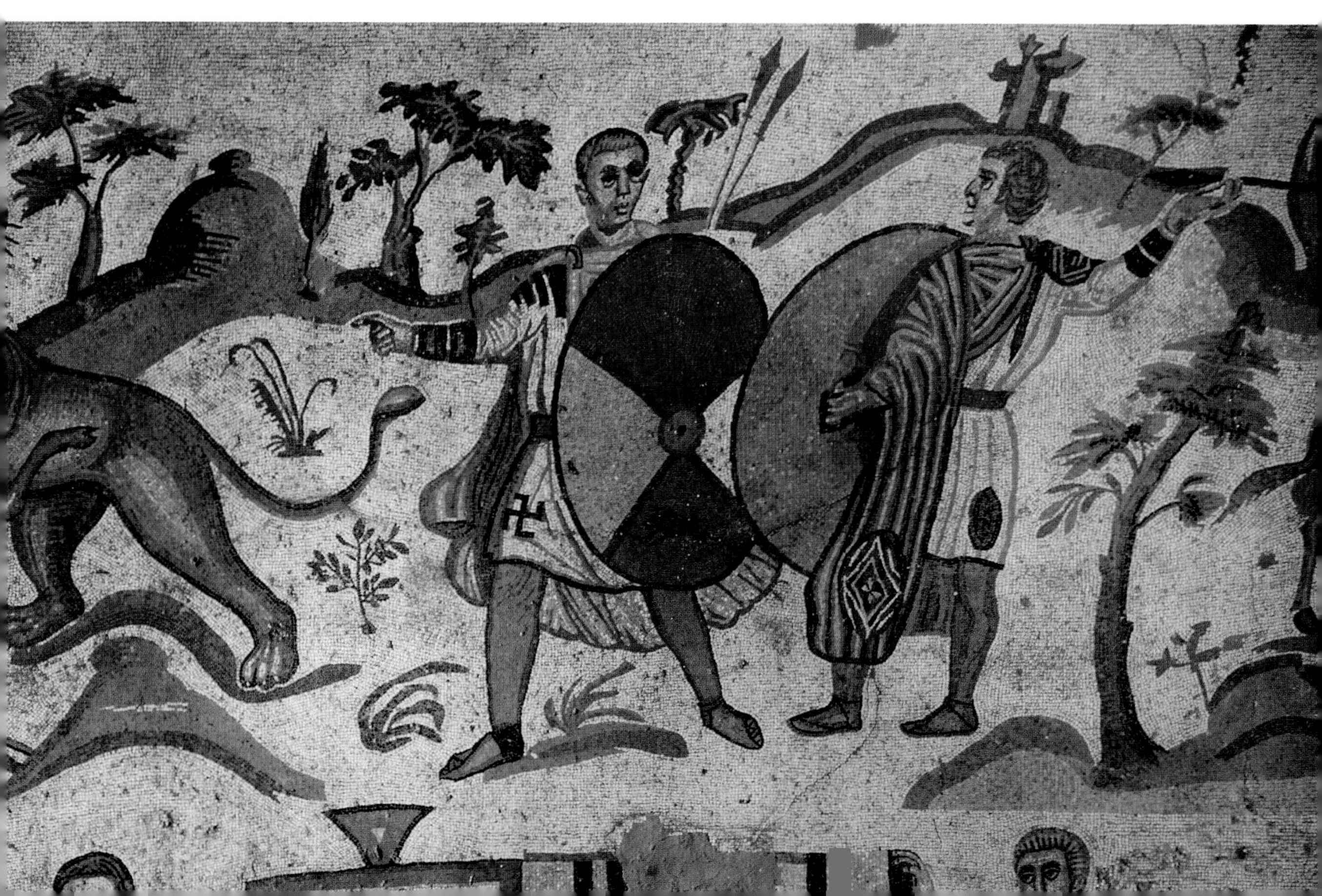

Chronology of Ancient Rome

and the major wars, campaigns, rebellions and disasters during their reigns

Period	Emperor	Date	Wars and campaigns	Major battles and events
Middle Republic		390 BC	Sack of Rome by the Gauls	
		343–290	Samnite wars	
		280–275	War with Pyrrhus	Asculum (279)
		264–241	First Punic war	
		218–202	Second Punic war	Cannae (216), Ilipa (206), Zama (202)
		214–205	First Macedonian war	
		200–196	Second Macedonian war	Cynoscephalae (197)
		192–189	War with Antiochus	Magnesia (190)
		172–167	Third Macedonian war	Pydna (168)
		149–146	Third Punic war	Destruction of Carthage (146)
		146	War between Romans and the Achaean League	Sack of Corinth (146)
		112–105	Jugurthine wars	Marius' first consulship (107)
		109–101	War against the Cimbri and Teutones	Aquae Sextiae (102), Vercellae (101)
Late Republic		91–88	Social war	
		64	Pompey's conquest of Syria	
		58–50	Julius Caesar's Gallic wars	Defeat of the Helvetii (58), Belgae and Nervii (battle of the Sambre, 57), Veneti and Morini (56), invasions of Britain (55 and 54), Vercingetorix's Revolt (battle of Gergovia and siege of Alesia, both in 52)
		53	Crassus' Parthian campaign	Carrhae (53)
		49–45	Civil war between Julius Caesar and Pompey and his successors	Dyrrhachium (48), Pharsalus (48), siege of Alexandria (48–47), Zela (47), Thapsus (46), Munda (45)
Late Republic (Triumviral period)		43–42	Antony and Octavian campaign against Caesar's assassins	Mutina (43), Philippi (42)
		41–40	Perusine war	Siege of Perugia (41–40)
		40–33	Antony's Parthian campaigns	
		38–36	Octavian's campaign against Sextus Pompey	Naulochus (36)
Principate	Augustus (31 BC–AD 14)	31	Civil war between Antony and Octavian	Actium (31)
		29–27	Conquest of Moesia	
		27–19	Cantabrian wars in Spain	
		26–24	Aelius Gallus' Arabian expedition	
		24–22	Publius Petronius' invasion of Nubia	
		19	Cornelius Balbus' victories over the Garamantes in Libya	
		16–15	Conquest of Noricum	
		15	Tiberius and Drusus defeat the Raeti and Vindelici, reaching the Danube	
		13–9	Drusus' campaigns in Germany	
		12–7	Tiberius' campaigns in Pannonia and Germania	
		4		Unrest in Judaea after the death of Herod the Great
		AD 4–5	Tiberius' campaigns in Germania	
		6–9	Revolt in Pannonia and Illyricum	
		9	Varian disaster	
		9–12	Tiberius' campaigns in Germany	
	Tiberius (14–37)	14	Revolt of the legions in Pannonia and Germany after the death of Augustus	
		14	Germanicus' campaigns against the Marsi	

Principate

Emperor	Date	Wars and campaigns	Major battles and events
Tiberius (14–37)	16	Germanicus' campaigns against the Chatti	
	17–24	Tacfarinas' Revolt in Numidia	
	21	Turoni Revolt in Gaul, led by Florus and Sacrovir	
	28	Revolt of the Frisii	
Gaius Caligula (37–41)	40–41	German campaign and expedition to the Channel	
Claudius (41–54)	42		Annexation of Mauretania
	43	Invasion of Britain	
	43–52	Campaigns in Britain, particularly against Welsh tribes (Silures, Ordovices and Deceangi)	
Nero (54–68)	47	Campaigns against the Frisii and Chauci in Germany	
	58–63	Campaigns of Corbulo and Caesennius Paetus against the Armenians in Parthia	
	60–61	Boudican Revolt in Britain	
	66–74	First Jewish Revolt ('The Great Revolt') and siege of Masada	Cestius Gallus' advance to and retreat from Jerusalem (66), Vespasian and Titus' Galilee campaign (67), siege of Jerusalem (70), siege of Masada (72–73 or 74)
	67–68	Vindex' Revolt in Gaul	
	68–69	**The Year of the Four Emperors** (Galba, Otho, Vitellius, Vespasian)	First and second battles of Bedriacum (near Cremona) (69)
Vespasian (70–79)	69–70	Batavian Revolt	
	71	Campaign against the Brigantes in Britain	
	72		Commagene annexed
Titus (79–81)	77–84	Agricola's campaigns in Britain	
Domitian (81–96)	83	War against the Chatti in Germany	
	87–89	Dacian war	
	92–93	Campaigns against the Suebians in Germany and the Sarmatians east of the Balkans	
Nerva (96–98)	97	Suebian war in Germany	
Trajan (98–117)	101–2	First Dacian war	
	105–6	Second Dacian war	
	106		Annexation of Nabataean kingdom as the Roman province of Arabia
	113–17	Parthian war	
	115–17	Jewish Revolt in Egypt	
Hadrian (117–38)	118	Sarmatian war	
	131–33	Second ('Bar Kochva') Jewish Revolt in Judaea	
	135	Arrian's campaign against the Alans?	
Antoninus Pius (138–61)	150	Campaign in Mauretania	
	155–58	Revolt in Britain	
	157–58	Campaigns against the Dacians	
Marcus Aurelius (161–80) co-emperor with Lucius Verus (161–69)	161–66	Lucius Verus' Parthian war	
	166–80	Marcomannic wars on the Danube frontier	Elegeia (161)
Commodus (180–92)	183	Dacian war	
The year 193 saw a succession of emperors: Pertinax, Didius Julianus, Septimius Severus			
Septimius Severus (193–211)	193–97	Civil wars against Pescennius Niger and Clodius Albinus	Siege of Byzantium (193–96), Lugdunum (196)

continued from previous page

	Emperor	Date	Wars and campaigns	Major battles and events
Principate	Septimius Severus (193–211)	195–97	Parthian wars	
		208–11	Campaigns in Britain and Caledonia	
	Caracalla (211–17)	213	War against the Alamanni	
		216–17	Parthian war	Nisibis (217)
	Elagabalus (218–22)	218	Civil war between Macrinus and Elagabalus	Imma (218)
	Severus Alexander (222–35)	231–33	Persian war	
		235	Campaign against the Alamanni	
'Third Century Crisis'	Maximinus Thrax (235–38)	235–36	Campaigns against the Alamanni, Dacians and Sarmatians	
	The dates of events between 238 and 275 are often uncertain; some short-lived emperors have been omitted			
	The year 238 saw a succession of emperors: Gordian I and II, Pupienus, Balbinus, Gordian III			
		238		Goths and Carpi attack across the Danube
	Gordian III (238–44)	243–44	Shapur I's first invasion of the Roman east	Rhesaina (243), Misiche (244)
	Philip (244–49)	245–47	War on the Danube frontier	
	Decius (249–51)	249–52	Renewed attacks by the Goths	
		252	Shapur I's second invasion of the Roman east	Sack of Antioch (252), Barbalissus (252)
	Valerian (253–60)	254	Marcomanni attack Pannonia; Goths attack Thrace	
		256	Franks attack Lower Rhine; Goths attack Asia Minor by sea	
		258 or 259	Valerian's son Gallienus defeats the Alamanni	
		260	Shapur I's third invasion of the Roman east	Valerian captured at Edessa (260)
	Gallienus (260–68)	260		Postumus proclaimed emperor in Gaul (killed 269)
		261–73		Growth of Palmyra's independent power in the East under Odenathus and Zenobia. Suppression and defeat of Palmyra by Aurelian (273)
	Claudius II 'Gothicus' (268–70)	268	Goths attack Thrace and Greece	
		269	Decisive victory over the Goths	
	Aurelian (270–75)	271		Trans-Danubian Dacia abandoned
	Probus (276–82)	276–77	Goths and Germans driven out of Gaul	
		278	Campaigns against Vandals on the Danube	
	Diocletian (284–305)	286–92	Campaigns against the Alamanni, Burgundians and Sarmatians	
Late Antiquity		286–93	Revolt of Carausius in Britain	
		293	Establishment of the Tetrarchy	
		296(?)–98	Persian invasion of Armenia	
		297/8	Revolt in Egypt	Roman army withdrawn from Nubia
	Constantine (306–37)	312	Civil war between Constantine and Maxentius	Battle of Milvian Bridge (312)
		322–23	The Sarmatians are driven from Pannonia, and the Goths from Thrace	
		357	War with Alamanni	Argentoratum (Strasbourg) (357)
	Julian (360–363)	359–63	Persian invasion of Mesopotamia; Julian's invasion of Persian empire	Siege of Amida (359)
	Valentinian I (364–75)	367	Britain attacked by Saxons, Picts and Scots	
	Theodosius (378–95)			
	Honorius (395–434)	395	Revolt of Alaric and the Visigoths	
		409	Spain invaded by Vandals, Alans and Suevi	Sack of Rome (410)
		429	Vandals overrun Africa	
		476	Romulus Augustulus, last Roman emperor in the West, deposed by Odovacer	

Glossary

acies A battle line. Legions typically fought in three lines (*triplex acies*) or two (*duplex acies*) each composed of subunits (maniples in the middle Republican period, cohorts in a late Republican or imperial legion).

ala (pl. *alae*) Literally a wing (as on a bird), but used to denote the flank of an army or the troops deployed there. Since these were often cavalry, in the imperial period the term was applied to regular units of about 300 or 1,000 auxiliary cavalry, equivalent to an infantry cohort.

aquila An eagle standard carried by a legion's *aquilifer* (standard-bearer).

auxilia Collective term for auxiliary units of the army, infantry and cavalry that supported the legions and were usually of lower status. In the Republican period they were provided on a largely ad hoc basis by allies, subjects and mercenaries. In the imperial period regular infantry cohorts and cavalry *alae* were recruited from free but mostly non-citizen inhabitants of the empire (peregrines).

beneficiarius A soldier who received exemption from certain duties and extra pay to serve on detached duty for a senior officer or official such as a provincial governor (often doing policing).

canabae A civilian settlement that developed next to a legionary fortress, whose population included traders and soldiers' family members.

castris 'From the camp', from Latin *castra*, a camp. A term denoting the origin of a recruit born to a soldier's family in a settlement such as *canabae*, close to a military base. The proportion of legionaries recruited *castris* increased over the imperial period.

colonia (pl. *coloniae*) A colony. In the late Republican and early imperial period these were normally cities (with their rural hinterlands) founded or re-settled by retiring legionary veterans. By the later 2nd century AD the title was a mark of status and political rights awarded to an existing city (often one associated with the army or Roman authority) rather than indicating a mass settlement of veterans.

comes (pl. *comites*) Literally 'a companion' (of the emperor). A title of high-ranking officials including certain provincial governors and military commanders in Late Antiquity. Often translated as 'Count'.

consul In the Republican period two consuls, elected from the senatorial order each year, served as the senior magistrates of the Roman state. They (along with the praetors) had *imperium*, the power to recruit and command armies, and sometimes actually commanded in the field. Consuls lost most of their executive powers to the emperor in the imperial period. However, the office continued to be held (often by more than two men each year) as a mark of status and distinction. In the imperial period provinces with more than one legion were governed by *consulares* ('consulars'), men who had held the office of consul in the course of their careers.

contubernium (pl. *contubernia*) The smallest subunit of a legion, made up of the eight men (*contubernales*) who shared a tent on campaign.

damnatio memoriae An attempt (sometimes the result of a formal decree of the senate) to erase the memory of an emperor or senior official from the historical record by erasing his name from inscriptions and destroying any images of him.

decimation Punishment of a unit for collective cowardice or similar offences by execution of every tenth member, often performed by the soldiers of the unit itself.

denarius (pl. *denarii*) A silver coin used in the western and central parts of the Roman empire from the late 3rd century BC to the mid-3rd century AD. In the imperial period a *denarius* equated to 100 bronze *sesterces* or 400 copper *asses*, and 25 *denarii* made up a gold *aureus*. An ordinary legionary soldier earned 225 *denarii* a year under Augustus.

dona militaria Military decorations awarded for particular exploits in battle or (for officers) more generally for service or participation in a campaign. In the imperial period they were awarded according to rank (see pages 40, 77, 86, 153 and 199).

dux Literally a 'leader' (hence English 'duke'), but used in a specific technical sense to denote the military commander in a province in Late Antiquity, when military and civil command structures had been separated.

equites (sing. *eques*) Literally 'horsemen', the term applied generally to cavalry in the Roman world. However, since wealthy individuals who could afford to maintain a horse provided the cavalry for early Roman armies, the term *equites* ('the equestrian order') was also used throughout Roman history for the group of wealthy individuals in the Roman political system ranking immediately below the senators. Through the early–middle imperial period, members of the equestrian order might serve as legionary tribunes or commanders of auxiliary units, but only commanded legions in the few unusual provinces with equestrian governors, such as Egypt and Mesopotamia. However, from the late 2nd century AD, militarily experienced *equites* increasingly held higher command positions, and from the reign of Gallienus (AD 253–68) all commanders of legions were drawn from the equestrian order.

hoplite A Greek heavy-infantry soldier, the core of archaic and classical Greek armies (*c.* 7th–4th centuries BC; also fielded by Greek-influenced cities including early Rome). They typically wore bronze armour and helmet, and were equipped with a large round bronze shield and thrusting spear (wielded single-handed). They fought in a phalanx formation.

immunes (sing. *immunis*) Legionary soldiers exempted ('immune') from heavy labour because they performed specialized duties. Most were technical specialists such as surveyors, clerks, craftsmen and medical orderlies.

imperium Legal-constitutional power to raise and command armies in the Roman state. In the Republican period, *imperium* was held by senior magistrates, the consuls and praetors, as well as former magistrates appointed with the title of proconsul or propraetor to govern provinces and command armies on the frontiers of the empire. In the imperial period, the emperor was supreme commander of the armies and holder of *imperium maius*, 'greater imperium'. His *imperium* outranked that of all others, and most commanders commanded only by virtue of a devolved grant of *imperium* from the emperor, rather than in their own name.

legatus ('legate') Used widely in the Roman world to denote the recipient of delegated powers of some kind (judicial, administrative as well as military). The most important kinds of legate with relation to legions were (1) the *legatus Augusti pro praetore* ('legate of the emperor with powers equivalent to a praetor's' or just 'imperial legate'), a senior senator who governed a province and commanded all the troops in it with a grant of powers delegated from the emperor who selected him; and (2) the *legatus legionis* ('legate of a legion' or 'legionary legate'), a senator who commanded a legion.

magister equitum / militum / peditum 'master of the horse' (cavalry) / 'of the soldiers' / 'of the infantry' – senior military officials in Late Antiquity, commanding regional field armies (like that of *Oriens*, the East) and the central field armies associated with the emperor.

maniple (*manipulus*) Literally 'a handful', the formation of 60 or 120 men that formed the main subunit of the 'manipular' legion from the 4th to late 2nd centuries BC, when it was superseded by the larger cohort.

municipium (pl. *municipia*) High-status cities in the Roman empire, second only to the *coloniae* in importance. They were governed according to a constitution formalized in law, typically set out in a public inscription.

oppidum A town, usually lacking the amenities of a full Roman-type city, such as baths and theatres. The term was applied by Caesar (and by modern scholars) to the proto-urban settlements he and later Roman invaders encountered in Gaul and Britain.

optio (pl. *optiones*) A junior officer who served as second-in-command of a century, subordinate to a centurion.

peregrinus (pl. *peregrini*; English 'peregrine') A free (i.e. non-slave) inhabitant of the Roman empire who was not a Roman citizen, and thus lacked certain rights and privileges. Typically inhabitants of the provinces, they might hold local rights and citizenship. For the most part peregrines were recruited into the *auxilia* of the imperial army while citizens joined the legions. However, peregrines were sometimes recruited into the legions in the early imperial period, particularly in the East, where there were relatively few citizens; and conversely by the 2nd century AD, many auxiliary recruits were Roman citizens.

phalanx A Greek word, denoting a close formation of heavy infantry. This is the formation in which hoplites fought, and early Roman armies (*c.* 6th century BC) may have employed a phalanx formation. Macedonian and Successor armies (late 4th–2nd centuries BC) used a deeper and more closely formed development of the phalanx in which the soldiers wielded a longer pike (sarissa) with both hands. Roman manipular armies of the middle Republican period (3rd–2nd centuries BC) often fought against such sarissa-equipped phalanxes.

praepositus Someone 'put in charge' or 'put in command' of something; a term used widely in administrative as well as military contexts. In a military sense, it could refer, for example, to the commander of a vexillation or a particular garrison.

praetor In the Republican constitution, praetors were the second-ranking magistrates after the consuls and were also elected on an annual basis. While many of their duties related to the lawcourts, praetors, like consuls, had *imperium* and could raise and command armies. Praetors continued to be elected during the imperial period and while they ceded many of their executive and military powers to the emperor, provinces with a single legion were usually governed by individuals of praetorian status, who had held the praetorship in Rome.

praetorian cohort / guard In the Republican period, magistrates and governors on campaign had a bodyguard (praetorian cohort) of picked legionaries, who served in that role on a temporary basis. However, in 27 BC Augustus created a permanent imperial guard that we generally call 'the praetorian guard', although Romans referred to it as 'the praetorian cohorts'. The number of cohorts and their size (500 or 1,000 men) changed over the imperial period, but by the 2nd century AD there were ten, of 1,000 men each. The guards had better terms of service than legionaries, and were normally recruited direct from Italian communities until Septimius Severus began to recruit them from experienced (typically Balkan) frontier legions. The praetorian cohorts were based in a camp in Rome, although they also fought with the emperor on campaign. The guard as a whole was commanded by one or two praetorian prefects appointed by the emperor from the equestrian order (*equites*). Given their proximity to the emperor, the cohorts and their officers often intervened in imperial politics.

praefectus ('prefect') Someone 'set in charge', in administrative or military terms. Equestrian governors of a few exceptional provinces such as Egypt were called prefects, as were the equestrian commanders of the legions who served under them. Likewise, the commanders of auxiliary units often bore the title prefect.

primi ordines 'men of the first rank', a term used collectively to describe the experienced and high-status centurions of a legion's first cohort.

principales Soldiers ranking between centurions and ordinary legionaries, who (unlike immunes) received extra pay (typically one and a half or two times the normal rate) because of their status and special duties they performed. They included the *optiones*, *tesserarii* (men who carried the watchword) and standard-bearers.

Principate The early and middle imperial period, from the reign of Augustus (31 BC) to the 3rd century AD (perhaps *c.* AD 235, the end of the Severan dynasty, or AD 284, the accession of Diocletian), derived from the term *princeps* ('leading citizen'), the usual title of the emperor at that time.

principia The headquarters area of a Roman camp, fort or fortress, where the cross-streets met. This usually included an open parade ground and headquarters block with *sacellum*, a chapel for the legionary standards.

proconsul An official with the powers of a consul, normally the governor of a province. In the Republican period he might be assigned to govern a frontier area with a substantial military force under his command and exercise considerable independence in its use, like Julius Caesar in Rome. In the imperial period, militarily active parts of the empire were instead governed by legates appointed by the emperor. Proconsuls of the imperial period, appointed by the senate, typically governed pacified parts of the empire and so, with the exception of the proconsul of Africa in the first decades of the 1st century AD, no longer commanded legions.

propraetor An official with the powers of a praetor, similar to a proconsul. In the Republic, a propraetor was typically a provincial governor, perhaps commanding an army including legions, while imperial propraetors were appointed by the senate to govern pacified provinces. However, the imperial legates appointed by emperors to govern warlike provinces and command legions also bore the title *legatus Augusti pro praetore* ('legate of the emperor with powers equivalent to a praetor's').

sestertius (pl. *sestertii*, English 'sesterce', 'sesterces') A bronze coin used in the western and central parts of the Roman empire. There were 100 sesterces in a *denarius.*

signum A standard carried by a *signifer* (standard-bearer).

vigiles The firemen or nightwatchmen of Rome, established by Augustus in AD 6 and organized as a paramilitary force made up of freedmen (ex-slaves) in seven cohorts, further divided into centuries. Augustus also created the three urban cohorts, a paramilitary policing force for the city of Rome.

Further Reading

The bibliography on the Roman army is immense, although – due to the variable nature of the evidence – some legions have received much more scholarly attention than others. What follows below is necessarily selective, but aims to guide the reader to a range of accessible reading and to some of the most important scholarly works.

General reading on the Roman army

The best introductions to the Roman army are Goldsworthy, A., *The Complete Roman Army* (London and New York: Thames & Hudson, 2003) and Keppie, L., *The Making of the Roman Army* (London: Routledge, 1998; Norman: University of Oklahoma Press, 1998) (which also serves as an important reference work for the origins of particular imperial legions).

Reference works and books on general topics relating to the Roman army

The most important and comprehensive reference work on the Roman legions is Ritterling, E., 'Legio'. *Paulys Realencyclopädie der classischen Altertumswissenschaft*, 12.1 (1925), 1186–1838, which is a classic legion-by-legion study focusing on the ancient evidence for their origins and activities. However, new discoveries of inscriptions and archaeological evidence mean Ritterling's study is out of date in some respects now and has been updated by Le Bohec, Y. (ed.), *Les légions de Rome sous le Haut-Empire. Actes du Congès de Lyon (17–19 Septembre 1998).* Collection du Centre d'Études Romaines et Gallo-Romaines, N.S., Vol. 20 (Lyon: De Boccard, 2000) (= *Les légions de Rome*).

Bishop, M.C. and J. C. Coulston, *Roman Military Equipment from the Punic Wars to the Fall of Rome* (Oxford: Oxbow Books, 2005; Oakville, CT: David Brown Book Co., 2006).

Brewer, Richard J. (ed.), *Roman Fortresses and their Legions* (London: Occasional Papers of the Research Committee of the Society of Antiquaries of London, 2000) (= *Roman Fortresses*).

Campbell, B., *The Roman Army, 31 BC–AD 337: A Sourcebook* (London and New York: Routledge, 1994).

Elton, H., *Frontiers of the Roman Empire.* (London: Batsford, 1996; Bloomington: Indiana University Press, 1996).

Erdkamp, P. (ed.), *A Companion to the Roman Army* (Oxford: Blackwell, 2007; Malden, MA: Wiley–Blackwell, 2011).

Feugere, M., *The Weapons of the Romans* (Stroud: Tempus Publishing, 2002).

Keppie, L. J. F., *Legions and Veterans.* Roman Army Papers 1971–2000 (Stuttgart: Franz Steiner Verlag, 2000 (= *Legions and Veterans*).

Le Bohec, Y., *The Imperial Roman Army* (London: Routledge, 2000).

Lendon, J. E., *Soldiers and Ghosts. A History of Battle in Classical Antiquity* (New Haven: Yale University Press, 2005).

Parker, H. M. D., *The Roman Legions* (Oxford: Oxford University Press, 1928; reprinted 1958 and 1971).

Rihll, T., *The Catapult: A History* (Yardley PA: Westholme, 2007).

Sabin, P., H. van Wees and M. Whitby (eds), *The Cambridge History of Greek and Roman Warfare* (2 volumes) (Cambridge: Cambridge University Press, 2007).

Sage, M. M., *The Republican Roman Army: A Sourcebook* (London and New York: Routledge, 2008).

Whittaker, C. R., *Frontiers of the Roman Empire: A Social and Economic Study* (Baltimore and London: Johns Hopkins, 1994).

Besides the sourcebooks edited by Campbell and Sage (above), many ancient sources can now be accessed on-line. One of the best collections is at Lacus Curtius, http://penelope.uchicago.edu/Thayer/E/Roman/home.html; see also the Perseus Project, http://www.perseus. tufts.edu/hopper/. For an almost complete corpus of Latin inscriptions, see the Clauss/Slaby Epigraphik-Datenbank, http://oracle-vm.ku-eichstaett.de:8888/epigr/epigraphikbeleg_en. For information about, and links to, papyri collections, see www.papyri.info.

Part I: The Legions in the Republican Period

Bell, M. J. V. ,'Tactical reform in the Roman Republican army.' *Historia* 14 (1965), 404–22.

Blois, L. de, *The Roman Army and Politics in the First Century before Christ* (Amsterdam: Gieben, 1987).

Daly, G. Cannae, *The Experience of Battle in the Second Punic War.* (London and New York: Routledge, 2002).

Forsythe, G., 'The army and centuriate organization in early Rome.' In Erdkamp, P. (ed.), *A Companion to the Roman Army* (Oxford: Blackwell, 2007; Malden, MA: Wiley-Blackwell, 2011), 24–41.

Goldsworthy, A., *The Roman Army at War, 100 BC–AD 200* (Oxford: Clarendon Press, 1998; New York: Clarendon Press, 1996).

Keppie, L. J. F., *Colonisation and Veteran Settlement in Italy, 47–14 BC* (London: British School at Rome, 1983).

Keppie, L. J. F., 'Mark Antony's Legions.' In *Legions and Veterans*, 75–96.

Potter, D., 'The Roman Army and Navy.' In Flower, H. J. (ed.), *The Cambridge Companion to the Roman Republic* (Cambridge and New York: Cambridge University Press, 2004), 66–88.

Rawlings, L., 'Army and battle during the conquest of Italy.' In Erdkamp, P. (ed.), *A Companion to the Roman Army* (Oxford: Blackwell, 2007; Malden, MA: Wiley-Blackwell, 2011), 45–62.

Rich, J., 'Warfare and the army in early Rome.' In Erdkamp, P. (ed.), *A Companion to the Roman Army* (Oxford: Blackwell, 2007; Malden, MA: Wiley-Blackwell, 2011), 7–23.

Sabin, P., 'The face of Roman battle.' *Journal of Roman Studies* 90 (2000), 1–17.

Sabin, P., 'The mechanics of battle in the Second Punic War.' In Cornell, T., B. Rankov and P. Sabin (eds), *The Second Punic War: A Reappraisal* (London: Institute of Classical Studies, 1996), 59–79.

Sage, M. M., *The Republican Roman Army: A Sourcebook* (London: Routledge, 2008; New York: Routledge, 2008).

Part II: The Legions in the Imperial Age

Campbell, B., *The Emperor and the Roman Army: 31 BC–AD 235* (Oxford and New York: Oxford University Press, 1984).

Campbell, B., 'The army.' In Bowman, A., P. Garnsey and A. Cameron (eds), *The Cambridge Ancient History, vol 11: The High Empire* (2nd ed., Cambridge and New York: Cambridge University Press, 2000), 110–30.

Forni, G., *Il reclutamento delle legion da Augusto a Diocleziano* (Milan-Rome: Fratelli Bocca Editori, 1953).

Gilliver, C. M., *The Roman Art of War* (Stroud: Tempus, 1999).

Goldsworthy, A., *The Roman Army at War, 100 BC–AD 200* (Oxford: Clarendon Press, 1998; New York: Clarendon Press, 1996).

Hassall, M., 'The army.' In Bowman, A., P. Garnsey and D. Rathbone (eds), *The Cambridge Ancient History, vol 12: The Crisis of Empire, A.D. 193–337* (2nd ed., Cambridge and New York: Cambridge University Press, 2005), 320–43.

Keppie, L. J. F., 'The army and the navy'. In *The Cambridge Ancient History, vol 10: The Augustan Empire* (2nd ed, Cambridge: Cambridge University Press, 1996; New York: Cambridge University Press, 2005), 371–96.

Keppie, L. J. F., *The Making of the Roman Army* (London: Routledge, 1998; Norman: University of Oklahoma Press, 1998).

Luttwak, E., *The Grand Strategy of the Roman Empire: from the First Century AD to the Third.* (Baltimore: Johns Hopkins, 1976; London: Weidenfeld & Nicholson, 1999).

Mann, J. C., *Legionary Recruitment and Veteran Settlement during the Principate*

(London: Institute of Archaeology Occasional Papers 7, 1983).
Mann, J. C., 'The raising of new legions during the Principate.' *Hermes* 91 (1963), 483–89.
Pollard, N. D., 'The Roman Army.' In Potter, D. S. (ed.), *A Companion to the Roman Empire* (Oxford: Blackwell, 2006; Malden, MA: Blackwell, 2006), 206–27.
Potter, D., *The Roman Empire at Bay AD 180–395* (London and New York: Routledge, 2004).
Syme, R., 'Some Notes on the Legions under Augustus.' *Journal of Roman Studies* 23 (1933), 14–33.
Syme, R., 'Guard Prefects of Trajan and Hadrian.' *Journal of Roman Studies* 70 (1980), 64–80.
Webster, G., *The Roman Imperial Army of the First and Second Centuries A.D.* (3rd ed., Norman: Oklahoma University Press, 1985).

Histories of individual legions:

The Legions of the Rhine Frontier and Gaul

Creighton, J. D. and R. J. A.Wilson (eds), Roman Germany. Studies in Cultural Interaction. *Journal of Roman Archaeology*, Supp. 32 (Portsmouth, RI, 1999).
Wells, C. M., *The German Policy of Augustus. An Examination of the Archaeological Evidence* (Oxford: Oxford University Press,1972).
Wells, C. M., 'The German policy of Augustus: 25 Years on'. In Gudea, N. (ed.), *Roman Frontier Studies.* Proceedings of the XVIIth International Congress of Roman Frontier Studies (Zalau, 1999), 3–7.

Augustus' Lost Legions: *XVII; XVIII; XIX*

Keppie, L. J. F., 'Legiones XVII, XVIII, XIX: Exercitus omnium fortissimus.' In *Roman Frontier Studies. Proceedings of the XVIth International Congress of Roman Frontier Studies 1995* (Oxford: Oxbow, 1997). Reprinted in *Legions and Veterans*, 161–65.
Murdoch, A., *Rome's Greatest Defeat. Massacre in the Teutoburg Forest* (Stroud: Sutton Publishing, 2006).
Schlüter, W., 'The Battle of the Teutoburg Forest: Archaeological Research at Kalkriese Near Osnabrück.' In: Creighton, J. D. and Wilson, R. J. A. (eds.), Roman Germany. Studies in Cultural Interaction. *Journal of Roman Archaeology*, Supplementary Series Nr. 32 (Portsmouth, RI, 1999) 125–59.
Schlüter, W. and R. Wiegels (eds), *Rom, Germanien und die Ausgrabungen von Kalkriese* (Osnabrück 1999).
Sommer, Michael, *Die Arminiusschlacht. Spurensuche im Teutoburger Wald* (Stuttgart: Kröner, 2009).
Wiegels, R., 'Legiones XVII, XVIII, XIX.' In *Les légions de Rome*, 75–78.

The Legions in the Batavian Revolt:
I Germanica; IIII Macedonica; XV Primigenia; XVI Gallica

IIII Macedonica

Gómez-Pantoja, J., 'Legio IIII Macedonica.' In *Les légions de Rome*, 105–17.
Morillo Cerdán, A., 'La legio IIII Macedonica en la península Ibérica. El campamento de Herrera de Pisuerga (Palencia).' In *Les légions de Rome*, 609–24.

XV Primigenia

Le Bohec, Y., 'Legio XV Primigenia.' In *Les légions de Rome*, 69.

The *Exercitus Germanae Inferioris*:
I Minervia; XXX Ulpia Victrix

Holder, P.A., '*Exercitus pius fidelis*: the army of Germania Inferior in AD 89.' *ZPE* 128 (1999), 237–50.

I Minervia

Eck, W., 'Die *legio I Minervia*. Militärische und zivile Aspekte ihrer Geschichte im 3. Jh. n.Chr.' In *Les légions de Rome*, 87–93.
Le Bohec, Y., 'Legio I Mineruia (Ier-IIe siècles).' In *Les légions de Rome*, 83–85.

XXX Ulpia Victrix

Le Bohec, Y., 'Legio XXX Vlpia.' In *Les légions de Rome*, 71–74.

Other Legions on the Rhine Frontier:
VIII Augusta; XXII Primigenia; V Alaudae; XXI Rapax

VIII Augusta

Keppie, L. J. F., 'Legio VIII Augusta and the Claudian Invasion.' *Britannia* 2 (1971), 149–55. Reprinted in *Legions and Veterans*, 166–72.
Keppie, L. J. F., 'Legio VIII in Britain: The beginning and the end.' In *Roman Fortresses*, 83–100. Reprinted in *Legions and Veterans*, 201–15.
Oldenstein-Pferdehirt, B., 'Zur Geschichte der Legio VIII Augusta.' *RGZM* 31 (1984), 397–431.
Reddé, M., 'Le camp de Mirebeau et l'histoire de la VIIIe légion Auguste sous le Flaviens.' In Goguey, R. and Reddé, M. (eds) *Le camp legionnaire de Mirebeau* (Mayence: RGZM, 1995).
Reddé, M., 'Legio VIII Augusta.' In *Les légions de Rome*, 119–26.

XXII Primigenia

Franke, T., 'Legio XXII Primigenia.' In *Les légions de Rome*, 95–104.
Piso, I., 'Les légions dans la province de Dacie'. In *Les légions de Rome*, 205–25.

V Alaudae

Franke, T., '*Legio V Alaudae.*' In *Les légions de Rome*, 39–48.
Strobel, K., 'Die Legio V Alaudae in Moesien.' *Historia* 37 (1988), 504–8.

XXI Rapax

Berard, F., 'La légion XXIe Rapax.' In *Les légions de Rome*, 49–67.
Rossi, L., 'Legio XXI Rapax... atque Infidelis?' In *Les légions de Rome*, 491–98.

The Legions of Roman Britain:
II Augusta; VI Victrix; IX Hispana; XX Valeria Victrix

Birley, A., *Fasti of Roman Britain* (Oxford: Clarendon Press, 1981).
Birley, E., *Roman Britain and the Roman Army: Collected Papers.* (Kendal: Titus Wilson, 1976).
Hassall, M., 'Legionary fortresses in Britain.' In *Les légions de Rome*, 441–57.
Holder, P. A., *The Roman Army in Britain* (London: Batsford 1981; New York: St. Martin's Press, 1982).

II Augusta

Keppie, L. J. F., *The Origins and Early History of the Second Augustan Legion* (Sixth Annual Caerleon Lecture) (Cardiff: National Museums and Galleries of Wales, 1993). Reprinted in *Legions and Veterans*, 123–59.
Keppie, L. J. F., 'Legiones II Augusta, VI Victrix, IX Hispana, XX Valeria Victrix.' In *Les légions de Rome*, 25–37.
Jarrett, M. R., 'Legio II Augusta in Britain'. In *Archaeologia Cambrensis* 113 (1964), 47–63.

VI Victrix

Birley, A., 'VI Victrix in Britain.' In Butler, R. M. (ed.) *Soldier and Civilian in Roman Yorkshire* (Leicester: Leicester University Press, 1971), 81–96.
Keppie, L. J. F., 'Legiones II Augusta, VI Victrix, IX Hispana, XX Valeria Victrix.' In *Les légions de Rome*, 25–37.
Morillo Cerdán, A. and V. Garcia Marcos, 'Nuevos testimonios acerca de las legiones VI Victrix y X Gemina en la region septentrional de la península Ibérica.' In *Les légions de Rome*, 589–607.

IX Hispana

Birley, E., 'The fate of the Ninth Legion.' In Butler, R.M. (ed.), *Soldier and Civilian in Roman Yorkshire* (Leicester, 1971), 71–80.
Eck, W., 'Zum Ende der legio IX Hispana.' *Chiron* 2 (1972), 459–62.
Keppie, L. J. F., 'The fate of the Ninth Legion – a problem for the eastern provinces?' In French, D. H. and Lightfoot, C. S. (eds), *The Eastern Frontier of the Roman Empire* (Oxford: British Archaeological Reports

International Series, 553, 1989), 247–55. Reprinted in *Legions and Veterans*, 173–81.
Keppie, L. J. F. ,'Legiones II Augusta, VI Victrix, IX Hispana, XX Valeria Victrix.' In *Les légions de Rome*, 25–37.

XX Valeria Victrix
Jarrett, M. G.,'Legio XX Valeria Victrix in Britain.' *Archaeologia Cambrensis* 117 (1968), 77–91.
Keppie, L. J. F., 'Legiones II Augusta, VI Victrix, IX Hispana, XX Valeria Victrix.' In *Les légions de Rome*, 25–37.
Malone, S. J., *Legio XX Valeria Victrix. Prosopography, archaeology and history.* BAR International Series 1491 (Oxford: Archeopress, 2006).
Manning, W., 'The fortresses of legio XX.' In Brewer R. (ed.) *Roman Fortresses*, 69–81.
Perea Yébenes, S., 'Hispania y la legio XX.' In *Les légions de Rome*, 581–87.

The Legions of Spain: *VII Gemina*
Jones, R. F. J., 'The Roman Military Occupation of North-West Spain.' *Journal of Roman Studies* 66 (1976), 45–66.
Le Roux, P., *L'armée romaine et l'organisation des provinces ibériques d'Auguste à l'invasion de 409* (Paris: Publications du Centre Pierre Paris 8, 1982).

VII Gemina
Legio VII Gemina (León: Cátedra de San Isidoro. Instituto Leonés de Estudios Romano-Visigóticos, 1970).
Le Roux, P., 'Legio VII Gemina (pia) felix.' In *Les légions de Rome*, 383–96.
Morillo, A. and V. Garcia-Marcos, 'Legio VII Gemina and its Flavian Fortress at León.' *Journal of Roman Archaeology* 16 (2003), 275–87.
Piso, I., 'Les légions dans la province de Dacie'. In *Les légions de Rome*, 205–25.

The Legions of Roman Africa: *III Augusta; I Macriana Liberatrix*
Cagnat, R., *L'armée romaine d'Afrique et l'occupation militaire de l'Afrique sous les empereurs* (Paris: Leroux, 1913).
Mattingly, D. J., *Tripolitania* (Ann Arbor: University of Michigan Press, 1994).
Speidel, M. P., 'The Roman Army in North Africa.' *Journal of Roman Archaeology* 5 (1992), 401–7.
Speidel M. P., *Emperor Hadrian's Speeches to the African Army: A New Text* (Mainz: Verlag des Romisch-Germanischen Zentralmuseums, 2006).

III Augusta
Le Bohec, Y., *La Troisième Légion Auguste* (Paris: CNRS, 1989).
Le Bohec, Y., 'Legio III Augusta.' In *Les légions de Rome*, 373–81.

I Macriana Liberatrix
Chausa, A., 'Legio I Macriana'. In *Les légions de Rome*, 369–71.

The Legions of Egypt: *XXII Deiotariana; II Traiana Fortis*
Alston, R., *Soldier and Society in Roman Egypt: a Social History.* (London and New York: Routledge, 1995).
Lehmann, C. M. and K. G. Holum, *The Greek and Latin Inscriptions of Caesarea Maritima* (Boston: American Schools of Oriental Research 2000), 71–77.
Sheehan, P., *Babylon of Egypt: The Archaeology of Old Cairo and the Origins of the City* (Cairo: The American University in Cairo Press, 2010).
Speidel, M., 'Augustus' Deployment of the Legions in Egypt.' *Chronique d'Égypte* 57.113 (1982), 120–24.
Speidel, M. P., 'Rome's Nubian garrison.' In *Aufstieg und Niedergang der römischen Welt* II.10.1 (1988), 767–79.

XXII Deiotariana
Daris, S. ,'Legio XXII Deiotariana.' In *Les légions de Rome*, 365–67.
Isaac, B and I. Roll, 'Judaea in the Early Years of Hadrian's Reign.' *Latomus* 38 (1979), 54–66.
Keppie, L. J. F., 'The history and disappearance of the legion XXII Deiotariana.' In *Legions and Veterans*, 225–32.
Mor, M., 'Two legions – same fate? (The disappearance of the Legions IX Hispana and XXII Deiotariana). *Zeitschrift für Papyrologie und Epigraphik* 62 (1986), 267–78.

II Traiana Fortis
Daris, S., 'Legio II Traiana Fortis.' In *Les légions de Rome*, 359–63.
Isaac, B. and I. Roll, 'Legio II Traiana in Judaea.' *Zeitschrift für Papyrologie und Epigraphik* 33 (1979), 149–56.
Isaac, B. and I. Roll, 'Legio II Traiana in Judaea – A Reply.' *Zeitschrift für Papyrologie und Epigraphik* 47 (1982), 131–32.
Rea, J. ,'Legio II Traiana in Judaea.' *Zeitschrift für Papyrologie und Epigraphik* 38 (1980), 220–21.
Villeneuve, F., 'L'armée romaine en mer Rouge et autour de la mer Rouge aux IIème et IIIème siècles apr. J.C. : à propos de deux inscriptions latines découvertes sur l'archipel Farasan'. In Lewin, A.S. and Pellegrini, P. (eds.) *The Late Roman Army in the Near East from Diocletian to the Arab Conquest* (Oxford: BAR International Series 1717, 2007), 13–27.

The Legions of the Roman East
Of particular importance for the study of the Roman army in the east is Isaac, B. *The Limits of Empire. The Roman Army in the East* (rev. ed., Oxford: Oxford University Press, 1993).

Dodgeon, M. H. and S. N. C. Lieu, *The Roman Eastern Frontier and the Persian Wars (AD 226–363): A Documentary History.* (New York and London: Routledge, 1991).
Kennedy, D. (ed.), *The Roman Army in the East* (Ann Arbor: Journal of Roman Archaeology Supp. 18, 1996).
Kennedy, D. and D. Riley, *Rome's Desert Frontier from the Air* (London: Batsford, 1990).
Keppie, L. J. F., 'Legions in the East from Augustus to Trajan.' In Freeman, P. and D. Kennedy (eds), *The Defence of the Roman and Byzantine East* (Oxford: BAR International Series, 297(i), 1986), 411–29. Reprinted in *Legions and Veterans*, 182–200.
Millar, F., *The Roman Near East 31 BC–AD 337* (Cambridge, MA: Harvard University Press, 1993).

Syria: *III Gallica; IIII Scythica; XVI Flavia Firma*
Kennedy, D. L., *The Roman Army in Jordan* (2nd ed., London: Council for British Research in the Levant, 2004).
Pollard, N. D., The Roman army as 'Total Institution' in the Near East? In Kennedy, D. (ed), *The Roman Army in the East* (Ann Arbor, Journal of Roman Archaeology Supplement 18, 1996), 211–27.
Pollard, N. D., *Soldiers, Cities and Civilians in Roman Syria* (Ann Arbor: University of Michigan Press, 2000).
Wheeler, E. L., 'The laxity of the Syrian legions'. In Kennedy, D. (ed.), *The Roman Army in the East* (Ann Arbor, Journal of Roman Archaeology Supplement 18, 1996), 229–76.

III Gallica
Dabrowa, E., 'Legio III Gallica.' In *Les légions de Rome*, 309–15.
French, D., 'Legio III Gallica.' In Dabrowa, E. (ed) *The Roman and Byzantine army in the East.* Proceedings of a colloqium (sic) held at the Jagiellonian University, Kraków in September 1992 (Kraków: Drukarnia Uniwersytetu Jagiellońskiego, 1994), 19–27.
Piso, I., 'Les légions dans la province de Dacie'. In *Les légions de Rome*, 205–25.

IIII Scythica
Kennedy, D. (ed), *The Twin Towns of Zeugma on the Euphrates: Rescue Work and Historical Studies* (Portsmouth RI: Journal of Roman Archaeology Supp. 27, 1998).
Speidel M. A., 'Legio IIII Scythica, its movements and men'. In Kennedy, D. (ed.), *The Twin Towns of Zeugma on the*

Euphrates: Rescue Work and Historical Studies (Portsmouth RI: Journal of Roman Archaeology Supp. 27, 1998), 163–203.
Speidel, M. A., 'Legio IV Scythica.' In *Les légions de Rome*, 327–37.
Wagner, J., *Seleukeia am Euphrat Zeugma* (Wiesbaden: Reichert, 1976).
Wagner, J., 'Legio IIII Scythica in Zeugma am Euphrat.' *Studien zu den Militärgrenzen Roms* 2 (Cologne-Bonn: Rheinland-Verlag, 1977), 517–39.

Judaea: *X Fretensis; VI Ferrata*

Eck, W., 'The Bar Kokhba revolt: the Roman point of view.' *Journal of Roman Studies* 89 (1999), 76–89.
Keppie, L. J. F., 'The legionary garrison of Judaea under Hadrian.' In *Legions and Veterans*, 219–24.
Lehmann, C.M and K. G. Holum, *The Greek and Latin Inscriptions of Caesarea Maritima* (Boston: American Schools of Oriental Research, 2000), 71–77.
Mor, M., 'The Roman Army in Eretz-Israel in the Years AD 70–132.' In Freeman, P. and Kennedy, D. (eds) *The Defence of the Roman and Byzantine East* (Oxford: BAR International Series, 297(ii), 1986), 575–602.
Schurer, E. (revised by Millar, F.; Vermes, G.; Goodman, M.), *The History of the Jewish People in the Age of Jesus Christ* (Edinburgh: T & T Clark, 1987).

X Fretensis

Arubas, B. and H. Goldfus, 'The kilnworks of the Tenth Legion Fretensis.' In Humphries, J. (ed) *The Roman and Byzantine Near East: Some Recent Archaeological Research* (Ann Arbor: Journal of Roman Archaeology, Supplement 14, 1995), 95–107.
Dabrowa, E., 'Legio X Fretensis.' In *Les légions de Rome*, 317–25.
Geva, H., 'The Camp of the Tenth Legion in Jerusalem: An Archaeological Reconsideration.' *Israel Exploration Journal* 34 (1984), 239–54.
Gichon, M., 'The siege of Masada.' In *Les légions de Rome*, 541–54.
Meshorer, Y., 'Two Finds from the Roman Tenth Legion.' *Israel Museum Journal* 3 (1984), 41–45.
Yadin, Yigael, *Masada: Herod's Fortress and the Zealots' Last Stand.* (London: Weidenfeld and Nicholson, 1966).

VI Ferrata

Cotton, H., 'The Legio VI Ferrrata,' In *Les légions de Rome*, 351–57.
Kennedy, D. L., 'Legio VI Ferrata. The annexation and early garrison of Arabia.' *Harvard Studies in Classical Philology* 84 (1980), 283–309.
Piso, I., 'Les légions dans la province de Dacie'. In *Les légions de Rome*, 205–25.
Tepper, Y., 'The Roman legionary camp at Legio, Israel.' In Lewin, A.S. and Pellegrini, P. (eds) *The Late Roman Army in the Near East from Diocletian to the Arab Conquest* (Oxford: BAR International Series 1717, 2007), 57–71.
Villeneuve, F., 'L'armée romaine en mer Rouge et autour de la mer Rouge aux IIème et IIIème siècles apr. J.C.: à propos de deux inscriptions latines découvertes sur l'archipel Farasan'. In Lewin, A.S. and Pellegrini, P. (eds) *The Late Roman Army in the Near East from Diocletian to the Arab Conquest* (Oxford: BAR International Series 1717, 2007), 13–27.
Yadin, Yigael, *Bar-Kokhba: The Rediscovery of the Legendary Hero of the Last Jewish Revolt against Imperial Rome* (London: Weidenfeld and Nicholson 1971).

Arabia: *III Cyrenaica*

Bowersock, G.W., *Roman Arabia* (Cambridge MA: Harvard UP, 1983).
Speidel, M. P., 'The Roman Army in Arabia'. In Roman Army Studies 1 (Amsterdam 1984), 229–72.

III Cyrenaica

Gatier, P-L., 'La Legio III Cyrenaica et l'Arabie.' In *Les légions de Rome*, 341–49.
Wolff, C., 'La legio III Cyrenaica au Ier siècle.' In *Les légions de Rome*, 339–40.

Cappadocia: *XII Fulminata; XV Apollinaris*

XII Fulminata

Bertrandy, G., and B. Rémy, 'Legio XII Fulminata.' In *Les légions de Rome*, 253–57.

XV Apollinaris

Wheeler, E., 'Legio XV Apollinaris: From Carnuntum to Satala – and beyond.' In *Les légions de Rome*, 259–308.

Severan Legions of Mesopotamia: *I Parthica; III Parthica*

Birley, E., 'Septimius Severus and the Roman Army.' *Epigraphische Studien* 8 (1969), 63–82.
Kennedy, D. L., 'The garrisoning of Mesopotamia in the late Antonine and early Severan period.' *Antichthon* 21 (1987), 57–66.
Mann, J.C., 'The raising of new legions during the Principate.' *Hermes* 91 (1963), 483–89.

I Parthica

Speidel, M. and J. Reynolds, 'A veteran of Legio I Parthica from Carian Aphrodisias.' *Epigraphica Anatolica* 5 (1985), 31–35.
Wolff, C., 'Legio I Parthica.' In *Les légions de Rome*, 247–49.

III Parthica

Wolff, C., 'Legio III Parthica.' In *Les légions de Rome*, 251–52.

The Legions of the Balkan Provinces

Moesia: *VII Claudia; XI Claudia; I Italica; IIII Flavia Felix*

VII Claudia

Fellman, R., 'Die 11. Legion Claudia Pia Fidelis.' In *Les légions de Rome*, 127–31.
Laporte, J-P., 'La *legio VIIa* et la déduction des colonies augustéenees de Césarienne.' In *Les légions de Rome*, 555–79.
Le Bohec, Y. and C. Wolff, 'Legiones Moesiae Superioris.' In *Les légions de Rome*, 239–45.
Piso, I., 'Les légions dans la province de Dacie'. In *Les légions de Rome*, 205–25.
Strobel, K., 'Zur Geschichte der Legiones V (Macedonica) und VII (Claudia pia fidelis) in der frühen Kaiserzeit und zur Stellung der Provinz Galatia in der augusteischen Heeresgeschichte.' In *Les légions de Rome*, 515–28.

XI Claudia

Fellmann, R., 'Die 11. Legion Claudia Pia Fidelis.' In *Les légions de Rome*, 127–31.

I Italica

Absil, M., 'Legio I Italica.' In *Les légions de Rome*, 228–38.

IV Flavia Felix

Le Bohec, Y. and C. Wolff, 'Legiones Moesiae Superioris.' In *Les légions de Rome*, 239–45.
Piso, I., 'Les légions dans la province de Dacie'. In *Les légions de Rome*, 205–25.

Pannonia: *X Gemina; XIV Gemina; I Adiutrix; II Adiutrix*

X Gemina

Gómez-Pantoja, J., 'Legio X Gemina'. In *Les légions de Rome*, 169–90.
Morillo Cerdán, A. and V. Garcia Marcos, 'Nuevos testimonios acerca de las legiones VI Victrix y X Gemina en la region septentrional de la península Ibérica.' In *Les légions de Rome*, 589–607.
Piso, I., 'Les légions dans la province de Dacie'. In *Les légions de Rome*, 205–25.

XIV Gemina

Franke, T., 'Legio XIV Gemina.' In *Les légions de Rome*, 191–202.
Piso, I., 'Les légions dans la province de Dacie'. In *Les légions de Rome*, 205–25.

I Adiutrix

Lörincz, B., 'Legio I Adiutrix.' In *Les légions de Rome*, 151–58.

Piso, I., 'Les légions dans la province de Dacie'. In *Les légions de Rome*, 205–25.

II Adiutrix

Lörincz, B., 'Legio II Adiutrix.' In *Les légions de Rome*, 159–168.

Piso, I., 'Les légions dans la province de Dacie'. In *Les légions de Rome*, 205–25.

Noricum: *II Italica*

Lörincz, B., 'Legio II Italica.' In *Les légions de Rome*, 145–49.

Winkler, G., 'Legio II Italica. Geschichte und Denkmäler.' *Jahrbuch des Oberösterreichischen Musealvereines* 116 (1971), 85–138.

Raetia: *III Italica*

Dietz, K., 'Legio III Italica.' In *Les légions de Rome*, 133–43.

Dacia: *V Macedonica, XIII Gemina*

Piso, I., 'Les légions dans la province de Dacie'. In *Les légions de Rome*, 205–25.

V Macedonica

Piso, I., 'Les légions dans la province de Dacie'. In *Les légions de Rome*, 205–25.

Strobel, K., 'Zur Geschichte der Legiones V (Macedonica) und VII (Claudia pia fidelis) in der frühen Kaiserzeit und zur Stellung der Provinz Galatia in der augusteischen Heeresgeschichte'. In *Les légions de Rome*, 515–28.

XIII Gemina

Piso, I., 'Les légions dans la province de Dacie'. In *Les légions de Rome*, 205–25.

Wolff, C., 'La *legio XIII Gemina* au Ier siècle.' In *Les légions de Rome*, 203–4.

A Legion in Italy: *II Parthica*

Balty, J. C., 'Apamea in Syria in the second and third centuries AD.' *Journal of Roman Studies* 78 (1988), 91–94.

Balty, J. C., *Apamea in Syria: the Winter Quarters of Legio II Parthica: Roman Gravestones from the Military Cemetery* (Brussels: VUB Press, 1993).

Birley, Anthony, *Septimius Severus: The African Emperor* (London and New York: Routledge, 1999).

Ricci, C., '*Legio II Parthica.* Una messa a punto.' *Les légions de Rome*, 397–410.

Van Rengen, W., 'La IIe Légion Parthique à Apamée.' In *Les légions de Rome*, 407–10.

Part III: The Legions in Late Antiquity

Bowman, A. K., 'The military occupation of Upper Egypt in the reign of Diocletian.' *Bulletin of the American Society of Papyrologists* 15 (1978), 25–38.

Campbell, B., 'The army.' In Bowman, A., P. Garnsey and A. Cameron (eds), *The Cambridge Ancient History, vol 12: The Crisis of Empire, A.D. 193–337* (2nd ed., Cambridge: Cambridge University Press, 2005), 110–30.

Dodgeon, M. H. and S. N. C. Lieu, *The Roman Eastern Frontier and the Persian wars AD 226–363* (London and New York: Routledge, 1991).

Duncan-Jones, R. P., *Structure and Scale in the Roman Economy* (Cambridge and New York: Cambridge University Press, 1990), 105–17; 214–21.

Elton, H., *Warfare in Roman Europe AD 350–425* (Oxford: Oxford University Press, 1997; New York: Clarendon Press, 1996).

Ferrill, A., *The Fall of the Roman Empire: The Military Explanation* (London and New York: Thames & Hudson, 1986).

Greatrex, G. and S. N. C. Lieu, *The Roman Eastern Frontier and the Persian Wars. Part II AD 363–630* (London: Routledge, 2002; New York: Routledge, 1991).

Johnson, S., *Late Roman Fortifications* (London: Batsford, 1983; Totowa, NJ: Barnes & Noble Books, 1983).

Kulikowski, M., 'The *Notitia Dignitatum* as a historical source.' Historia 49 (2000), 358–77.

Lee, A. D., 'The army.' In Cameron, A. and Garnsey, P. *Cambridge Ancient History, vol. 13: The Late Empire AD 337–425* (2nd ed) (Cambridge: Cambridge University Press 1998), 211–37.

Pollard, N. D., *Soldiers, Cities and Civilians in Roman Syria* (Ann Arbor: University of Michigan Press, 2000).

Potter, D., *The Roman Empire at Bay AD 180–395* (London and New York: Routledge, 2004).

Southern P. and K. R.Dixon, *The Late Roman Army* (New Haven, Yale University Press, 1996; London: Batsford, 1996).

Abbreviations in quotation references

Quotations from ancient sources have been translated from the Latin or Greek by Nigel Pollard.

AE *L'Année épigraphique.*

BGU Berlin Greek Papyrus.

BHL *Bibliotheca Hagiographica Latina Antiquae et Mediae Aetatis* (*Subsidia Hagiographica 6:* Brussels, 1898–1901).

CBI E. Schallmayer, K. Eibl, J. Ott, G. Preuss, E. Wittkopf, *Der römische Weihebezirk von Osterbruken I: Corpus der griechischen und lateinischen Beneficiarier-Inschriften des Römischen Reiches* (Stuttgart, 1990).

CIL *Corpus inscriptionum latinarum.*

CIRPZamora Á. Alonso Ávila - S. Crespo Ortiz de Zárate, *Corpus de inscripciones romanas de la provincia de Zamora* (Valladolid, 2000).

CJ *Codex* of Justinian.

CTh *Theodosian Code.*

EJ V. Ehrenberg and A. H. M. Jones, *Documents illustrating the Reigns of Augustus and Tiberius* (2nd ed., Oxford University Press, Oxford, 1955).

IBR = F. Vollmer, *Inscriptiones Baivariae Romanae, sive inscriptiones provinciae Raetiae adiectis Noricis Italicisve* (München, 1915).

IDR *Inscriptiones Daciae Romanae*, Bukarest 1975–present.

IGLS *Inscriptions grecques et latines de la Syrie.*

IGR *Inscriptiones graecae ad res romanas pertinentes.*

ILS H. Dessau, ed., *Inscriptiones latinae selectae* (1892–1916).

IMS Inscriptions de la Mésie Supérieure, Belgrad 1976–present.

IRP Palencia L. Hernandez Guerra, *Inscripciones romanas en la provincia de Palencia* (Valladolid, 1994).

P.Mich. Michigan Papyrus.

RIB *Roman Inscriptions of Britain.*

SB *Sammelbuch griechischer Urkunden aus Aegypten.*

SEG *Supplementum epigraphicum graecum.*

SHA *Scriptores Historiae Augustae.*

Smallwood E. M. Smallwood, *Documents illustrating the Principates of Nerva Trajan and Hadrian* (Cambridge: Cambridge University Press, 1966).

ZPE *Zeitschrift für Papyrologie und Epigraphik.*

Atiquot *Journal of the Israel Department of Antiquities.*

Classical Texts

English translations of most of these ancient works (see table right) are available online now, particularly on the Lacus Curtius (http://penelope.uchicago.edu/Thayer/E/Roman/Texts/home.html) and Perseus Project (http://www.perseus.tufts.edu/hopper/collection?collection=Perseus:collection:Greco-Roman) websites.

Alternatively, many can be found in the Penguin Classics and Loeb Classical Library series. Relevant translated extracts from ancient works can also be found in source books such as those edited by Michael Sage and Brian Campbell listed in the bibliography.

Notes on the table

The works *The Alexandrian War* and *The African War* traditionally have been attributed to Julius Caesar as a continuation of his *Civil War* (hence [Caesar]), but probably were written by another near-contemporary author, perhaps Caesar's legate Hirtius, who was the consul killed fighting Mark Antony at Mutina.

The work *Concerning the Fortification of a Camp* had traditionally been attributed to the early 2nd-century AD writer of technical treatises on surveying, but is probably a later work by an unknown author, hence 'Pseudo-Hyginus'.

Scriptores Historiae Augustae ('The Writers of the Augustan/Imperial Histories', abbreviated to *SHA*) is the term usually used to denote the author(s) of a series of imperial biographies starting with Hadrian. The texts themselves claim they were written by different authors writing in the late 3rd century AD. However, detailed analysis suggests they were written by a single author at the end of the 4th century AD.

Compilations, *corpora* by multiple authors

Codex of Justinian, *c.* AD 530
The Digest, *c.* AD 530
Notitia Dignitatum, Oriens (*Or.*), *c.* AD 395 (for *Oriens*, the eastern half of the *Notitia Dignitatum*)
Notitia Dignitatum, Occidens (*Oc.*), *c.* AD 420 (for *Occidens*, the western half of the *Notitia Dignitatum*)
Theodosian Code, AD 429–38

Writer	Title of work	Date writing (approximate)
Ammianus Marcellinus	*Histories*	(Late 4th cent. AD)
Appian	*Civil War*	(Mid-2nd cent. AD)
Arrian	*Battle Formation Against the Alans*	(First half 2nd cent. AD)
Augustus	*Res Gestae Divi Augusti (Achievements of the Divine Augustus)*	(*c.* AD 14)
Julius Caesar	*Gallic War*	(Mid-1st cent BC)
	Civil War	(Mid-1st cent BC)
[Caesar]	*African War*	(Mid-1st cent BC)
	Alexandrian War	(Mid-1st cent BC)
Cicero	*Letters to his Friends*	(Mid-1st cent. BC)
Cassius Dio	*Roman History*	(Late 2nd–early 3rd cent AD)
Dionysius of Halicarnassus	*Roman Antiquities*	(Late 1st cent. BC)
Herodian	*Roman History*	(First half 3rd cent. AD)
Hyginus / 'Pseudo-Hyginus'	*Concerning the Fortification of a Camp*	(3rd cent. AD?)
Josephus	*The Jewish War*	(Later 1st cent. AD)
Julian	*Orations*	(Mid-4th cent. AD)
Libanius	*Orations*	(Second half 4th cent AD)
Livy	*History of Rome from the Foundation of the City*	(Late 1st cent BC–early 1st cent. AD)
Pliny the Elder	*Natural History*	(Mid-1st cent AD)
Pliny the Younger	*Letters*	(Early 2nd cent. AD)
Plutarch	*Life of Mark Antony*	(Early 2nd cent. AD)
	Life of Gaius Gracchus	
	Life of Romulus	
Polybius	*The Histories*	(Mid-2nd cent. BC)
Procopius	*The Buildings*	(Mid-6th cent. BC)
Sallust	*Jugurthine War*	(Third quarter 1st cent. BC)
Scriptores Historiae Augusta (*SHA*)	*Aurelian*	(Late 4th cent. AD)
	Caracalla	(Late 4th cent. AD)
	Probus	(Late 4th cent. AD)
	(Septimius) *Severus*	(Late 4th cent. AD)
	Severus Alexander	(Late 4th cent. AD)
Strabo	*Geography*	(Mid-2nd cent AD)
Suetonius	*Augustus*	(Early 2nd cent. AD)
	Caesar	
	Vespasian	
Tacitus	*Agricola*	(Late 1st–early 2nd cent. AD)
	Annals	
	Histories	
Theophylact Simocatta	*History*	(1st half of 7th cent. AD)
Vegetius	*Epitome of Military Science*	(Late 4th–early 5th cent. AD)
Zosimus	*New History*	(Early 6th cent. AD)

Acknowledgments

We would like to thank Lawrence Keppie and Philip Matyszak for reading early drafts of our manuscript and for making helpful comments. We are very grateful to David Mattingly, Roger Wilson and Mike Bishop for providing photographs to be used in the book. Greg Schwendner was very helpful in tracking down an ostracon.

Our thanks also go to Colin Ridler, Alice Reid, Sally Nicholls, Rowena Alsey and Celia Falconer at Thames & Hudson for their patience, support and hard work.

Sources of Illustrations

a=above, **b**=below, **l**=left, **r**=right
Maps and diagrams on pp **10–11, 16, 22, 37, 49, 51, 54, 84, 108, 113, 122, 132, 174, 214** drawn by ML Design, © Thames & Hudson Ltd, London.
1 akg-images/Erich Lessing; **2** akg-images/Erich Lessing; **3** akg-images/De Agostini Picture Library; **4** British Museum, London; **6** The Art Archive/Alamy; **8** akg-images/Erich Lessing; **9** Mauritius Images GmbH/Alamy; **12–13** E & S Ginsberg/Alamy; **15** Photo Scala, Florence; **17** The Art Archive/Museo di Villa Giulia Rome/Collection Dagli Orti; **18a** Antikensammlungen, Staatliche Museen zu Berlin; **18bl** Museo Archaeologico Nazionale, Naples; **18br** Photo Scala, Florence; **19** Museo Archaeologico Nazionale, Chieti; **20a** British Museum, London; **20b, 21b** © RMN/Hervé Lewandowski; **22a** British Museum, London; **23** British Museum, London; **24** akg-images; **27a** akg-images/Peter Connolly; **27b** Ny Carlsbergy Glyptotek, Copenhagen; **28** British Museum, London; **29** Bankes Collection, Kingston Lacey; **31** British Museum, London; **32–33** Vittoriano Rastelli/Corbis; **34** akg-images/De Agostini Picture Library; **35** Alan Crawford/istockphoto.com; **38** Giovanni Lattanzi; **40** Landesmuseum Mainz; **41** Ermine Street Guard; **42a** Landesmuseum Mainz; **42b, 43, 44b** Cristian Chirita; **44a** Francis G Mayer; **44bl** Ermine Street Guard; **45** Landschaftsverband Rheinland/Archäologischer Park/Regional Museum Xanten; **47** Dr. D.J. Woolliscroft, The Roman Gask Project, The University of Liverpool; **48** Independent Picture Service/Alamy; **52–53** akg-images/Bildarchiv Steffens; **56a** Rheinisches Landesmuseum, Bonn; **56b** British Museum, London; **58a** Museum Kalkriese; **58b** Roger Wilson; **59** akg-images/Museum Kalkriese; **60** Museo Archaeologico, Venice; **61l** www.romancoins.org; **61r** Rheinisches Landesmuseum, Bonn; **62** Courtesy of Professor Lawrence Keppie; **63** Jona Lendering; **64** Araldo de Luca/Corbis; **66, 67** Jona Lendering; **68, 69** Roger Wilson; **70** akg-images/Bildarchiv Steffens; **71** Courtesy David Blain; **73** Saalberg Museum; **74a** Roger Wilson; **74bl** Saalberg Museum; **74br** Roger Wilson; **75a** www.romancoins.org; **75b** British Museum, London; **76** Roger Wilson; **77a, 77b** Landesmuseum Mainz; **78a, 78b** British Museum, London; **79** Roger Wilson; **81** Jona Lendering; **82–83** Adam Woolfitt/ Corbis; **85** British Museum, London; **87a, 87b** Exeter Archaeology; **88** Skyscan/Corbis; **90a** Hunterian Museum & Art Gallery, Glasgow; **90b** Mike Bishop; **91a** Alan Crawford/istockphoto.com; **91b** Corpus Inscriptionum Latinarum (CIL), Berlin-Brandenburgische Akademie de Wissenschaften; **92** Hunterian Museum & Art Gallery, Glasgow; **93** Statens Historiska Museum, Stockholm; **94** Hunterian Museum & Art Gallery, Glasgow; **96a, 96b** Roger Wilson; **97** Anthony Baggett/istockphoto.com; **98, 99** British Museum, London; **100** The Virtual Experience Company; **101** Castle Museum, Colchester; **104–5** Grosvenor Museum, Chester; **104b** Roger Wilson; **105b** Hunterian Museum & Art Gallery; **106–7** DeAgostini Picture Library/Scala, Florence; **109** Caligatus; **110** Håkan Svensson; **111** Alfredo Dagli Orti/Art Archive/Corbis; **112–13** akg-images/Gilles Mermet; **114** *Corpus Inscriptionum Latinarum* (*CIL*), Berlin-Brandenburgische Akademie de Wissenschaften; **115** Roger Wilson; **116** Hemis/Alamy; **117a** British Museum, London; **117b** Jona Lendering; **118** Corbis; **119** Roger Wilson; **120–21** Terry Lawrence/istockphoto. com; **125** Mike P. Shepherd/Alamy; **126, 127** Photo Scala Florence; **128a, 128b** British Museum, London; **129** Nigel Pollard; **130–31** Michele Falzone/JAI/Corbis; **133a, 133b** British Museum, London; **135** State Hermitage Museum, St. Petersburg; **136** Michael Major/istockphoto.com; **137** Museo Capitolino, Rome; **139** Nigel Pollard; **140** Stéphane Compoint; **141a** Yale University Art Gallery; **141b** Nigel Pollard; **142** akg-images; **143** Bernard Gagnon; **144a** David Mattingly; **144b** Lonely Planet Images/Alamy; **145** akg-images/Erich Lessing; **147** akg-images/Peter Connolly; **148** akg-images/Israelimages; **149** Avishai Teicher; **150a** akg-images/bildarchiv Steffens; **150b** Israel Antiquities Authority; **153** imagebroker/Alamy; **154** Aivolie/istockphoto.com; **155** Aerial Photographic Archive of Archaeology in the Middle East (APAAME), www.humanities.uwa.edu.au/research/cah/aerial-archaeology; **157** Witold Ryka/istockphoto.com; **158** British Museum, London; **159** Yahya Arhab/epa/Corbis; **160** Aerial Photographic Archive of Archaeology in the Middle East (APAAME), www.humanities.uwa.edu.au/research/cah/aerial-archaeology; **161** Sally Nicholls; **163** The Art Archive/Alamy; **164** Israel Antiquities Authority; **165a** Norma Joseph/Alamy; **165b** Grandmaster; **167a** imagebroker/Alamy; **167b** Matthias Kabel; **168** Jona Lendering; **169** Krzystof Slusarczyk/istockphoto.com; **171** Charles & Josette Lenars/Corbis; **172–73** akg-images/De Agostini Picture Library; **174** www.romancoins.info; **175** Ante Perkovic; **176** akg-images; **177** akg-images/Peter Connolly; **178** Mike Bishop; **179a** Courtesy Ilian Boyanov; **179b** Svilen Enev; **180** Roger Wilson; **182a, 182b, 183** Warsaw Institute of Archaeology; **184** www.romancoins.info; **185** Peter Erik Forsberg/Alamy; **186** Stephane Gautier/Sagaphoto.com/Alamy; **188** Roger Wilson; **189a** Wien Museum, Vienna; **189b** Roger Wilson; **191** Photo Scala Florence; **192** Terra Sigillata-Museum Rheinzabern; **193a** www.romancoins.info; **193b** Jona Lendering; **194** Roger Wilson; **195ar, 195b** Civertan; **195al** Mike Bishop; **196l** The Art Archive/Museo della Civilta Romana, Rome/Gianni Dagli Orti; **196r** Photo Scala, Florence; **197a** www.romancoins.info; **197b** Rossignol Benoit; **198** Sandro Vannini/Corbis; **199** Roger Wilson; **200** Cristian Chirita; **202** Roger Wilson; **203** Apulum Archaeology, Romania; **204–5** Superstock/Alamy; **206** Araldo da Luca/Corbis; **207** Deblu68; **208** www.romancoins.info; **209** Nigel Pollard; **210–11** Giovanni Lattanzi; **212** Erich Lessing/akg-images; **213** Aerial Photographic Archive of Archaeology in the Middle East (APAAME), www.humanities.uwa.edu.au/research/cah/aerial-archaeology; **215** Bayerische Staatsbibliothek, Munich; **218** dbimages/Alamy; **222** Museum of Vojvodina, Novi Sad, Autonomous Province of Vojvodina; **223** akg-images/Erich Lessing.

Index

Roman names are typically listed under their *cognomen* (the last name) unless they are more familiar by another element e.g. emperors and ancient writers in particular.

Roman first names (*praenomina*) are few in number and formulaic, so they are often abbreviated. They include: Aulus (abbreviated as A.), Gaius (C.), Gnaeus (Cn.), Lucius (L.), Marcus (M.), Publius (P.), Quintus (Q.), Sextus (S.) and Titus (T.).

Page numbers in *italic* refer to illustrations, and in **bold** to maps.